THE STUDIA PHILONICA ANNUAL
Studies in Hellenistic Judaism

SBL

Society of Biblical Literature

THE STUDIA PHILONICA ANNUAL
Studies in Hellenistic Judaism

Editors
David T. Runia
Gregory E. Sterling

THE STUDIA PHILONICA ANNUAL
Studies in Hellenistic Judaism

Volume XXII

2010

EDITORS
David T. Runia
Gregory E. Sterling

ASSOCIATE EDITOR
David Winston

BOOK REVIEW EDITOR
Ronald Cox

Society of Biblical Literature
Atlanta

THE STUDIA PHILONICA ANNUAL
Studies in Hellenistic Judaism

The financial support of

C. J. de Vogel Foundation, Utrecht
Queen's College, University of Melbourne
University of Notre Dame
Pepperdine University

is gratefully acknowledged

ISBN: 978-1-58983-525-2
ISSN : 1052-4533

The cover photo, *Ezra Reads the Law*, is from a wall painting in the Dura Europos synagogue and used with permission from Zev Radovan (www.BibleLandPictures.com).

Printed on acid-free, recycled paper conforming to ANSI/NISO Z39.48-1992 (R1997) and ISO 9706:1994 standards for paper permanence.

∞

THE STUDIA PHILONICA ANNUAL
STUDIES IN HELLENISTIC JUDAISM

Contributions should be sent to the Editor, Prof. Gregory E. Sterling, Dean of the Graduate School, 502 Main Building, University of Notre Dame, Notre Dame, IN 46556, USA; email: sterling.1@nd.edu. Please send books for review to the Book Review Editor, Prof. Ronald Cox, Religion Division, Pepperdine University, 24255 Pacific Coast Highway, Malibu, CA 90263-4352; email: rcox@pepperdine.edu.

Contributors are requested to observe the "Instructions to Contributors" located at the end of the volume. These can also be consulted on the Annual's website: http://www.nd.edu/~philojud. Articles which do not conform to these instructions cannot be accepted for inclusion.

The Studia Philonica Monograph series accepts monographs in the area of Hellenistic Judaism, with special emphasis on Philo and his *Umwelt*. Proposals for books in this series should be sent to the Editor, Prof. Thomas H. Tobin S.J., Theology Department, Loyola University Chicago, 1032 West Sheridan Road, Chicago, IL 60660-1537, U.S.A.; email: ttobin@luc.edu. See further News and Notes.

CONTENTS

Note. The editors wish to thank the typesetter Gonni Runia once again for her tireless work on this volume. They wish to express their thanks to Tamar Primoratz (Melbourne) for her assistance with the bibliography, and also to Sister Lisa Marie Belz OSU, ABD and Lauren O'Connell for meticulously proof-reading the final manuscript. As in previous years we are deeply grateful to our publisher, The Society of Biblical Literature, and to Leigh Andersen and Kathie Klein, for making the publication of the Annual possible.

ABBREVIATIONS

The abbreviations used for the citation of ancient texts and modern scholarly literature generally follow the guidelines of the Society of Biblical Literature as published in *The SBL Handbook of Style* (Hendrickson: Peabody Mass. 1999) §8.4. In addition to the abbreviations listed in the Notes to contributors at the back of the volume, please note the following:

MSU	*Mitteilungen des Septuaginta-Unternehmens*
RA	*Revue d'assyriologie et d'archéologie orientale*
SGLG	Sammlung griechischer und lateinischer Grammatiker
SO	*Symbolae Osloenses*
STCPF	Studi e testi per il Corpus dei papiri filosofici greci e latini

The Studia Philonica Annual 22 (2010) 1–51

ALLEGORICAL INTERPRETATION OF THE PENTATEUCH IN ALEXANDRIA: INSCRIBING ARISTOBULUS AND PHILO IN A WIDER LITERARY CONTEXT

EKATERINA MATUSOVA

To the memory of Martin Hengel

It is known that Philo was not the first to write an allegorical commentary on the Pentateuch—such an attempt had already been made in the second century B.C. in Alexandria by Aristobulus, a Jewish philosopher of the period of Ptolemy Philometor.[1] Philo's own works also contain references both to other allegorical interpretations of the Scripture and to other allegorists. These two facts, especially the latter, have encouraged scholars to view Philo's commentary as part of a tradition—to postulate a succession of Jewish commentators on the Scripture, working throughout the two centuries that separate Aristobulus and Philo (this despite the lack of evidence for these commentators in the sources: the early Christian authors do not know Jewish allegorical exegetes of the LXX except for Aristobulus and Philo). P. Borgen, for instance, in his 1997 study, *Philo of Alexandria, an Exegete for His Time*, summarized the results of previous research in this direction as follows: Philo was one of several Pentateuch commentators within the Jewish community in Alexandria; his works reflect the differences of opinion and points of agreement between these commentators; Philo's method was based on the practice of scriptural interpretation in the synagogues. Borgen described this view of things as "the growing trend in Philonic scholarship."[2] This position, which many scholars adopted, is quite

---

[1] Clement of Alexandria, *Strom.* 1.72.4. The authenticity of the Aristobulus fragments has been proved by N. Walter, *Der Thoraausleger Aristobulos* (TU 86; Berlin: Akademie, 1964) and is accepted by most scholars.

[2] P. Borgen, *Philo of Alexandria, an Exegete for His Time* (NovTSup 86; Leiden: Brill, 1997), 2–9.

understandable: an evident connection that exists between the works of Aristobulus and Philo—whatever we may have in between—provokes to link these extremes by reconstructing a tradition of commentary. Equally understandable is the desire to define this tradition as essentially Jewish and distinctive of the exegetical culture in Alexandria. At present, that "growing trend" of more than ten years' standing has grown almost into an orthodoxy,[3] although no new facts or serious arguments to support it have come to light. However, this theory, in the form it has been developed, entails so many difficulties, that it challenges the correctness of simple decisions, which lie near at hand.

In this article I would like, first of all, to draw attention to some problems which this, already traditional approach to Philo's activity entails. Secondly, I would like to propose some new perspectives which may help better to understand the cultural background of the exegetical tradition that links Aristobulus and Philo.

1. *The synagogue origin thesis*

1.1. *The evidence from Qumran and from the New Testament*

In order to elucidate the picture of how Philo was related to the Jewish interpretative tradition, it is worth comparing Philo's method with the non-Alexandrian Jewish material authentic to the period. First of all, I mean documents and texts discovered in the caves of the Dead Sea. In my opinion, the choice of this material is justified by the approach, shared by several scholars, and, particularly, formulated by M. Bernstein, according to whom "although it is clear that the Qumran scrolls are geographically isolated as a collection, it must be stressed that they nevertheless constitute a perhaps nonisolated selection of Jewish literature in late antiquity, and, as has been noted, this is as true in the area of biblical interpretation as in any other."[4]

Among all types of commentary found in Qumran we will discuss only those examples which can be compared with allegorical exegesis, particularly the examples of *indirect* interpretation of a text. These are pesharim—

---

[3] See, for instance, the article by M. Niehoff, "Homeric Scholarship and Bible Exegesis in Ancient Alexandria: Evidence from Philo's 'Quarrelsome Colleagues'," *CQ* 57.1 (2007): 166–82.

[4] Cf. M. Bernstein, "Interpretation of Scripture," in *Encyclopedia of the Dead Sea Scrolls* (2 vols.; ed. L. H. Shiffman and J. VanderKam; Oxford: Oxford University Press, 2000), vol. 1, 376–383, 382, cf. also 376, 377.

or the "actualizing midrash"—a commentary that either rephrases a text, or makes it "relevant" by assigning to it a historical significance connected with the end of history. It is very important to note that this kind of interpretation was applied, first and foremost, to prophecies, and partly to poetic texts in general (often also considered prophetic). This fact is entirely understandable—the very nature of prophecy demanded some kind of concretizing exegesis. The prophecies had become less clear over time, or, as the Qumranites may have thought, had never been entirely clear even to the prophets who uttered them. Thus, the "pesharim" type of commentary was applied in the first instance to the dark poetic texts referring to future times (which, according to the commentators, had already arrived). It tried to explain them historically, according to the demands of the text. However, the interpretations proposed usually are not intended to shift the original meaning of the word (which is allegorical interpretation in the strict sense), they only fill it with a concrete historical meaning, being actually interpretations, but not allegorizations of the material. (For instance, "the city" is Jerusalem (1QpHab XII, 7), a wicked one is the wicked priest, a righteous one is the teacher of righteousness (1QpHab XI, 4–5)). The pesharim do contain elements of allegorical interpretation, since they sometimes require one to read one significance through another (cf., for instance, 1QpHab II, 12–13; XII, 4; 4Q169 III, 8–9). However, in this type of commentary allegorical interpretation is not applied to a text systematically, but it is rather a way of explaining individual difficulties, which occur when a proper noun in a prophetic text doesn't fit a historical context created by the interpretation. Anyway, the pesharim do not offer allegorical interpretations of a prosaic text, even less it is a philosophical allegory.

Menahem Kister, in his article on Biblical commentary in the Qumran manuscripts writes: "I would like now to turn to another observation, namely the significant absence of any literature of continuous or thematic midrash other than the pesharim."[5] "Most Qumranic interpretations of legal passages in the Penateuch," M. Kister continues, "consist of paraphrases." This despite the fact that, as the author notes, "The Qumran sectarians were, no doubt, deeply engaged in interpretation of the Pentateuch and considered it as the main source of their law." Kister also notes that it was this very interpretative activity of the sect which prompted the

---

[5] M. Kister, "A Common Heritage: Biblical Interpretations at Qumran and Its Implications," in *Biblical Perspectives: Early Use and Interpretation of the Bible in Light of the Dead Sea Scrolls: Proceedings of the First International Symposium of the Orion Center for the Study of the Dead Sea Scrolls and Associated Literature, 12-14 May, 1996* (ed. M. Stone and E. Chazon; Leiden: Brill, 1998), 101–111, 105.

Rabbinical midrash to formulate its own interpretations as a response.[6] Overall, however, the rabbinic halakha is based to a much lesser extent on interpretation of the Scripture than the sectarian law " . . . and yet we only find [in Qumran] scattered examples of explicit interpretations of verses of the Law, and these are not presented in the form of hermeneutical compositions (as is the case with the pesharim). . . . Commentaries on portions of the Pentateuch did not, perhaps, take shape as a literary genre, although exegesis was surely inherent in the study of the Bible."[7]

In the Qumran manuscripts there are only two or three occasions where indirect interpretation is applied to prose texts. However, this happens only where the text either contains a poetic expression (as CD VI, 3–10; III, 16, where allegorical interpretation is applied to the famous "Song of Wells" in Num 21:18) or is related to a passage from a prophetic book (as 11QMelch, where two prosaic contexts, Lev 25: 9–13 and Deut 15:2, are explained through Isa 61: 1–2).[8] The author concludes: "This allegorical interpretation of the poetic passage could potentially have led to an allegorical exegesis of the preceding narrative verse, but the far-reaching exegetical potential of this allegorical midrash was most probably not realized by the Qumran sect or by the rabbis."[9]

As scholars have noted, echoes of this interpretative technique can be seen in all sorts of different branches of post-Hellenistic Jewish tradition— from the Evangelists, to the Apostles, to the Rabbinical midrash.[10] For instance, let us study a few remarkable examples from the New Testament.

The Apostle Paul in I Cor 10: 1–13 refers to the events of the Exodus, saying that all these events were as examples for us, "to the intent we should not lust after evil things, as they also lusted" (I Cor 10:6).[11] This context is sometimes cited to prove the hypothesis that in ancient Judaism there was some sort of interpretation of the Torah which was comparable to Philo's interpretation, since the Apostle Paul interpreted the Exodus. Sometimes this is called a typological interpretation, because the Apostle uses the word "typos"—i.e. "example". But what is important to note here is the fact that the Apostle's interpretation reproduces faithfully that of Ps. 77 (according to the LXX, and 78, according to the MT), where the events of

[6] Kister, "A common heritage,"106, n. 17.
[7] Kister, "A common heritage," 106.
[8] As D. Flusser has argued, we have, probably, a similar transferring in 1QS IV, 19–20, See D. Flusser, "A Pre-Gnostic Idea in DSS," in *Jerusalem Studies in Jewish Thought 9: Studies. in Honor of Shlomo Pines 2*, (Jerusalem, 1989), 165–175 (in Hebrew).
[9] Kister, "A common heritage," 110.
[10] Cf. M. Bernstein, "Interpretation of Scripture," 382.
[11] Here and below, all biblical quotations are taken from the KJV.

the Exodus are already grouped in the way St. Paul assembles them, and all the moral conclusions he makes are drawn. Generations to come should remember what had happened at the time of the Exodus, "Lest they should be like their fathers," says the Psalmist (Ps 77:8). The Psalm and the Epistle both use the expression "our fathers," an expression which, for obvious reasons, is absent from the text of Exodus. What is even more remarkable, even the opening words of the apostolic chapter are identical to the first verses of the Psalm in their moral message. St. Paul says, "Brethren, I do not want that you should be ignorant (ἀγνοεῖν) that our fathers were all under the cloud . . ." (I Cor 10:1). And this is the idea of the opening verses of the Psalm: "and he ordered our fathers to teach it to their children (γνωρίσαι), that it should be known (γνῶ) by the future generation." It seems to me, therefore, that it is quite clear that the Apostle, in discussing the semantics of the images of Exodus, is using the Psalm. The transfer of the events of the Exodus into a Psalm gave them another dimension. As elements of a poetic and prophetic text, they could receive an explicative interpretation which, in its turn, was projected back onto the text of the Exodus. As I have said, essentially the Apostle keeps to an interpretation that is already contained in the Psalm. What is new in his explanations is that he specifies that the generation which needs to draw a lesson from these events is the *last* generation—"and they are written for our admonition, upon whom the ends of the world are come" (I Cor 10:11); as well as the comparison of Christ with the rock "for they drank of that spiritual Rock that followed them: and that Rock was Christ." (I Cor 10: 4). Thus, his own interpretation can be reduced to the concretization of the elements of the Psalm by the events and personalities of his time, which he, like those commentators at Qumran, considered the history of the end of the world.

The other example is from Gal 4:24–31, where the Apostle tells us that Sarah and her childbearing and Hagar and hers are the images of the two Covenants, the Old and the New. But just like 11QMelch, the Apostle considers this passage of Genesis through the medium of the Prophet Isaiah, whom he also cites. The Prophet says (Isa 54:1,4) that the childbearing of a sterile woman will be more fruitful than that of a married woman—a passage which was undoubtedly understood as a reference to Sarah and Agar. Immediately after this, he says that that which no longer nourishes must be relinquished and one must turn to another Covenant, new and eternal (Isa 55:2–3). New, because he talks of a covenant not only after Moses, but even after David. It is clear, therefore, that St. Paul is here talking once again of an interpretation of the Prophet, an interpretation which is basically a historical concretization of his words. This interpretation could then be projected back onto the text of Genesis.[12]

Thus, it would be impossible to deny that in Jewish tradition outside Alexandria prosaic texts of the Scripture could be submitted to indirect interpretation (even called by the Apostle Paul allegorical). However, the remarkable feature is that the examples from Qumran and the New Testament passages show evident traces of the same interpretative technique. This is a historically related interpretation which actualizes and makes concrete, and which is essentially applied to prophetic texts. It is only afterwards that this interpretation can be projected back onto the prosaic texts, intimately connected—in the eyes of the commentators—with these poetic passages. The presence of this technique in different branches of Second Temple Judaism shows that it was part of their common exegetical background. At the same time, in none of these branches we can see any traces of a systematical application even of this kind of exegesis to the entire prosaic text of the Law. Thus, discussing Philo's undertaking, we have to acknowledge that occasional applications of the pesharim type of commentary is our best *textual* evidence of applying indirect interpretation to the text of the Pentateuch in Jewish exegetical tradition outside Alexandria.

I do not think that it is impossible to find in Philo's work echoes of a similar approach, when Philo interprets some passages of the Scripture with the allusion to others, probably, poetic ones (though not only to them,

---

[12] It is my pleasure to refer to the article by Steven di Mattei, "Paul's Allegory of the Two Covenants (Gal 4. 21–31) in Light of First-Century Hellenistic Rhetoric and Jewish Hermeneutics," *NTS* 52 (2006): 102–122. The author, analyzing Gal 4: 21–31 in comparison with Isa 54:1, independently comes to practically the same conclusions. Especially, see p. 17: "It is through Isaiah's portrayal of Jerusalem (above) as barren and through his linking together the theme of Zion's joy, since soon the barrenness will show itself as plentitude, with the covenant promises made to Abraham and his seed, that Paul is able to see in Genesis 16-17 an allegory of two covenants. Isaiah's exhortation to Jerusalem to rejoice in the new covenant is allegorically represented in God's proclamation to Abraham and Sarah that she shall not go childless. What Paul's hermeneutic seems to be doing, then, is allegorically reading Isaiah's heavenly Jerusalem in Genesis' Sarah." And p. 21: "Paul's exegetical claim, therefore, is that Scripture, in speaking of the elements of then (τότε), discloses, allegorically, the events which are now (νῦν) currently being revealed. On a comparative level, we may conclude by noting that, as pesher exegesis applies prophetic texts to the current eschatological present, and as haftarah liturgical reading practices make use of prophetic texts to read Torah eschatologically, so too it would seem Paul's method reads Genesis 16–17 and 21:10 as speaking allegorically of what shall befall those living in the final generation, but not through historical 'types' [. . .] but rather trough the divine word."

For another example of this actualizing interpretation of the Prophet in the New Testament tradition, see also in Luke 4:16–22.

but also to other texts). Nor do I think that we cannot find in his writings a few interpretations, known from the Jewish exegetical tradition outside Alexandria,[13] and—looking further—any other evidences of his knowledge of this tradition. However, I want to emphasize that from the methodological point of view, and drawing on the *textual* study of the relevant sources available to us, we see that the general exegetical picture which presents itself in the case of Aristobulus and Philo is significantly different. In this case we meet with an approach which systematically interprets allegorically prosaic texts of the Law, without correlating it—as a rule—to prophetic texts or giving to it any historical interpretations, but translating its significance into the language of Greek philosophy.

In this kind of interpretation, the kinship between different branches of Jewish tradition manifests itself also on the level of generalization of exegetical approach. The pesher Habakkuk famously asserts that the ability to interpret the words of the prophets is not a task of everybody, but a spiritual gift, given by God to the priest of the community, almost like the ability to prophesy that was given to the prophets (1QpHab II, 6–10).[14] All other people have to accept and to keep these explanations, but they are not allowed to invent their own plausible interpretations. We see the same idea in the words of the apostle Peter addressed to a Christian community, undoubtedly engaged in the interpretation of Scriptures: "We have also a more sure word of prophecy; whereunto ye do well that ye take heed, as unto a light that shineth in a dark place, until the day dawn, and the day star arise in your hearts: *knowing this first, that no prophecy of the scripture is of any private interpretation* (πᾶσα προφητεία γραφῆς ἰδίας ἐπιλύσεως οὐ γίνεται). For the prophecy came not in old time by the will of man: but holy men of God spake as they were moved by the Holy Ghost" (2 Pet. 1: 19–21). In the Gospels all the examples of the apostles' own attitude to these matters perfectly illustrate this picture: Jesus often spoke in the prophetic way allegorically, with intention to be understood indirectly, but none of his pupils dared to propose any explanation (Matt 13:11; Mark 4:11, Luke 8:10). They waited until Jesus himself would explain to them the meaning of an image. It is true that Philo alludes several times to the capacity of prophesizing which his soul acquires when giving most profound allegorical explanations.[15] In my opinion, this is a sign of his knowledge of this tradition of exegesis. However, his normal exegetical practice highlights itself

---

[13] Cf. for instance, Kister, "A common heritage,"110.

[14] Cf. M. Horgan, *Pesharim: Qumran Interpretations of Biblical Books* (CBQMS 8; Washington, D.C.: Catholic Biblical Association of America, 1979), 229–259.

[15] *Cher.* 27, cf. *Mos.* 1. 286.

against this background even more clearly, showing that this kind of allusion serves mainly rhetorical purposes. Philo's exegetical method not only admits several completely different interpretations of the same textual element,[16] but also—what is more important—consists in systematical, thorough correlating of the LXX with the dialogues of Plato and several most important works of Aristotle (e.g. Nichomachean Ethics, Eudemian Ethics, Categories and some other), as well as with the philosophical texts of the tradition contemporary to Philo. This procedure requires technical skills and is based on a deep professional knowledge of the material, which renders the understanding of Philo so difficult for modern readers, since most of us have not equal training in ancient philosophy.

This suggests to us another consideration. Whatever the intimate balance (or the distance) between the year of Jubilee and the last judgment in 11QMelch, or between Sarah and Hagar and the two Covenants in Gal 4: 24–31, the logic of interpretation still remained clear for Jewish readers due to the clear exegetical procedure which the commentators followed: they still remained in the realm of senses which were interconnected in Jewish religious consciousness. However, when Philo interprets the LXX through the texts of Plato and Aristotle, the balance between literal and indirect meaning of the texts of the Law is completely destroyed in the eyes of an ordinary reader (whatever connection between the LXX and Plato might have existed in the opinion of Philo). The interpretation becomes allegorical in the strict sense of the word (according to the classical definition of Heraclitus, i.e. when a text is supposed to mean something different (ἄλλο) from what it actually says).[17] Indeed, Philo systematically imposes on the Scripture philosophical notions which are in no way provoked or invited by its plain meaning. Moreover, often he is quite insensitive and even violent to the direct meaning of the text, which he forcibly distorts and interprets in conformity with his own philosophical ideas and system of symbols. For instance, interpreting Egypt as a symbol for the corporal senses, Philo interprets Joseph as a type of soul that is not mature for the life of a philosopher, while his treacherous brothers, on the other hand, are understood as representatives of philosophical reasoning (sic! *Det.* 11–16). Everybody who is familiar with Philo's arguments can cite many similar examples. And we cannot neglect the fact that in Philo's writings allegory is often polemically opposed to literal understanding and used to eliminate completely the literal meaning of the text, rather than elucidate it on any

---

[16] For instance, *Cher* 21–30; *Deus* 104–107; *Mos.* 2. 98; *Spec.* 2. 56–57.
[17] Heraclitus, *All.* 5.2.

level whatever.[18] Thus, the actual distance between both levels of the text, the literal and the hidden, become vast, compared to the normal practice of the pesharim type commentaries.

The problem I want to emphasize consists not in that Philo, humanly, was reluctant to read or to understand the Scripture literally, or even that he could not, when he felt it appropriate, to allude to literal understanding in his works, as he does in *QG* and in *QE* and sometimes in other writings. The problem is that his general exegetical approach to the LXX, according to which almost everything in the Law of Moses can be understood allegorically (*Jos.* 28), can not be sufficiently explained from what we know about the genuine Jewish hermeneutics as a matter of fact. This, first of all, should make one vigilant against the idea of the alleged connection between Philo's exegesis and the normal synagogue practice. As our discussion below will show, I think that, in spite of the tendencies to unify and to smooth the picture of exegetical development in Alexandria, it is worth studying it bearing in mind the differences between both traditions. It may help to understand much better not only Philo's place in a literary process, but also some historical and literary nuances of the cultural development in the Alexandrian Diaspora.

Therefore, this article is devoted not to the study of some common or similar elements, which can be found in the Qumran—New Testament—Midrash exegetical traditions, from one side, and in Philo's allegory, from the other. Nor does it discuss the extent to which Philo was familiar with any Jewish literary traditions of his time, apart the LXX. I am going to speak only of Philo's general methodological approach to the LXX that, whatever his personal attitude may have been to the norms of his ancestral religion, is clearly visible in the majority of his works. This principle of interpretation, then, which leads Philo to interpret the entire Pentateuch in terms of Greek philosophy regardless of the plain meaning of the text and of its allegorical import, the origins and the tradition of this exegetical approach are the main concern of this article.

Thus, let us repeat that, in this methodological way, when we compare the Palestinian scriptural commentaries and Philo's exegetical works, we find that Philo's commentaries differ from the Palestinian:

1. in the material which is interpreted (legal prose first and foremost, then all texts)

2. in the technique which is applied (systematic, non-historical allegory)

---

[18] Cf. Philo *Deus* 133; *Leg.*2. 19; *Det.* 95; *Agr.* 131.

3. in the aim which is pursued (not to elucidate the text, but to create a parallel, self-sufficient system of interconnected meanings).

If we postulate that Philo's method originated in the synagogues of Alexandria, that is in the milieu of probably more Hellenized, but still Jewish, religious communities, then we have to ask ourselves what it was that occurred in those synagogues which so radically altered their methodology and created such a wide gulf between Palestinian and Alexandrian exegesis?

1.2. *The school of wisdom thesis*

In fact we know almost nothing, except what has been said, of the activities in the synagogues of Philo's time. The idea that Philo's commentary originated in the synagogue was proposed by V. Nikiprowetzky, who, in his Ph.D. dissertation,[19] set out to prove, as one of his main aims, that Philo's commentary was indeed a commentary in the proper meaning of the word, and primarily linked to the Jewish synagogue tradition. Basing his arguments mainly upon the treatises, *Every Good Man Is Free* and *On the Contemplative Life*, Nikiprowetzky thought that descriptions of the Essenes and *Therapeutai*, who, according to Philo, engage in commentary on holy books, reflected real practices in the synagogues of Philo's own time. He calls them "wisdom schools" and devotes a whole chapter to a description of their activities based on these two works.[20] Let us turn, then, to these two treatises, which are so important to the origin of the theory.

We must note that it is only in *Prob.* 75–91 that Philo talks of Jews and, in particular, the Essenes, as of a distinct national and religious community. It is important to remember that even in this description he is clearly playing down the specifically national characteristics, and emphasizing the universal features of the ideal of the "practical life" (he says so himself in *Contempl.* 1), basing this description on a traditional description of a Pythagorean *thiasos*.[21] Nevertheless, he does not say that allegorical commentary was practiced in the Jewish (in this case the Essene) synagogues. He says only that "one takes the books and reads aloud and another . . . comes forward and expounds what is not understood," because much in their "philosophy" is expressed through "symbols."[22] Both of these terms must

---

[19] V. Nikiprowetzky, *Le commentaire de l'Écriture chez Philon d'Alexandrie* (ALGHJ 11; Leiden: Brill, 1977).

[20] Nikiprowetzky, *Le commentaire,* 177–192.

[21] Cf. also M. Petit, Introduction to *Quod omnis probus liber sit*, in PAMP 28 (Paris: Éditions du Cerf, 1974), 17–132, 60–61.

[22] *Prob.* 82. This phrase was mistranslated by Colson in the Loeb edition.

here be understood as "translations" of Jewish realities into the language in which the Greeks described them (I will discuss this at more length below), but allegorical interpretation need not be meant here. However, it is true that in the Holy Books, mainly in the prophets, much is said darkly and cryptically, and requires explanation. Such explanations were in fact given, for example those contained in the pesharim found at Qumran. That same practice of explaining the prophecies with reference to current events in front of the public in a synagogue is reproduced in the Gospel of St. Luke (4:16–22) and—in relation to the new Christian community—by St. Paul in his epistles (see above). This does not tell us, however, that the synagogues practiced allegorical, systematical, still less philosophical commentary on the Scripture: in that the evidence of the Qumran library, the Gospels' description, and Philo's description of the Essene synagogue and of a non-Essene synagogue in *Somn.* 2.127 all coincide.

Also, when Philo emphatically, if very vaguely, talks of the allegorical interpretation of archaic texts, he deliberately stresses that, firstly, he is *not speaking of the Essenes* (*Contempl.* 1), and, secondly, that he is describing not a particular ethnic group ("this kind exists in many places in the inhabited world—because both Greece and the barbarian world were to participate in the perfect good," *Contempl.* 21), but rather a kind of ideal community living according to the ideal of the *vita contemplativa*. In the second case, Philo has simply reproduced the Greek philosophical ideal of the contemplative life (Βίος θεωρητικός), which had been part of the literary tradition since Aristotle.[23] Thus, when he talks in this connection of allegorical interpretation we should examine how large a place the topos of allegory occupied within the framework of the *vita contemplativa* topos, rather than taking this as a direct description of synagogue practice. All this compels me to regard the approach proposed by Nikiprowetzky as unreliable in the very conception which served as the starting point of his argument.

1.3. *The other allegorists: the evidence from Philo*

It is worth emphasizing once more that what disposes scholars to speak of a tradition of Jewish allegory preceding Philo and contemporary to him, is not so much simply the existence of Aristobulus fragments as a precedent

[23] See, O. L. Levinskaya, "The *Therapeutai* and the Philosophic Tradition of Dissertations in *Utramque Partem*," in *Mathesis* (ed I. Rozhansky; Moscow: Nauka, 1991), 176–193 (in Russian). One can also compare the description of the *Therapeutai* in *On the Contemplative Life* to the description of Egyptian priests by one of Philo's contemporaries, an allegorist named Chaeremon. Cf. G. E. Sterling, "Platonizing Moses: Philo and Middle Platonism," *SPhA* 5 (1993): 96–111, 105.

for Philo's work (since Aristobulus alone does not amount to a tradition), as Philo's own many references to other allegories and allegorists. Among the modern scholars who have gone down the road of trying to discover and describe this presumed Jewish allegorizing tradition are, e.g., R. Radice, T. Tobin, B. L. Mack, D. T. Runia, D. M. Hay and R. Goulet.[24]

In particular I would like to note Hay's article, "Philo's References to Other Allegorists," in which Hay is concerned with the statistical analysis and classification of all such references. The results of his study are decidedly puzzling, however: why do the overwhelming majority of "non-Philonic" allegories turn out to be so clearly secular and non-religious, even compared to Philo himself?

In his discussion of allegories of the soul, Hay writes:

> Whereas, however, most of Philo's psychological allegorizing is God-orien-tated, a large proportion of the psychological interpretations of the other allegorists are secular in the sense of having little or no reference to the divine-human relation.[25]

and, elsewhere:

> One of the most intriguing facts about these other allegorists is that they seem often to have found in Scripture not religious, but secular teaching. A large proportion of the interpretations Philo credits to others concern non–religious cosmology, mathematics, metaphysics and psychology.[26]

If the foundations of allegorical commentary are to be found, as the scholars listed above believe, in the synagogues, how are we to explain the fact that these allegorists have in fact strayed so far (even compared to the deeply Hellenized Philo) from their spiritual background? Some resear-chers go so far as to postulate an entire class of secular Jewish Pentateuch commentators, of whom Philo happened to be the most religious.[27] But

---

[24] R. Radice, *Platonizmo e Creazionismo in Philone di Alessandria* (Milano: Vita e pensiero, 1989); T. Tobin, *The Creation of Man: Philo and the History of Interpretation* (CBQMS 14; Washington, D.C.: Catholic Biblical Association of America, 1983); B. L. Mack, "Philo Judaeus and the Exegetical Traditions in Alexandria," in *ANRW* II 21.1 (Berlin-New York: W. de Gruyter, 1984), 554–586; D. T. Runia, *Philo of Alexandria and the "Timaeus" of Plato* (Leiden: Brill, 1986), 504–505 ; idem, "Philo: Alexandrian and Jew," in D. T. Runia, *Exegesis and Philosophy: Studies on Philo of Alexandria* (Collected Studies 332; Aldershot, Hampshire, Eng.: Variorum, 1990–1991), 1–18; D. M. Hay, "Philo's References to Other Allegorists," *SPhA* 6 (1979–80): 41–75; R. Goulet, *La philosophie de Moïse. Essai de reconstitution d'un Commentaire philosophique préphilonien du Pentateuque* (Histoire des doctrines de l'Antiquité classique 11; Paris: Librairie philosophique J. Vrin, 1987), 27 f.

[25] Hay, "Philo's references," 55.

[26] Hay, "Philo's references," 59.

[27] The idea was first put forward by R. Goulet, *La philosophie de Moïse,* 40 f.

· even if these mysterious commentators were Jewish (although the fact that they studied the text of the Septuagint does not seem to me sufficient grounds for this conclusion),[28] how was their interpretative activity connected with the synagogues? Indirectly, it appears, if at all.

2. *Stoic influence*

Now, let us turn to another point, which is significant in our discussion of Philo's allegory, namely the alleged Stoic influence. Allegory as such had obviously been a part of Greek literary activity from very early times. It is well known that this method of interpretation became particularly popular at one point among the Stoics. Consequently, the similarity between Philo's commentary and the Stoic allegorical commentaries on Homer has often been remarked upon, with two well-preserved Stoic texts cited most often—Heraclitus' *Homeric problems* and Cornutus' *On the Nature of the Gods*. The parallels of particular interpretations and terminology are well analyzed in the works of Zeller, Leisegang and Bréhier.[29] Most scholars, including Dörrie, Dillon, Pepin, Runia, Tobin, Radice and others, believe that Philo's allegory was Stoic in origin.

Those who hold that Philo's commentary arose from the Jewish tradition combine both views, positing the influence of Stoic allegorizing as the formal origin of this method, but situating its development within a Jewish environment. Thus, Tobin believes that Hellenistic Jews began to use techniques originating in the ancient tradition of Stoic interpretation of Homeric epic. He points to the resemblance between the anti-anthropo-morphic interpretations of Philo and those of Aristobulus, as well as the similarity of both authors to Heraclitus, Cornutus and ps. Plutarch's *The Life and Poetry of Homer*.[30] D. Runia expresses the same opinion:

---

[28] One of the clearest examples of how the Septuagint had penetrated non-Jewish cultural consciousness are the Doric Pythagorean Pseudepigrapha. In these W. Burkert and B. Centrone have discovered several characteristic and fairly significant borrowings from the Old Testament. W. Burkert, "Zur geistgeschichtlichen Einordnung einiger Pytha-goria,"in *Pseudepigrapha I* (Entrétiens sur l'antiquité classique 18; Vandeuvres-Génève: Fondation Hardt, 1971), 23–56; B. Centrone, *Pseudopythagorica ethica. I trattati morali di Archita, Metopo, Teage, Eurifamo* (Naples: Bibliopolis, 1990), 30–33.

[29] E. Zeller, *Philosophie der Griechen* 3 (Leipzig, 1923), 330–336; H. Leisegang, "Philon," *RE* 41. 20. Sp. 36–39; E. Bréhier, *Les idées philosophiques et religieuses de Philon d' Alexandrie* (Paris: Librairie philosophique J. Vrin, 1950, ³ first published in 1908), 60–83.

[30] T. Tobin, *The Creation of Man*, 20–35.

> . . . the greater part of the interpretative techniques employed by Philo are adapted to the requirements of Biblical exegesis of an authoritative text and have their origin in the traditions of the Hellenistic synagogue. These Jewish traditions were initially much indebted to the innovatory techniques of allegory and etymology developed in the exegesis of Homer and Hesiod by Stoic philosophers and other scholars, but soon (one surmises) proceeded to follow their own intuitions.[31]

This position, however, which links the allegorical method of Aristobulus and Philo to a specifically Jewish origin and specifically Stoic formal consequences, also raises many unanswered questions.

2.1. *Objections from content*

It is interesting that both Philonic and "non-Philonic" allegories cited in his writings clearly bear the stamp of Platonic philosophy. The picture, which these scholars have to draw, therefore becomes even more complicated. Tobin comments as follows:

> The anti-anthropomorphic interpretations in Philo also differ from those essentially Stoic allegories in that a good number of them are heavily influenced by Platonism. In addition, the interpretations become more and more Platonic as time goes on, while the Stoic elements either drop out or are revised. This indicates that a significant shift has begun to take place and that shift was connected with the revival of interest in the interpretation of Plato. While still using the techniques of their predecessors (e.g. Aristobulus) which were derived from the Stoic interpretation of Homer, Hellenistic Jewish exegetes began to draw the content of their interpretations from Platonic, rather than from Stoic sources.[32]

R. Radice's thinking also proceeds along exactly the same lines.[33]

If, however, we draw a line of tradition from Stoic origins to the later Platonizing development, and if we place this line of tradition in a specially Jewish environment, we should be able to explain the reasons why Jewish thought took this particular direction. Why were the Jewish commentators at first attracted by Stoicism, and why did they then turn to Platonism? From the point of view of a classicist, such a phenomenon is too remarkable to remain unexplained or unremarked upon. And there is also another difficulty which I want to stress: if we are to suppose that Philo's commentary is related through its origins to Stoic allegory, we ought to be able to find not only a few coincidences of interpretation, but also an identical exegetical principle in both. This, however, is extremely difficult. We can see

---

[31] D. Runia, *Philo of Alexandria and the "Timaeus,"* 504–505.
[32] T. Tobin, *The Creation of Man*, 54.
[33] R. Radice, *Platonizmo e Creazionismo*, 99, 204, 208.

this clearly if we take such an important notion as *physical* interpretation, which in Philo's system is almost synonymous with the notion of *allegorical interpretation* as such.[34] Scholars have already noted that none of Philo's "physical" allegories is physical in the Stoic meaning of the word. This term includes for Philo a characteristic complex of ideas inextricably linked with the Middle Platonic and neo-Pythagorean tradition.[35] On the contrary, when Philo cites an interpretation very much in the spirit of Stoicism, in which the tree of life is likened to the human heart,[36] he rejects it on the grounds that it is not *physical*, φυσική, but rather *medical*, ἰατρική.[37] A certain amount of Stoic terminology in Philo's writings is not a witness of a particular Stoic influence: at that period Stoic terminology was a common element in Middle-Platonic ethics, though its philosophical impact remained rather superficial.[38]

Besides, of course, we must be certain that Aristobulus at least had a direct connection with the Stoic method of interpretation, since many scholars see the tradition as progressing from Stoic origins, represented by Aristobulus, to the Platonic-influenced allegory of Philo.

However, we find that, even less than in Philo, does anything in Aristobulus' philosophical interpretations point to a specifically Stoic influence. N. Walter already, though pointing at the Stoic origin of Aristobulus' exegesis, had to acknowledge this fact: ". . . sein Gottesgedanke ist nicht der stoische, seine allegorische Auslegung antropomorphischer Züge ging daher auch nicht auf physische Grössen, sondern auf Gottes geschichtliches Handeln."[39] We can add that the philosophy of Aristobulus' explanations is close to the Pseudo-Aristotelian treatise *De Mundo* and to some of the Pythagorean pseudepigrapha.[40]

---

[34] Cf. Hay, "Philo's References," 47.

[35] Cf. J. Dillon, "The Formal Structure of Philo's Allegorical Exegesis," in *Two Treatises of Philo of Alexandria. A Commentary on the De Gigantibus and Quod Deus sit immutabilis* (ed. D. Winston and J. Dillon; Brown Judaic Studies 25; Chico, California: Scholars Press, 1983), 81. See also my 'Introduction' to the Russian Philo (*Филон Александрийский. Толкования Ветхого Завета* (Москва: ГЛК Ю. А. Шичалина, 2000), 7–50, 30–36. Cf. Steven di Mattei, "Moses' Physiologia and the Meaning of Physikos in Philo of Alexandria," *SPhA* 18 (2006): 3–32, 24.

[36] This is strongly reminiscent of Chrysippus, who wished to demonstrate that Hesiod's account of the birth of Athena from the head of Zeus did not conflict with the Stoic teaching that the heart is the seat of intelligence (Galen, *De plac. Hipp. Et Plat.* 3.8.2–21 = *SVF* 2.908–909).

[37] *Leg.* 1.59. Something similar occurs in *QG* 1.10.

[38] J. Whittaker, "Platonic Philosophy in the Early Centuries of the Empire," in *ANRW* II, Bd. 36.1 (1988), 116.

[39] Walter, *Der Thoraausleger Aristobulos,* 136.

[40] E. Matusova, "Philosophical Exegesis of the Old Testament in the Works of Philo of Alexandria: the Sources and the Tradition" (Ph.D. diss., Russian Academy of Sciences,

2.2. *Objections from form and method*

Even more problematic than the argument from content is the argument from the method of Philo's exegesis as compared with Stoic patterns. It has been noted that Philo's exegesis resembles the neo-Platonic commentaries closely in the following respects: all text is divided into lemmata—short passages ranging from a single line to a paragraph; the text of the lemma is analyzed phrase by phrase, and the text of the phrase—word by word; and lemmata are grouped into sections of commentary.[41] The text of the LXX is analyzed *thoroughly*, i.e., practically every word of every sentence is considered as apt to be interpreted allegorically. This coincides with Philo's own statement, that almost everything in the Law of Moses can be understood allegorically.[42]

However, it is important to realize that this approach to a literary text was, it seems, not typical of Stoic exegesis of Homer. What interested the Stoics was interpreting aspects of a *myth* presented within a text, rather than the text itself as a literary phenomenon. This was demonstrated by A. Long and J. Porter in their analysis of the Stoic methods of literary criticism.[43] In particular, J. Porter emphasizes, "I am wholeheartedly in agreement with A. Long in his critique of the assumption, which has gone unquestioned for too long, that the Stoics were interested in allegory as a form of literary interpretation,"[44] i.e., in allegorical interpretation of a *literary* text. As such, the text only interested the Stoics within the boundaries of the sort of philological criticism legitimized by Aristotle's Poetics (allegory was not among such methods). Long does not consider Heraclitus, the author of the *Homeric Problems*, a true Stoic. Nevertheless, even Heraclitus is in no way ready to interpret allegorically the *whole* text of the Iliad, or *every* fragment of it. Only those passages which look impious can be, as a last resort, interpreted allegorically in order to rescue their moral content and to defend Homer from the charge of impiety (*Quaest. Hom.* 6).

The interest of the Stoics in the myths, which underlie a poetic narrative, was legitimized by the approach already familiar to the Greek

---

Institute of Philosophy, 2000), 80–83 (in Russian); eadem, "Aristobulus," in *Ancient Philosophy. Encyclopaedic Dictionary* (ed. M. Solopova; Moscow: Progress-Traditzia, 2008), 152–154 (in Russian).

[41] J. Dillon, "The Formal Structure," 78.

[42] *Jos.* 28.

[43] A. A. Long, "Stoic readings of Homer," in *Homer's Ancient Readers: the Hermeneutics of Greek Epic's Earliest Exegete* (ed. R. Lamberton and J. Keaney; Princeton, NJ: Princeton University Press, 1992), 41–60; James I. Porter, "Hermeneutic Lines and Circles: Aristarchus and Crates on the Exegesis of Homer," *ibid.*, 67–114.

[44] Porter, "Hermeneutic Lines," 86, n. 52.

philosophy. For instance, Plato in the *Timaeus* (22 c–d) says that ancient myths conceal some cosmological truth and gives an example of how these mythological events can be interpreted. From the viewpoint of this approach, allegorical interpretation is possible because every myth bears some hidden information in itself, independently of the literary form, which it has. Consequently, the Stoics, who essentially followed this idea expressed by Plato, did not consider the author of the text as an *intentional* allegorist[45] (and consequently did non apply allegorical interpretation to his literary innovations). Even Heraclitus, who unlike other Stoics, claims that Homer could really intend to say something allegorically, does not insist on this idea. He only says: "So, since the trope of allegory is familiar to all other writers (actually, Heraclitus is talking about metaphors—E.M.) and known even to Homer, *what should prevent us mending his alleged wrong notions about the gods by this kind of justification?*"[46] However, Philo constantly credits Moses, who, according to the tradition reflected in the *Jubilees*, is the author of the Pentateuch, with the intention to write allegorically,[47] and he was not the first to make this claim. Already Aristobulus says that Moses often intentionally talks allegorically.[48] Consequently, Aristobulus too says that he will systematically unfold every truth hinted by Moses ("I shall begin then to interpret each particular signification, as far as I may be able").[49]

There is also another significant difference between Philonic and Stoic exegesis, which Long's study elucidates. At the level of the interpreter it is reasonable to distinguish two positions, one of explicating or unfolding a meaning which in one way or another is present within the text, and another of ignoring or completely effacing this meaning and replacing it with another parallel one. It is this second possibility which is *allegorization*, or allegorical interpretation, properly so called, while the former is better termed *interpretation*, or interpreting explanation. Long thinks that Stoic exegesis, examined from this point of view, is best described as interpretation, applied to mythical facts and not to literary texts. It always has the etymology of names and verbs as a starting point and retains the link with the plain meaning of the text—e.g., Hera is air, Metis is intellect, mind and so on.[50] The same is true of Heraclitus, whose interpretative principle is very close to the explicative and etymologically based interpretation of the

---

[45] This idea is particularly stressed by A. Long, "Stoic readings," 43 ff.
[46] Heraclitus, *All.* 6.1 (Transl. by D. A. Russell and D. Konstan.).
[47] *Prob.* 29 ; *Det* 15 ; *Fug.* 194; *Deus* 23; 94–95; 128.
[48] Eusebius, *Praep. ev.* 8. 10. 1–4
[49] Eusebius, *Praep. ev.* 8. 10. 6.
[50] Long, "Stoic readings," 56–59.

Stoics. However, the very opposite is true of Philo. As has been said, Philo works with a system of metaphysical and ethical terms which he forcedly brings together with the text of the Pentateuch, what often creates a gulf between literal and allegorical meaning (the wives of the patriarchs are virtues; daughters of men are pleasures, giants are degenerated human souls, masculine seed is logos, Joseph is always soul attached to the body etc.). And even when using etymology, Philo, unlike the Stoics, does not depend on etymological suggestions in his philosophical explanations, what has been rightly stressed by D. Runia.[51] What Philo is doing in the great majority of cases is, in Long's terms, *allegorization,* or *allegorical inter-pretation,* properly so called. Aristobulus too, clearly identifies a gap between surface meaning and hidden meaning, and what he does is, therefore, certainly *allegorization* of the LXX.

Long himself, comparing Philonic and Stoic methods of interpretation, concludes that the Stoic influence on Philo's allegorical methodology "if it existed at all, was marginal to Philo's main concerns and only superficially related to Stoicism."[52] And despite some doubts which have been expressed as a reaction on his position,[53] I still think that Long's opinion is valuable as coming from an expert in Stoic philosophy: Long could not fail to see that what we have in Philo is not essentially Stoic.

2.3. *Historical objection*

Finally, a purely historical objection comes into force here. It seems that Homeric allegory became a formal method of criticism in the Stoic school no earlier than in the time of Crates of Mallos[54] (Heraclitus and Cornutus were his followers). Prior to that, it appears only sporadically in the history of the Stoa, no more often than it does in other schools of Greek philosophy as part of a general Greek interest in allegorical interpretation, already

---

[51] D. T. Runia, "Etymology as an Allegorical Technique in Philo of Alexandria," *SPhA* 16 (2004): 101–121, 113: "Firstly, in many cases there appears to be quite a distance between the etymology and the symbol that the name represents. Symbols cannot be derived directly from the etymology, but are the result of interpretation in terms of a larger allegorical scheme. The chicken precedes the egg." That is true: the chicken of philosophical interpretation always precedes the egg of etymology, and this is hardly compatible with what we know about the Stoic approach.

[52] A.A. Long, "Allegory in Philo and Etymology in Stoicism: a Plea for Drawing Distinctions," *SPh* 9 (1997): 198–210, 198. Cf. also 199, 206.

[53] D.T. Runia, "Etymology as an Allegorical Technique," 119.

[54] R. Pfeiffer, *History of Classical Scholarship from the Beginnings to the End of the Hellenistic Age* (Oxford: Clarendon, 1968), 140, 237.

evinced by the pre-Socratics.[55] However, the Stoic Crates of Mallos was an approximate contemporary of Aristobulus (first half of the second century B.C.) and belonged to the philological school of Pergamum, which at this time had parted company with the Alexandrian school—the theoretical debates between the two had become notorious. In such a situation, it becomes difficult to talk of Aristobulus as drawing directly on Crates and his school. In his analysis of the philosophical situation in Alexandria in the second century B.C., Frazer concludes that it is unlikely that Aristobulus could have been influenced by the Stoics.[56]

Thus, I think we have too many unanswered questions. (1) From the point of view of material, method and purpose, the principles of Philo's commentary cannot be sufficiently explained from within the Jewish interpretative tradition, as known to us from Qumran, Midrash and New Testament texts, which agree more among themselves than with Philo. (2) All interpretations cited by Philo are purely secular and do not point toward a specifically Jewish environment. (3) The Stoic origin of Philo's method is not confirmed either by an analysis of the fragments of the first known allegorical commentary of the second century B.C., nor by an analysis of his own works.

And until all these questions have been answered and all these contradictions have been reconciled I will allow myself to continue doubting that the conception of Philo's commentary as originating within a Jewish environment of textual interpretation in synagogues, and based on Stoic allegory, is the most adequate attempt to explain this great and outstanding cultural phenomenon.

3. *The Greek tradition of allegorical exegesis: a new perspective*

As we have mentioned, most works on Philonic allegory are based on the hypothesis that all Hellenistic allegory is traceable to Stoic roots. However, this hypothesis is, essentially, mistaken.

It is worth noting again that allegorical interpretation was actually practiced long before Stoicism came into being and continued to be used by several philosophical schools in Hellenistic times.

If we turn, for instance, to the historical and literary facts, we shall find that attempts to interpret a "barbarian" text allegorically are not unique in

---

[55] F. Wehrli, *Zur Geschichte der allegorischen Deutung Homers in Altertum* (Borna, Leipzig: R. Noske, 1928), 15–30.

[56] D. M. Frazer, *Ptolemaic Alexandria* (3 vols.; Oxford: Clarendon, 1972), vol. 2, n. 108.

the Greek-speaking world. There are in fact several parallels in the period from the second century B.C. to the second century A.D. As mentioned above, in the second century B.C., Aristobulus,[57] who dedicated his work to Ptolemy Philometor, wrote a philosophical commentary in the spirit of Peripatetic/ Pythagorean philosophy. In Philo's time, again in Alexandria, Chaeremon,[58] a Stoic and an Egyptian priest, wrote an allegorical commentary to Egyptian myths. In the second century A.D., Plutarch, a Platonist close to neo-Pythagorean circles, also wrote a commentary on Egyptian myths (the *On Isis and Osiris*), referring extensively to other interpretations of the myth, Pythagorean as well as Stoic. Finally, in the second century A.D., we find another allegorizing commentary on the Old Testament, composed by a Pythagorean, Numenius of Apamea, who had no direct connection to Judaism. Numenius interprets the Old and even the New Testament in the spirit of Platonic/Pythagorean philosophy, and famously asks: "Who is Plato, but Moses speaking Attic Greek?"[59]

We have therefore five examples of allegorical commentary on Eastern —"barbarian"—texts, one of which belongs to an author, designated elsewhere as a Stoic, and the others to authors who are either specifically designated as Pythagoreans by the sources, or who were in close contact with Pythagoreanism. I would like to note here that Clement of Alexandria —a literate and well-informed Alexandrian of the not-so-distant future— also calls Philo a Pythagorean. He does this especially when discussing his literary undertaking.[60] His testimony, though its reliability is a matter for discussion,[61] has, in my view, received too little attention.

---

[57] Clement of Alexandria, *Strom.* 5.14.97; Eusebius, *Praep. ev.* 13.12.

[58] P. W. van der Horst, *Chaeremon: Egyptian Priest and Stoic Philosopher* (EPRO 101; Leiden: Brill, 1984); M. Frede, "Chaeremon der Stoiker," in *ANRW* II 36.3 (Berlin-New York: W. de Gruyter, 1989), 2067–2103.

[59] Scholars such as Waszink (J. H. Waszink, "Porphyrios und Numenios," in *Porphyre* (Entrétiens sur l'antiquité classique 12; Vandeuvres-Génève: Fondation Hardt, 1966), 35ff and Dodds (E. R. Dodds, "The *Parmenides* of Plato and the Origin of the Neoplatonic *One*," *CQ* 22 (1928): 140, n.1; Idem, *Pagan and Christian in an Age of Anxiety* (Cambridge: Cambridge University Press, 1965), 130, n.2) believe that Numenius knew Philo's works. However, J. Whitaker rightly points out that this cannot be proven, since the Septuagint attracted the Greeks' attention quite independently of Judaism (J. Whitaker, "Moses Atticizing," *Phoenix* 21 (1967): 196–201). He gives particular prominence to this idea in his article, though touching only on the later tradition (after the first century B.C.). Cf. also P. Merlan, "Philo and the beginnings of Christian thought," in *The Cambridge History of Later Greek and Early Medieval Philosophy* (ed. A. H. Armstrong; Cambridge: Cambridge University Press, 1967), 96–106.

[60] Clement of Alexandria, *Strom.* 1.72: τούτων ἁπάντων πρεσβύτατον μακρῷ τὸ Ἰουδαίων γένος, καὶ τὴν παρ' αὐτοῖς φιλοσοφίαν ἔγγραπτον γενομένην προκατάρξαι τῆς παρ' Ἕλλησι

When, early in the third century A.D., Origen wrote the first Christian allegorical commentary to the Old Testament, Porphyry, in his polemic *Against the Christians*, asserted that Origen's work was modeled on the writings of neo-Pythagoreans such as Numenius, Cronius, Apollophanes, Longinus, Moderatus, Nicomachus and other famous Pythagoreans, as well as on the books of the Stoics Chaeremon and Cornutus.[62]

Clearly, allegorical commentaries could be written by both Stoics and Pythagoreans, but the examples cited above, as well as the names listed by Porphyry, point to the Pythagoreans as being more prominent in allegorical criticism. For instance, although few examples of Pythagorean commentaries have come down to us, ancient literature gives many indications of their existence. Pythagoreans wrote commentaries on Homeric epic,[63] on sculptures and paintings,[64] on the sayings of Pythagoras himself (this last is the largest category—see below) and, what concerns us most, commentaries on the myths or texts of barbarian nations (Numenius, Plutarch).

The Pythagorean activity in allegorical criticism can hardly be reduced to the Stoic influence. Apparently, it was another branch of Hellenistic tradition deriving from an ancient source. I want to draw attention to the fact that, when studying the history of Greek allegory, we should probably concentrate not so much on with which school an author was affiliated, but more on his basic principles of allegorical approach to the text. Reconstruction of a principle that differs from the Stoic attitude to Homer can lead us to a better understanding of the phenomenon and to a more detailed conception of the history of this *literary genre*.

A very important indication of an approach to the text different from the interpretative explanation of the Stoics is provided by Porphyry's testimony concerning Origen. *Having borrowed from the Greek authors their method of interpreting Greek mysteries,* Origen, according to Porphyry, *applied it to the Hebrew scriptures.*[65] Porphyry affirms the connection between allegorization and interpretation applied in Greek tradition to some elements of mystery cults. His statement made in the third century A.D. can be

---

φιλοσοφίας διὰ πολλῶν ὁ **Πυθαγόρειος** ὑποδείκνυσι Φίλων; *Strom.* 2.100: ὡς φησιν ὁ **Πυθαγόρειος** Φίλων τὰ Μωυσέως ἐξηγούμενος .

[61] See, for instance, D. T. Runia, "Why does Clement of Alexandria call Philo 'The Pythagorean'?," *VC* 49 (1995): 1–22.

[62] Porphyry, *Christ.* fr. 39 Harnack (= Eusebius, *Hist. eccl.* 6.1. 4–8).

[63] Origen, *Cels.* 7. 6. 33–40.

[64] Plutarch, *Is. Os.* 318E. The so-called *Tabula Cebetis* has also been written in Pythagorizing circles.

[65] Porphyry, *Christ.* fr. 39 Harnack (=Eusebius, *Hist. eccl.* 6.19. 8).

exemplified by the theoretical preamble of a commentary, written, as early
as in the fifth or forth century B.C., namely, the Derveni Papyrus.

3. 1. *The Derveni Papyrus*

The Derveni papyrus contains a commentary on a theogonic Orphic poem.
This commentary is essentially allegorical; it transposes elements of the
poem into the level of Greek physical philosophy. It is not difficult to see
that in fact the wish to interpret the poem indirectly arises because the content of the poem, being sometimes extremely obscene, is incompatible with
the theological norms established by Greek philosophical thought. However, the author of the commentary proposes his own theoretical foundation of this approach, which has fortunately come down to us. The author
claims that the text of the poem belongs to a mystery cult and is intended
only for those who have been initiated. Thus, in the col. 7 we read:[66]

> ... hymn saying *sound and lawful things* (ὑγιῆ καὶ θεμιτά). For he was [telling a
> holy discourse] by his poetry. For it is not possible to state what way the *words
> are used* (τὴν ὀνομάτων θέσιγ) and at the same time *the text itself* (τὰ ῥηθέντα).[67]
> His poetry is something *strange* (ξένη) and *riddling* (αἰνιγματώδης) for people.
> But Orpheus did not intend to tell them captious riddles, but *momentous things*
> (μεγάλα) in riddles. Indeed, he is **telling a holy discourse** (ἱερ[ολογ]εῖται) *from
> the first and up to the last word* (καὶ ἀπὸ τοῦ πρώτου καὶ μέχρι τοῦ τελευταίου
> ῥήματος). As he also makes clear in the well-chosen verse: for having ordered
> them to put doors to their ears he says that he is [not legis]lating for the many
> ... [? but only for] those pure in hearing ...

Let us observe the exegetical principles of this commentary to the extent
they can be useful for our discussion.

The starting point of the approach seems to be the notion of **telling a
holy discourse** (ἱερολογεῖσθαι). This verb is derived from the collocation
ἱερὸς λόγος, **a holy discourse**. As far as we know, this collocation was
initially a *terminus technicus* in religious language used to designate a

[66] I adopted the translation by G. Betegh (G. Betegh, *The Derveni Papyrus: Cosmology,
Theology and Interpretation* (Cambridge: Cambridge University Press, 2004), 17).
[67] I adopted the reconstruction proposed by Janko (cf. R. Janko, "The Derveni
Papyrus: an Interim Text," *ZPE* 141 (2002): 1–61, 14). Another reconstruction and translation by K. Tsantsanoglou–G.M. Parassoglou: «And one cannot state the solution of the
words (τὴν ὀνομάτων λύσιγ) though they are spoken (καίτοι ῥηθέντα)» (*The Derveni Papyrus*
(ed. Theokritos Kouremenos, George M. Parássoglou, Kyriakos Tsantsanoglou; STCPF 13;
Firenze: Leo S. Olschki editore, 2006), 74–75, 130–131).

narrative connected to mystery rituals, fully known only to the initiates.[68] Basing himself upon this crucial idea of the connection between holy discourse and secret rites, the author of the commentary claims that no ordinary man can rightly understand Orpheus' Theogony because this text is also *a kind of holy discourse* intended only for the initiates (apparently because it was, according to the common opinion, written by Orpheus, whose name was closely associated with mysteries).

Therefore every reader who wants to understand the true meaning of the text needs some special explanations, which introduce him into its secret content like an initiate is introduced into the mysteries. *Thus the main metaphor of the genre we are going to trace comes into being: allegorical interpretation of an Orphic poem is compared to initiation into the mysteries.* Without such an interpretation the reader sees its "momentous" (μεγάλα) content just as "strange" (ξένη) and "riddling" (αἰνιγματώδης).

At the same time the author of the commentary stresses that an Orphic *holy discourse* is not only inevitably, but even *intentionally* allegorical (cf. col.7. 10–11: "[Orpheus] is [not legis]lating for the many . . . [? but only for] those pure in hearing . . . " col. 13.5: "in his whole poetry he speaks about facts through the hints"). This indirect way of expression was chosen in order not to be understood by everybody, but only by those who are capable of it.

The author insists that the indirect way of expression is peculiar to the poem as a whole and that the discrepancy between surface and inner meaning concerns every particular element of the poem: Orpheus is talking allegorically "from the first and up to the last word" (7.7–8: καὶ ἀπὸ τοῦ πρώτου καὶ μέχρι τοῦ τελευταίου ῥήματος). And "one has to speak about each verse in turn (καθ' ἔπος ἔκαστον) that in his whole poetry he speaks about facts through the hints (αἰνίζεται)," (col. 13. 5–6: ὅτι μὲν πᾶσαν τὴν ποίησιν περὶ τῶν πραγμάτων αἰνίζεται καθ'ἔπος ἔκαστον ἀνάγκη λέγειν). Thus, the nature of an Orphic poem is described as totally allegorical.

One of the main concerns of the author is to persuade readers that the things said by Orpheus are *sound and lawful*. This assertion, however, blatantly contradicts the reality, since Orphic poems in general, and this one, in particular, do say utterly shameful things about the gods (cf. coll. 8, 13 etc.). The only way to avoid this evident inconsistency was to claim that what is literally said does not coincide with what is meant under the words. Consequently, it creates a methodological approach of interpretation which

---

[68] Herodotus, *Hist.* 2. 51, 62, 81. Cf. R. Baumgarten, *Heiliges Wort und Heilige Schrift bei den Griechen. Hieroi Logoi und verwandte Erscheinungen* (Tübingen: Gunter Narr Verlag, 1998), 122 ff.

consciously separates two levels of a text. Whatever reconstruction of the third sentence of the column we accept (τῶν ὀνομάτων θέσιν or τὴν ὀνομάτων λύσιν), the idea of the author remains the same: the written or spoken level of the text does not coincide with its deep content. It is clearly reformulated in the col. 20, where concerning τὰ λεγόμενα of the mysteries it is said that "it is not possible to hear and at the same time to understand them" (20.3: οὐ γὰρ οἷόν τε ἀκοῦσαι καὶ ὁμοῦ μαθεῖν τὰ λεγόμενα).

The particular explanations proposed by the author of the Derveni papyrus perfectly illustrate this statement. While equating the deities of the Theogony with the forces of nature and thus giving all the mythological events in the poem physical and theological sense, he does not accept a minimalist interpreting explanation invited by the meanings already contained in the text, neither does he care to rescue any literal meaning of any passage (the manner which is typical of Stoic exegesis of Homer). On the contrary, he rather forcibly subordinates all elements of the narrative to his philosophical idea, which is much more important to him than anything in the text of the poem. For instance, Olympus is not heaven, as people may think, but Time (col. 12); the Ocean is neither river nor water, but Air (col. 23). In interpreting the text he does not follow anything but the logic of his philosophical vision. And even when using etymology, he does not follow its obvious suggestions, but rather makes it serve his sometimes rather extravagant explanations, which fit the general picture he draws. Thus Kronos is not connected to chronos, time, though that would be a reasonable and etymologically well-founded explanation in the spirit of the later Stoics. He interprets it as *Mind*, because this "strikes," or "pushes together" (κρούει), all things (col. 14). Using the distinction made by A. Long (see above), we can say that the author of the Derveni papyrus prefers the allegorical interpretation properly so called, refusing the possibility of exploring any interpreting explanation.

As for the secret content of the text, many examples of the allegorical interpretation proposed by the author of the commentary show us that he was looking mainly for physical and astronomical explanations, equating Zeus with the air and interpreting all other deities as its aspects.[69] In the Derveni commentary physical interpretations prevail to the extent that it becomes clear how the notion of physical interpretation could potentially converge with the notion of allegorical interpretation as such. We will see exactly this convergence in many examples of allegorical interpretations in the subsequent period, and particularly in Philo himself. Philo, as we know, on many (around 75) occasions uses the term *natural*, φυσικός, to refer to

---

[69] Columns 9; 10.10–13; 11.1–4; 12; 13; 14; 17.

allegorical interpretation as such, and often to emphasize that the Scripture aims to speak allegorically.[70] It is in the line of this very reasoning that at several points he refers to the allegorists themselves as φυσικοὶ ἄνδρες.[71]

Let us repeat the main points of the approach, proposed in the Derveni papyrus.

1. The text is termed a *hieros logos* (or the manner in which a text speaks is claimed to be typical of *hieros logos*)
2. The terminology of mysteries accompanies exegesis and constitutes its main metaphor.
3. The text is considered as being thoroughly allegorical, from the first to the last word.
4. It is considered as being intentionally (and inevitably) allegorical.
5. The hidden meanings of the events, words and expressions, used in the text, are often considered completely alien to their plain meaning.
6. Therefore allegorizing and not interpreting explanation is the main principle of the commentary.
7. The interpretation proposed is philosophical and, particularly, physical in character.

As we see, all points of this approach, except for the last one, represent a picture, which is diametrically opposed to that of Stoic exegesis of Homer and suspiciously similar to the approach typical of Philo's exegesis of the LXX. Particularly, I want to stress the importance of the two first elements. Exceptionally, and to an extent that is attested neither before nor after him, Philo designates the LXX as a *hieros logos*. In total he applies this concept more than one hundred times, a statistic comparable with his use of the concepts of *physiologia* and *physikos*, which for Philo, (as said), signifies allegorical interpretation in general. This concept of the *hieros logos* has no direct parallel in Jewish culture and language; it will, after Philo, also be carefully avoided by Christian authors, with the exception of the Alexandrians Clement and Origen who use it in contexts relating to allegorical

---

[70] *Leg.* 1.39; 3.177; *Conf.* 60; *Fug.* 19; *Abr.* 241; *QG* 2.81.

[71] *Post.* 7; *Abr.* 99. The technical connotations of the notion had been observed by scholars (see Hay, "Philo's references," 46–47, cf. also di Mattei, "Moses' Physiologia," 4, nn.5,6). In my opinion, Steven di Mattei's critique of the possibility of technical implications of the term is not very convincing ("Moses' Physiologia," 5–9). My impression is that in order to realize the literary dimension of the notion we have to locate it in a right perspective which reveals itself through the tradition which follows the Derveni commentary (see below).

interpretation. Also, Philo constantly describes the process of comprehending the hidden meaning of the LXX , termed a *hieros logos*, as an initiation into the mysteries (*Sacr.* 60; *Cher* .42; *Somn.* 1.164; *Det.* 11–16), using the terminology which has sometimes been so trying to some scholars. I will return to the detailed analysis of these contexts below. At present, I suggest that this terminology, as well as all other points of this exegetical approach which we have highlighted, must be understood through the perspective of a literary genre.

3.2. *Allegorical interpretation of hieroi logoi in development*

First of all, it is important to state that the commentary of the Derven papyrus is one of many examples of allegorical interpretation of the Orphic poems which have come down to us in fragments and in the citations of ancient authors. An allegorical commentary on an Orphic poem is attributed to a certain Epigenes, who probably lived in the fourth century B.C.[72] We find also citations of allegorical exegesis of Orphic *hieroi logoi* in the fragments of Denis Thrace, an Alexandrian grammarian of the second or first century B.C. [73] Finally, Clement of Alexandria, a Christian exegete of the second century A.D., proposed an interpretation of an Orphic poem, written in the Hellenistic period and called the *Testamentum Orphei*, which bears some evident traces of allegorical technique.[74] This last example demonstrates the popularity which the genre of indirect philosophical interpretation of Orphic poems had in the Hellenistic, and particularly, in the Alexandrian tradition.

As far as we know, in the Hellenistic period the term *hieros logos* was generally applied to Orphic poems of various content and origin. This fact is better explained not by the poems' connection to real mystery cults (which, in my opinion, is difficult to prove even in the case of the Orphic Theogony of the Derveni papyrus), but by an influence of the literary tradition.[75] In particular, and among other reasons, as a development of the idea exposed in the Derveni commentary, i.e., by their widely acknowledged fitness for allegorical interpretation. If our suggestion is right, it testifies to the fact that in the field of the Orphic literature there was a transformation or an extension of the notion of *hieros logos* from a *terminus*

---

[72] Clement of Alexandria, *Strom.* 5.8.49; Cf. M. L. West, *The Orphic Poems* (Oxford: Clarendon, 1983), 9.

[73] Clement of Alexandria, *Strom.* 5.8.45.

[74] Clement of Alexandria, *Strom.* 5.8.124–126.

[75] Baumgarten, *Heiliges Wort*, 98 f.

technicus used in the language of religion to a designation of a text which speaks allegorically and demands, therefore, allegorical interpretation.[76] This kind of text was only conventionally related to mystery rites. Thus, the notion of *hieros logos* became significant not in the religious area only, but also in the field of literary genres, whereas the terminology of mysteries accompanied this term as an indispensable part of the genre.[77]

The suggestion of how this Orphic tradition could be extended onto another material, we find in the theoretical preamble of the Derveni papyrus itself. It is very important that the Derveni papyrus already emphasizes that the enigmatic quality of the Orphic text seems *somewhat "foreign"* (ξένη).[78] This epithet may hint at the Thracian origin of the singer, but at the same time, just before this statement, we are told that the mysteries of the Greeks are organized on the pattern of the magi, who, whatever they were, nevertheless were associated with barbarian priests.[79] This thought can be inscribed in the wider circle of similar ideas of the generic kinship between the Greek and the barbarian mysteries. These ideas were very popular in the Greek world, beginning with Herodotus, who identifies Orphic and Pythagorean sacred rites with those of the Egyptians (2.81), and through to Strabo, who generalizes the problem, commenting, in relation to the mysteries that, "Greeks and barbarians have" these "as a common habit" (10. 3, 9). Viewing the comparison clearly expressed in the Derveni papyrus in the context of the history of a literary genre, we have to note that this parallel invites the possibility of transferring the interpretative methods applied to the Orphic text onto sacred texts of comparable status within any barbarian culture. As early as the turn of the fourth century B.C., we can attest the possibility of transferring the related concepts of "holy discourse" and "riddling" into "foreign," that is barbarian, texts connected, at least in the eyes of the Greeks, with the mysteries. Consequently, this kind of text, being a *holy discourse*, was to be interpreted allegorically.

[76] In some of the later texts the notion of *hieros logos* sometimes completely loses its connection to any other context than a literary one, what had rightly been suggested by R. Janko (cf. for instance the use of the terms ἱερολογεῖσθαι, ἱερολογία, ἱερολόγος in the sense of "speak in allegories" in Lucianus, *Syr. D*.26 and *Astr.* 10 and in Herennius Philo, FGrH 790 F.1, 49). Cf. R. Janko, "The Derveni Papyrus (Diagoras of Melos, *Apopyrgizontes Logoi*?): a new translation," *CP* 96 (2001): 1–32, 3.

[77] Incidentally, this corresponds to the conclusion arrived at by Christoph Riedweg, though he does not bring up the question of the genre of interpretation of *hieroi logoi*. Cf. Ch. Riedweg, *Mysterionterminologie bei Platon, Philon und Klemens von Alexandrien* (Berlin: W.de Gruyter, 1987), 90–92.

[78] Column 7. 4–7.

[79] Column 6. 1–10.

The idea of connection of any barbarian religion with some mystery rites and consequently the notion of barbarian mysteries was in fact one of the Greeks' preconceived and firmly entrenched ideas. For instance, the particular connection which, as the Greeks thought, existed between Orphic texts and the Egyptian legends connected to mystery cults, is attested by a fragment of Plutarch which comes from his lost treatise *On the Daedalian Festivals*:

> Among the ancients, Greeks as well as barbarians, the science of nature (φυσιο-λογία) was presented in the form of a scientific discourse (φυσικὸς λόγος) hidden in myths more often as a theology which appeared mysterious, concealed by riddles and implications (δι'αἰνιγμάτων καὶ ὑπονοιῶν), in which what was expressed was, for the mob, clearer than what was kept silent, but what was kept silent had more meaning than what was expressed. That is what appears clearly in the Orphic poems (τὰ ὀρφικὰ ἔπη), in the Egyptian and Phrygian legends (οἱ Αἰγύπτιοι καὶ Φρύγιοι λόγοι), and it is above all the liturgies of initiation to the mysteries and symbolic rites of sacrifice that show the thought of the ancients.[80]

As we see, Plutrarch groups Orphic poems and barbarian, especially Egyptian, legends (discourses) together as far as their mode of conveying information is concerned. Both types of text conceal theological, physical truth, which is accessible only to a few "initiates." All other people, the mob, see in them only riddles, but not their hidden meaning. The idea of this mode of expression being congenial to one typical of mystery rituals follows from the last words of the quotation above, as well as from the epithet *mysterious* applied to the notion of theology concealed in the text. Obviously, the term *mysterious* as defining the character of the theology hidden in the narratives is here rather a term of genre (as well as the division into the mob and a few "initiates" suggested by the author)—the terminology of mysteries had by that time become indispensable for discussion of allegorical meaning of *hieroi logoi*. In this passage two important terms remain unspoken, but clearly hinted at, being the basic notions of the discourse. Firstly, here we see again that the idea of *physical* (or theological) content of the text coincides with the idea of its *allegorical* nature. Secondly, equating the Orphic poems, usually termed *hieroi logoi*, with the Egyptian *logoi*, usually considered as being connected to mystery festivals, naturally in this context presupposes the extension of the notion of *hieros logos* onto the Egyptian myths.

We find an earlier testimony of this transfer in an Orphic poem, the *Argonautica*. This poem explicitly mentions the *holy discourse (hieron logon) of*

---

[80] Fr.157, Sandbach.

the Egyptians,[81] showing how the Orphic tradition absorbs some elements of the Egyptian.

In accordance with what Plutarch says in the fragment quoted above, Plutarch himself in his treatise *On Isis and Osiris* refers to the myth of Isis and Osiris as a *hieros logos* (351F, 352B). Consequently, allegorical explanation is in his eyes the only legitimate way to approach this text. Plutarch says that in order to penetrate into the hidden theological meaning of this narrative "we must take *philosophical reasoning* as our guide and *mystagogue*" (378A). He refers, therefore, to an initiation into the mysteries as the main metaphor of an allegorical interpretation of the text, which, as we have noted, directly follows from the reasoning of the Derveni commentary. At the same time he claims the philosophical interpretation to be the only way of explanation. His interpretations are mainly purely physical and astronomical in nature. In agreement with the ideology of the Derveni papyrus, he announces that the narrative must be purified of all superstition and indecency, because "the wisdom contained in their *theology* is *riddling*" (354 C). Thus, the deep theological level of the text is regarded as covered with a strange, riddling form, which looks indecent and even shameful. In the same treatise Plutarch tells us that the enigmatic, symbolic form of an allegorical text is expressed through *words* (ὀνόματα) which cannot be understood in their proper meaning (370 F). Thus he refers to the distinction, reflected in the papyrus, between the expression and the content level of the text. In complete agreement with the approach of the Derveni text again, Plutarch specifies that in such a text (which is a *hieros logos*), *nothing* of what has been said (τῶν λεγομένων) can be taken in its direct sense: every detail, every event and person has to be understood allegorically (355 B; 378 A).

However, the logic of the Derveni text does not confine the development to any particular barbarian tradition. It mentions Persian magi who perform rites in a way analogous to the Greek mysteries, which theoretically could lead to a corresponding treatment of their texts had they been sufficiently known to the Greeks. Plutarch, for his part, mentions some Phrygian legends along with the Egyptian ones, showing that allegorical interpretation was also attempted in relation to this material. The process, as Plutarch shows, which took place in the melting pot of Hellenistic Egypt in relation to the local Egyptian culture, could—and for many historical reasons would be quicker to touch—the culture of the Egyptian Jews, especially since the Greeks of the early Hellenistic period were inclined to regard Jewish culture as a barbarian culture of deep philosophical

---

[81] *Arg.* 43: ἠδ' ὅσον Αἰγυπτίων ἱερὸν λόγον ἐξελόχευσα.

meaning.[82] It is very important to realize that the Jews of Hellenistic Egypt in the third and second centuries B.C. had a social and cultural position, which differed in many ways from their position in the subsequent period, when cultural climate changed under the influence of the Roman rule and with the intensification of the religious ideology of the Maccabees. In earlier periods, these people enjoyed a privileged position and often a high social status, and were in the eyes of the Greeks much closer to the Greeks and Macedonians themselves than to the local Egyptian population. Consequently, they had many more grounds for assimilating their culture with the culture of the dominant social class than even the Egyptians.[83] From the moment when, in the second century B.C., the *Letter of Aristeas* fixed the status of the Septuagint as the sacred text of the Jews, the generalizing thought of the Greeks had every right to treat it as a sacred text, placing it on the same level as the sacred texts of other barbarian peoples and drawing it into the orbit of their own traditions connected with sacred material. The Hebrews on their part, at least the most lettered of them, evidently did not wish to miss the opportunity to raise the prestige of the Pentateuch to the level of a philosophical text

3.2.1. The Jewish contribution: Aristobulus

It is not insignificant that our first allegorical commentary on the LXX, written by a philosopher Aristobulus and dedicated to Ptolemy VI Philometor (185–146 B.C.), is approximately contemporaneous with the *Letter of Aristeas*. I want to draw attention to some interesting details in the fragments of Aristobulus' commentary, which can prove this line of thinking.

From our viewpoint it is important, that *an Orphic poem* of Hellenistic origin, which Aristobulus quotes extensively in his commentary, serves

---

[82] M. Hengel, *Judentum und Hellenismus* (Tübingen: J. C. B. Mohr (Paul Siebeck), 1988³), 464–472; J. Mélèze Modrzejewski, *The Jews of Egypt from Rameses II to Emperor Hadrian* (Philadelphia: Jewish Publication Society, 1995), 49–50.

[83] J. Mélèze Modrzejewski, *The Jews of Egypt*, 82–83. The study of papyri and inscriptions shows a very high degree of assimilation among the Jews of Early Hellenistic Egypt, cf. V. Tchericover, "Prolegomena," in V. Tchericover, M. Fuks, M. Stern, ed., *Corpus Papyrorum Judaicarum* (CPJ) (3 vols.; Cambridge, MA: Harvard University Press, 1957–1964), vol. 1, 22–36; J. M. S. Cowey, "Das ägyptische Judentum in hellenistischer Zeit—neue Erkenntnisse aus jüngst veröffentlichten Papyri," in *Im Brennpunkt: Die Septuaginta. Studien zur Entstehung und Bedeutung der Griechischen Bibel, Bd. II* (ed. S. Kreuzer and J. P. Lesch; Stuttgart: W. Kohlhammer, 2004), 40–41. Cf. also J. Barclay, *Jews in the Mediterranean Diaspora*: From Alexander to Trajan (323 BCE–117 CE) (Edinburgh: T&T Clark, 1996), 24–25, 103–117.

him as main point of cultural reference. The author of this poem certainly knew the LXX and worked some quotations from it into his text.[84]

This is probably the reason why Aristobulus writes:

> . . . as well as Orpheus in the poem, uttered (or *called*) by him on the pattern of the *Holy Discourse* (τῶν κατὰ τὸν ἱερὸν λόγον αὐτῷ λεγομένων).

As C. Riedweg suggests, and I fully agree, the term "holy discourse," ἱερὸς λόγος, indicates here the LXX.[85] It was a deliberate metaphor used by Aristobulus in order to emphasize the *generic* relationship between the Old Testament and *an Orphic poem* quoted by him. At the same time we know that the term ἱερὸς λόγος was in the Greek tradition used properly as a designation of the Orphic poems. Thus, we have again an example of transferring this term from the Orphic into the barbarian material, this time into the holy text of the Jews. As said above, this transfer could be made according to the logic of the literary genre in order to ground the claim to interpret a text allegorically.

It is exactly this claim that Aristobulus makes in relation to the Old Testament. His main goal was to purify the LXX from any suspicion of anthropomorphism, absolutely incompatible with the philosophical tradition of the Academic provenance prevailing at that time in Alexandria. Thus, he maintains that in reading the LXX we have "to hold fast the fitting conception of God" (Eusebius, *Praep. ev.* 8.10.1), emphasizing that "all the philosophers agree that we ought to hold pious opinions concerning God" (Eusebius, *Praep. ev.* 13.12.8). This idea corresponds to the rigorous statement of the Derveni commentary, which postulates that, whatever we may read in the Orphic text, it says "sound and lawful things (ὑγιῆ καὶ θεμιτά)" (col.7.1) (cf. also Plutarch, *Is. Os.* 354 C).

The author of the Derveni commentary explains the "enigmatic" and "cryptic" nature of the poem by Orpheus' intention to conceal things from the multitude: "he is [not legis]lating ([νομο]θετεῖν) for the many" (col.

---

[84] C. Riedweg, *Jüdisch-hellenistische Imitation eines orphischen Hieros Logos. Beobachtungen zu OF 245 und 247 (sog. Testament des Orpheus)* (Classica Monacensia 7; Tübingen: G. Narr Verlag, 1993), 55–62.

[85] Riedweg, *Jüdisch-hellenistische Imitation*, 45. If we translate "uttered," the content of the poem is alluded to; if we translate "called," obviously, the poem's title is meant. Envisaging this second possibility, it is worth noting that other Greek authors refer to this very Orphic poem, terming it Διαθῆκαι, "Testaments" ([Justin], *Monarch.* 2.4; Theophilus, *Autol.* 3.2.). It is probable that Aristobulus knew this title. In this case he wished to stress that the name "Testament" is applied to the holy discourse (*sensu proprio*) of Orpheus on the pattern of the Testament (*sensu proprio*), which is the Holy Discourse of the Jews. Philo testifies to the possibility of using the word διαθήκη as a designation of the Scripture and, particularly, as a synonym to the word νόμος, see Philo *Det.* 6; *Somn.* 2.223, 237.

7.10). As we see, the reconstruction of the verb [νομο]θετεῖν is plausible enough. In the same way, Aristobulus explains the cryptic nature of the LXX by the intention of "our legislator" (sic! ὁ νομοθέτης ἡμῶν) to say something different from what he means: "'For our lawgiver Moses . . . announces certain arrangements of nature and preparations for mighty deeds, by adopting phrases applicable to other things, I mean to things outward and visible" (Eusebius, *Praep. ev.* 8.10. 1–4). Thus, both commentators underline the intentional allegory of the discourse and I think that the epithet "legislator" or "lawgiver," applied to Moses, though traditional in Jewish Hellenistic culture, is not purely accidental in this context.

Aristobulus, in accordance with the strategy of the Derveni commentary, develops the idea of the two parallel semantic levels: "But to those who are devoid of power and intelligence, and only cling close *to the letter* (τῷ γραπτῷ), he does not appear to explain *"any grand idea"* (μεγαλεῖόν τι) " (Eusebius, *Praep. ev.* 8.10. 5). The expression "to the letter" clearly points to another level of the text, i.e., its deep content hidden under the letters, which corresponds to the distinction between "the words" (τὰ ὀνόματα) and their "momentous" content, drawn in the Derveni papyrus (col. 7. 3–4, 7) (cf. also Plutarch, *Is .Os.* 370 F). The description of this hidden content as some "grand idea" (μεγαλεῖόν τι) faithfully reproduces an analogous "momentous" (μεγάλα) epithet applied to the content of the Orphic theogony in the Derveni papyrus (col. 7. 7). The analogy is almost complete. According to it, we can reasonably suppose that the proper epithet to the written level of the text of the LXX would be "riddling."

However, the correspondence does not stop there. Having said that the text of the LXX has two levels and that the content of the hidden one is grand, Aristobulus promises: "I shall begin then *to interpret each particular signification* (λαμβάνειν καθ᾽ ἕκαστον σημαινόμενον), as far as I may be able." This promise literally corresponds to the program set out by the author of the Derveni commentary who says: "one has to speak *about each verse in turn* (καθ᾽ ἔπος ἕκαστον) that in his whole poetry *he speaks about facts through the hints* (αἰνίζεται)" (col. 13.5–6) (cf. also Plutarch, *Is .Os.* 355 B; 378 A). The meaning of the verb σημαίνω, used by Aristobulus, is close here to the verb αἰνίζεται, "to hint," the expression καθ᾽ ἕκαστον was copied almost without changes. We do not know, whether Aristobulus was ready to interpret allegorically the whole text of the LXX, as the author of the Derveni commentary claims to do, but it is very probable that he alluded to this program statement.

In accordance with the strategy of the Derveni commentary, Aristobulus proposes "to take the interpretations *in a natural way* (φυσικῶς)," proposing theological, i.e., physical, explanations of the passages under commentary. It is worth noting that even the pantheistic theology of both commentaries is somewhat akin: the author of the Derveni text equating all deities with the air (Zeus) says that Zeus penetrates all; Aristobulus says that the power of God penetrates all and contains all (Eusebius, *Praep. ev.* 8.10.15–16; 13.12.7).

Finally, one of the minor explanations preserved in the fragments of the Jewish author is suspiciously similar to one preserved in the Derveni text. He says that the meaning of the word "hands" as used of God has to be understood metaphorically as his power, because this is the meaning of this word in the common contemporary speech (Eusebius, Praep. ev. 8.7.10). The author of the Derveni text too, makes the very same kind of reference to a common expression when interpreting the verb "flow" (col. 23.5–10).

Thus, the number and the character of the parallels indicate that they are not purely accidental. We cannot be sure whether Aristobulos was guided by the text of the Derveni papyrus itself (since the fragments of Aristobulus reflect main methodological points rather than particular philosophical explanations), or the pattern preserved in the Derveni papyrus strongly influenced subsequent commentaries on Orphic poems, some of which were known to Aristobulus. However, the comparison shows that the fragments of the first allegorical commentary to the LXX contain clear references to the tradition of the allegorical interpretation of the Orphic *hieroi logoi*. What Plutarch, in development of the strategy of the Derveni commentary, says about the mode of conveying information typical of the Orphic poems and Egyptian *logoi* (fr. 157 Sandbach), we also see alluded to in the first allegorical commentary on the LXX. Aristobulus applies the term ἱερὸς λόγος to the LXX with a clear reference to an Orphic poem in order, as I think, to substantiate the case for its allegorical interpretation.

3.2.2. The Egyptian element enhanced

As I have mentioned, it is not necessary that allegorical interpretation of the LXX originated under the direct influence of Egyptian literary patterns. In the first half of the second century B.C., the Jews were in the position to establish their own links with Greek culture, without any intermediary. However, gradually it seems, this balance was destroyed. In the Egyptian priesthood there appeared more and more people who abandoned their cultural seclusion and tried to find their own way into the Greek intellectual circles. In different ways they developed and supported the Greek assumption that Egyptian culture was *totally symbolical.*[86] Particularly, this development is attested in the area of interpretation of the hieroglyphics: the Egyptian priests even vied with each other in inventing new symbolical meaning of hieroglyphic signs.[87] The Greeks, on their part, enthusiastically repeated and, probably, developed these interpretations at their own risk. It is reasonable to suppose that in the area of the interpretation of *hieroi logoi* there was an analogous development. Plutarch in *Is. Os.* constantly refers to the interpretations borrowed from the Egyptian priests, whereas study of the Egyptian papyri testifies to the fact that these interpretations had been developed in the temple circles.[88] The fragments of Philo's contemporary Chaeremon show how this local tradition was transmitted to the wider public, and Chaeremon, according to the testimony of Porphyry, was not alone to interpret Egyptian myths allegorically.[89] By Philo's time Egyptian culture became in Egypt highly significant as a symbolical culture and the barbarian culture par excellence.[90]

[86] See, for instance, the classical book of E. Iversen, *The Myth of Egypt and Its Hiero-glyphs in European Tradition* (Copenhagen: Gad, 1961; repr., Princeton: Princeton University Press, 1993), and idem, "Egypt in Classical antiquity: a Résumé," in *Hommage à Jean Leclant: Études Isiaques* (ed. C. Berger et al.; Bibliothèque d'étude de l'IFAO 106/3; Le Caire: Institut Français d'Archéologie Orientale, 1994), 295–305.

[87] E. Hornung, "Ancient Egyptian Religious Iconography," in *Civilizations of the Ancient Near East* (4 vols.; ed J. M. Sasson; New York: C. Scribner's Sons, 1995), vol. 3, 1718–1726, 1724.

[88] Cf. below n. 99.

[89] Porphyry, *Aneb.* 2. 12–13 = Chaeremon, Fr. 5 Van der Horst.

[90] I would like to emphasize the importance, which the genre of allegorical interpre-tation of the Egyptian sacred narratives/texts still had in the eyes of the first Christian exegetes in Alexandria, when they tried to legitimate allegorical interpretation of the Old Testament. Clement, in eulogizing how the Old Testament speaks in veiled terms, tells us that "the Egyptians did not trust to first-comers the mysteries, but held them back, and did not communicate to the profane the knowledge of divine things... It is in this way that their *riddles* (αἰνίγματα) are like those of the Hebrews" (*Strom.* 5.7. 41). "That is why the mode of expression in veiled language, which is truly divine and which is deposited as the most needful thing for us in the secret sanctuary of truth, a *discourse* absolutely *holy* (ἱερὸς λόγος), was designated indirectly by the Egyptians by means of what they call their 'sanctuaries,' and by the Hebrews, by means of the veil." (*Strom.* 5.4.19). By this complicated metaphor Clement means that the *hieros logos* of the Egyptians, which is enigmatic and guarded in their sanctuary (ἄδυτα) and forbidden to the profane, is the model according to which the Hebrews guard their most holy text behind a veil which separates their sanctuary from the rest of the Temple.

Origen in his polemic against Celsus asks why the latter denies the Old Testament the possibility of being allegorically interpreted, if all the Greeks recognize that Egyptians and other barbarians who "participate in *mysteries* and in the truth" have this right: "Is it only the Greeks who are permitted to find philosophical truths beneath hidden meanings, as well as the Egyptians and all those of the barbarians who participate in *mysteries* and in the truth, while the Jews alone, their Law-giver and their writers seem to you the most stupid

This locates Philo in a special set of circumstances in which, when using the tradition of allegorical interpretation of *hieroi logoi*, he could not avoid clear allusions to the Egyptian context as paradigmatic for his approach. This helps to understand why Philo explains the allegorical purport of the Scripture by the reference to the fact that Moses was educated in Egypt and consequently acquired the technique of symbolic representation (that is, one that allows and invites allegorical interpretation) from the local tradition: "These (the learned Egyptians) further instructed him in the philosophy conveyed in symbols . . .," he says.[91] But the very same complex of evident cultural circumstances made Philo's undertaking even more problematic in the eyes of people who either did not historically belong to the old cultural traditions of the Egyptian Diaspora, or consciously refrained from using them under the new ideological influences reaching the Diaspora from Jerusalem.

Whatever the social origin and status of Philo's opponents inside the Jewish community of Alexandria may have been, only the tension between them and Philo explains why the contexts of the legitimating of an allegorical approach to the LXX bear the traces of sharp polemics. Let us turn now to the analysis of Philo's contexts.

4. *Philo's contexts legitimizing allegorical approach to the LXX*

In interpreting the appearance of God to Abraham as an intellectual penetration beneath the surface of things—closely connected for Philo to the idea of allegorical interpretation[92]—Philo describes it using the following imagery:

> Sarah . . . **initiated** (μύστης) to the greatest of **mysteries** (μυστήρια), she does not reveal them thoughtlessly to anyone, but that, guarding them in her reserve and in silence, she should keep them secret . . . for an initiate of the mysteries must keep hidden **the holy discourse** (ἱερὸς λόγος) of the Uncreated Being and

---

of men, and that this is the only nation which has received no divine power...?" (*Cels*. 4.38). And "if the Egyptians unfold the myths, that is philosophy through *riddles* (αἰνίγματα) and *mysteries*, but if Moses, who wrote histories for his whole people, leaves them stories and laws, his words are empty fable and admit of no allegory!" (*Cels*. 1.20.19). Thus, the earliest Christian allegorists justify allegorical interpretation of the Old Testament by reference to an Egyptian *hieros logos*, which is *riddling*, hidden from the profane and connected to *mysteries*. Their words serve here as indicators of a literary genre, well known to the Alexandrian public.

[91] *Mos* 1.23. Here and below I have adopted the Loeb translation by Colson, with some emendations.

[92] Cf. *Contempl.* 78; *Somn.*1.164.

of his Powers, because it does not belong to everyone to guard the treasure of the divine rites (*Sacr.* 60).

Sarah here signifies Virtue, a quality of the soul of Abraham. This passage shows that when describing the penetration into the hidden meaning of things, Philo makes use of interconnected notions of the *hieros logos, mysteries* and *initiates,* introduced for the first time in connection with allegorical interpretation in the Derveni text.

This passage is closely linked to another passage where this terminology of initiation into the sense of *holy discourses* is applied to the allegorical exegesis of the Law:

> Now is it not fitting that even *blind minds* should become sharpsighted in these and similar circumstances, being endowed with the power of sight by the **most sacred oracles**, so that we **should judge according to the nature of things** (φυσιογνωμονεῖν) and **not hold to the literal meaning only** (τοῖς ῥητοῖς). As for us, even if, having allowed the eyes of the soul to close, we do not have the wish or the power to recover our sight, yourself... lift us up, **Hierophant**, command us, ... become our **mystagogue** and introduce us to the secret light of the **holy discourses** (ἱερῶν λόγων) and make us see the splendours kept under lock and key and invisible to the **uninitiated** (ἀτελέστοις). (*Somn.* 1.164)

Philo states that an epistemological transfiguration, this time represented by Abraham and Jacob, should guide one who has experienced it to the non-literal understanding of the Scripture. This is the reason why the LXX is here termed *hieroi logoi.* We see also a clear division into the literal (here: τὰ ῥητά) and non-literal level of the text. This is typical of the tradition of interpretation of *hieroi logoi* starting from the Derveni commentary (see above: Aristobulus apud Eus., *Praep. ev.* 8.10.5; Plutarch, *Is. Os.* 370 F, 378 A). The non-literal meaning of the text is supposed to be physical, since the non-direct understanding of the LXX—*hieroi logoi*—is described by the word φυσιογνωμονεῖν. Moses is compared to the priest introducing into the mysteries (ἱεροφάντης, μυσταγωγῶν), people who are not able to follow him are uninitiated (ἀτέλεστοι). It is remarkable that the comparison of Moses with a mystagogue is very similar to that of Plutarch where he writes that, "one must take as a guide and a mystagogue philosophical reasoning," to understand a holy discourse (see above: *Is. Os.* 378A).

This could be taken just as an exhortation to extend our understanding of the Scripture beyond the limits of its literal sense, if those who are incapable of doing that had not been termed *blind minds* (οἱ τυφλοὶ διάνοιαν).

The opposition between Philo and people who do not accept his method manifests itself in the following passage, where Philo refuses to understand literally the accounts of the lives of the Patriarchs and suggests we should interpret them allegorically. This suggestion is conceived as a program:

When we speak of the conception and the birth of the Virtues, let the *super-stitious* **stop their ears** (ἀκοὰς ἐπιφραξάτωσαν) or *remove* themselves. We explain **the divine initiations** to those **initiates** who are worthy to know **the holiest of mysteries**, to those who practise with modesty true piety, that piety which is truly without *vanity*. But we **will not reveal holy things** (οὐχ ἱεροφαντήσομεν) to those who, prisoners of an incurable disease, appreciate that which is holy and sacred only according to the measure of *grandiloquence and scrupulous keeping to exact words and formal pedantry of their customs.* (*Cher.*42)

The exhortation to the non-initiates to stop their ears is a traditional element of every Orphic *hieros logos*.[93] Using this traditional exhortation Philo explicitly gives the text under discussion, namely, the LXX, the status of a *hieros logos*. Here, again, in accordance with the ideology described above we find an elaborate terminology of mysteries (τελεταί, ἱεροφαντέω, μύσται), which is destined to convey the idea of allegorical understanding of this text.

At the same time, basing on the traditional claim that a *hieros logos* is intended for initiates only, Philo stresses that he understands by the uninitiated a group of people with particular characteristics. Philo speaks of those who are not capable of any deep understanding, because they are superstitious, vain, and, at the same time, too attached to customs. The reference to the scrupulous attachment to the literal execution of customs rather points to the environment of the synagogues. In this connection the charge of superstition (δεισιδαίμονες) sounds especially provocative here, being the most common charge against the Jews at that period.[94] At the same time, Philo particularly stresses that these people are attached to the literal understanding of words. This means that allegorical interpretation is opposed here to the attitude adopted by these people. In addition to the reasons expressed above this evidence also contradicts the idea of Philo's method being welcomed in the circles close to the synagogues at least in Philo's time.

Another very instructive passage where allegory is sharply opposed to a literal interpretation is found in *Det.* 11–16. Jacob there represents a protreptic to philosophy. This exhortation is to make Joseph see reality in philosophical terms, something he did not know how to do before. To do this Jacob sends his son to his brothers. But Joseph had always thought that his education was sufficient to understand everything. He is not sure that he needs to learn again. Jacob does not want to press this young man, but he is nevertheless absolutely convinced that Joseph must learn again. The

---

[93] Cf. *Derv. P.* Col. 7. 9–10 ; See also Riedweg, *Jüdisch-hellenistische Imitation*, 50.
[94] See Hengel, *Judentum und Hellenismus*, 470, 475 n. 27.

fact that an interpretation of the LXX is being discussed is evident from the following words:

> If, then, O my thought, you examine in this fashion **the discourses (words)** of God, **revealed by the hierophant** (ἱεροφαντέντες λόγοι), which are also the laws of men who love God, you will be obliged to refuse to allow anything that is **low or unworthy of their greatness.** In fact, even the story which we are discussing, **how could anyone with any sense allow it?...**"

According to Philo, it is impossible that Jacob, although he had many servants, chose to send his beloved son to look for his brothers.

> And you see that the Scripture goes even so far as to indicate the place from which he sent him, which is practically the same as clearly telling us **to avoid a literal interpretation,** since Hebron, from which Joseph was sent, is a symbol of the body, which hinders one from penetrating to the truth.

The expression ἱεροφαντέντες λόγοι is a Philonian neologism. In it he has linked the idea of a holy discourse to that of the initiation into the mysteries (the hierophant is someone who initiates into mysteries). Philo explicitly says that these *logoi* are the laws of the Jewish people. Then, in accordance with the interpretative ideas we have discussed above, he consistently asserts that the laws of the Jewish people, being *hieroi logoi*, not only invite allegorical, but *do not allow* literal interpretation.

I would like to emphasize Philo's attitude to Joseph, expressed through the mouth of Jacob. Joseph is depicted as a man educated in the spirit of literal understanding of the Law and who is sure that his attitude this text is right and sufficient. Philo stresses his unwillingness to adopt an allegorical vision of the Penateuch and he undoubtedly blames Joseph for his blindness and narrow-mindedness.

As mentioned above, the idea of not allowing literal interpretation is strongly connected with the notion of indecent meaning of a text. These reflections which we find first in the Derveni papyrus (cf. Derv. P. 7. 1; 13. 4–6) later constitute a part of the literary tradition of allegorical interpretation of *hieroi logoi*, which presupposed that the text under commentary was in one way or another indecent in its direct sense (cf. Aristobulus apud Eus., *Praep. ev.* 8.10.1; Plutarch, *Is. Os.* 354 C). Thus, we have good reason to think that in this passage we find another detail, which testifies to the kinship of Philo's attitude with the interpretative tradition we are now discussing. I mean his somewhat exaggerated indignation, which he shows towards the direct sense of the Pentateuch. What he says about the impossibility of accepting the literal meaning concerns usually only minor points.[95] I believe that Philo, working within the constraints of this tradition, felt obliged to admit the presence of something "low or unworthy" in the literal sense of the text, as a tribute to the tradition.

However, even taking in consideration some literary conventions, we should not dismiss Philo's main *methodological* concern in his approach to the LXX, which equally follows from this very tradition. I mean his idea of interpreting the *whole* text of the Scripture, possibly *avoiding* its literal interpretation (not in the sense that a literal understanding is impossible, but in the sense that in the literary domain of his exegesis it is not aimed at). In Philo's writings, besides the passages under discussion, we have several fairly significant places, where the allegorical approach is sharply opposed to the literal and the adherents of the latter one are treated by Philo with deep contempt and scorn. These people who "are accustomed scrupulously to study the literal and obvious interpretations" (*Sobr.* 33) and "who are in the habit of, and fond of pursuing such investigations" (*Deus* 133) do not actually have any deep understanding. In Philo's opinion, they "strain at a gnat." He calls them "the sophists (a very pejorative word in Philo's language) of the literal interpretation" (*Somn.* 1. 102), "the highbrow" (eadem), "those who study evil cunning through their ingenuity in devising excuses [sc. for the plain meaning of the Scripture]" (*Agr.* 157). And the last example is particularly revealing, because in it Philo explicitly says that these people never dare to use allegorical exegesis.[96] At the same time, Philo says that in applying of his method of interpretation to the LXX he not only follows the "right reason" (*Sobr.* 33), but also *the rules of allegory* (οἱ ἀλληγορίας νόμοι, *Somn.* 1. 102). This testifies to the fact that Philo was absolutely aware of applying to the LXX some strict exegetical rules.

So, the analysis of the passages under discussion shows that

1. In justifying the allegorical approach to the Scripture Philo always evokes the terminology of the pagan tradition of allegorical interpretation of *hieroi logoi*. He identifies the Scripture with a *hieros logos* and describes the process of comprehending its hidden meaning as an initiation into the mysteries. Thus, he locates his exegetical approach in a very precise literary tradition, which everyone who belonged to Alexandrian culture could not fail to recognize.

2. At the same time, almost all of the passages which contain this terminology are imbued with polemics, sometimes very sharp and pejorative,

---

[95] *Deus* 133, 140; *Agr.* 131; *Somn.* 1.102; *Sobr.* 33.

[96] "As no one studying evil cunning dares in devising excuses, we will say using allegory that. . ." (*Agr.* 157. Translation is mine).

against people who, being faithful executors of the Jewish Law, did not accept Philo's method.

In order to anticipate any misunderstanding which this discussion may provoke, I would like to repeat what has been said in the beginning of this article. The polemics we have highlighted are not a kind of conflict that has to be treated in religious terms (at least not in the limits of our actual discussion). This tension is not a sign of impossibility for Philo to take literally the sense of the Pentateuch, or even to use it sometimes in his works, but it is rather some kind of exegetical, and also social, polemics, justifying application to the Scripture of one or another *literary* method of interpretation. First of all, it testifies to the fact that whatever the situation with the interpretation of the LXX in Alexandria at the time of Aristobulus (when the tendencies to integrate were not yet hindered by the slowly increasing influence of Maccabean ideology), it is clear that it was far from being serene by Philo's time. Philo's opponents are unwilling to adopt his approach to the interpretation of the LXX. Philo, for his part, is sometimes scornful of their attitude to such an extent that later he had good reason to apologize for that, at least seemingly, as he did in *Migr.* 86–94.[97] Secondly, if

---

[97] The context, often cited by scholars as an indication of Philo's loyalty to the literal understanding of the Law, is in fact very problematic. At first sight (especially when one reads it in any modern translation) it says two obvious things: Philo praises good fame and coming to terms with people and reproaches those, who, being engaged in an allegorical interpretation of the Law, do not follow its literal prescriptions. However, in this passage Philo uses philosophically highly remarkable terminology which has very precise meaning in all his writings. To describe this situation Philo uses such terms as "the many" (οἱ πολλοί) (90,93), "the opinions of the many" (τὰ δοκοῦντα τοῖς πολλοῖς) (90), "the realm of seeming" (τὸ δοκεῖν) (86,88), "bastard wealth perceptible by the outward senses" (αἰσθητὸς καὶ νόθος) (95), "feminine reasoning" (οἱ θηλύτεροι λόγοι) (95) which are all genuine Platonic technical philosophical terms of highly negative purport. In *Migr.* 95 he explicitly says that these people (whose recognition he is forced to seek) are endowed with "feminine reasonings which are in every respect overcome by those things which are visible, and which are unable to comprehend any object of contemplation which is beyond them." Cf. *Gig.* 4 with notes of J. Dillon, in Winston and Dillon, ed., *Two Treatises*, 235; cf. also R. A. Baer, *Philo's use of the categories of Male and Female* (Leiden: Brill, 1970). Thus, even in this context, Philo moves from the hidden philosophical disapproval of what he seemingly praises to the open blame of people who forced him to this discussion. On the contrary, in "reproaching" those who are fond of allegory he uses such terms as "unexpected joy" (ἀσμενισμός) (88), "plain naked truth by itself" (ἡ ἀλήθεια γυμνὴ αὐτὴ ἐφ' ἑαυτῆς) (90), "souls unconnected with the body" (ἀσώματοι ψυχαί) (90), which are direct quotations from Plato and/or technical terms describing in Philo's writings the highest level of epistemology and ethics. And even the reproach of "living in desert" (90) is not only a very positive moral achievement of a person in the rest of Philo's writings, but also a particular feature of the ideal community of *Therapeutai* (*Contempl.* 20.2; 24.5). Thus, Philo, while reproaching people, described them as ideal and true philosophers. One probably should not delude oneself: not a bit does Philo in this context change his attitude

we take in consideration the beginning of our discussion, that is the principles of allegorical interpretation typical of the Jewish tradition outside Alexandria, we will see that the situation, which manifests itself in Philo's writings, can be inscribed in a wider context. As we have suggested, the exegetical traditions outside Alexandria do not know systematical allegorical approach to the prosaic text of the Law. Even those single applications of allegorical interpretation to prosaic texts which have come down to us, are organized according to certain exegetical rules, which are clearly visible already in the earliest examples of indirect interpretation at Qumran. Philo doesn't essentially follow these patterns—his interpretations are not historically related and they are not—as a rule—based on the texts of the Jewish prophets and psalms. Moreover, he practices a thorough philosophical allegorical interpretation of the Jewish Law, including all special laws and even drawing in his discussion the Ten Commandments (cf. *Decal.* 1.5). His undertaking has no case in the non-Alexandrian exegetical culture and may look even provocative from a viewpoint of those people who had close connections with the original national tradition of exegesis. This made his opponents so reluctant to accept his approach. Their reluctance, in its turn, made Philo so eager to point at a tradition behind him, a tradition of many centuries standing, which had been applied to the Scripture, at least occasionally, in Alexandrian culture, and which justified—in the eyes of the genuine Diaspora members—such an approach. By this reason his contexts of justifying allegorical approach to the LXX are intimately connected with polemics. Thus, in the line of our discussion, we have to bear in mind that the main reason why Philo makes reference to the tradition of allegorical interpretation of *hieroi logoi* is to indicate the exegetic tradition to which he attaches himself in applying to the Pentateuch a total allegorical interpretation. In the literary domain, classifying a text as a *hieros logos* meant the almost automatic application of the allegorical, philosophical (physical) interpretation to the text as a whole, without any connection to its literal meaning—because this kind of text was

---

to the allegorical and to the literal interpretation of the Scripture—he definitely prefers allegory to any literal understanding. This is the reason why also in this context he, even "reproaching" allegorists, explicitly calls the Scripture *hieros logos* (*Migr.* 90): Philo wants to stress that this text *demands* allegorical exegesis. But what, then, is the aim of this discussion? I believe that Philo intentionally writes this passage on two semantic levels, like the Law of Moses, he claims, has been written: for those who understand and for those who do not. On the literal level it is intended for people who were unable to distinguish between two completely different things—Philo's exegetical approach, sanctified by a literary tradition, and his personal attitude to the norms of ancestral religion.

presumed never to speak directly, but always through symbols from the
first to the last word.

5. *Philo's further steps for the development of the genre*

From Plutarch's *On Isis and Osiris* we learn that one of the most popular
ways of interpreting "holy discourses," especially Egyptian ones, was to
use astronomy: the sun, moon, hemispheres, new moons, lunar cycles, the
movement of the moon relative to the sun, eclipses, horizons—that is the
main meaning of Egyptian myths according to his allegorical interpretation.[98] The explanations, given by Plutarch, are, probably, even less theological than those of the Derveni text. Only at the end of the treatise does he
allow himself some theological interpretations, which correspond to the
Academic idea of what the highest form of physics is. The increase of the
astronomical allegory, used for the explanations of the Egyptian *hieros logos*,
though it does not theoretically contradict the principles of the genre
(already in the Derveni papyrus there are many examples of purely astronomical interpretations), has, probably, its particular and special reason.
When interpreting the Egyptian myth Plutarch based himself on the
previous interpretations known to him, and especially on those which came
from the milieu of the Egyptian priesthood (so he often says himself). As far
as we can judge from the Egyptian papyri available to us, this was the
tradition of interpretation of sacred texts developed in the purely Egyptian
milieu.[99] It is reasonable to suppose that with time this local tradition
became known to the Greeks and influenced their attitude to sacred Egyptian texts. For instance, an example of this local tradition of interpretations
translated into Greek and presented to Greek society is given in the
fragments of Philo's contemporary Chaeremon. Porphyry, describing his
interpretative activity, says the following: "Chaeremon and *his like* put
nothing before the visible worlds; they place on the level of principles the
gods of the Egyptians and admit of no other gods, as they call planets,
which compose the Zodiac and all that rise next to them, the divisions into
decanes, the horoscopes, those they call "powerful chiefs," whose names
are also reported in the Salmeschiniaca, with medical cures, the risings, the

[98] Plutarch, *Is. Os.* 41–4.
[99] Cf., for instance, H. O. Lange and O. Neugebauer, ed., *Papyrus Carlsberg No. 1. Ein
hieratisch-demotischer kosmologischer Text* (Køpenhagen, 1940), and Jacques Vendier et al,
eds., *Le Papyrus Jumilhac* (Paris: Centre National de la Recherche Scientifique, 1961).

settings, the signs that portend the future."[100] Thus, as the interpretations of Plutarch show and the fragments of Chaeremon prove, astronomical interpretations had a largely prevailing status among physical interpretations, applied to the Egyptian myths, starting at least from Philo's time. Several passages from Clement of Alexandria[101] give additional examples of this astronomical allegory in the Egyptian context.

It is reasonable to suppose that if the allegorical interpretation of the LXX developed against the background of this local tradition, Philo would reflect the influence of its special features and react to it. It is interesting that Philo knows of such astronomical allegories being applied to the LXX. However, often they are not his own but belong to certain other authors whom he cites, those same allegorists we mentioned at the start of our discussion. Thus, some interpret the Cherubim on the mercy seat of the Ark of the Covenant as the two hemispheres: "Some hold that, since they [the Cherubim] are set facing each other, they are symbols of two hemispheres, one above the earth and one under it, for the whole heaven has wings . . . But I should myself say that . . . ."[102] Or: "Some give it [the Sabbath] the name of the 'season,' since seven is a factor common to all the phenomena which stand highest in the world of sensible things . . . such are the seven planets, the Great Bear, the Pleiades and the cycles of the moon, as it waxes and wanes, and the movements, harmonious and grand beyond description, of the other heavenly bodies."[103] *Some* understood heavenly bodies to be referred to by the *Fathers* who are mentioned in Genesis (15:15): "the sun, moon and other stars to which it is held that all things on earth owe their birth and framing."[104] Philo himself also demonstrates his skill in this kind of interpretation, as, for instance, in the interpretation of the vestments of the High Priest of Jerusalem in *On the Life of Moses*, or in the treatise *On the Cherubim*, where an elaborate astronomical explanation of the Cherubim serves as an example of allegorical interpretation par excellence.[105] However, it is clear that Philo is not an ardent adept of this kind of exegesis. He rather resorts to astronomical explanations as to a "done thing." Of course, his academic idea of physics was much more profound and wide than the

---

[100] Porphyry, *Aneb.* 2. 12–13 = Chaeremon, Fr. 5 Van der Horst.

[101] Clement of Alexandria, *Strom.* 5. 7. 41, 43.

[102] *Mos.* 2.98; an expanded version of this interpretation is given in *Cher.* 25–7.

[103] *Spec.* 2.56–57.

[104] *Her.* 280.

[105] *Mos.* 2.117–135; *Cher.* 21–24. Interestingly, *Mos.* 2.117–135 and *Cher.* 25–26 bear evident traces of generic kinship with the interpretations of the Egyptian sacred statues, preserved by Porphyry (*De cultu simulacrorum* fr. 10 = Chaeremon fr. 17 D van der Horst) and Clement of Alexandria (*Strom.* 5. 7. 43).

limited area of astronomy, especially when this astronomy was devoid of any theological implications. Consequently, the concentration of the physical exegesis on the highest part of physics, i.e., on theology, understood in terms of the philosophy of Middle Platonism, is one of the developments, and one which distinguishes Philo's attitude. However, methodologically, it is fully in the tradition of the genre and deserves study rather as an aspect of the history of philosophy.

However, there is another turn in Philo's method, which looks unexpected from the point of view of the tradition of interpretation of *hieroi logoi*. I refer to his preference, expressed in many ways, for ethical interpretations. This is clearly visible already in the treatise *On the Cherubim*, cited above, where Philo, having given an exemplary astronomical interpretation of the Cherubim, moves onto an ethical interpretation of them, introducing it by the following phrase: "But I have also perceived in the past a meaning more profound, in listening to the voice of my soul, which is often inspired by God and the divine" (*Cher.* 27). Philo's orientation towards the ethical interpretation of the Scripture is one of the most distinctive features of his exegesis of the LXX. There is one place in his work where he gives this change of method—from astronomical to ethical exegesis—almost a programmatic significance. In *On Dreams*, terming the Scripture a *hieros logos*, Philo imagines it speaking as it calls for an end to the search for truth in the sphere of astronomy and says that truth is instead to be found in the sphere of ethics:

> Accordingly *the holy discourse* (ἱερὸς λόγος) addresses to the explorer of the facts of nature certain questions—"Why do you carry on investigations about the sun, as to whether it is a foot in diameter, whether it is larger than the whole earth, whether it is many times its size? And about the illuminations of the moon, whether it has a borrowed light, or whether it employs one entirely its own? And why do you search into the nature of the other heavenly bodies, or into their revolutions or the ways in which they affect each other and affect earthly things? . . . Why do you take up astronomy and pay such full and minute attention to the higher regions? Mark, my friend, not what is above and beyond your reach but what is close to yourself, or rather make yourself the object of your impartial scrutiny.[106]

The term *hieros logos*, serving as a marker of a text requiring allegorical interpretation, here indicates the need to reject the astronomical interpretation of the Scripture and to adopt the ethical.[107] At the same time we

---

[106] *Somn.* 1.53–54.

[107] It is not impossible that Philo is here drawing also on *Jub*.12:17, which could have been known to him in a Greek translation: "And a word came into his heart and he said: all the things of the stars, and the things of the moon and of the sun are all in the hand of the

have not seen so far any traces of ethical interpretation applied to any kind of *hieros logos* before Philo. It is true that it was not unnatural for Philo to search for the ethical implications of the Scripture, as this text is the basis of all kinds of behavior in Jewish tradition, and an ethical element is very strong in all kinds of Jewish exegesis outside Alexandria. However, if our reasoning is right, and it was important for Philo to retain a link with the Greek exegetical tradition under question, we should expect that he would search for justification of this shift. Thus, the question that arises is: what particular literary tradition is Philo exploring in applying to a *hieros logos* the ethical interpretation and does he himself give in his work any hints at his theoretical basis?

In *Prob.* 80–83, eulogizing exercises in the "ethical philosophy" favored with the community of the Essenes, Philo says: "But the ethical part they study very industriously, taking for their coaches the laws of their fathers, which could not possibly have been conceived by the human soul without divine inspiration (82). . . . because the most of their *philosophy* is formulated in *symbols* (φιλοσοφεῖται διὰ συμβόλων) *as the old fashion was* (ἀρχαιο-τρόπῳ ζηλώσει)." We will turn back to the expression "as the old fashion was" later. For now I want to emphasize the idea that their exercises in ethical philosophy are based on the laws of their fathers, which are a *philosophy* expressed in *symbols*.

In the Greek philosophical tradition there is an obvious parallel to this description. Pythagoras' teachings were famously expressed via "akous-mata" or "symbols," which were difficult to interpret even for the early Pythagoreans themselves. This gave rise from the earliest times to a tradition of exegesis that was clearly allegorical in nature. Interpreting Pythagorean symbols became a distinct traditional genre of Pythagorean literature and philological scholarship from very early times.[108] One of the earliest collections of such symbols, already provided with an allegorical interpretation, belongs to Aristotle.[109] Another early commentary to Pythagorean symbols was written in the first half of the fourth century by one Anaxi-

---

Lord. Why do I search them out?" (Cf. also Sir 3:21 –24). But the replacement of "word" with "holy discourse" and the discussion which follows on the different parts of Greek philosophy—physics and ethics—clearly points to the fact that the context of Jubilees merely serves as a springboard for transferring the argument onto a new plane. Philo is an author who usually treats the same theme on several levels simultaneously. Cf. my article "1 Enoch in the Context of Philo's Writings," in *The Dead Sea Scrolls in Context: Integrating the Dead Sea Scrolls in the Study of Ancient Texts, Languages, and Cultures* (2 vols.; ed. A. Lange, E. Tov, and M. Weigold, with the assistance of Bennie H. Reynolds III; Leiden: Brill, 2010), vol. 1, 385–397.

[108] Iamblichus, *VP* 23.105.

[109] Porphyry, *VP* 41; DL 8.34–36 = Aristotle, Fr. 195 Rose = Fr. 5 Ross.

mander, who was, according to the Suda lexicon, the son of Anaximander of Miletos.[110] A certain Pythagorean is also known in Hellenistic times to have composed a book entitled *On Pythagorean Symbols* under the name of Androcides (the physician of Alexander the Great).[111] A similar work was possibly written by Alexander Polyhistor.[112] The popularity and the wide dissemination of this tradition is later attested in written form by Porphyry[113] and, especially, Iamblichus[114] and was also practiced *orally* in circles influenced by Pythagoreanism.

Thus, Plutarch tells us about a discussion on Pythagorean symbols he attended during his visit to Rome:

> (1) Sulla the Carthaginian, having proclaimed a welcome-dinner (as Romans call it) to celebrate my arrival in Rome after a long absence, invited a small number of close friends, including a certain pupil of Moderatus the Pythagorean, named Lucius, who was a native of Etruria. When he saw my friend Philinus abstaining from the flesh of living creatures, he was naturally led to speak about *the doctrines of Pythagoras* (τοὺς Πυθαγόρου λόγους) . . . He stressed in support the *symbola*, like those . . . not to receive swallows as guests in the house. . . . He said that though the Pythagoreans have handed these precepts down in oral and written tradition, the Etruscans are the only people who in fact carefully observe and abide by them. (2) After Lucius' discussion of these topics, we commented that the rule about the swallows seemed especially strange . . . The explanation which some of the ancients had regarded as sufficient in itself to explain the hidden meaning, that the precept conceals a reference to slanderous, whispering associates, was rejected by Lucius himself . . . (4) My words seem to have amounted to a removal of inhibitions for the rest, *for now they confidently attacked the other symbols*, proposing *plausible ethical explanations* (ἠθικὰς ἐπιεικῶς ποιούμενοι τὰς λύσεις αὐτῶν).[115]

As far as we can judge from the collections of symbols, available to us, as well as from Plutarch's description, the allegorical interpretation of the Pythagorean symbols *was traditionally ethical*.

Philo's indication of the tradition of allegorical interpretation of Pythagorean symbols as the foundation of his own ethical interpretation of the LXX is clearly expressed in the same treatise, which contains references to the ethical exercises of the Essenes and to their ancestral "philosophy of symbols" in *Every Good Man is Free*. Philo begins by citing a Pythagorean symbol and interpreting it ethically:

---

[110] Suda, s.v. Ἀναξίμανδρος.
[111] Iamblichus, *VP* 28.145.
[112] Clement of Alexandria, *Strom.* 1.15.70.
[113] *VP* 42–45.
[114] *Protr.* 21.106, 18; *VP* 23.103.
[115] *Quaest. conv.* 8.7.

Now we are told that the saintly *thiasos* of the Pythagoreans teaches among other excellent doctrines this also: 'walk not on the highways.' This does not mean that we climb steep hills—the school was not prescribing foot-weariness —but *it hints by symbol* (αἰνιττόμενος διὰ συμβόλου) that in our words and deeds we should not follow popular and beaten tracks.[116]

The discussion of the Pythagorean symbol, and particularly of this symbol, at the beginning of the treatise has a programmatic significance. A little later, Philo gives a similar allegorical interpretation of the words of Moses, who, as we are supposed to have understood, was expressing himself cryptically in order to avoid "the highways of words":

The law-giver of the Jews describes the wise man's hands as heavy (Ex 17:12), *hinting by this symbol* (διὰ συμβόλου . . . αἰνιττόμενος) that his actions are not superficial, but firmly based, the outcome of a mind that never wavers.[117]

And later still, another similar interpretation:

Yet what need is there of long journeying on the land or voyaging on the seas to seek and search for virtue, whose roots have been set by their Maker ever so near us, as the wise legislator of the Jews also says "in thy mouth, in thy heart and in thy hand" (Deut 30:14), thereby *hinting by symbols* (αἰνιττόμενος διὰ συμβόλων) at words, thoughts and actions?[118]

The significant fact that Philo uses a Pythagorean symbol at the beginning of his work, as well as his emphatic use of the same terminology (cf. the expression "hint using symbols") later on in connection with the "sayings" of Moses, indicates that the words of Moses were intentionally represented by Philo as symbolic utterances like those of Pythagoras and, as such, subject to corresponding allegorical interpretation.[119]

If we compare the terminology employed by Philo, Plutarch (when discussing Pythagorean symbols) and Iamblichus (in his *Life of Pythagoras* and *Protreptic*), we see that each of them uses the same technical terms. The contexts of all three authors contain the expression consisting of the word "symbol" (σύμβολον) together with the verb "hint" (αἰνίττομαι) or a cognate:

Philo: αἰνιττόμενος διὰ συμβόλου (*Prob.* 2–3; 29; 68).
Plutarch: τὸ σύμβολον ἠνιγμένον (*Quaest. Conv.* 7.7.2).

---

[116] *Prob.* 2–3.
[117] *Prob.* 29
[118] *Prob.* 68.
[119] Cf. *Conf.* 107 ff; *Spec.*3.178 ff.

Iamblichus: συμβόλων ἐμφάσεις τοῦ **αἰνιγματόδους** ἐλευθερωθεῖσαι (*VP* 23.103)

Such a "hinting symbol" needs, according to Plutarch, a "solution":

ᾤοντο **λύειν** τὸ σύμβολον (*Quaest. Conv.* 7.7.2)
ποιούμενοι **τὰς λύσεις** (*Quaest. Conv.* 7.7.2)

Iamblichus, along with the cognate ἐπίλυσις (ἑκάστου συμβόλου **τὰς ἐπι-λύσεις**—*Protr.* 105) uses as technical terms the words διαπτύσσω, ἀποκαλύπτω and ἀνάπτυξις:

Εἰ μή τις αὐτὰ τὰ σύμβολα ἐκλέξας **διαπτύξειη** (*VP* 23.105; *Protr.* 106.10)
συμβόλων ἐμφάσεις...**ἀποκαλυφθεῖσαι** (*VP* 23.103).
ἀνάπτυξις τῶν συμβόλων (*Protr.* 6.5)

The same terminology plays a key role in Philo's *On the Contemplative Life* where he describes the allegorical method of the mysterious *Therapeutai*, whose rational soul "*unfolds and removes the symbolic coverings* (τὰ μὲν σύμβολα **διαπτύξασα** καὶ **διακαλύψασα**)."[120] If we look at the wider context of this phrase, we will see that on the lexical level alone, many other expressions, apart from the technical terms we have highlighted, strongly recall phrases used by Iamblichus.[121] All that taken together testifies to the fact that Philo and Iamblichus belong to the same literary and exegetical tradition, which is essentially the tradition of allegorical interpretation of Pythagorean symbols.

Through this tradition we can adequately interpret some of Philo's statements, which are perplexing when taken as referring to a Jewish

---

[120] *Contempl.* 78.
[121] *Contempl.* 78: "They explain the sacred texts allegorically, searching for their hidden meaning. For to these people the whole complex of laws seems to resemble a living creature with the literal ordinances for its body and for its soul *the invisible mind laid up in its wording* (τὸν ἐναποκείμενον ταῖς λέξεσι ἀόρατον νοῦν). It is in this mind especially that the rational soul begins to contemplate the things akin to itself and looking through the words as through a mirror *beholds the marvelous beauties of the concepts* (κάλλη νοημάτων ἐμφαινόμενα), *unfolds and removes the symbolic coverings* (τὰ μὲν σύμβολα διαπτύξασα καὶ διακαλύψασα) and brings forth the thoughts and sets them bare to the light of day for those who need but a little reminding to enable them to discern the inward and hidden through the outward and visible." Thus "beholds the marvelous beauties of the concepts" (κάλλη νοημάτων *ἐμφαινόμενα*) corresponds to Iamblichus' ἵνα τὰ ῥήματα *ἐκφανῆ* γένηται (*Protr.* 106.13) and συμβόλων *ἐμφάσεις* (*VP* 23. 103); "the invisible mind laid up in its wording" (τὸν ἐναποκείμενον ταῖς λέξεσι ἀόρατον νοῦν) is close in meaning to the expression *ἀπορρήτους ἐννοίας* (*VP* 23.103).

context. For instance, describing the community of the Essenes, he says that they study the ethical part of their philosophy very industriously, "... because most of their *philosophy* is formulated in *symbols* (φιλοσοφεῖται διὰ συμβόλων) *as the old fashion was* (ἀρχαιοτρόπῳ ζηλώσει)."[122] The question arises what kind of old fashion does Philo refer to, speaking, most probably, about the laws, and not about the prophetic writings, as it becomes clear from *Prob.* 80 (cf. "the laws of their fathers;" cf. also *Prob.* 83 –84)? This statement is best explained by reference to how Iamblichus explains the Pythagorean manner of talking symbolically: "Most indispensable for him (Pythagoras) was his manner of teaching by means of "symbols." For this style of teaching was treated with respect by nearly all Hellenes inasmuch *as it was of ancient origin* (παλαιότροπος ὢν ἐσπουδάζετο)."[123] We see that the explanations of the two authors coincide even on the lexical level: παλαιότροπος in the phrase of Iamblichus corresponds to Philo's ἀρχαιότροπος and ἐσπουδάζετο (from σπουδή) to ζήλωσις.

Thus, Philo's reference to the ethical content of the "philosophy of symbols" is only meaningful in the eyes of educated Greek readers. Philo refers to the philosophy of the holy texts which is "formulated in symbols as the old fashion was" not in order accurately to represent the real state of things inside the community of the Essenes, but in order to "translate" that reality into the "Greek" language—that is *to explain to Greeks why the main focus of the Essenes is on ethics* and, most importantly, in order to *create a theoretical basis for his own ethical allegory of the Scripture.*

So when Philo sees the Scripture as a collection of ethical symbols and gives them an allegorical meaning, he is also transposing onto the LXX the practice and method of interpreting Pythagorean symbols, together with an entire complex of concomitant ideas.

It is probably worth noting that the neo-Pythagorean tradition, as represented at its later stage by Porphyry and Iamblichus, explains Pythagoras' manner of speaking symbolically through his imitation of initiates into the mystery cults. Thus, Porphyry says that "Certain things he declared symbolically in imitation of the mysteries."[124] This idea is also repeated by Iamblichus.[125] So Pythagoras' teaching was understood as, in some sense, connected to mysteries, or organized on the pattern of mysteries, and, consequently, as a kind of *hieros logos*. (The attributing to him in the Hellenistic period of a certain writing called by that name testifies to the popularity of

---

[122] *Prob.* 82–83.
[123] *VP* 23.103 (transl. by J. Dillon); cf. *VP* 34. 247.
[124] Porphyry, *VP* 41: ἔλεγε δέ τινα καὶ μυστικῷ τρόπῳ συμβολικῶς.
[125] Iamblichus, *VP* 23.104.

these ideas[126]). Certainly, Porphyry and Iamblichus show that this kind of explanation of the symbolic nature of the philosophy of Pythagoras was largely influenced by the Egyptian context: both, as Philo had done in the case of Moses, directly connect Pythagoras' ability to speak allegorically with the idea of him being instructed by the Egyptian priests.[127] However, we do not know how early this tradition arose. It is possible that Philo was already aware of these tendencies to explain the allegorical nature of the Pythagorean material and consequently felt he was entitled to adopt the theoretical basis of the Pythagorean tradition to explain the allegorical meaning of the LXX, defined by him as a *hieros logos*.

However, Clement of Alexandria has preserved valuable evidence of the tendency within Hellenistic culture to "lump together" Pythagorean symbols and the Old Testament, independently of Philo's project. This may also have formed the background out of which his work grew. Such a tendency pointed to the dependence of Pythagoras on the Old Testament (as one of the most important texts of the barbarian tradition). Clement informs us for instance that Pythagoras' injunction "not to let a swallow live indoors" was traced by one commentator to the Prophet Jeremiah (8:7), and so were the other symbols.[128] Elsewhere he refers to certain individuals who believe that Pythagoras borrowed his symbolic style from Ezekiel.[129] It is not surprising, then, that in this context literary exegetical methods which had long been applied by Pythagoreans to Pythagorean texts also came to be applied to the LXX. That is one of the reasons why Philo is called in our sources "the Pythagorean"—in connection, I repeat, with his literary undertaking. Philo's innovation in allegory may have been simply the systematic application of this technique to the LXX—it is, at least, the earliest example of such an application to have come down to us.

6. *Conclusion*

To recapitulate all we have said, I would like to stress that trying to explain one significance in terms of another (what we call allegorical interpretation) cannot serve as a marker of a national tradition, or of a particular branch inside a national tradition. The inclination to allegory, broadly understood, cannot, by itself, indicate to which exegetical culture the author belongs.

---

[126] Diogenes Laertius, *VPh* 8.7; Diodorus, *Bibl.* 1.98.2; Iamblichus, *VP* 28.146.
[127] Porphyry, *VP* 11.9; Iamblichus, *VP* 20.2; 23.1; 23.103.
[128] Clement of Alexandria, *Strom.* 5.5.27–30.
[129] *Strom.* 1.15.70.

The tendencies in some way to allegorize a text were present in Jewish communities. It is possible, and even probable, that this played a certain part in the appearance of Philo's great undertaking. However, every community in exploring these intuitions develops its own principles of commentary: that is how a method comes into being. In the absence of other historical and literary data, we must study the method, its tradition, sphere and area of application. In the case of Philo's allegorical method, we must conclude that his allegorical commentary on the LXX arose within the context of a general Greek Hellenistic approach to barbarian texts, which expected allegorical interpretation of barbarian ἱεροὶ λόγοι. All ἱεροὶ λόγοι were usually interpreted "physically," and this was what made Aristobulus and Philo include the "physical" interpretation in their commentaries as an essential element. In Philo's commentary it is present on two levels: 1) rudimentary remnants of crude astronomical allegories of the LXX mentioned by Philo, and his own elaborate astronomical interpretations, 2) Philo's own understanding of the notion of allegory in terms of *physiologein* and *physiologia*. Philo justified the change to an ethical allegorical interpretation, which was not typical of commentaries on Holy Discourses (and not present in the fragments of Aristobulus), by reference to the tradition of interpreting Pythagorean symbols. The allegorical principle he uses reproduces, at the technical level, the manner in which Pythagorean symbols were interpreted.

This we can state as a matter of fact. In answer to the question of how far such a practice could have influenced or penetrated into Hellenistic-Jewish circles—including even the synagogues—I prefer to say that it would be wiser to let this remain in the realm of hypotheses and a matter for the intuition of each individual scholar.

Russian State University
Moscow

The Studia Philonica Annual 22 (2010) 53–82

L'«EXTASE MYSTIQUE» DANS LA TRADITION PLATONICIENNE: PHILON D'ALEXANDRIE ET PLOTIN[*]

TATJANA ALEKNIENÉ

I. *Philon d'Alexandrie et Plotin: quelques remarques sur l'histoire de la recherche*

Les études mettant en comparaison les œuvres de Plotin et de Philon d'Alexandrie n'ont jamais été en honneur. Après quelques démarches enthousiastes dans ce domaine, vers la fin du XIXe et pendant la première moitié du XXe siècle,[1] des critiques très sévères ont été exprimées[2] à l'égard de ceux qui avaient osé songer que la pensée de Plotin, un philosophe de la noble lignée de la philosophie grecque, pourrait être marquée en quoi que ce soit par l'influence d'un auteur d'une culture «hybride» et horriblement

---

[*] Je remercie chaleureusement les professeurs Dominic O'Meara et Jean-Daniel Dubois, grâce aux quels j'ai pu présenter les résultats de mes recherches sur la notion d'extase, respectivement, à l'Université de Fribourg, en mai du 2007, et à Paris, en février 2008 (pendant une séance du séminaire «Plotin et les gnostiques», dirigé par Jean-Daniel Dubois et Philippe Hoffmann). Je tiens aussi à les remercier pour le précieux soutien de mes études sur Philon et Plotin, qu'ils m'ont accordé, soit en approuvant mes conclusions, soit en les critiquant d'une manière bienveillante et encourageante. La première version de cet article est parue en lituanien, dans une revue *Religija ir kultūra* (éditée par l'Université de Vilnius, Lituanie) 3 (2006): 7–36.

[1] Cf. surtout Henry Guyot, *Les réminiscences de Philon le Juif chez Plotin. Étude critique* (Paris: Félix Alcan, 1906) (je reviendrai dans la suite sur cet ouvrage.); Idem, *L'infinité divine depuis Philon le Juif jusqu'à Plotin (Ier s. av. J.-C.–IIIe s. ap. J.-C.). Avec une introduction sur le même sujet dans la Philosophie grecque avant Philon le Juif* (Paris: Félix Alcan, 1906). Un autre partisan résolu de l'hypothèse, selon laquelle Philon avait exercé une influence importante sur la pensée de Plotin, était Harry Austryn Wolfson. Cf. son *Philo, Foundations of religious Philosophy in Judaism, Christianity and Islam* (Cambridge, Mass.: Harvard University Press, 1947), II, 156–160 *et al.*; "Albinus and Plotinus on Divine Attributes." *HThR* 45 (1952): 115 *sq.* Étienne Vacherot pensait que l'œuvre de Philon a inspiré la philosophie alexandrine par l'intermédiaire de Numénius, *Histoire critique de l'École d'Alexandrie* (Paris: Landrange, 1846), I, 166 *sq.*

[2] Cf. surtout Eric Robertson Dodds, "The *Parmenides* of Plato and the Neo-Platonic 'One'," *CQ* 22 (1928): 129–142.

éclectique.[3] Depuis, la grande majorité des historiens de la philosophie restent attachés à l'opinion selon laquelle, dans l'histoire de la philosophie grecque, les écrits de Philon n'ont aucune valeur propre, ne serait-ce qu'en tant que mine des informations sur le platonisme alexandrin des premiers siècles d'après J.-C.[4] Et comme ce gîte est considéré comme extrêmement vaste, mal ordonné et de nature trop singulière, peu nombreux sont ceux qui s'aventurent à l'exploiter.

Cela étant dit, c'était autour de la notion d'«extase» que le plus grand mouvement s'est produit, pendant la première moitié du siècle passé, sur ce champ généralement peu animé.

II. ἔκστασις *dans l'œuvre de Plotin*

Il serait sans doute utile, avant de proposer l'aperçu de cette discussion, jeter un coup d'œil sur les principaux textes de Philon d'Alexandrie et de Plotin, qui en ont servi de la base. Il convient de commencer par celui des *Ennéades*, car c'est surtout à propos de l'œuvre de Plotin que le rapport entre les deux auteurs a été envisagé.

Il nous faudra donc se rappeler un beau texte de la fin du *Tr.* 9 (VI, 9). C'est le seul cas dans les *Ennéades* où le mot ἔκστασις est employé en relation avec l'expérience spirituelle qu'on pourrait appeler mystique, ou au moins mystérieuse.[5] A cet endroit du *Tr.* 9 (VI, 9), Plotin, encore une fois, retrace les tout derniers pas de la montée de l'âme humaine vers le but suprême de son cheminement spirituel. Cette fois-ci, il s'adresse à ceux qui ont déjà fait auparavant cette expérience de l'unité absolue et indiscernable. Celui qui a vu ce but désiré et a vécu cet état, n'a qu'à s'en souvenir, se

---

[3] E. R. Dodds, *ibid.* 131: «Nor is anything really analogous to the close reasoning and intellectual subtlety of Plotinus to be found [...] in hybrid products like the works of Philo, the *Hermetica* and the *de Mysteriis*»; *ibid.* 132: «his [Philo's] eclecticism is that of the jackdaw rather than the philosopher».

[4] Cf. cependant la récente notice dans l'*Oxford Classical Dictionary* (edd. Simon Hornblower and Antony Spawforth, Oxford: Oxford University Press, 1996[3]), rédigée par Tessa Rajak, professeur d'histoire ancienne à l'université de Reading (UK), selon laquelle «Philo's voluminous works were a formative influence on Neoplatonism». Exceptionnelle aussi est l'attitude de Roberto Radice qui se rebelle contre le «présupposé méthodologique» qui consiste à «interpréter de manière univoque» les rapports de Philon «avec le monde philosophique païen gréco-latin: autrement dit, en allant de la philosophie grecque —en particulier platonicienne—à Philon, et jamais en sens inverse», "Le judaïsme alexandrin et la philosophie grecque," trad. C. Lévy, in *Philon d'Alexandrie et le langage de la philosophie* (ed. Carlos Lévy, Turnhout: Brepols, 1998), 483.

[5] Cf. *Tr.* 9 (VI, 9), 11.1–4 et Pierre Hadot, *Plotin, Traité 9 (VI, 9)*, introduction, traduction et notes par P. H. (Paris: Cerf, 1994), 112, n. 216.

souvenir de soi-même au moment de cette union. Là-bas, il n'avait plus rien dans son âme, aucun mouvement, aucune activité, rien que lui appartienne, «il n'était même plus du tout lui-même, […] mais comme ravi, comme possédé paisiblement par un dieu, il était entré dans la solitude et dans un état de tranquillité parfaite, (ne penchant d'aucun côté en son être propre, et ne tournant pas autour de lui-même), étant totalement en repos et, en quelque sorte, devenu le repos lui-même».[6] Dans cet état, il avait dépassé et le beau lui-même et le chœur des vertus.[7] Plotin compare cette mystérieuse expérience avec la vision du dieu, qu'on peut éprouver dans un sanctuaire: «comme quelqu'un qui a pénétré à l'intérieur du sanctuaire, ayant laissé derrière lui les statues qui se trouvent dans le temple, qui seront les premières pour lui lorsqu'il sortira du sanctuaire, après l'objet de vision qu'il a contemplé à l'intérieur et le commerce qu'il y a eu, non pas avec une statue ou une image, mais avec Lui».[8]

Les philosophes platoniciens étaient habitués, depuis les dialogues de Platon, à décrire l'expérience de la réalité divine comme une vision ou une contemplation. Toutefois, ce sont plutôt les notions ayant trait au toucher ou à une autre espèce du contact plus immédiat que Plotin choisit pour parler d'une rencontre qui dépasse le domaine de l'intellect, avec toutes ses magnifiques vertus.[9] Dans notre texte aussi, il ne tarde guère à se corriger: «Mais peut-être n'était-ce pas un objet de vision qu'il a contemplé; mais il s'agit d'une autre manière de voir; sortie de soi, épanouissement de soi, intensification de soi, aspiration vers le contact et le repos; tendance à la coïncidence, si quelqu'un veut contempler ce qui est dans le sanctuaire: s'il regarde d'une autre manière, alors rien ne lui est présent».[10] Cette description de l'état d'union suprême est une des plus célèbres dans l'œuvre de

---

[6] *Tr.* 9 (VI, 9), 11.11–16, traduction de Pierre Hadot (n. 5).

[7] *Tr.* 9 (VI, 9), 11.16–17.

[8] *Ibid.*, 11.17–21.

[9] Cf. *Tr.* 9 (VI, 9), 9.18, 54–55; 10.14–18; 11.4–7 et P. A. Meijer, *Plotinus on the Good or the One (Enneades VI 9): An Analytical Commentary* (Amsterdam Classical Monographs 1; Amsterdam: J. C. Gieben, 1992), 304–306.

[10] *Tr.* 9 (VI, 9), 11.22–26: τὸ δὲ ἴσως ἦν οὐ θέαμα, ἀλλὰ ἄλλος τρόπος τοῦ ἰδεῖν, ἔκστασις καὶ ἅπλωσις καὶ ἐπίδοσις αὐτοῦ καὶ ἔφεσις πρὸς ἀφὴν καὶ στάσις καὶ περινόησις πρὸς ἐφαρμογήν, εἴπερ τις τὸ ἐν τῷ ἀδύτῳ θεάσεται. εἰ δ' ἄλλως βλέποι, οὐδὲν αὐτῷ πάρεστι. Je cite la traduction de P. Hadot, qui s'appuie sur sa version du texte grec corrigé. Hadot adopte la conjecture περίνευσις de W. Theiler pour περινόησις. Personnellement, je préfère la traduction «déploiement» ou «ouverture», pour ἅπλωσις, à lieu d' «épanoussement» (de soi), et «abandon de soi», à lieu du «intensification de soi», pour ἐπίδοσις αὐτοῦ. J'en traite dans mon article "Mystérieuse ἅπλωσις dans l'*En.* VI, 9 (9) de Plotin," *Philologus* 154/1 (2010): 57–77.

Plotin.[11] En tant que l'expression d'une expérience que Plotin lui-même qualifie d'inexprimable,[12] elle est en même temps très singulière et pose beaucoup de problèmes aux interprètes, quand il s'agit de préciser le sens des notions évoquées.[13]

L'établissement du texte grec pose également quelques problèmes. Pour notre mot ἔκστασις, il y a, dans la tradition manuscrite, de légères oscillations, car dans un manuscrit (*Monacensis Graecus* 449), un -τ est ajoutée au-dessus du -στ, ce qui suggère qu'il faudrait lire ἔκτασις au lieu du ἔκστασις. Ces deux mots, en effet, sont souvent confondus dans les manuscrits. Les éditeurs sont confrontés au même choix à deux autres endroits des *Ennéades*, notamment dans le *Tr.* 53 (I, 1), 5.23[14] et dans le *Tr.* 38 (VI, 7), 17.40.[15]

Il ne serait pas sans doute difficile de comprendre ἔκτασις dans le contexte d'une comparaison avec le sanctuaire. Dans ce cas-là, il s'agirait d'un mouvement de celui qui s'élève et s'étend vers le Principe, comme on étend les mains dans la prière. Plotin parle ainsi dans le *Tr.* 10 (V, 1), 6.8 *sqq* d'une prière qui n'est pas prononcée à haute voix, mais qui s'exprime dans un élan de l'âme qui se tend et s'étend pour pouvoir seule prier le Dieu seul.[16] Ce texte du *Tr.* 10 (V, 1) n'est pas seulement chronologiquement proche de notre *Tr.* 9 (VI, 9), mais il s'agit aussi dans celui-là du Principe, demeurant en soi comme dans un sanctuaire, et des statues (ἀγάλματα) érigées à l'extérieur.[17]

Les deux autres cas d'emploi du mot ἔκστασις dans les *Ennéades* ne sont pas source des mêmes hésitations. Dans le *Tr.* 44 (VI, 3), 2.20, il s'agit de

---

[11] Cf. P. A. Meijer, *op. cit.* (n. 9), 280: «Here we encounter one of the most famous descriptions and the most famous row of descriptive terms ever to be met in Plotinus with regard to the union».

[12] *Tr.* 9 (VI, 9), 10.19–11.4.

[13] Cf. Christian Tornau, *Plotin, Ausgewälte Schriften* (Stuttgart: Philipp Reclam, 2001), 345, n. 63: «Eine Reihe experimenteller Ausdrücke, mit denen Plotin das Unsagbare zu sagen versucht»; P. A. Meijer, *op. cit.* (n. 9), 281, n. 801: «Plotinus introduces several hapaxes or hapaxical uses of signification to denote the union (ἔκστασις, ἅπλωσις, ἐπίδοσις [. . .] περινόησις and ἐφαρμογή), now that words of seeing are set aside as inappropriate. It is characteristic for this aporetical situation».

[14] ὅτι καὶ ἡ ἐπιθυμία τοῦ ἐπιθυμητικοῦ καὶ ὁ θυμὸς τοῦ θυμικοῦ καὶ ὅλως τοῦ ὀρεκτικοῦ ἡ ἐπί τι ἔκτασις (ainsi Paul Henry et Hans-Rudolf Schwyzer, *editio maior* et la plupart des manuscrits) ou ἔκστασις (HS, *editio minor*, *Monacensis Graecus* 449).

[15] ἴχνος οὖν καὶ νοῦς ἐκείνου· ἐπεὶ δὲ ὁ νοῦς εἶδος καὶ ἐν ἐκτάσει (W. Theiler, *mss:* ἐν ἐκστάσει *seu* ἐκστάσει) καὶ πλήθει, ἐκεῖνος ἄμορφος καὶ ἀνείδεος.

[16] *Tr.* 10 (V, 1), 6.8–11: Ὧδε οὖν λεγέσθω θεὸν αὐτὸν ἐπικαλεσαμένοις οὐ λόγῳ γεγωνῷ, ἀλλὰ **τῇ ψυχῇ ἐκτείνασιν ἑαυτοὺς** εἰς εὐχὴν πρὸς ἐκεῖνον, εὔχεσθαι τοῦτον τὸν τρόπον δυναμένους μόνους πρὸς μόνον.

[17] *Tr.* 10 (V, 1), 6.12–15: Δεῖ τοίνυν θεατήν, ἐκείνου ἐν τῷ εἴσω οἷον νεῷ ἐφ᾽ ἑαυτοῦ ὄντος, μένοντος ἡσύχου ἐπέκεινα ἁπάντων, τὰ οἷον πρὸς τὰ ἔξω ἤδη ἀγάλματα ἑστῶτα, μᾶλλον δὲ ἄγαλμα τὸ πρῶτον ἐκφανὲν θεᾶσθαι πεφηνὸς τοῦτον τὸν τρόπον; cf. *Tr.* 9 (VI, 9), 11.17 *sqq*.

l'incapacité de la matière à se déplacer (τῆς ὕλης τὴν οὐκ ἔκστασιν), et dans le *Tr.* 49 (V, 3), 7.13, il est affirmé que «pour l'Intellect le 'repos' n'est pas une sortie (ἔκστασις) de l'Intellect: le 'repos' de l'Intellect est un acte en vacance de tous les autres actes».[18] Selon Eric Robertson Dodds, dans ce dernier texte, le mot ἔκστασις «a son sens habituel et vague, qui décrit pour quelqu'un la sortie de sa condition mentale ordinaire».[19]

Si nous avions à choisir entre ἔκστασις et ἔκτασις dans le *Tr.* 9 (VI, 9), il faudrait dire que le premier conviendrait sans doute mieux dans le contexte du chapitre 11, où l'expérience de l'union a déjà été décrite comme semblable à un «ravissement» (ὥσπερ ἁρπασθείς) et à une «possession» (ἐνθουσιάσας).[20] Celui qui a éprouvé cet état, il s'était retiré et s'était éloigné de tout et de soi-même, s'était enfui, comme Plotin le dira dans toutes dernières lignes du traité.[21]

Willy Theiler[22] avait proposé une correction plus radicale du texte, notamment de remplacer ἔκστασις par στάσις et de supprimer στάσις à la ligne 24: στάσις καὶ ἅπλωσις καὶ ἐπίδοσις αὐτοῦ καὶ ἔφεσις πρὸς ἁφὴν καὶ περίνευσις[23] πρὸς ἐφαρμογήν. Ainsi disparaîtrait la juxtaposition déconcertante de στάσις et ἔκστασις, et la deuxième partie, «dynamique», de la description deviendrait plus homogène: ἔφεσις πρὸς ἁφὴν [καὶ στάσις] καὶ περινόησις <περίνευσις ?> πρὸς ἐφαρμογήν.[24] Nous ne pouvons évidemment pas étudier ici le caractère «statique» ou «dynamique» (nous pourrions l'appeler «extatique») de toute cette phrase.[25] Qu'il nous suffise pour

---

[18] *Tr.* 49 (V, 3), 7.13 *sqq:* ἡσυχία οὐ νοῦ ἐστιν ἔκστασις, ἀλλ᾿ ἔστιν ἡσυχία τοῦ νοῦ σχολὴν ἄγουσα ἀπὸ τῶν ἄλλων ἐνέργεια· ἐπεὶ καὶ τοῖς ἄλλοις, οἷς ἐστιν ἡσυχία ἑτέρων, καταλείπεται ἡ αὐτῶν οἰκεία ἐνέργεια καὶ μάλιστα, οἷς τὸ εἶναι οὐ δυνάμει ἐστίν, ἀλλὰ ἐνεργείᾳ. Traduction de Bernard Ham, *Plotin, Traité 49 (V, 3)*, introduction, traduction et notes par B. H. (Paris: Cerf, 2000).

[19] *Pagan and Christian in an Age of Anxiety, Some Aspects of Religious Experience from Marcus Aurelius to Constantine* (Cambridge: University Press, 1965), 72, n. 1. Traduction de Henry-Dominic Saffrey (*Païens et chrétiens dans un âge d'angoisse. Aspects de l'expérience religieuse de Marc-Aurèle à Constantin* (Claix: La Pensée Sauvage, 1979), 88, n. 1.

[20] *Tr.* 9 (VI, 9), 11.12 *sq.*

[21] *Tr.* 9 (VI, 9), 11.51: φυγή.

[22] Willy Theiler, *Plotins Schriften* (Hamburg: Felix Meiner, 1971), VI, 174.

[23] Περίνευσις est une conjecture de W. Theiler pour περινόησις. Cf. n. 10 *supra*.

[24] Plg. P. A. Meijer, *op. cit.* (n. 9), 280 *sq*, n. 798. P. Hadot, *op. cit.* (n. 5), 67, 112, n. 219 corrige στάσις en στάσιν: ἔφεσις πρὸς ἁφὴν καὶ στάσιν, d'où sa traduction: «aspiration vers le contact et le repos». Chr. Tornau, *op. cit.* (n. 13) ne cherche pas à améliorer le texte transmis qu'il rend ainsi: «ein Außer-sich-Geraten, Sichentfalten, Sichaufgeben; ein Streben, es zu berühren, ein Stillstehen, ein Um-es-herum-Denken, um mit ihm in Deckung zu kommen».

[25] Les éléments d'une telle étude ont été proposés par René Arnou, *Le désir de Dieu dans la philosophie de Plotin* (Paris: Félix Alcan, 1921), 236 *sq* et Pierre Hadot, *op. cit.* (n. 5), 207.

l'instant d'observer que, dans le contexte de la réflexion de Plotin sur l'union avec la suprême Divinité, ἔκστασις n'est pas nécessairement un opposé de στάσις: la sortie de soi est un mouvement de celui qui va s'établir dans la stabilité absolue du son Principe.[26]

Quoi qu'il en soit, nous ne pouvons évidemment pas corriger toujours les textes grecs pour les rendre plus logiques et plus cohérents. Dans notre cas, outre le témoignage quasi unanime des manuscrits, nous pouvons considérer comme un argument complémentaire en faveur du texte transmis le fait que Proclus et pseudo Denys l'Aréopagite emploient le mot ἔκστασις dans les contextes qui rappellent le *Tr. 9* (VI, 9).[27]

La célèbre «description de l'état mystique» comporte encore une difficulté considérable. Comme Plotin tient pour inexprimable l'état qu'il veut évoquer, il recourt à une comparaison.[28] Cela ne facilite guère la tâche des interprètes, car il s'agit ici d'une expérience qui est très proche mais non pas identique à celle d'un philosophe, tel Plotin lui-même. Celui qui a compris le sens de l'énigme du rite religieux, dit Plotin, n'a pas besoin d'aller dans un sanctuaire pour éprouver le véritable mystère du contact avec la divinité.[29]

---

[26] Cf. R. Arnou, *Le désir de Dieu* (n. 25), 238: «Ce mode supérieur de connaître Dieu est à la fois ἔκστασις et στάσις: Il faut tenir compte du sens spécial de ce mot στάσις dans les Ennéades. Sortie de soi, l'âme se trouve en un état supérieur, loin du monde où l'on ne peut trouver qu'un repos éphémère (ἠρεμία), elle se trouve dans la stabilité (στάσις), propre aux êtres véritables qui ne connaissent pas le changement, plus haut encore et comme édifiée et plantée en Dieu».

[27] Cf. Proclus, *In Ti.* 1.212.20–25 Diehl: καὶ ἐλπίδα τῶν ἀγαθῶν ἄτρεπτόν τε ὑποδοχὴν τοῦ θείου φωτὸς καὶ **ἔκστασιν** ἀπὸ πάντων τῶν ἄλλων ἐπιτηδευμάτων, ἵνα **μόνος τις τῷ θεῷ μόνῳ συνῇ** καὶ μὴ μετὰ πλήθους τῷ ἑνὶ **συνάπτειν** (cf. *Tr. 9* (VI, 9), 8.9, 19, 27 *sq*) ἑαυτὸν ἐγχειρῇ· πᾶν γὰρ τοὐναντίον ὁ τοιοῦτος δρᾷ καὶ ἀφίστησιν ἑαυτὸν τῶν θεῶν· ὡς γὰρ οὐ θέμις μετὰ τοῦ μὴ ὄντος τῷ ὄντι προσομιλεῖν, οὕτως οὐδὲ μετὰ πλήθους **τῷ ἑνὶ συνάπτεσθαι** δυνατόν; Pseudo Denys l'Aréopagite, *Myst.* 1: τῇ περὶ τὰ μυστικὰ θεάματα συντόνῳ διατριβῇ καὶ τὰς αἰσθήσεις ἀπόλειπε καὶ τὰς νοερὰς ἐνεργείας καὶ πάντα αἰσθητὰ καὶ νοητὰ καὶ πάντα οὐκ ὄντα καὶ ὄντα καὶ πρὸς τὴν ἕνωσιν, ὡς ἐφικτόν, ἀγνώστως ἀνατάθητι τοῦ ὑπὲρ πᾶσαν οὐσίαν καὶ γνῶσιν· τῇ γὰρ ἑαυτοῦ καὶ πάντων ἀσχέτῳ καὶ ἀπολύτῳ καθαρῶς **ἐκστάσει** πρὸς τὸν ὑπερούσιον τοῦ θείου σκότους ἀκτῖνα, πάντα ἀφελὼν καὶ ἐκ πάντων ἀπολυθείς, ἀναχθήσῃ. Toutefois, la variante ἔκτασις se rencontre également dans la tradition manuscrite de l'œuvre de Proclus.

[28] *Tr. 9* (VI, 9), 11.16: ὥσπερ τις [...]; *ibid.* 11.26: ταῦτα μὲν οὖν μιμήματα· καὶ τοῖς οὖν σοφοῖς τῶν προφητῶν αἰνίττεται, ὅπως θεὸς ἐκεῖνος ὁρᾶται.

[29] *Tr. 9* (VI, 9), 11.30–32. Cf. Porphyre, *Plot.* 10.33–38.

III. ἔκστασις dans les écrits de Philon

Dans l'œuvre de Philon, c'est un texte du *Quis rerum divinarum heres sit* 249 *sqq* qui est le plus souvent évoqué dans la discussion sur l'histoire de la notion d' «extase mystique». Ici, Philon commente «une scène fameuse du ch. 15 de la *Genèse:* Abraham interroge Dieu sur son héritier; Dieu répond en promettant un descendant autre que 'le fils de la servante', il demande à Abraham de préparer un sacrifice; au coucher du soleil, une *extase* (c'est le mot grec qui est employé dans le texte grec de la *Septante*) tomba sur Abraham; révélation lui est faite du sort qui attend sa postérité; puis le sacrifice est consumé par le feu et Dieu renouvelle sa promesse d'une terre, entre l'Égypte et l'Euphrate».[30]

Le commentaire qui nous intéresse principalement porte sur les mots de la *Genèse* 15:12: «Au coucher du soleil une extase (ἔκστασις) tomba sur Abraham et voici, une grande frayeur obscure tombe sur lui». C'est par le mot «extase» que Philon commence son exégèse. Dans ce texte de la *Septante*, ἔκστασις est une traduction de l'hébreu *tardémah* qui est rendu habituellement en langues modernes par le «profond sommeil». Philon note que le mot grec ἔκστασις peut avoir quatre significations différentes. Il explique que «'Extase' signifie tantôt (1) la fureur délirante qui provoque la folie, sous l'effet de la sénilité, ou de la mélancolie, ou pour tout autre raison analogue; tantôt (2) la stupéfaction que l'on éprouve devant des événements survenant à l'improviste, alors que l'on ne s'y attend pas; tantôt encore (3) le calme (ἠρεμία) de l'intelligence (διάνοια), si vraiment il est dans sa nature de se reposer parfois; tantôt enfin, (4) ce qui est le mieux, la possession et le délire d'origine divine, comme l'éprouve la race prophétique (ἡ δὲ πασῶν ἀρίστη ἔνθεος κατοκωχή τε καὶ μανία)».[31]

Pour illustrer ces quatre sens du mot grec ἔκστασις, Philon cite les textes des Écritures où sont employés soit le substantif ἔκστασις, soit le verbe ἐξίσταμαι.[32] L'exemple donné pour la troisième signification est tiré de Genèse 2:21 où il s'agit de la naissance de la femme: «'Car Dieu', est-il écrit, 'envoya une extase sur Adam et il dormit'. 'Extase' désigne ici le repos et le calme de l'intellect (ἔκστασιν τὴν ἡσυχίαν καὶ ἠρεμίαν τοῦ νοῦ παραλαμβάνων). Le sommeil de l'intellect, en effet, correspond à l'éveil de la sensibilité et inversement, l'éveil de l'intelligence correspond à l'inaction de

---

[30] J'emprunte la description de l'épisode de la *Genèse* à Marguerite Harl, *Quis rerum divinarum heres sit*, introduction, traduction et notes par M. H. (PAMP, Paris: Cerf, 1966), 13.

[31] *Her.* 249. Traduction de Marguerite Harl (voir la note précédente).

[32] *Her.* 250–251, 257.

la sensibilité».[33] Il semble que les commentateurs n'ont pas encore observé que l'affirmation du *Tr.* 49 (V, 3), selon laquelle «pour l'Intellect le 'repos' n'est pas une sortie de l'Intellect: le 'repos' de l'Intellect est un acte en vacance de tous les autres actes (ἡσυχία οὐ νοῦ ἐστιν ἔκστασις, ἀλλ' ἔστιν ἡσυχία τοῦ νοῦ σχολὴν ἄγουσα ἀπὸ τῶν ἄλλων ἐνέργεια)»,[34] ressemble à une réplique polémique à une telle définition d'«extase» que nous trouvons chez Philon.

Encore plus profond est, aux yeux de Philon, le contact avec Dieu qui s'établit dans une âme digne d'éprouver la meilleure des quatre espèces d'extase, «la possession et le délire d'origine divine, comme l'éprouve la race prophétique», ἡ δὲ πασῶν ἀρίστη **ἔνθεος κατοκωχή** τε καὶ **μανία**, ᾗ τὸ προφητικὸν γένος χρῆται.[35] Dans cet état, l'intellect cède sa place non à la sensation, comme cela se passait dans le cas de la troisième espèce d'extase, mais à Dieu lui-même. Selon Philon, c'était une extase de cette sorte, cet «état d'un homme possédé par Dieu, inspiré par Dieu» (ἐνθουσιῶντος καὶ θεοφορήτου τὸ πάθος) qui était celui d'Abraham au coucher du soleil.[36]

Philon ajoute que c'est seulement une âme parfaitement sage et vertu-euse qui peut éprouver une telle inspiration prophétique, car «le prophète n'exprime aucune parole qui lui soit personnelle; tout est d'autrui, un autre parlant en lui. Au méchant, il n'est pas permis d'être l'interprète de Dieu, si bien qu'aucun homme mauvais n'est inspiré de Dieu au sens propre; cela convient seulement au sage, puisque, seul, il est l'instrument sonore de Dieu, dont Dieu frappe invisiblement les cordes avec son plectre».[37] C'est pourquoi tous les justes, dont parle Moïse, sont aussi «possédés de Dieu et prophétisent».[38]

Philon explique que la mention du «coucher du soleil» est un indice qui convient admirablement à l'état de l'homme inspiré de Dieu, car «ce qu'est en nous le raisonnement (λογισμός), le soleil l'est dans le monde; l'un et l'autre sont porteurs de lumière [...]. Or donc, tant que notre intellect brille

---

[33] *Her.* 257. Dans un autre ouvrage (*Leg.* 2.31 *sq*) Philon explique, à propos du même texte de la *Genèse*, que «l'extase et la diversion (τροπή) de l'intelligence (τοῦ νοῦ), c'est le sommeil de cette faculté; elle est en extase lorsqu'elle ne s'occupe pas des intelligibles qui la concernent et, lorsqu'elle n'a plus cette activité, elle dort», traduction de Claude Mondésert (PAPM, Paris: Cerf, 1962). Ici, comme dans le *Quis heres*, «extase» est expliquée en termes de la philosophie grecque comme un écartement, une diversion de l'intelligence par rapport à ses propres activités.

[34] *Tr.* 49 (V, 3), 7.13–15.

[35] *Her.* 249.

[36] *Her.* 258.

[37] *Her.* 259; cf. *ibid.* 266.

[38] *Ibid.* 260: πάντας γοῦν ὁπόσους ἀνέγραψε δικαίους κατεχομένους καὶ προφητεύοντας εἰσήγαγεν.

et accomplit en nous son évolution [...], étant en nous-mêmes, nous ne sommes pas possédés (ἐν ἑαυτοῖς ὄντες οὐ κατεχόμεθα); mais lorsqu'il vient au couchant, alors tout naturellement, c'est l'"extase' et 'tombent' sur nous la possession et le délire divins (ἡ ἔνθεος κατοκωχή τε καὶ μανία). [...] Cela arrive à la race prophétique: l'intellect, en nous, est chassé au moment, où arrive le souffle divin; lorsque celui-ci repart, le notre est réintroduit; car il n'est pas permis que le mortel cohabite avec l'immortel (θέμις γὰρ οὐκ ἔστι θνητὸν ἀθανάτῳ συνοικῆσαι). C'est la raison pour laquelle le coucher du raisonnement, accompagné de ténèbres, engendre 'l'extase' et le délire venu de Dieu (ἔκστασιν καὶ θεοφόρητον μανίαν)».[39]

IV. *La discussion à propos de la notion d' «extase» chez Philon et Plotin au cours du XXᵉ siècle*

Après avoir évoqué les principaux textes de deux auteurs, nous pouvons maintenant nous tourner vers la discussion concernant l'origine de la notion de «l'extase mystique», que ces textes ont nourrie. Quant à la «mystique», nous n'avons pas évidemment ici l'intention d'étudier le phénomène lui-même ou ses espèces. Il nous faudra toutefois garder ce terme, car la plupart des historiens qui ont étudié la notion d' «extase» chez nos deux auteurs, utilisent ce terme convenu pour distinguer un emploi du mot «extase», dans les cas où celui-ci désigne l'expérience d'un contact direct avec la suprême Divinité. Ce n'est pas l'expérience elle-même qui nous intéressera mais plutôt l'histoire de l'emploi et de la «promotion» du mot ἔκστασις dans le domaine de l'expérience psychique. Bien que certains chercheurs aient attiré l'attention sur le vocable lui-même, quand ils parlaient de «l'extase mystique» chez Plotin et ses prédécesseurs, il semble que, jusqu'à présent, aucune étude suivie n'a été proposée là-dessus.

L'ouvrage qui a servi du point de départ à la discussion sur la relation de la notion d' «extase» philonienne et celle de Plotin est paru à Paris en 1906. Il a pour auteur Henri Guyot et porte un titre éloquent: *Les réminiscences de Philon le Juif chez Plotin.*[40] Cette recherche est d'une étendue modeste (92 pages), manque beaucoup de précision et n'autorise pas à adhérer à la ferme conclusion tirée par l'auteur, selon laquelle, «Philon et, par lui, les croyances judéo-orientales ont exercé» sur la philosophie grecque postérieure «*une influence* plus grande que les historiens, particu-

---

[39] *Ibid.* 263–265. Cf. encore *Spec.* 4.49.
[40] Henry Guyot, *Les réminiscences de Philon le Juif chez Plotin. Étude critique* (Paris: Félix Alcan, 1906).

lièrement M. Ed. Zeller, ne l'ont accordé, et *qu'il faut même qualifier de prépondérante*».[41] On n'a pas à s'étonner si l'avis d'H. Guyot n'a pas eu de partisans résolus.[42] Son étude a tout de même soulevé une petite vague de réactions,[43] surtout le chapitre portant sur la notion d'extase, qui était à cette époque-là un sujet très en vogue parmi les historiens de la philosophie et des religions.

Tout en admettant que le fait même de l'occurrence de mot grec ἔκστα-σις soit important pour qu'on puisse parler d'une «doctrine de l'extase»,[44] H. Guyot, en fait, appuie ses conclusions sur plusieurs textes des deux auteurs, qui ne contiennent pas toujours le mot ἔκστασις mais mentionnent différents aspects de l'état que l'âme connaît à l'approche de Dieu et à l'instant de sa rencontre avec lui. Guyot réunit diverses descriptions de cet état, qu'il trouve dans les écrits de Philon et de Plotin, sous le titre commun de «la doctrine de l'Extase». De l'étude comparative de ce choix de textes, il tire la conclusion que, en écrivant «sur l'Extase», «Plotin s'est *souvenu* aussi» de Philon,[45] et il décrit cette expérience de «l'extase», que les deux auteurs auraient conçue d'une manière identique, comme un événement au cours duquel «Dieu vient vers l'âme, ou plutôt il la tire à lui. Celle-ci sort d'elle-même. Les deux s'unissent, se mêlent et ne font plus qu'un».[46]

---

[41] *Ibid.* 89, c'est moi qui souligne.

[42] Cependant, le travail de H. Guyot n'est pas oublié et peut encore servir de bon point de départ pour une étude portante sur l'origine de certaines notions philosophiques et théologiques. Cf., par exemple, Albert-Kees Geljon, "Divine Infinity in Gregory of Nyssa and Philo of Alexandria," *VC* 59/2 (2005): 152–177.

[43] C'est pourquoi il est assez surprenant, que l'ouvrage de Henry Guyot n'est guère mentionné par David T. Runia qui brosse un aperçu fort utile de l'histoire des recherches sur le rapport entre Philon et la tradition platonicienne,—"Witness or Participant? Philo and the Neoplatonist Tradition," in *Philo and the Church Fathers. A Collection of Papers by D. T. Runia* (Leiden: Brill, 1995), 183–189. D. T. Runia commence par «the grandiose and idiosyncratic perspective on the history of philosophy developed by the Jewish-American scholar Harry Austryn Wolfson», qui, dans sa version de l'histoire de la philosophie, avait accordé à Philon le rôle de l'initiateur d'une deuxième et centrale période, celle de la philosophie religieuse. Toutefois, on a l'impression que D. T. Runia lui-même à en vue la discussion inaugurée par H. Guyot, quand, en résumant ses réflexions, il écrit (*op. cit.* 202): «It needs not, therefore, be a mirage, if we were to perceive far in the distance behind the word *hestôs*—but perhaps also the word *ekstasis*—the figure of the Patriarch Abraham, i.e. Pentateuchal texts as expounded by Philo, even if Plotinus may not have been conscious of texts when he wrote his treatise».

[44] Cf. *Les réminiscences de Philon le Juif* (n. 40), 81: «La doctrine de Philon et de Plotin est une doctrine de l'extase. Le nom y est écrit et répété».

[45] *Ibid.* 84. H. Guyot pense que la source directe dont Plotin s'inspire, quand il traite de «l'Extase», soit Numénius.

[46] *Ibid.* 81.

Nous pouvons remarquer d'emblée qu'une telle définition convient mal à la pensée de Philon, comme elle est exprimée dans le texte du *Quis heres* que nous avons évoqué, où il est dit que c'est l'intellect (ou «le raisonnement»; νοῦς ou λογισμός) de l'âme qui en sort pour céder sa place à Dieu, et qu'il est obligé de se comporter ainsi, car aucun être mortel ne peut s'unir, encore moins s'identifier à la Divinité suprême. Quant à Plotin, bien qu'il parle parfois de la Divinité qui «remplit» ou «envahit» l'âme, le plus souvent il accorde l'initiative à l'âme,—c'est elle qui est encouragée à se lancer, en s'abandonnant, vers son origine.

D'une manière générale, on peut se demander si le terme «extase», qui évoque des traditions de spiritualité distinctes de celle des philosophes platoniciens, est bien choisi pour nommer la notion de l'union la plus intime entre une âme et son Principe, comme cette notion se dessine dans les écrits de Plotin. D'autant plus que, comme nous l'avons remarqué, dans le texte du Traité 9 (VI, 9) qui sert de point d'appui pour parler de la notion de «l'extase» dans les *Ennéades*, Plotin décrit une certaine expérience religieuse qu'il *compare*, sans l'identifier, avec celle d'un philosophe.[47]

C'est René Arnou, semble-t-il, qui a été le premier à répondre d'une manière explicite aux suggestions d'H. Guyot. Dans son ouvrage, paru chez le même éditeur (*Librairie Félix Alcan*) quinze ans après celui de Guyot, Arnou critique le travail de son prédécesseur en tant qu'il «s'en tient trop exclusivement à des similitudes de langage, base trop fragile pour les conclusions qu'il en tire. Que Plotin emploie ἔκστασις comme Philon, qu'est-ce que cela prouve, alors qu'on sait de Philon lui-même que de son temps ce mot était assez employé pour qu'on pût lui donner quatre sens différents».[48] Arnou remarque que des autres expressions de Philon et de Plotin, rapprochées par Guyot, notamment les formes du verbe ἐνθουσιάζω (ou, chez Philon, ἐνθουσιάω), ou l'affirmation que «l'extase se produit avec soudaineté», «se trouvent déjà dans Platon». «Pourquoi», conclut l'auteur, «parler d'une réminiscence de Philon, s'il suffit d'en appeler à Platon que ses lointains disciples se flattaient de suivre pas à pas?»[49] Bien qu'il réprouve la méthode employée dans l'étude de Guyot, Arnou soutient énergiquement la conclusion générale de son collègue. Il indique de nouveaux textes de Philon, qui parlent de la vision de Dieu, autant que cela est accessible pour une âme, et résume que «c'est plus qu'il n'en faut pour parler avec raison d'une influence de Philon sur Plotin, que cette influence

---

[47] Cela est bien mis en relief par P. Hadot, *Plotin, Traité* 9 (n. 5), 203 *sqq.*

[48] R. Arnou, *Le désir de Dieu* (n. 25), 260. L'auteur indique (260, n. 2) le texte du *Quis heres* que nous avons déjà évoqué.

[49] *Ibid.*

se soit exercée directement ou par un intermédiaire, Numénius ou Ammonius Sakkas».[50]

Toutefois, Arnou observe une grande différence entre l'attitude des
deux auteurs. Selon lui, tandis que l'un «se contente d'affirmer ses idées,
qu'il rattache plus ou moins heureusement aux textes de l'Écriture, Plotin
systématise la doctrine de l'extase en la déduisant des principes de sa
philosophie».[51] Nous pouvons observer que l'ironie consiste dans le fait,
que, dans le cas de la «doctrine de l'extase», ce n'est pas le texte de Plotin
mais celui du *Quis heres* 249 *sqq*, de Philon, qui a l'air d'un système.

Quelques années plus tard E. R. Dodds s'est opposé fermement à l'avis,
selon lequel on pourrait quasiment identifier les deux notions d'«extase». Il
souligne que «à la différence de celle de Philon, extase de Plotin survient au
bout d'un travail intellectuel intérieur, et non pas comme un résultat d'une
abnégation de la raison ou d'une intervention magique de l'extérieure; c'est
de la réalisation suprême de soi-même, qu'il s'en agit ici, plutôt que du
renoncement au soi-même».[52]

Plus tard, dans son célèbre ouvrage *Pagan and Christian in an Age of
Anxiety*, E. R. Dodds ajoute d'utiles précisions au sujet de l'emploi du mot
grec ἔκστασις. Il note, avec juste raison, que ce mot amène souvent à la
confusion, lorsqu'on traite des faits de l'expérience mystique, car à lui seul,
dans la langue grecque classique, ce mot a plusieurs sens, qui n'ont rien à
voir avec l'état de l'*unio mystica*, lorsqu'il désigne de brusques et «anor-
maux» changements de l'état psychique et l'égarement de l'esprit sous
l'effet de l'étonnement ou de la frayeur, ou encore «l'hystérie» et «la
psychopathie» (c'est ainsi que le mot ἔκστασις est souvent employé chez
Aristote et dans les traités médicaux). Ultérieurement, ἔκστασις commence
à signifier «obsession», ou bien une obsession divine des prophètes de
l'Écriture juive, ou l'obsession diabolique (c'est ainsi qu'Origène parle de
l'*extase* de la Pythie).[53] Après avoir cité un passage du *Quis heres* 265 *sq*,[54]
Dodds conclut que l'ἔκστασις dont parle Philon ne doit pas être confondue
avec l'expérience de «l'union mystique».[55] Selon lui, ce que décrit Philon, ce
n'est pas «l'union mystique», mais «un état de 'l'obsession temporaire' ou

---

[50] *Ibid*. 263.

[51] *Ibid*. 264.

[52] E. R. Dodds, "The *Parmenides* of Plato" (n. 2), 142. Cf. R. Arnou, *Le désir de Dieu*
(n. 25), 251 *sqq*.

[53] E. R. Dodds, *Pagan and Christian* (n. 19), 70–71.

[54] «'The mind in us', he says, 'is banished from its house upon the coming of the
divine spirit, and upon its withdrawal is again restored; for mortal and immortal may not
share the same house'».

[55] *Pagan and Christian* (n. 19), 71.

ce qu'on appelle aujourd'hui une transe médiumnique».[56] «C'est l'esprit surnaturel qui descend dans un corps humain et non pas l'homme qui s'élève lui-même ou qui est élevé au-dessus du corps».[57]

Ainsi en brossant l'histoire de la notion de «l'extase mystique», E. R. Dodds observe que, à sa connaissance, «la plus ancienne application de ce mot à l'expérience mystique au sens strict, se trouve dans une célèbre phrase de Plotin [...], où l'union mystique est décrite comme 'une *ekstasis*, une simplification et un abandonnement [...] de moi, un désir du contact qui est à la fois un repos et un effort spirituel d'adaptation'».[58] «C'est apparemment de Plotin, à travers Grégoire de Nysse, que le mysticisme chrétien a tiré cet emploi du mot *ekstasis*».[59]

Un autre éminent connaisseur de la tradition de la philosophie grecque, le traducteur de l'œuvre de Plotin en anglais Arthur Hilary Armstrong, ne partage que partiellement l'avis de son collègue. D'une part, A. H. Armstrong note, avec juste raison, ce que semblent ne pas avoir observé les partisans de l'hypothèse de l'influence de Philon sur Plotin: «Il n'y a aucun doute que, de manière générale, l'image des relations entre l'âme et Dieu proposée par Philon est très différente de celle que présente Plotin. La manière dont Philon souligne la profonde dissemblance entre Dieu et toutes ses créatures [...], son entière inaccessibilité pour la raison humaine [...], et les motifs d'une telle attitude seraient complètement étrangers à l'esprit de Plotin».[60] «Devant Dieu, Philon est plein de la profonde humilité, il Le craint et il L'aime en se rendant compte de sa propre nullité. [...] En cela, il appartient entièrement à la tradition juive. Quant à Plotin, il a toute la confiance en soi qu'un philosophe Grec éprouvait en présence de la Divinité».[61]

Toutefois, «même cette prodigieuse assurance recule à l'instance de l'union mystique suprême».[62] C'est pourquoi A. H. Armstrong considère

---

[56] *Ibid.* 72. Je cite la traduction française de H. D. Saffrey (n. 19). Cf. E. R. Dodds, "The *Parmenides* of Plato" (n. 2), 142.

[57] *Pagan and Christian,* 72.

[58] *Ibid.*: «an *ekstasis*, a simplification and surrender of the self, an aspiration toward contact which is at once a stillness and a mental effort of adaptation».

[59] *Ibid.*

[60] Arthur Hilary Armstrong, *The Architecture of the Intelligible Universe in the Philosophy of Plotinus. An Analytical and Historical Study* (Cambridge: University Press, 1940), 71. Traduction française de Josiane Ayoub et Danièle Letocha (*L'Architecture de l'univers intelligible dans la philosophie de Plotin,* Ottawa: l'Université d'Ottawa, 1984).

[61] *Ibid.* 72.

[62] *Ibid.*: «Even his tremendous self-confidence, however, falters when it comes to the supreme mystical union».

que la distinction que Dodds fait entre l'attitude de Philon et celle de Plotin est trop rigide: pour Plotin aussi, l'état de l'union avec Dieu n'est pas toujours celle d'une «suprême réalisation de soi-même»; le plus souvent, il l'évoque comme une expérience foncièrement différente, voire étrangère à la connaissance intellectuelle, et l'attitude de l'âme est parfois décrite par lui comme une état purement passif, dans l'attente de l'apparition soudaine de l'Un, qui l'envahit et l'illumine.[63] De l'avis d'Armstrong, «tout cela ressemble singulièrement à la description de l'extase proposée par Philon, dans un texte de Philon [*Quis heres* 264–265] que Dodds avait cité».[64]

À l'appui de cette opinion d'A. H. Armstrong, nous pouvons ajouter que ce n'est pas seulement dans un passage assez controversé du *Tr.* 49 (V, 3), 14.8[65] que Plotin compare l'expérience intérieure de l'Un avec l'état des gens inspirés et des possédés,[66] mais aussi dans le même chapitre 11 du *Tr.* 9 (VI, 9), où il s'agit de l'état de l'union absolue avec «Lui»: ἀλλ᾽ ὥσπερ ἁρπασθεὶς ἢ ἐνθουσιάσας ἡσυχῇ.[67]

Armstrong note que Philon et Plotin, quand ils évoquent l'expérience qui dépasse le niveau intellectuel, développent tous les deux les images du *Phèdre* et du *Banquet* platoniciens. Il s'étonne, en même temps, que «deux hommes aussi différents quant aux lignes générales de leur pensée religieuse et philosophique s'expriment sur ce point d'une manière aussi semblable».[68] De son avis donc, bien qu'il soit impossible d'indiquer un lien repérable historiquement entre l'œuvre de Philon et celle de Plotin, les similitudes de leurs descriptions de l'état de l'union mystique plus que

---

[63] *Ibid.* 72–73.

[64] *Ibid.* 73. Cf. E. R. Dodds, "The *Parmenides* of Plato" (n. 2), 142, n. 4.

[65] Cf. E. R. Dodds, *ibid.* 142, n. 3, A. H. Armstrong, *The Architecture* (n. 60), 73, B. Ham (n. 18), 238 *sq.*

[66] *Tr.* 49 (V, 3), 14.8–13: Ἔχειν δὲ οὐ κωλυόμεθα, κἂν μὴ λέγωμεν. Ἀλλ᾽ ὥσπερ οἱ ἐνθουσιῶντες καὶ κάτοχοι γενόμενοι ἐπὶ τοσοῦτον κἂν εἰδεῖεν, ὅτι ἔχουσι μεῖζον ἐν αὑτοῖς, κἂν μὴ εἰδῶσιν ὅ τι, ἐξ ὧν δὲ κεκίνηνται καὶ λέγουσιν, ἐκ τούτων αἴσθησίν τινα τοῦ κινήσαντος λαμβάνουσιν ἑτέρων ὄντων τοῦ κινήσαντος, οὕτω καὶ ἡμεῖς κινδυνεύομεν ἔχειν πρὸς ἐκεῖνο.

[67] *Tr.* 9 (VI, 9), 11.12–13. Curieusement, ni E. R. Dodds, ni par la suite A. H. Armstrong ne prennent pas en considération ce texte du ch. 11. De l'avis de Dodds "The *Parmenides* of Plato" [n. 2], 142, n. 3), le fait même que dans le *Tr.* 49 (V, 3) il s'agit d'une *comparaison* avec l'état des possédés montre suffisamment que, aux yeux de Plotin, cet état est «différent de son extase». Il vaut donc la peine de rappeler, une fois de plus, que la fameuse description de «l'union mystique» du *Tr.* 9 (VI, 9) est également présentée dans le contexte d'une *comparaison*. Autrement dit, «l'extase» qui, à côté d'autres termes, est évoquée ici, désigne une expérience semblable mais non identique à celle du philosophe, comme dans le cas des comparaisons avec l'état des possédés.

[68] *The Architecture* (n. 60), 73.

toute autre chose dans les *Ennéades* peuvent témoigner de l'influence que Philon aurait exercée sur Plotin.[69]

Il semble que, depuis l'ouvrage de Dodds,[70] aucun auteur ne s'est prononcé sur ce sujet controversé. Et lorsque nous prenons les études sur Plotin, parues vers la fin du XXᵉ siècle, nous pouvons constater que la discussion concernant la généalogie et la typologie de la notion d'«extase mystique» ne jouit plus d'aucune faveur auprès des interprètes, et que la notion même d'«extase» n'est plus, et avec bonne raison, considérée comme essentielle pour la pensée de Plotin.[71]

Toutefois, je crois que l'histoire de cette notion peut être instructive, surtout pour pouvoir mieux juger de la place que Philon a pu avoir dans la tradition platonicienne. Par conséquent, il vaut la peine de reconsidérer les principaux témoignages.

V. Classement des espèces de la folie (μανία) divine dans le Phèdre platonicien

Tout d'abord, pour reprendre l'investigation ébauchée par nos collègues pendant la première moitié du XXᵉ siècle, il faudra ajouter à notre dossier un autre texte important de la tradition platonicienne. Il est assez surprenant que ce texte n'ait jamais été évoqué dans le débat concernant le rapport possible entre «l'extase» chez Philon et chez Plotin. C'est surtout Hans Leisegang qui, dans son ouvrage sur la connaissance mystique dans la philosophie et la religion grecques, a indiqué un parallèle, selon lui évident, entre les *quatre* espèces d' «extase» distinguées par Philon et la fameuse division en *quatre* formes de la folie divine (μανία), qui est proposée par Socrate dans le *Phèdre* platonicien (244 a–245 a, et récapitulation en 265 b *sqq*).[72]

---

[69] *The Architecture* (n. 60), 73–74. En outre de la notion d' «extase», A. H. Armstrong souligne la similitude de la conception de la contemplation «pluralisante de l'unité divine par l'intellect» (*the pluralizing contemplation of the divine principle by the intellect*) dans l'œuvre de deux auteurs.

[70] Il s'agit du *Pagan and Christian in an Age of Anxiety*, paru en 1965. A. H. Armstrong répondait principalement à l'article considérablement plus ancien du même auteur ("The *Parmenides* of Plato" [n. 2], 1928).

[71] L' «extase» n'est guère évoquée dans l'excellente étude de Dominic O'Meara, *Plotin, Une introduction aux Ennéades*, traduit de l'anglais (*Plotinus, An Introduction to the Enneads,* Oxford: Clarendon, 1993) par Anne Banateanu (Fribourg: Academic Press, Paris: Cerf, 2004²). Pierre Hadot, dans le vaste commentaire à sa nouvelle traduction du *Tr.* 9 (n. 5), ne mentionne ἔκστασις qu'une seule fois, dans une paraphrase du développement du ch. 11.22–26 (*Traité 9*, 207).

[72] Hans Leisegang, *Heilige Geist: Die vorchristlichen Anschauungen und Lehren vom Pneuma und der mystisch-intuitiven Erkenntnis* (Leipzig: Teubner, 1919), Bd. I, Th. 1, 166: «lässt sich hier eine Vergleichung mit einem der Hauptstücke des platonischen Dialogs

Il faut donc rappeler brièvement cette classification du *Phèdre*, selon laquelle sont salutaires les dons de la folie (1) mantique, c'est-à-dire divinatoire et prophétique; (2) télestique; celle-ci inspire les gens qui savent faire recours aux rites de purification et d'initiation pour écarter les maux; (3) poétique, qui vient des Muses (τρίτη δὲ ἀπὸ Μουσῶν **κατοκωχή τε καὶ μανία**);[73] enfin, (4) la meilleure de toutes les formes de la possession divine, la folie érotique éprouvée par les philosophes (αὕτη **πασῶν τῶν ἐνθουσιάσεων ἀρίστη** τε καὶ ἐξ ἀρίστων τῷ τε ἔχοντι καὶ τῷ κοινωνοῦντι αὐτῆς γίγνεται).[74] C'est elle qui fait l'objet principal de toute la palinodie de Socrate, qui comporte aussi la célèbre image du ὑπερουράνιος τόπος, la «plaine de la vérité» qui est au-dessus du ciel.[75]

H. Leisegang note que, de même que chez Platon l'énumération des espèces profitables de la «folie» aboutit à l'éloge de la folie divine des philosophes, inspirée par Éros, de même l'analyse de Philon s'achève par une louange de l'extase prophétique du sage.[76] Outre cette correspondance de la structure générale des deux développements, ce sont les emprunts lexicaux qui montrent à l'évidence la dépendance de Philon à l'égard de Platon. Du point de vue du contenu, il est important de noter que, pour les deux auteurs, seul l'esprit du sage peut être saisi par une «extase» ou une «folie» divine.[77] Leisegang conclut que «l'extase chez Philon est une notion qui n'est guère étrangère à la spiritualité grecque, ni empruntée au prophétisme juif ou aux spéculations orientales; plutôt, prise dans son contenu global (*ihrem ganzen Inhalt nach*), elle n'est rien autre que θεία μανία platonicienne».[78]

Nous pouvons observer que cette analyse efface trop aisément la différence apparente entre la folie érotique du *Phèdre* et l'extase prophétique de Philon. Néanmoins, l'auteur a eu raison de souligner la dépendance du classement de Philon par rapport à celui du *Phèdre*. Le fait de cette

---

Phaidros kaum von der Hand weisen». Henri-Charles Puech, dans un article, sur lequel je reviendrai plus loin ("ΜΟΡΜΩΤΟΣ. A propos de Lycophron, de Rab et de Philon de Alexandrie," *REG* 46 [1933]: 329, n. 2), signale que, de façon générale, cette thèse est déjà formulée par Erwin Rohde (*Psyche*, II⁵, 48, 3). Dans la littérature plus récente, c'est l'ouvrage d'Anita Méasson—*Du char ailé de Zeus à l'Arche d'Alliance. Images et mythes platoniciens chez Philon d'Alexandrie* (Paris: Études augustiniennes, 1986), qui contribue d'une façon substantielle à l'étude de la relation entre l'exégèse de Philon et les dialogues de Platon, ainsi dans le cas de la «doctrine de l'extase»; voir surtout les pp. 222–230 et 411 *sq.*

[73] *Phdr.* 244 a–245 a.
[74] *Ibid.* 249 e.
[75] *Ibid.* 245 b *sqq.*
[76] *Heilige Geist* (n. 75), 166.
[77] *Ibid.* 166–167.
[78] *Ibid.* 167.

dépendance prouve suffisamment que le développement de Philon ne doit pas être considéré comme une pièce complètement hétérogène dans la tradition platonicienne. D'une façon générale, il vaut vraiment la peine qu'on se souvienne de ce dialogue de Platon dans le contexte de notre étude: en plus des correspondances manifestes indiquées par le savant allemand, il faut se rappeler que la palinodie de Socrate, avec son image de l'âme ailée, est un des textes platoniciens préférés de Philon, et que les motifs du *Phèdre* sont bien perceptibles dans la partie finale du *Tr.* 9 (VI, 9) de Plotin.[79]

Plus important encore pour notre propos, est le fait que le *Phèdre* platonicien est parfois indiqué, et non sans raison, comme un texte où apparaît pour la première fois la notion d'extase «philosophique». Socrate parle ici d'une âme qui se souvient de la réalité qu'elle avait jadis contemplée: l'homme qui ne cesse pas, par le souvenir, de s'attacher à cette réalité est ainsi toujours initié aux mystères parfaits et devient lui-même vraiment parfait, «mais comme il s'est détaché [ou: 's'écarté'] de ce à quoi tiennent les hommes (ἐξιστάμενος τῶν ἀνθρωπίνων σπουδασμάτων) et qu'il s'attache à ce qui est divin (πρὸς τῷ θείῳ γιγνόμενος), la foule le prend à partie en disant qu'il a perdu la tête, alors qu'il est possédé par un dieu (ἐνθουσιάζων), ce dont ne se rend pas compte la foule».[80] Un peu plus loin Socrate explique que, quand les âmes, qui gardent assez ferme le souvenir, «aperçoivent quelque chose qui ressemble aux choses de là-bas, ces âmes sont projetées hors d'elles-mêmes et elles ne se possèdent plus (ἐκπλήττονται καὶ οὐκέτ᾽ αὐτῶν γίγνονται)».[81] C'est vers la réalité qui s'étend hors du ciel (ἔξω τοῦ οὐρανοῦ), que de telles âmes partent par leurs pensées, vers cette réalité qu'elles avaient contemplée, quand elles avaient elles-mêmes dépassé la voûte céleste et s'étaient établies sur «le dos du ciel» (ἔξω πορευθεῖσαι ἔστησαν ἐπὶ τῷ τοῦ οὐρανοῦ νώτῳ).[82]

---

[79] Cf. *Tr.* 9 (VI, 9), 9.1: Ἐν δὲ ταύτῃ τῇ χορείᾳ καθορᾷ πηγὴν μὲν ζωῆς, πηγὴν δὲ νοῦ, ἀρχὴν ὄντος, ἀγαθοῦ αἰτίαν, ῥίζαν ψυχῆς («et dans cette danse, l'âme contemple la source de la vie, la source de l'Intellect, le principe de ce qui est, la cause du bien, la racine de l'âme») et *Phdr.* 247 d5: ἐν δὲ τῇ περιόδῳ καθορᾷ μὲν αὐτὴν δικαιοσύνην, καθορᾷ δὲ σωφροσύνην, καθορᾷ δὲ ἐπιστήμην; 9.23: τὸ γὰρ ἐνταῦθα καὶ ἐν τούτοις ἔκπτωσις καὶ φυγὴ καὶ πτερορρύησις («chute, fuite, perte des ailes») et *Phdr.* 246 c2, 248 c8; 11.17: ὑπερβὰς ἤδη καὶ τὸν τῶν ἀρετῶν χορόν, et *Phdr.* 247 d7; enfin, 11.49: Καὶ οὗτος θεῶν καὶ ἀνθρώπων θείων καὶ εὐδαιμόνων βίος, ἀπαλλαγὴ τῶν ἄλλων τῶν τῇδε, βίος ἀνήδονος τῶν τῇδε, φυγὴ μόνου πρὸς μόνον («Et telle est la vie des dieux et des hommes divins et bienheureux») et *Phdr.* 248 a1: καὶ οὗτος μὲν θεῶν βίος· αἱ δὲ ἄλλαι ψυχαί, ἡ μὲν ἄριστα θεῷ ἑπομένη καὶ εἰκασμένη ὑπερῆρεν εἰς τὸν ἔξω τόπον τὴν τοῦ ἡνιόχου κεφαλήν, καὶ συμπεριηνέχθη τὴν περιφοράν.

[80] *Phdr.* 249 c5–d3. Traduction de Luc Brisson (*Platon, Phèdre*, traduction inédite, introduction et notes par L. B., Paris: Flammarion, 1995²).

[81] *Ibid.* 250 a6.

[82] *Phdr.* 247 b6–c2. Cf. 247 e3–4: δῦσα πάλιν εἰς τὸ εἴσω τοῦ οὐρανοῦ. Certains textes de Philon montrent, qu'il a bien retenu cette image d'une âme qui se tient fermement

Nous pouvons donc discerner dans le mythe du *Phèdre* les germes des deux notions d' «extase» philosophique ou plutôt d'une double «extase», en tant qu'une âme (1) *se retire* (ἐξιστάμενος) de toutes les occupations d'ici-bas pour de nouveau être capable d' (2) *aller au-delà* du ciel visible (ἔξω τοῦ οὐρανοῦ), car c'est dans cette vie déjà qu'une âme parfaite peut éprouver le parfait mystère de la réalité intelligible.[83] Cette expérience pourrait sans doute être appelée «mystique», surtout que, à côté des mots et des expressions désignant l'état de délire et d'obsession philosophique, les images des rites mystérieux y sont également évoquées.[84] D'autre part, dans le mythe du *Phèdre*, l'âme, bien qu'elle s'efforce de s'élever au-dessus de la rationalité normale des gens ordinaires (οἱ πολλοί), n'est pas encore exhortée à aller au-delà de ses capacités intellectuelles, contrairement à ce qu'envisage Plotin, quand il parle de l'expérience de celui qui a dépassé même ce «chœur des vertus»[85] qui dans le *Phèdre* est le but suprême des aspirations d'une âme parfaite.[86]

VI. *De la folie poétique du Phèdre à la notion de l'extase prophétique dans l'œuvre de Philon*

En revenant sur la comparaison entre les quatre espèces de la folie selon le *Phèdre* et les quatre significations du mot «extase», exposées dans le *Quis heres*, il faut tout d'abord souligner que, du point de vue lexical et textuel, ce dernier classement est principalement basé sur le texte grec de la *Septante*. Cette dépendance textuelle a été justement mise en relief par

---

debout près, où dans la divinité. Cf. *Cher.* 19, *Abr.* 58 *sq* (οὐδὲν γὰρ ἀνωτέρω θεοῦ, πρὸς ὃν εἴ τις τὸ τῆς ψυχῆς ὄμμα τείνας ἔφθακε, μονὴν εὐχέσθω καὶ στάσιν, κτλ), *QE, incerti sedis fr.* 12 Petit (ἀκλινῶς καὶ ἀρρεπῶς ἐν μόνῳ θεῷ στῆναι) et Plotin, *Tr.* 9 (VI, 9), 9.51 (ἐν μόνῳ στῆναι τούτῳ).

[83] *Phdr.* 249 c6–8: τοῖς δὲ δὴ τοιούτοις ἀνὴρ ὑπομνήμασιν ὀρθῶς χρώμενος, τελέους ἀεὶ τελετὰς τελούμενος, τέλεος ὄντως μόνος γίγνεται.

[84] *Phdr.* 249 c6–8 (v. la note précédente); 250 b–c: ὅτε σὺν εὐδαίμονι χορῷ μακαρίαν ὄψιν τε καὶ θέαν, ἑπόμενοι μετὰ μὲν Διὸς ἡμεῖς, ἄλλοι δὲ μετ' ἄλλου θεῶν, εἶδόν τε καὶ ἐτελοῦντο τῶν τελετῶν ἣν θέμις λέγειν μακαριωτάτην, ἣν ὠργιάζομεν ὁλόκληροι μὲν αὐτοὶ ὄντες καὶ ἀπαθεῖς κακῶν ὅσα ἡμᾶς ἐν ὑστέρῳ χρόνῳ ὑπέμενεν, ὁλόκληρα δὲ καὶ ἁπλᾶ καὶ ἀτρεμῆ καὶ εὐδαίμονα φάσματα **μυούμενοί** τε καὶ ἐποπτεύοντες ἐν αὐγῇ καθαρᾷ, καθαροὶ ὄντες.

[85] *Tr.* 9 (VI, 9), 11.17: ὑπερβὰς ἤδη καὶ τὸν τῶν ἀρετῶν χορόν.

[86] Chez Proclus, dans le *Commentaire sur Timée de Platon* (*In Ti.* 1.212.23), ἔκστασις, non plus, n'est pas une notion très «ambitieuse». Elle ne désigne qu'un «écartement» «de tous autres affaires», ἔκστασιν ἀπὸ πάντων τῶν ἄλλων ἐπιτηδευμάτων. Néanmoins, son but corresponde à celui envisagé dans le *Tr.* 9 (VI, 9) plotinien: «pour qu'on puisse seul être avec le Dieu seul», ἵνα μόνος τις τῷ θεῷ μόνῳ συνῇ.

Henri-Charles Puech,[87] dans sa polémique contre la conclusion de H. Leisegang, quoi que on ne peut pas adhérer à son affirmation, selon laquelle «les
§§ 249–266 de l'Héritier des biens divins puisent en partie à une source
empruntée au rabbinisme alexandrin, à une source judéo-hellenistique».[88]
En effet, il semble que le mot même ἔκστασις qui dans l'explication de
Philon est dérivé du texte de la Septante n'a jamais été employé dans la
littérature grecque antérieure avec le sens d'«obsession divine».[89] En
général, c'est plutôt le verbe ἐξίστημι et les expressions ἔξω εἶναι, ἔξω
γίγνεσθαι qui, dans cette tradition, désignent l'état de l'égarement de
l'esprit.[90]

Concernant la correspondance plus précise entre les termes des deux
classements en question, Puech note que le parallélisme s'évanouit vite dès
qu'on entre dans le détail. De son avis, «tout au plus peut-on dire que les
quatre catégories platoniciennes ont été contractées en une seule par Philon
et utilisées par lui à des degrés divers pour traiter de sa quatrième ἔκστασις.
Le fait que les parties sont quatre ici et là ne constitue qu'une analogie toute
formelle».[91] Cette dernière observation me paraît assez juste.[92] D'autre part,
le fait de cette correspondance formelle semble témoigner d'une volonté de
l'auteur d'aligner sa propre division sur le modèle platonicien. En même
temps, cela lui permet rendre plus visible la particularité de son propre
classement, et nous pouvons essayer de préciser la nature de l'amalgame
des quatre catégories de folie, opéré par Philon. S'il y a une «contraction»,

---

[87] "ΜΟΡΜΩΤΟΣ" (n. 72), 327 sqq.

[88] Ibid. 333. Les études récentes ne permettent pas de considérer la notion du «rabbinisme alexandrin» comme convenable du point de vue historique. Selon toute vraisem-
blance, les textes que Puech tient pour les échos d'une classification de formes d'extase,
antérieure à celle de Philon et indépendante de lui, dans la tradition rabbinique (à partir du
début du IIIᵉ siècle) et dans la littérature chrétienne (il s'agit surtout d'Épiphane de
Chypre, Didyme et des textes qui ont trait à la polémique antimontaniste), (op. cit. 316, 327,
331–332), sont héritiers de l'œuvre de Philon.

[89] Quoi que extrêmement sceptique à l'égard de l'histoire de la notion de «l'extase
mystique», qui serait antérieure à Plotin, E. R. Dodds admet que c'est dans la Septante que le
mot ἔκστασις commence à signifier l'obsession divine et qu'après Philon cet emploi
devient commun,—Pagan and Christian (n. 19), 71.

[90] Plg. Gorgias, fr. 11.107 (τινες ἰδόντες φοβερὰ καὶ τοῦ παρόντος ἐν τῷ παρόντι χρόνῳ
φρονήματος ἐξέστησαν), Euripides, fr. 265 (νοῦ δ' οἶνος ἐξέστησέ μ'), Or. 1021 (ἐξέστην
φρενῶν), Ba. 359 (μέμηνας ἤδη, καὶ πρὶν ἐξεστὼς φρενῶν), IA 136 (οἴμοι, γνώμας ἐξέσταν),
Xenophon, Mem. I.3.12 (τοῦ φρονεῖν ἐξίστησι). Cf. encore Aristote, EN 1149b35 (ἐξέστηκε
τῆς φύσεως, ὥσπερ οἱ μαινόμενοι τῶν ἀνθρώπων) et Fr. Pfister, RAC, Bd IV, s. v. 'Ekstase' 948
sq.

[91] ΜΟΡΜΩΤΟΣ (n. 72), 330–331.

[92] Toutefois, la troisième forme d'extase (cf., à ce propos, M. Harl, Quis rerum [n. 30],
39 sq, n. 4) et peut-être déjà la deuxième, dans le schéma de Philon, ne sont pas forcement
négatives.

ce serait plutôt celle de trois premières espèces, qui sont toutes des états de la *possession* divine en sens propre, tandis que la folie philosophique, inspirée par Éros, implique un genre différent de la relation avec la réalité divine; c'est seulement par analogie, ou aux yeux des gens ordinaires, non initiés que cet état aussi peut avoir l'air d'une «possession». Autrement dit, l'esprit des philosophes est ailleurs, mais il ne s'agit pas, dans leur cas, d'une possession temporaire, comme elle est éprouvée par les prophètes, les prêtres et les poètes, comme l'a justement observé Dodds.[93]

Il est encore plus important que cette forme de l'extase prophétique comme possession divine d'espèce plutôt traditionnelle soit élevée par Philon au rang supérieur dans la division en quatre catégories, au point de lui assigner la place de la meilleure folie, qui dans le *Phèdre* était celle de la folie philosophique. Donc c'est l'expérience de la possession, au dehors et au-delà du pouvoir intellectuel, qui est considérée ici comme une forme la plus parfaite et la plus excellente d'un état psychique extra-ordinaire et comme une rencontre la plus immédiate avec la Divinité qu'un auteur comme Philon pouvait envisager. D'autre part, en prenant la place de la folie «philosophique», cette «extase» prophétique lui emprunte comme son nouveau trait essentiel l'exigence de la perfection éthique[94].

L'expérience de la folie philosophique exaltée dans le *Phèdre* ne serait pas conforme aux relations avec Dieu, telles qu'elles sont conçues par Philon. En outre, il ne devait pas sans doute aimer son aspect (homo) sexuel prononcé. Quant aux trois autres catégories de la division platonicienne, la formule même que Philon choisit pour nommer son quatrième genre d'extase semble indiquer sa préférence: il emprunte en effet pour cela l'expression grecque κατοκωχή τε καὶ μανία, qui dans le *Phèdre* désigne la folie *poétique*.[95] Le mot κατοκωχή que Philon emploie volontiers, quand il parle de la «possession» prophétique,[96] n'est pas fréquent dans la littérature grecque. Platon, chez lequel ce mot se rencontre pour la première fois, outre dans le *Phèdre*, l'utilise dans l'*Ion*, où il s'agit également de la «possession» poétique. Nous pouvons supposer que ce n'est pas par hasard que Philon choisit cette appellation pour sa meilleure «extase», car à un autre endroit du même ouvrage il emploie les autres termes présents dans la même définition de la folie poétique dans le *Phèdre*: il parle des «âmes vierges,

---

[93] *Pagan and Christian* (n. 19), 72.

[94] Ce fait a été souligné par Hans Leisegang, *Heilige Geist* (n. 72), 167–169.

[95] *Her.* 249, 264; *Phdr.* 245 a2.

[96] Cf. *Spec.* 4.48 *sq:* τῆς ἐνθέου κατοκωχῆς καὶ προφητείας; *Mos.* 1.277, 281; 2.246 *et alibi* (16 occurences). L'expression κατοκωχή τε καὶ μανία, en outre du *Her.*, se rencontre dans le *Migr.* 84: τὸ γὰρ ἑρμηνεῦον τὰ θεοῦ προφητικόν ἐστι γένος ἐνθέῳ κατοκωχῇ τε καὶ μανίᾳ χρώμενον.

tendres (ἄβατοι καὶ ἀπαλαί) et nobles» qui «reçoivent aisément les marques magnifiques et tout à fait divines de la vertu».[97] D'autre part, Philon souligne volontiers l'aspect sonore et le caractère musical de l'extase prophétique.[98]

En effet, ce n'est pas tant aux philosophes de l'école de Socrate que ressemblent les protagonistes de l'œuvre de Philon, qu'aux poètes inspirés qui, avec les rhapsodes, servent parfois de cible à l'ironie socratique.[99] Le héros des écrits de Platon n'est pas un prophète ou un poète de la profession, mais leur émule,—un homme du nouveau type spirituel, un philosophe, tel Socrate, tandis qu'aux yeux de Philon rien n'égale l'autorité spirituelle et l'expérience du rapport avec Dieu dont jouissent les prophètes de l'Écriture juive. C'est donc leur expérience de la possession extatique qu'il élève au-dessus de toute autre forme de la «folie».

Anita Méasson, dans l'ouvrage, paru en 1986, où elle étudie d'une manière précise l'emploi des images des dialogues platoniciens dans les écrits de Philon,[100] ne tient pas assez compte, me semble-t-il, de cette substitution, quand elle observe, d'ailleurs avec juste raison, que plutôt que celle du *Phèdre*, la définition de l'extase prophétique dans le *Quis heres* suit l'*Ion*, où il s'agit de l'état des poètes inspirés et de leurs interprètes.[101] La description de l'état de l'inspiration poétique est en butte d'ironie du philosophe Socrate. Socrate ne tient pas cette inspiration pour mauvaise ou nuisible, mais il ne la met pas non plus, contrairement à Philon, en rapport avec la perfection éthique. Selon le protagoniste du dialogue, un excellent ouvrage peut être produit par l'intermédiaire d'un poète qui n'est pas parfait, non seulement du point de vue éthique (qualités éthiques ne sont pas de tout prises en considération par Socrate), mais aussi par ses capacités professionnelles.[102]

---

[97] *Her.* 38. A. Méasson (*Du char ailé* [n. 72], 225, n. 74) montre en outre comment l'image de l'aimant, emprunté à la description de l'inspiration poétique dans l'*Ion*, est utilisé par Philon à propos de l'ascension spirituelle d'Abraham,—cf. *Ion* 533 d4–6, 536 a1–3 et *Her.* 70.

[98] Cf. *Her.* 259, *Spec.* 4.49.

[99] Cf. *Ion* 535 e *sqq.*

[100] Cf. la note 75 *supra.*

[101] Cf. surtout 536 c1–5: οὐ γὰρ τέχνη οὐδ' ἐπιστήμη περὶ Ὁμήρου λέγεις ἃ λέγεις, ἀλλὰ **θείᾳ μοίρᾳ καὶ κατοκωχῇ**, ὥσπερ οἱ κορυβαντιῶντες ἐκείνου μόνου αἰσθάνονται τοῦ μέλους ὀξέως ὃ ἂν ᾖ τοῦ θεοῦ ἐξ ὅτου ἂν κατέχωνται; 533 e5 –534 a7; 534 b4–6 *sqq*: οὐ πρότερον οἷός τε ποιεῖν πρὶν ἂν ἔνθεός τε γένηται καὶ ἔκφρων καὶ ὁ νοῦς μηκέτι ἐν αὐτῷ ἐνῇ; A. Méasson, *Du char ailé* (n. 72), 224–226, 411.

[102] Cf. *Ion* 534 c5 –535 a1: ὁ θεὸς ἐξεπίτηδες διὰ τοῦ φαυλοτάτου ποιητοῦ τὸ κάλλιστον μέλος ᾖσεν.

D'autre part, Philon ne veut pas non plus identifier cette expérience des prophètes hébreux aux espèces apparemment similaires de la folie «prophétique»[103] et «télestique» de l'inventaire du *Phèdre*. Nous pouvons supposer que c'est en tant que moins précise du point de vue de la croyance religieuse et comme plus universelle que la définition de la possession *poétique* convenait mieux à l'exégète juif qui a bien exprimé sa répugnance à l'égard des pratiques religieuses traditionnelles des Grecs.[104] En effet, il était lui-même un tel homme—imbu de la culture des Grecs, mais sans être adepte de leur religion.

En outre, les prophètes extatiques de Philon ne sont pas les devins ou les prêtres anonymes, comme le sont «la prophétesse de Delphes, les prêtresses de Dodone» et les autres experts en matière de la religion, évoqués dans le *Phèdre*.[105] Pour Philon, il s'agit des personnages les plus éminents de l'histoire des relations entre le peuple hébreu et son Dieu, et leurs prophéties concernent les moments essentiels de cette histoire, les moments que Philon est désireux d'expliquer comme les principaux épisodes de la vie de l'âme et de ses «migrations» à la rencontre de Dieu. Ainsi, le protagoniste du *Quis heres* Abraham, sous l'emprise d'une «extase», reçoit l'annonce que ses héritiers auront à vivre de longues années de captivité, après lesquelles ils seront libérés et rentreront dans leur patrie,[106] ce qui pour Philon équivaut à un message sur l'enfermement provisoire de l'âme dans le corps, son affranchissement et le retour dans sa patrie spirituelle.[107]

Nous pouvons donc en résumé dire que dans l'œuvre de Philon, grâce à la rencontre du texte commenté de la *Septante* et des idées des dialogues platoniciens, familières à cet exégète, apparaît une nouvelle notion d' «extase»: le mot grec ἔκστασις commence à désigner une expérience du contact le plus immédiat avec la divinité, une expérience qui dépasse les capacités

---

[103] Cf. *Phdr.* 244 b–e: ἥ [. . .] ἐν Δελφοῖς **προφῆτις** [. . .] ἡ μανία ἐγγενομένη καὶ προφητεύσασα.

[104] Cf. *Spec.* 1.319 *sq*; 3.40; 4.48–52 (ici Philon reprouve sévèrement les «pseudo-prophètes» grecs, selon lui, incapables de céder la place de ses conjectures humaines à l'esprit divin), *et alibi*; cf. encore H. Leisegang, *Heilige Geist* (n. 72), 172 *sq*.

[105] *Phdr.* 244 b–e.

[106] *Gen.* 15:13–14.

[107] Il est notable que ce motif exégétique, que nous rencontrons pour la première fois dans l'œuvre de Philon, est développé d'une manière magnifique dans la partie finale du *Tr.* 1 (I, 6) de Plotin (8.16 *sqq*), où le point de départ lui est donné par une citation de l'*Iliade*: «Fuyons vers notre chère patrie». J'étudie l'histoire de ce thème exégétique, que je mets en relation avec l'exégèse philonienne, dans mon article "L'énigme de la 'patrie' dans le Traité 1 de Plotin: héritage de l'exégèse philonienne?," *RA* 35 (2007): 1–46.

intellectuelles et qui est éprouvée par une âme déjà arrivée au sommet de la perfection éthique.[108]

VII. *L'exégèse des verbes ayant la signification «extatique» dans les écrits de Philon*

D'une manière générale, il est très important, pour une étude de la notion philonienne d' «extase», d'observer que les textes de la *Genèse* où le mot ἔκστασις est employé ne sont pas les seuls à offrir à cet auteur l'occasion de traiter de «l'évasion» et de «la sortie» de l'âme. Ainsi, dans le même ouvrage *Quis heres*, c'est déjà à propos de *Genèse* 15:4 «Celui qui sortira de toi (ἐξελεύσεται ἐκ σοῦ), celui-ci héritera de toi», que Philon explique qu'une âme désireuse d'hériter les biens divins abandonnera non seulement le corps avec tous ses sens, non pas uniquement le langage, mais aussi *soi-même*, pour tout offrir à Dieu qui en est la véritable source:

> «Qui donc sera l'héritier ? Ce n'est pas l'esprit (λογισμός) qui reste enfermé, de son propre gré, dans la prison du corps, mais celui qui aura été délivré de ses chaînes, qui aura été libéré, et sera sorti hors (ἔξω) des murs et se sera, si l'on peut dire, abandonné lui-même (αὐτὸς ἑαυτόν). [. . .] Si donc, ô mon âme, quelque désir entre en toi d'hériter des biens divins ce n'est pas seulement 'la terre', c'est-à-dire le corps, ni la 'parenté', c'est-à-dire la sensation, ni 'la maison de ton père' (*Gen* 12:1), le langage, que tu abandonnera, mais fuis-toi toi-même, sors de toi-même (ἔκστηθι σεαυτῆς), comme les possédés et les corybantes, saisie de l'ivresse des bacchantes, transportée par Dieu d'une sorte d'enthousiasme prophétique. C'est l'intelligence qui est emplie de Dieu et qui n'est plus en elle-même (οὐκέτ' οὔσης ἐν ἑαυτῇ διανοίας), qui est excitée par l'amour céleste, rendue comme folle, conduite par Celui qui Est véritablement, attiré en haut vers lui[109] [. . .] qui recevra cet héritage».[110]

---

[108] Il est intéressant de remarquer que l'auteur du commentaire néoplatonicien alexandrin tardif du *Phèdre* (*Hermiae Alexandrini in Platonis Phaedrum scholia*, ad 244 a, 84, 18 *sqq* Couvreur) aligne les formes de la folie, du bas en haut, selon une autre hiérarchie qui rabaisse la folie poétique à tout dernier degré dans le classement: μουσική, τελεστική, μαντική, ἐρωτική. D'autre part, dans ce commentaire le mot ἔκστασις apparaît déjà à côté de la μανία platonicienne.

[109] Dans les manuscrits, «Celui» vers qui «est attirée» intelligence est désigné par un pronom soit de la forme neutre (ἄνω πρὸς **αὐτό**), soit en masculin (ἄνω πρὸς **αὐτόν**). En tout cas, ces mots de Philon semblent contredire l'affirmation, citée précédemment de E. R. Dodds, selon laquelle la notion philonienne d' «extase» présuppose que «C'est l'esprit surnaturel qui descend dans un corps humain et non pas l'homme qui s'élève lui-même ou qui est élevé au-dessus du corps», *Pagan and Christian* (n. 19), 72 (traduction de H. D. Saffrey [n. 19]). À ce propos, cf. encore les explications de M. Harl, *Quis rerum* (n. 30), 132, n. 1.

[110] *Her.* 68–70. Traduction de M. Harl (n. 30), dont je corrige la dernière phrase.

Celui, vers qui se précipite comme vers son suprême but l'âme pensante, est «Celui qui est véritablement»,[111] et, par conséquent, ne dépasse pas le lieu «supra-céleste» du *Phèdre*. Toutefois, l'intelligence qui aspire à lui est incitée à sortir non pas seulement hors de toutes les choses qu'elle possède ici-bas, mais aussi hors *d'elle-même*.

La suite du texte du *Quis heres* déroule ce thème de la migration de l'âme. Ici Philon s'adresse à l'intelligence (διάνοια) qui a quitté le corps, la sensation et le langage, pour finalement s'échapper d'elle-même et sortir d'elle-même (§ 74: ὑπέξελθε καὶ μετανάστηθι σεαυτῆς). Cela veut dire, explique l'exégète, que l'intelligence n'a pas à garder pour elle-même ses facultés de pensée, de raisonnement et de compréhension, mais elle doit les apporter et les offrir «à Celui qui est la Cause de la pensée exacte et de la compréhension sans erreur».[112] Cette explication anticipe donc la notion d'extase qui ne sera clairement nommée que bien plus avant dans le même ouvrage. Mais avec les mots ἔκστηθι σεαυτῆς on en est tout près.[113] D'autre part, cette notion est assez différente de celle de la suite de l'ouvrage. Cette fois-ci, il s'agit non pas de l'intellect qui abandonne sa place en nous (ἐξοικίζεται), lorsqu'arrive le souffle divin, mais de l'intelligence (appelée λογισμός ou διάνοια) qui s'abandonne elle-même (οὐκέτ' οὔσης ἐν ἑαυτῇ διανοίας), pour effectuer son ultime migration à la rencontre de Dieu.

Soulignons-le encore une fois: une telle notion de la sortie de l'intelligence *hors d'elle-même* en vue d'une migration vers sa source divine n'apparaît pas dans les dialogues de Platon, même s'agissant de la «folie» des philosophes ou de celle des poètes inspirés. Toutefois, cette notion ressort clairement à la fin du *Tr.* 9 (VI, 9) de Plotin.[114] Je ne suis pas première pour observer[115] que, en général, chez Philon la structure de l'univers est haussée d'un «étage» supplémentaire, au dessus du lieu intelligible du *Phèdre*

[111] *Ibid.* 70.
[112] *Her.* 74.
[113] Comme l'observe M. Harl, *Quis rerum* (n. 30), 28, «Philon passe tout simplement du texte biblique ἐξελεύσεται ἐκ σοῦ à la belle doctrine de l'extase, avec l'expression ἔκστηθι σεαυτῆς».
[114] Cf. surtout *Tr.* 9 (VI, 9) 10.14–17: τότε μὲν οὖν οὔτε ὁρᾷ οὐδὲ διακρίνει ὁ ὁρῶν οὐδὲ φαντάζεται δύο, ἀλλ' οἷον ἄλλος γενόμενος καὶ **οὐκ αὐτὸς οὐδ' αὐτοῦ** συντελεῖ ἐκεῖ, **κἀκείνου γενόμενος** ἕν ἐστιν ὥσπερ κέντρῳ κέντρον συνάψας; 11.10–12: οὐκ ἐπιθυμία ἄλλου παρῆν αὐτῷ ἀναβεβηκότι – ἀλλ' οὐδὲ λόγος οὐδέ τις νόησις **οὐδ' ὅλως αὐτός, εἰ δεῖ καὶ τοῦτο λέγειν**.
[115] Cf. A. Méasson, *Du char ailé* (n. 72), 382: «Dans le *De praemiis*, comme dans le *De opificio mundi*, un étage s'ajoute à l'espace mythique du *Phèdre*, celui du monde intelligible qui devient, à l'instar du monde sensible, un lieu qu'enveloppe une réalité supérieure. Que Philon désigne allégoriquement cette réalité, dans le *De opificio mundi*, par le Grand Roi, ou, dans le *De praemiis*, par le Père et Sauveur, on sait qu'elle est pour lui l'Être incréé dont parle le *De gigantibus* , § 14 [...]. Dans tous les cas, c'est Dieu qui est ainsi désigné».

platonicien.[116] C'est parce que Dieu, dont il parle, est la source de toute réalité, y compris intelligible, source qui est supérieure à tout le reste.

Donc, ce n'est pas uniquement ἔκστασις, mais aussi les autres mots ou les expressions indiquant un mouvement «extatique», qui offrent à l'exégète, fort habile à trouver dans les mots et les images de l'Écriture d'éminentes leçons spirituelles, une occasion de développer son thème privilégié de la sortie et de la migration de l'âme vers son but ultime.[117] C'est surtout, apparemment, à propos de la migration d'Abraham et autour des textes de la *Genèse* 12:1 et 15:5 que nous rencontrons de tels développements exégétiques, mais de nombreux autres textes des Écritures juives permettent à Philon d'évoquer ce motif.[118] Dans le cas de l'exégèse de *Gen.* 15:4 dans le *Quis heres*, «l'extase» de l'âme apparaît clairement comme une ultime migration d'Abraham, dont l'auteur rappelle les étapes précédentes, telles qu'elles sont conçues dans ses commentaires allégoriques.[119]

---

[116] Cf. *Her.* 76: ὅτι δ᾽ ὁ ὑπεξελθὼν ἐξ ἡμῶν (ἐξ ἡμῶν νοητῶν,—*Pap.*, Wendland) καὶ γλιχόμενος ὀπαδὸς εἶναι θεοῦ (cf. *Phdr.* 248 a) τοῦ φύσεως ἀοιδίμου πλούτου κληρονόμος ἐστί, μαρτυρεῖ λέγων· ἐξήγαγεν δὲ αὐτὸν ἔξω καὶ εἶπεν· ἀνάβλεψον εἰς τὸν οὐρανόν (*Gén.* 15.5).

[117] A. Méasson signale le passage du *Her.* 68 *sqq* comme un cas, quand l'exégèse «fait violence au texte de l'Écriture pour lui imposer une interprétation platonicienne»,—*Du char ailé* (n. 72), 453, «Index analytique», *s. v.* «Exégèse»; voir aussi *ibid.* 223–228 et 411 *sq.* Mais il me semble qu'elle sous-estime ainsi la tendance amplement illustrée par l'œuvre de Philon d'interpréter d'une façon allégorique les mots désignant diverses sortes de mouvement. Il est vrai que, dans le cas du *Her.*, l'exégèse des §§ 68 *sqq* anticipe les explications ultérieures. Toutefois, les autres écrits de Philon offrent des très nombreux exemples de l'exégèse comparable des mots ayant la signification «extatique» (ὑπεξέρχεσθαι, μετανίστασθαι, μετοικίζεσθαι, ἐκπορεύεσθαι, etc.; cf., à ce propos, M. Harl, *Quis rerum* [n. 30], 130, n. 1). Il vaudrait la peine de bien analyser l'ensemble de telles explications, pour pouvoir discerner leurs principaux traits. D'autre part, A. Méasson semble ne pas tenir compte de la nouveauté importante de la notion de la sortie de l'intelligence, qui apparaît dans les §§ 68–75.

[118] Dans le *Migr.* 1 *sq* et 190 *sq*, il s'agit, à propos de la *Genèse* 12:1, de la triple migration de l'âme au dehors du corps («la terre»), de la sensation («la parenté») et du langage («la maison de ton père»); cf. *Her.* 69. *Leg.* 3.39 *sqq* traitent de l'ultime sortie de l'intelligence au dehors d'elle-même, qui doit s'ajouter aux migrations précédentes (voir n. 124–125 *infra*). Plus avant, dans le même écrit, ce sont les mots de *l'Exode* 33:7, qui fournissent une occasion de parler d'une pareille sortie: καὶ γὰρ «πᾶς ὁ ζητῶν κύριον ἐξεπορεύετο» (cf. *Ex.* 33:7), παγκάλως· εἰ γὰρ ζητεῖς θεόν, ὦ διάνοια, **ἐξελθοῦσα ἀπὸ σαυτῆς** ἀναζήτει, μένουσα δὲ ἐν τοῖς σωματικοῖς ὄγκοις ἢ ταῖς κατὰ νοῦν οἰήσεσιν ἀζητήτως ἔχεις τῶν θείων, κἂν ἐπιμορφάζῃς ὅτι ζητεῖς. [. . .] οὕτως ὁ μὲν φαῦλος ἀρετήν γε φεύγων καὶ θεὸν ἀποκρυπτόμενος ἐπ᾽ ἀσθενῆ βοηθὸν καταφεύγει τὸν ἴδιον νοῦν, ὁ δὲ σπουδαῖος ἔμπαλιν **ἑαυτὸν ἀποδιδράσκων** ἀναστρέφει πρὸς τὴν τοῦ ἑνὸς ἐπίγνωσιν, καλὸν δρόμον καὶ πάντων ἄριστον ἀγώνισμα τοῦτο νικῶν. Dans le *Ebr.* 100–102, comme dans le *Her.* 43, le thème de «la sortie» de l'intelligence est développé à propos du *Ex.* 9:29 (ἐπειδὰν ἐξέλθω τὴν πόλιν, ἐκπετάσω τὰς χεῖρας πρὸς τὸν κύριον).

[119] *Her.* 69. Cela est bien mis en relief par A. Méasson, *Du char ailé* (n. 72), 222 *sq.*

Plus loin dans le texte du *Quis heres*, Philon fournit un bon commentaire de sa propre méthode exégétique qui consiste à discerner dans les mots désignant les déplacements spatiaux les mouvements essentiels de la vie intérieure de l'âme. Selon lui, la suite du récit de la *Genèse* (*Gen.* 15:5): «il le fit sortir au-dehors», ἐξήγαγεν αὐτὸν ἔξω, a «également une portée morale».[120] «Bien des gens»,—observe Philon,—«par manque de culture (ὑπ' ἀμουσίας ἤθους), ont coutume de rire en disant: 'quelqu'un peut-il sortir au-dedans ou inversement rentrer au-dehors ?'». «Oui»—riposte l'auteur—«esprits ridicules et superficiels ! Vous n'avez pas appris à dépister les démarches de l'âme; c'est pour les corps seulement que vous étudiez les mouvements. Voilà pourquoi il vous paraît invraisemblable que l'on sorte au-dedans ou qu'on entre au-dehors ! Nous, au contraire, les familiers de Moïse, nous ne voyons aucune absurdité dans ces expressions».[121]

Philon continue son dialogue imaginaire, en évoquant l'expérience qui devrait être compréhensible même pour tels gens superficiels:

«N'accepteriez-vous pas de dire, si le grand prêtre manque de perfection, que, lorsqu'à l'intérieur du saint des saints (ἐν τοῖς ἀδύτοις) il célèbre les rites ancestraux, il est à la fois au-dedans (ἔνδον) et au-dehors (ἔξω), au-dedans par son corps visible, au-dehors par son âme qui vagabonde et s'égare ? Inversement, s'il s'agit d'un homme qui n'appartient pas à la race sacerdotale, mais qui aime Dieu et que Dieu aime, ne direz-vous pas, alors qu'il se tient en dehors des lieux de lustration, qu'il demeure tout à fait au-dedans (ἐσωτάτω), puisqu'à ses yeux la vie corporelle tout entière est un exil, et que, lorsqu'il peut vivre par l'âme seule, il a le sentiment de résider dans sa patrie ? Vraiment tout insensé se trouve hors du seuil, même si, de toute la journée, il ne s'éloigne pas un seul instant, tout sage, au contraire, est au-dedans, même s'il se trouve séparé, je ne dis pas seulement par des pays, mais par d'immenses espaces terrestres. Selon Moïse, [. . .] le prêtre 'ne sera pas homme', quand il entre dans le saint des saints, 'jusqu'à ce qu'il en sorte' (*Lév.* 16.17): en cela, il ne s'agit pas du corps, mais des mouvements de son âme (οὐ σωματικῶς, ἀλλὰ ταῖς κατὰ ψυχὴν κινήσεσιν)». Philon conclut de cette manière son explication: «C'est donc avec raison qu'il est dit: 'il le fit sortir au-dehors' des prisons du corps, des cavernes des sens, des sophismes du langage trompeur, et, par-dessus tout, hors de lui-même (αὐτὸν ἐξ ἑαυτοῦ)».[122]

Apparemment, ce commentaire de Philon n'explique pas le sens pléonastique de l'expression qui est plus manifeste en grec: ἐξήγαγεν . . . ἔξω.[123] Au lieu de cela, il choisit de commenter la relation paradoxale qui peut exister entre la position au dedans ou en dehors d'un objet, selon qu'il s'agit de la position du corps ou de la disposition de l'âme. On comprend donc qu'on

---

[120] *Her.* 81.
[121] *Ibid.*
[122] *Ibid.* 82–85.
[123] Il s'agit, en effet, d' «un hébraïsme».

peut simultanément être au-dedans (par son corps visible) et en dehors (par son âme) et inversement, mais cela ne nous apprend pas, pourquoi il a fallu ajouter ἔξω, ni comment il serait possible «sortir au-dedans» ou inversement «rentrer au-dehors». En outre, ce commentaire attribue à ἔξω une signification négative, car il s'agit là d'une âme qui s'égare en dehors des lieux sacrés. Une explication plus satisfaisante est avancée dans autre ouvrage de Philon (*Leg.* 3.39 *sqq*). Ici, en commentant la même phrase de la *Genèse* 15:5, l'auteur reprend le thème principal du *Quis heres* 68 *sqq* pour expliquer que ἔξω, terme apparemment superflu, doit être tenu pour un indice que, dans ce texte de l'Écriture, il s'agit de la sortie la plus radicale, qui mène «jusqu'au lieu le plus extérieur» (εἰς τὸ ἐξώτατον), au-delà de toutes choses et hors de l'intelligence (νοῦς) elle-même.[124] Autrement, explique Philon, l'intelligence pourrait abandonner le corps mais se réfugier dans la sensation, et ainsi de suite, comme l'on peut quitter une pièce de la maison, mais se trouver *dans* une autre.[125]

En revenant sur le texte du *Quis heres* 81 *sqq*, il faut observer que les propos de Philon concernant l'expérience du saint des saints, qui doit être éprouvée à l'intérieur de l'âme plutôt que dans un espace visible du sanctuaire, incitent à les rapprocher de la remarque que Plotin fait à propos de sa comparaison avec la vision de Dieu dans le sanctuaire. Il dit en effet: «Mais le prêtre sage, qui comprend le sens de l'énigme, peut bien réaliser la véritable vision, en pénétrant à l'intérieur du sanctuaire. Et s'il n'y entre pas, parce qu'il considère que ce sanctuaire est quelque chose d'invisible et qu'il est source et principe, il saura, lui, que c'est par le principe qu'on voit le Principe et que c'est au Semblable que s'unit le semblable».[126] Autrement dit, ce n'est pas la position du corps par rapport au sanctuaire (ἔνδον ou ἔξω) qui compte, mais la véritable relation avec ce qui peut être éprouvé là-dedans.[127] Les textes de Philon et de Plotin que nous comparons suggèrent que, pour avoir une telle expérience, il faut sortir au dehors (ἔξω) de toutes les choses, y compris au dehors de soi-même, voire de soi-même pensant.

---

[124] *Leg.* 3.40: οὕτως οὖν ἀκουστέον· τὸν νοῦν εἰς τὸ ἐξώτατον ἐξήγαγε. τί γὰρ ὄφελος ἦν καταλιπεῖν αὐτὸν τὸ σῶμα, καταφυγεῖν δὲ ἐπ' αἴσθησιν; τί δὲ αἰσθήσει μὲν ἀποτάξασθαι, λόγῳ δὲ ὑποστεῖλαι τῷ γεγωνῷ; χρὴ γὰρ τὸν μέλλοντα νοῦν ἐξάγεσθαι καὶ ἐν ἐλευθερίᾳ ἀφίεσθαι πάντων **ὑπεκστῆναι**, σωματικῶν ἀναγκῶν, αἰσθητικῶν ὀργάνων, [κατα]λόγων σοφιστικῶν, πιθανοτήτων, τὰ τελευταῖα καὶ **ἑαυτοῦ**.

[125] *Leg.* 3.40–41.

[126] *Tr.* 9 (VI, 9), 11.25–32, traduction de P. Hadot (n. 5).

[127] Cf. encore *Tr.* 9 (VI, 9), 8.29–45 et *Tr.* 1 (I, 6), 8.21 *sqq*.

VIII. _Philon d'Alexandrie et Plotin: les principaux points du contact_

Notons que c'est surtout dans les cas où nous rencontrons chez Plotin les développements exégétiques _portant sur les notions désignant les mouvements spatiaux_ pour en tirer les leçons sur l'odyssée de l'âme,[128] que nous avons droit de supposer que l'œuvre de Philon a pu laisser ici sa trace. La notion d'«extase», qui a été l'objet d'un débat animé concernant l'influence possible, directe ou indirecte, de Philon sur Plotin, en est, à mon avis, un exemple éloquent. Surtout que le dernier chapitre du _Tr._ 9 (VI, 9) montre le même intérêt prononcé d'un exégète à l'égard des notions du mouvement dans un espace sacré et à l'approche de Dieu, qui est un trait distinctif de l'œuvre de Philon. Toute la comparaison avec l'entrée et la sortie du sanctuaire en est un témoignage. Dès lors nous ne nous étonnerons pas beaucoup du fait que P. Hadot, dans son commentaire sur le _Traité_ 9 (VI, 9), indique à ce propos un parallèle avec un texte de Philon. De l'avis de cet auteur, «des comparaisons opposant l'entrée dans le sanctuaire (début de la contemplation et de la vision) et la sortie du sanctuaire (interruption de la vision)» probablement étaient «traditionnelles dans le platonisme».[129] Comme seul témoin de cette «tradition» est allégué un passage tiré du _De somniis_ de Philon d'Alexandrie: «Lorsque l'intellect est possédé par l'amour divin, lorsqu'il tend de tous ses efforts pour parvenir jusqu'à _l'adyton_, lorsqu'il se porte en avant de tout son élan et de tout son zèle, entraîné par Dieu, il oublie tout, il s'oublie lui-même, il ne se souvient que de (Dieu) et il est suspendu à lui… Mais lorsque l'enthousiasme tombe et que le désir se relâche de sa ferveur, il redevient homme en s'éloignant des choses divines, rencontrant alors les choses humaines qui sont aux aguets dans les propylées…».[130]

Nous rencontrons dans ce texte de Philon d'autres motifs qui entourent, ici comme dans le _Tr._ 9 (VI, 9), l'image du sanctuaire, notamment les notions de repos immuable, de «possession», etc. Chez Philon l'image du sanctuaire apparaît à propos du texte de l'Écriture (_Lév._ 16.17). Observons encore qu'il s'agit du même texte que Philon évoque dans le _Quis heres_ 84,

---

[128] Dans le _Tr._ 1 (I, 6), l'explication porte sur le texte d'Homère, et dans le _Tr._ 9 (VI, 6), l'objet de l'exégèse est l'ambiance d'un sanctuaire.

[129] _Traité_ 9 (n. 5), 205.

[130] _Somn._ 2.232. Traduction de P. Hadot (n. 5). D'ailleurs, déjà Émile Bréhier (Plotin, _Ennéades_ VI, 2, texte établi et traduit par É. B., Paris: Les Belles Lettres, 1938, 189, n. 2) notais, à propos de la même comparaison, que «Plotin se réfère ici à une tradition symbolique qui existe sous de multiples formes» et évoquait comme un exemple de «l'exégèse allégorique des cultes des mystères» l'œuvre de Philon d'Alexandrie.

dans le contexte de sa réflexion sur la signification spirituelle d'un mouvement extatique.[131]

Il est également notable que c'est précisément à propos des passages
«exégétiques» (où il s'agit de l'exégèse autre que celle des textes de Platon),
peu nombreux dans les écrits de Plotin, que les rapprochements avec
l'œuvre de l'exégète juif ont été proposés. Un autre parallèle, avec *les Legum
allegoriae* 2.56 de Philon, a été suggéré par E. R. Dodds, à propos du chapitre
7.4-7 du *Tr.* 1 (VI, 6), où Plotin compare la pureté de ceux qui montent vers
le Dieu avec la nudité exigée à l'entrée des *sacra sacrorum*.[132]

Bien sûr, il serait exagéré de tenir toutes les métaphores et tous les
thèmes exégétiques du mouvement spirituel qui se rencontrent chez Philon,
pour le résultat de son travail d'exégète. Comme nous le savons bien, dans
les dialogues de Platon aussi, l'âme «descend», «monte», «s'enfuie», et ainsi
de suite. Ce sont précisément telles images et notions des dialogues qui ont
nourri l'exégèse de Philon et qui en sont une condition absolument nécessaire. Néanmoins, le plus souvent les platoniciens, comme l'a justement
observé R. Arnou,[133] cherchent à rester fidèles au vocabulaire du Maître
dans ce domaine des usages métaphoriques. Mais «l'extase» ne faisait pas
partie de ce lexique «canonique». D'autre part, le récit de l'histoire des relations des patriarches du peuple juif avec leur Dieu est extrêmement riche en
notions spatiales et «cinétiques», pour offrir à un diligent exégète d'innom-
brables occasions d'appliquer et développer les métaphores et les allégories
platoniciennes. Et nous pouvons penser que parfois Philon rattache si
habilement, et d'une manière si originale, au texte commenté les propos de
son philosophe préféré,[134] que les résultats de telle synthèse exégétiques
deviennent connus et trouvent des adeptes, même assez lointains.

Dès lors, nous pouvons conclure qu'il est fort probable que Plotin,
quand il mentionne ἔκστασις dans le texte du *Tr.* 9 (VI, 9), fait référence à
un tel emploi de ce mot, qui apparaît et est développé dans l'œuvre de

---

[131] Voir n. 122 *supra*.

[132] *Pagan and Christian* (n. 19), 94. Cette référence a été reprise dans l'*Index fontium* de
l'*editio minor* de P. Henry et H.-R. Schwyzer, OCT (Oxonii: e typographeo Clarendoniano,
1964), 347. Voir, à ce sujet, T. Aleknienė, "L'énigme de la 'patrie'" (n. 107): 32 *sq*, 38 *sq*.

[133] R. Arnou, *Le désir de Dieu* (n. 25), 260.

[134] L'observation de R. Arnou, selon laquelle «Philon se contente d'affirmer ses idées,
qu'il rattache plus ou moins heureusement aux textes de l'Écriture» (*ibid*. 264), va dans
même sens, si nous y remplaçons les «idées» propres de Philon par celles de Platon, et
soulignions que parfois ses synthèses exégétiques paraissent être très fécondes. Dans notre
cas précis, le mot ἔκστασις pouvait bien rester un élément du texte grec de l'Écriture, sans
entrer dans un amalgame avec les notions de la philosophie grecque, et *vice versa*.

Philon, mais non pas avant lui.[135] D'autre part, cette notion s'intègre parfaitement bien dans la description de la partie finale du *Tr.* 9 (VI, 9), où
Plotin rappelle plus d'une fois à celui qui veut vraiment attendre son
origine, l'exigence d'abandonner tout, y compris soi-même. Un autre texte
de Plotin, celui du *Tr.* 49 (V, 3) montre bien qu'il pouvait considérer l'état
de la possession comme une comparaison pertinente et une image suggestive pour parler de cette expérience ineffable. En même temps, il est intéressant d'observer que dans le même *Tr.* 49 (V, 3), le mot ἔκστασις est employé
dans une phrase qui a l'air d'une réplique polémique à une autre définition
d' «extase», que nous trouvons dans le *Quis heres* de Philon.[136]

Quant à la possibilité d'un rapport historique entre les œuvres de deux
auteurs, je pense que ces deux mondes n'étaient pas si impénétrables
comme ils le sont dans les têtes de la plupart des historiens éclairés du XXe
siècle. Je crois que, au contraire, il est tout à fait probable que Plotin ait pu
connaître l'œuvre de Philon pendant son long séjour à Alexandrie.[137] Il se
peut que ce n'soit pas un hasard si les notions et les motifs qui font penser à
Philon se trouvent surtout dans ses écrits d'une première décade: *Tr.* 1 (I,
6); *Tr.* 9 (VI, 9), mais aussi dans le *Tr.* 5 (V, 9).[138] Il s'agirait là sans doute
non pas de l'expérience que Plotin aurait empruntée à son collègue hétéro-
doxe, mais de notions qui ont servi à l'exprimer et à l'interpréter.[139]

Vilnius Pedagogical University
Lithuania

---

[135] Comme le pense aussi David T. Runia ("Witness or Participant ?" [n. 39], 202), qui
pose la question du rôle que Philon pouvait jouer dans la tradition platonicienne et cherche
une réponse en étudiant la notion de *stasis*. Selon la conclusion de cet auteur, «It needs not,
therefore, be a mirage, if we were to perceive far in the distance behind the word *hestôs* —
but perhaps also the word *ekstasis* — the figure of the Patriarch Abraham, i.e. Pentateuchal
texts as expounded by Philo, even if Plotinus may not have been conscious of texts when
he wrote his treatise». Toutefois, il faut préciser que, pour D. T. Runia, l'œuvre de Numénius serait un chaînon important dans l'histoire de la transmission des notions de Philon
d'Alexandrie.

[136] Voir n. 34 *supra*.

[137] Cf. Porphyre, *Plot.* 3.6–21.

[138] Voir à ce propos T. Alekniené, "L'énigme de la 'patrie'" (n. 107): 5–7, 39, n. 186.

[139] Cf. l'observation d' E. R. Dodds, à propos de la signification de la notion de l'Un
dans la pensée de Plotin: «A recent German writer [...] has even suggested that Plotinus'
personal experience of the *unio mystica* determined his conception of the One. [...] It is
perhaps truer to say that his conception of the One determined, not indeed the personal
experience itself, but the interpretation which Plotinus attached to that experience» ("The
Parmenides of Plato" [n. 2]: 140 *sq*).

The Studia Philonica Annual 22 (2010) 83–85

SPECIAL SECTION

PHILO'S *DE AGRICULTURA*

INTRODUCTION

GREGORY E. STERLING

One of the most enduring contributions made by ancient Alexandrian philologists was the introduction of commentaries on important texts. The ὑπόμνημα ("commentary" or "explanatory notes") was a separate scroll that accompanied the ἔκδοσις ("edition"). The ὑπόμνημα was considered to be distinct from a monograph or σύγγραμμα that tackled specialized problems. The format of the ὑπόμνημα typically followed the lemma–exegesis model in which the commentator worked through the text sequentially, moving lemma by lemma with annotations that varied in nature and length. Perhaps the best known philologist in the Hellenistic world was Aristarchus of Samothrace (ca. 216–14 B.C.E.) whose influence was exponentially raised through the forty or so students associated with his school in Alexandria.[1] The commentary tradition developed by the philologists spread to other intellectuals, including philosophers. Among the latter, allegory became an important means for annotating texts. The history and nature of the use of allegory among Hellenistic philosophers has been widely debated in recent decades, including by Philonists.[2]

How should we understand the commentaries of Philo? The Pentateuch exegete wrote three major commentaries: *The Questions and Answers on Genesis and Exodus*, the Allegorical Commentary, and the Exposition of the Law. While the last two names are constructs that we use for the series,[3] the

---

[1] Franco Montanari, "Aristarchus (4)," *Brill's New Pauly* 1:1090–93.

[2] E.g., see the special section in *SPhA* 16 (2004): 96–187, esp. L. Michael White, "Introduction," 96–100.

[3] The Allegorical Commentary is a construct based on the treatises that begin the series known as *The Allegories of the Laws* (see Eusebius, *HE* 2.18.1). The Exposition of the Law is a modern construct that does not have a verbal basis in Philo's corpus.

series were of Philo's design. All three works follow the sequence of the biblical text and overlap one another in the process. In the case of the Exposition, Philo gave us the plan of the work in three places.[4] The independent nature of each commentary series has not always been appreciated, but they are very different and the differences should be respected.

The Allegorical Commentary was Philo's *magnum opus*—at least it contains his most profound expositions of the biblical text. The nature and extent of the commentary series are points of dispute. Did Philo follow an existing model for his commentaries or were they *sui generis* in their attempt to develop a theme for each treatise?[5] What was the role of the question and answer technique?[6] How does Philo use the biblical text in secondary and tertiary lemmata? Where did the series begin and end? Should we posit a treatment of Gen 1?[7] Does the series end with *On God* at Gen 18:2 or should we include the partial and thematic *On Dreams*?[8] We could extend the list of questions, but the point is that we still need to do a good deal of work on Philo's commentaries.

This is largely due to the fact that while scholars have explored concepts in Philo, they have not devoted enough attention to his thought in the form in which he expressed it, i.e., his exegesis. One of the goals of the Philo of Alexandria Commentary Series is to provide detailed analyses of his individual treatises with the hope that we will be able to answer the larger questions about his corpus when the detailed work on specific treatises is complete. Albert Geljon and his *Doktorvater*, David T. Runia, have agreed to undertake a commentary on *De agricultura*. They were fortunate to have the unpublished dissertation of A. L. Kilaniotis to assist

---

[4] Philo, *Abr.* 2–5; *Praem.* 1–3. See also *Mos.* 2.45–47.

[5] For attempts to address this question see John Dillon, "The Formal Structure of Philo's Allegorical Exegesis," in *Two Treatises of Philo of Alexandria: A Commentary on* De gigantibus *and* Quod Deus sit immutabilis sit (ed. John Dillon and David Winston; BJS 25; Chico, CA: Scholars Press, 1983), 77–87; David T. Runia, "The Structure of Philo's Allegorical Treatises: A Review of Two Recent Studies and Some additional Comments," *VC* 38 (1984): 209–56; idem, "Further Observations on the Structure of Philo's Allegorical Treatises," *VC* 41 (1987): 105–38. Runia's essays were reprinted in *Exegesis and Philosophy: Studies on Philo of Alexandria* (CSCS 332; Aldershot: Variorum, 1990), nos. 4 and 5.

[6] Valentin Nikiprowetzky, "La Bible de Philon dans le *De gignatibus* et le *Quod Deus*," in *Two Treatises of Philo of Alexandria*, 91–118, argued that Philo used the question and answer technique extensively in the Allegorical Commentary.

[7] E.g., Thomas H. Tobin, "The Beginning of Philo's *Legum Allegoriae*," *SPhA* 12 (2000): 29–43.

[8] See the cautious and judicious comments of James R. Royse, "The Works of Philo," in *The Cambridge Companion to Philo* (ed. Adam Kamesar; Cambridge: Cambridge University Press, 2009), 44–45.

them in their work.[9] Although they are creating their own commentary, they have Kilianotis' permission to include material from his research. In keeping with the practice of the commentary series and the Philo of Alexandria unit in the Society of Biblical Literature, a session was organized at the annual meeting of the Society to explore specific aspects of the treatise. The papers are intended to assist the authors with the commentary. We offer them here as contributions to some of the issues posed by *On agriculture* and the larger Allegorical Commentary of which the treatise is a part.

University of Notre Dame

---

[9] A. L. Kilaniotis, "Philo of Alexandria, *De agricultura*: An Analytical Commentary" (Ph.D. diss., Trinity College, Dublin, 1989). The dissertation was supervised by John Dillon. One other work worthy of mention is Roberto Radice, *Filone di Alessandria, La migrazione verso l'eterno: L'agricultura, La piantagione di Noè, L'ebrietà, La sobrietà, La confusione delle lingue, La migrazione di Abramo* (I Classici del Pensiero, Sezione di filosofia classica e tardo-antica; Milan, 1988).

The Studia Philonica Annual 22 (2010) 87–109

THE STRUCTURE OF PHILO'S ALLEGORICAL TREATISE *DE AGRICULTURA*

DAVID T. RUNIA

1. *Introduction*

The subject of the structure of Philo's allegorical treatises is one of the more important in Philonic studies. After all, this group of treatises makes up almost half of Philo's writings and we bump up against the topic every time we read them. In 1985 in Anaheim California, at the very first Society of Biblical Literature annual meeting that I ever attended, I presented a paper with the title "Vivisection: further observations on the structure of Philo's allegorical treatises, with special reference to *De gigantibus* and *Quod Deus immutabilis sit.*"[1] The striking term "Vivisection," which was not used for the published version, referred to Philo's image of scripture as a living being consisting of body and soul (*Contempl.* 78). This paper formed part of a considerable body of research carried out in the seventies and eighties of the last century on the structure of Philo's allegorical treatises, stimulated by the research of excellent scholars such as Valentin Nikiprowetzky, Robert Hamerton-Kelly, Jacques Cazeaux, John Dillon, Roberto Radice and others.[2] Since then things have gone rather quiet. Recently there has been a

---

[1] Subsequently published as "Further Observations on the Structure of Philo's Allegorical treatises," *VC* 41 (1987): 105–38; reprinted in *Exegesis and Philosophy: Studies on Philo of Alexandria* (Variorum Collected Studies Series; London: Variorum, 1990), chapter V. It is not mentioned in the listing of the seminar's papers by Gregory E. Sterling, "A History of the Philo of Alexandria Program Units in the Society of Biblical Literature," in *In the Spirit of Faith: Studies in Philo and Early Christianity in Honor of David Hay [= SPhA 13 (2001)]* (ed. David T. Runia and Gregory E. Sterling; BJS 332; Providence RI, 2001), 25–34, because it was not on the official program. But see the note in "Further Observations," 134.

[2] Valentin Nikiprowetzky, *Le commentaire de l'Écriture chez Philon d'Alexandrie: son caractère et sa portée; observations philologiques* (ALGHJ 11; Leiden: Brill, 1977); Robert G. Hamerton-Kelly, "Some Techniques of Composition in Philo's *Allegorical Commentary* with Special Reference to *De agricultura*: a Study in the Hellenistic Midrash," in *Jews, Greeks and Christians: Religious Cultures in Late Antiquity: Essays in Honor of W. D. Davies* (ed. Robert Hamerton-Kelly and Robert Scroggs; SJLA 21; Leiden: Brill, 1976), 45–56; Jacques Cazeaux, *La trame et la chaîne: ou les Structures littéraires et l'Exégèse dans cinq des Traités de Philon*

stimulating article by Uri Gershowitz and Arkady Kovelman on teleological structure in Philo and the rabbis,[3] to which I will return below.
Scholars of the calibre of Folker Siegert and Maren Niehoff continue to
work on the Alexandrian background to Philo's exegesis.[4] But it certainly
needs no justification to return to questions that relate to the structure of
Philo's allegorical treatises.

In the present article I will be focusing on the method and structure of
one particular treatise, the *De agricultura*, as part of the preparation for the
commentary that Albert Geljon and I are writing together for the Philo of
Alexandria Commentary series.[5] My aim is to revisit key issues that come
to the surface as we read the treatise and try to determine how Philo has
structured it, looking primarily at the treatise on its own, but also taking
into account its context in the Allegorical Commentary as a whole. I shall
first look at more general aspects, before focusing specifically on the
treatise's structure and its main themes. Finally I shall speak briefly about
what I think the implications of our findings are for how the commentary
on this particular allegorical treatise should proceed.

---

d'*Alexandrie* (ALGHJ 15; Leiden: Brill, 1983); *idem, La trame et la chaîne, II: Le cycle de Noé
dans Philon d'Alexandrie* (ALGHJ 20; Leiden: Brill, 1989); John M. Dillon, "The Formal
Structure of Philo's Allegorical Exegesis," in *Two Treatises of Philo of Alexandria: a
Commentary on De gigantibus and Quod Deus sit immutabilis* (eds. David Winston and John
M. Dillon; BJS 25; Chico California, 1983), 77–88; Roberto Radice, "Introduzione," in *Filone
di Alessandria: Le origini del male. I Cherubini, I sacrifici di Abele e di Caino, Il malvagio tende a
sopraffare il buono, La posterità di Caino, I Giganti, L'immutabilità di Dio* (eds. Claudio
Mazzarelli and Roberto Radice; I classici del pensiero: Sezione I Filosofia classica e tardo
antica; Milan: Rusconi, 1984), 5–44.

[3] Uri Gershowitz and Arkady Kovelman, "A Symmetrical Teleological Construction
in the Treatises of Philo and in the Talmud," *Review of Rabbinic Judaism* 5 (2002): 228–46.

[4] Folker Siegert, "Early Jewish Interpretation in a Hellenistic Style," in *Hebrew Bible /
Old Testament. The History of Its Interpretation* (ed. Magne Sæbø; Göttingen: Vandenhoeck &
Ruprecht, 1996), 62–89; "Hellenistic Jewish Midrash," in *Encyclopedia of Midrash: Biblical
Interpretation in Formative Judaism* (eds. Jacob Neusner and Alan J. Avery Peck; Leiden:
Brill, 2005), 1.199–250; Maren R. Niehoff, "Homeric Scholarship and Bible Exegesis in
Ancient Alexandria: Evidence from Philo's 'Quarrelsome' Colleagues," CQ 57 (2007): 166–
82; "Recherche homérique et exégèse biblique à Alexandrie: un fragment sur la Tour de
Babel préservé par Philon," in *Philon d'Alexandrie. Un penseur à l'intersection des cultures
gréco-romaine, orientale, juive et chrétienne* (ed. Baudouin Decharneux and Sabrina Inowlocki;
Monothéismes et philosophie; Turnhout: Brepols, forthcoming).

[5] As yet no commentaries on treatises in the Allegorical Commentary have been published. We are eagerly awaiting the commentary on *Quod deterius* being prepared by Adam
Kamesar.

2. *The Allegorical Commentary as running commentary*

Let me start with an entirely uncontroversial assertion. The Allegorical Commentary is a running commentary on scripture, commencing at Gen 2:1 in *Legum allegoriae* 1.1 and ending in the treatises still extant at *De mutatione nominum* 270 which gives exegesis of Gen 17:22.[6] But even this straightforward statement immediately gives rise to questions. In the first place, what is the status of the treatises *De somniis*, which in all editions follow straight on from *Mut.*? Although these treatises cite substantial amounts of scripture and treat some passages verse by verse, they are not organized as a running commentary but rather by means of a systematic tripartite division of dreams. And because we lack the first book of the work, we do not know whether it was directly connected with the Allegorical Commentary, and if so, how this was done.[7]

A second question relates to the subject of this paper more closely, because it focuses on the three treatises *De agricultura, De plantatione* and *De ebrietate*. These three (and the missing other book of *Ebr.*[8]) all focus on just a single scriptural text, Gen 9:20–21. So in this case too, is it legitimate to speak of them as being part of a running commentary on scripture? We note too that all three have titles that differ from earlier titles in the series (from *Leg.* to *Deus*) in their systematic focus—Περὶ γεωργίας, Περὶ

---

[6] But this was not the end of the Commentary series, as the fragment *De Deo* on Gen 18:2 shows. As Folker Siegert, *Philon von Alexandrien Über die Gottesbezeichnung "wohltätig verzehrendes Feuer" (De Deo): Rückübersetzung des Fragments aus dem Armenischen, deutsche Übersetzung und Kommentar* (WUNT 46; Tübingen: J. C. B. Mohr (Paul Siebeck), 1988), 6 rightly argues, this was most likely from a lost treatise in the Allegorical Commentary. At least six books of the running Commentary have been lost (and another three if *Somn.* is included); see Jenny Morris, "The Jewish Philosopher Philo," in *The History of the Jewish People in the Age of Jesus Christ (175 B.C. – A.D. 135)* (ed. Eduard Schürer, Geza Vermes *et al.*; vol. 3 part 2; Edinburgh: T&T Clark, 1987), 868. James Royse points out to me that it is also possible that the structure of the lost Περὶ διαθηκῶν was similar to that of *Somn.*, i.e. that a discussion of the Noachitic covenant was the springboard for a more general exposition on covenants in the Pentateuch. But it is certainly very possible that the lost treatises gave a running commentary on Gen 8:21–9:17 parallel to *QG* 2.54–64, if not on an even longer section of the biblical text on the story of Noah.

[7] Morris, "The Jewish Philosopher Philo," 840 suggests that the missing first book may have treated the dream of Abimilech in Gen 20:3, which is not far removed from the end of the Allegorical Commentary as we have it. But Sofía Torallas Tovar, "Philo of Alexandria on Sleep," in *Sleep* (eds. T. Wiedemann and K. Dowden; Nottingham Classical Studies 8; Bari: Levante Editori, 2003), 41–52, argues that the book probably dealt with the dream of Isaac in Gen 26:2–5.

[8] It is disputed whether the extant book of *Ebr.* was the first or the second; see Morris, "The Jewish Philosopher Philo," 836.

φυτουργίας, and Περὶ μέθης—and also from the treatises that follow them
(*De sobrietate* to *Mut.*).[9]

At this point it is fitting to draw renewed attention to the largely forgotten study by Maximilian Adler published eighty years ago.[10] The
starting-point of his research was the contents of the missing other book of
Ebr. He argued that to reach a sound conclusion on this question, it was
necessary to look at the literary and stylistic features of the Allegorical
Commentary as a whole, an aspect that Cohn had overlooked in his authoritative treatment of the organization of the three major scriptural commentaries of the Philonic corpus. Adler argues in fine detail that the progression
of treatises from *Leg.* to *Ebr.* reveals a clear developmental progress from a
text-bound lemmatic exegesis in *Leg.* that only gradually brings in verses
from elsewhere in scripture to a fully-fledged systematically organized
treatise structure in *Agr.* and the following treatises. It is a development
from the kind of piece-meal exegesis found in the *Quaestiones* to a wholly
new and fully independent literary achievement.[11]

There is no need to delve into the details of Adler's argument, which
contain many sharp observations but in their totality are not convincing. It
is remarkable how scholars can be influenced by the scholarly fashions of
their time. Adler was writing at a time when developmental explanations
were very much in vogue. One need only think of Werner Jaeger's hugely
influential book on Aristotle's development, which sent Aristotelian scholarship in a wrong direction for half a century.[12] It has always seemed
puzzling to me why Adler did not recognize that the literary structure of
the treatises subsequent to *Ebr.* (except *Somn.*) reverted back to the kind
of structure that we find in earlier treatises in the Commentary. This

[9] The Latin title of *Sobr.* is misleading here. The Greek title reads Περὶ ὧν νήψας ὁ Νῶε
εὔχεται καὶ καταρᾶται, i.e. a descriptive and not a "systematic" title.

[10] Maximilian Adler, *Studien zu Philon von Alexandreia* (Breslau: M. & H. Marcus,
1929). On Adler, a holocaust victim who died in Auschwitz, see Daniel R. Schwartz,
"Philonic Anonyms of the Roman and Nazi Periods: Two Suggestions," *SPhA* 1 (1989): 73.

[11] See esp. Adler, *Studien*, 51: "Wir haben also in den zwei Büchern Περὶ γεωργίας zum
ersten Male einen solchen Grad schriftstellerischer Selbständigkeit feststellen können, daß
wir Philons Kommentar zu Gen. 9, 20 als eine von der bisherigen Behandlungsweise völlig
verschiedene, neue literarische Leistung würdigen müssen." Why has Philo now shown
independence? Is it from his exegetical predecessors? The main problem in my view is that
the method in *Leg.* 1–2 (originally one book) is somewhat deviant compared with the other
treatises. The method in *Leg.* 3 already resembles the rest of the Commentary quite
strongly.

[12] Werner Jaeger, *Aristoteles: Grundlegung einer Geschichte seiner Entwicklung* (Berlin:
Weidmannsche Buchhandlung, 1923).

observation alone would have to call into question the general conclusion that he reaches on Philo's development as a writer.

It is more convincing to argue that the Allegorical Commentary is a running commentary, but one that reveals a constantly varying interplay between direct textual exegesis and more systematic treatment. The piece-meal exegesis found in the first two books of *Leg.* are located at one end of the spectrum, the tight thematic structure of the three treatises *Agr.*, *Plant.* and *Ebr.* at the other. There is no need to postulate a development between them. When writing *Somn.* Philo goes a step further and no longer maintains the continuous running commentary on Genesis, although in some cases, when he cites the text of a dream, he then proceeds to comment sequentially on verses of the text cited.[13]

3. *Exegetical methods*

I turn now to the exegetical methods that Philo uses in composing his running commentaries on scripture. Whether one regards him as a rambler (Colson) or a highly methodical and organized writer (Cazeaux),[14] there can hardly be any doubt that he makes use of a series of distinctive exegetical techniques which form the basis for the structure of his treatises. There is an overwhelming consensus in Philonic scholarship that these techniques were not primarily the invention of Philo himself, but that he took them over from exegetical traditions that had developed in Alexandria over a long period of scholarly biblical study. This view is not only inherently plausible, but can also be demonstrated with a high degree of probability from the frequent references to exegetical predecessors and colleagues (always anonymous) in Philo's treatises.[15]

---

[13] Thus in *Somn.* 1 he cites Gen 28:12–15 in §3 and then at §61 proceeds to give a running commentary on v. 11 (which was not cited and is called the προοίμιον in §133) and then a briefer commentary on the verses cited in §§133–188.

[14] The extremes of interpretation as set out in my study, "The Structure of Philo's Allegorical Treatises: a review of two recent studies and some additional comments," *VC* 38 (1984): 209–56; reprinted in *Exegesis and Philosophy: Studies on Philo of Alexandria* (Variorum Collected Studies Series; London: Variorum, 1990), chapter IV.

[15] See especially the research of David M. Hay, "Philo's References to Other Allegorists," *Studia Philonica* 6 (1979–1980): 41–75; "References to Other Exegetes," in *Both Literal and Allegorical: Studies in Philo of Alexandria's Questions and Answers on Genesis and Exodus* (ed. David M. Hay; BJS 232; Atlanta, 1991), 81–97; and Thomas H. Tobin, *The Creation of Man: Philo and the History of Interpretation* (CBQMS 14; Washington: The Catholic Biblical Association of America, 1983).

It has also long been noted that Philo's exegetical methods bear more than superficial resemblance to exegetical modes and techniques that were developed in Palestine, first by the scribal predecessors of the rabbis and then by the rabbis themselves. The best overview of this complex field of study in recent years has been given in a Cambridge dissertation by David Instone Brewer.[16] In the first part of his study he presents a long list of scribal *middoth*, consisting of four modes and twenty-one techniques of exegesis. This forms an excellent background for looking at the exegetical methods found in Philo. After summarizing the state of scholarly research and limited amount of direct evidence from Philo's writings, he reaches the following conclusion:[17]

> Philo therefore knew many exegetical techniques which were similar to those outlined in the later [rabbinic] lists of middoth, as well as others which were not. However, we cannot conclude that these techniques were brought to Palestine from Alexandria or vice versa because . . . parallels do not necessarily indicate dependence. Perhaps we should take note of the third option . . . , that both Palestine and Alexandria learned from each other. This is certainly what Philo would have advocated.

This careful conclusion is persuasive. In addition, as Instone Brewer also reminds us, we should not overlook the debts that Philo and the traditions he takes over may have had to Greek interpretative methods, e.g. allegorical exegesis and the various techniques developed in Alexandrian Homeric scholarship.

It seems to me that in the quest for the historical background of Philo's exegesis there are limits to what can be attained. In a brilliant article on the techniques of composition in Philo's allegorical treatises with particular reference to *Agr.*, to which I have been much indebted in my own research on the subject, Robert Hamerton-Kelly argues that the basic structure of the treatise can be explained by a combination of the Jewish technique of *gezerah shawa* (inference by verbal analogy) and the Greek method of diaeresis.[18] There are most certainly strong similarities between the way that Philo links biblical texts and the technique of *gezerah shawa*,[19] but in the

---

[16] David Instone Brewer, *Techniques and Assumptions in Jewish Exegesis before 70 C. E.* (TSAJ 30; Tübingen: Mohr Siebeck 1992).

[17] Instone Brewer, *Techniques and Assumptions*, 211. For the point about parallels he refers to the famous article by Samuel Sandmel, "Parallelomania," *JBL* 81 (1962): 1–13.

[18] Hamerton-Kelly, "Some techniques of composition."

[19] Instone Brewer, *Techniques and Assumptions*, 17–18 distinguishes between two kinds of *gezerah shawa*. The first is "the definition of an ill-defined phrase or word in one text by its use in another text where its meaning is clearer." The second is "the interpretation of one text in the light of another text to which it is related by a shared word or phrase." What we find in Philo is closer to the second kind.

absence of specific references to the method in Philo, we cannot be certain that the two methods in fact have the same origin, especially given the quite different contexts in which they occur.

The difficulty that Philo's writings confront us with is the lack of explicit descriptive detail on the exegetical methods he uses. As noted at the beginning of the paper, we know that he compares scripture to a living being with the literal commands as its body and the invisible meaning as its soul (*Contempl.* 78). From this statement it may be reasonably deduced that he sees scripture as a unified whole whose parts can be linked together in the exegetical process. There are numerous comments on the relation between the literal and the allegorical meaning, on the application of the allegorical method, on the use of etymologies, on the brilliance of Moses, and so on. But nowhere does Philo give us any kind of theoretical reflection that would allow us to relate all these methods to the way he structures his allegorical treatises.[20]

In the light of this absence I believe we have no alternative but to adopt an *empirical* approach when studying our subject.[21] This means we must carefully analyse how Philo constructs his treatises and identify the methods he uses on the basis of his actual praxis. Ideally this might be done for the entire Allegorical Commentary, giving us insight into the entire scope of his methodology. But that would be a vast undertaking, a labour of love that might take even a life time to complete. In the meantime a piece-meal approach must prevail, focusing on the single treatise or a short sequence of treatises, as in fact I am doing now. I find myself in agreement with Jacques Cazeaux, who in his second volume of analyses dealing with the cycle of Noah from *De gigantibus* to *De sobrietate* states that "the principle guiding the exegete of Philo should in the first instance be to employ a solid empiricism."[22] I agree too with his criticism of Nikiprowetzky, who had argued that the backbone of a Philonic allegorical treatise is a series of questions and answers which link it with the *Quaestiones* commentary.[23]

---

[20] I still firmly believe, against Cazeaux, *La trame et la chaîne*, 511–15, that *Sacr.* 82–85 cannot be understood as referring to the way Philo structures his commentaries; see "Further Observations," 218.

[21] Cf. my claim in "The Structure of Philo's Allegorical Treatises," 239: "The task facing research on Philo's exegetical structures is first of all to make detailed analysis of the diverse treatises . . . The approach must be as empirical as possible, observing the actual *praxis* of Philo's exegesis."

[22] Cazeaux, *La trame et la chaîne II*, 2: "Aussi le principe guidant l'exégète de Philon devra-t-il tout d'abord s'accommoder d'un solide empirisme."

[23] Cazeaux, *La trame et la chaîne II*, 2, 270–75, commenting on Valentin Nikiprowetzky, "L'exégèse de Philon d'Alexandrie dans le *De gigantibus* et le *Quod Deus sit immutabilis*," in Winston and Dillon, *Two Treatises of Philo of Alexandria*, 5–76.

Even though his analysis works quite well for the treatise *Gig.–Deus*, it is simplistic to suggest that the method of the question and answer forms the structural basis of *all* the allegorical treatises. For example, in the case of *Agr.*, its structure of is obviously not explained by the single *quaestio* found at *QG* 2.65.

In their stimulating article Gershowitz and Kovelman, building on the work of Cazeaux, argue that analysis of Philo's treatises shows that he makes conscious use of the principles of symmetry and teleology not only in his philosophy (as shown by *Her.* 120–122), but also in the way he structures his biblical commentaries.[24] This is a bold claim, particularly as it is supported by only one example (*Leg.* 1.1 and 3.251). Nevertheless it is one that should be tested as we embark on our empirical examination of the structures of particular treatises. The further question that it presupposes is the degree of structural and thematic coherence underlying Philo's project. On this topic I crossed swords with Cazeaux many years ago, because I did not find the manner in which he postulated the total coherence of Philo's structures convincing. But here too there should be no dogmatism.[25] The question of the coherence of Philo's structures, both within a treatise and in their sequence, also needs to be part of our investigations, to be carried out in an empirical approach.

4. *The primacy of the biblical text*

In my first essay on the subject of the structure of Philo's allegorical treatises I set out a number of principles that had to be recognized when reading Philo's exegesis. The first and most important of these was the primacy of the biblical text.[26] It is now almost universally recognized that Philo is first and foremost a commentator on scripture. In the running commentary which is the Allegorical Commentary, the biblical text of Genesis is very clearly the starting-point of every treatise. It is then connected, to a greater or a lesser degree, with other scriptural texts, and together these texts—which I called the main and the secondary biblical lemmata respectively—form the skeleton as it were on which the biblical

---

[24] Gershowitz and Kovelman, "A Symmetrical Teleological Construction." The authors argue for a parallelism between Philo and the Talmud in the use of symmetry and teleology. Their debt to Cazeaux is expressed on p. 230.

[25] "The Structure of Philo's Allegorical Treatises," to which he gives a generalized reply in *La trame et la chaîne II*, 2.

[26] "The Structure of Philo's Allegorical Treatises," 237. The other principles were the opacity of the biblical text, the finality of Philonic text and the modesty of the Philonic text.

commentary is draped. I am therefore strongly persuaded that analysis of the structure of a Philonic allegorical treatise should always start with the biblical texts that he cites.

Of course it must be immediately recognized that not all the biblical texts referred to by Philo work in the same way or at the same level. Aside from the main biblical lemmata, the most important texts are those that are quoted at length and then form the basis for a significant exegetical development. There are a number of clear examples of this method in *Agr*. For example, at §148 Deut 20:5–7 is cited virtually *verbatim* (quite a long quote) and it then forms the basis for the commentary right up to §168. In other cases it is just a single word or brief phrase that interests Philo, such as when at §§42–43 he quotes Gen 30:36 and Exod 3:1 in order to illustrate the role of the shepherd. Noteworthy too is how citations of and references to the key biblical texts are used to frame sections of the commentary. Thus the main biblical lemma Gen 9:20 is cited at §1, §20, §125 and §181. As we shall see, these citations are strategically placed to commence the exegesis in the two main parts of the treatise (at §1 and 125) and to close it off in the initial chapter (at §§20–25) and at the end of the treatise (§181).[27]

A further question about the "skeleton" of biblical texts is how they are connected together. In my earlier work I was forcibly struck by how often the connections are based on verbal parallels or similarities which establish what I called a "verbal mode of transition."[28] Striking examples can be adduced from *Agr*. Returning to the biblical quote Deut 20:5–7 in §148, we might wonder what stimulated Philo to focus on this particular text in order to illustrate those practisers of virtue who have only attained a "half-solidified wisdom" (§146). It seems to me no coincidence that this text contains exactly the same phrase ἐφύτευσεν ἀμπελῶνα that occurs in the main biblical lemma Gen 9:20.[29] Less certain is whether the repeated reference to an ἄνθρωπος in this text recalls Noah the ἄνθρωπος in Gen 9:20. Philo appears to do rather little with this term in his main text, though one must suspect that the references to the ἡγεμὼν ἄνθρωπος and ἄνθρωπος ὁ ἐν ἑκάστῳ ἡμῶν in §§8–9 are inspired by it.

My emphasis on these verbal stimuli for linking up texts should not be misunderstood. Of course these links also have a thematic aspect and are ultimately motivated by the line of exegetical argument—however complex

[27] I presuppose a division into parts, chapters and sections, to which I shall return below at the end of the paper.

[28] The terminology was introduced in "The Structure of Philo's Allegorical Treatises," 239.

[29] The phrase occurs only three times in the Pentateuch: Gen 9:20, Deut 20:6, Deut 28:30. The last text is part of the curses and is obliquely referred to in *Praem*. 139.

or even convoluted—that Philo wishes to pursue in his treatise. What they draw attention to are two important elements of Philo's exegetical method. Firstly, they demonstrate his assumption of the unity of scripture, as implied in the image of scripture as a living being to which I have already twice referred. This will in the first instance apply to the Torah of Moses, but can be complemented by the writings of those disciples of Moses who have studied the Torah, such as the Psalmist referred to in *Agr.* 50. Secondly, they demonstrate the importance for Philo of biblical terminology. It is clear that he has studied the terms used for various activities and concepts in the Pentateuch very carefully, perhaps using some kind of concordance for this purpose.[30] These studies allow him to link up similar terms and phrases across the biblical text or place them in opposition as the case may be. There are many cases of this practice in *Agr.*, particularly in the first part where the distinctions are made between three sets of terms.[31] It is this feature of his exegesis that recalls the use of the method of *gezerah shawa* by the scribes and rabbis, though I would maintain that what Philo does cannot be reduced to that method.[32] It is natural to describe this method of linking texts as a "process of association" and to regard Philo as an "associative thinker." I have done so myself in my earlier research.[33] The danger is that we regard the process as too mechanical and so overlook the development of exegetical and philosophical themes in the treatise. In this perspective, it is important, using our empirical approach, to identify the presence of proleptic or teleological motifs, as postulated by Cazeaux and Gershowitz–Kovelman, since it would be an indication of how Philo plans and carries out the structure of his treatises.

---

[30] The examples of uses of the decad by Moses at *Congr.* 89 suggests at the very least a list of passages and perhaps a listing in a concordance. I postulated the use of some kind of concordance in "The Structure of Philo's Allegorical Treatises," 245. Naomi G. Cohen, *Philo's Scriptures: Citations from the Prophets and Writings: Evidence for a Haftarah Cycle in Second Temple Judaism* (JSJSup 123; Leiden: Brill, 2007), 113–16, 137, has also suggested Philo's use of a concordance that extended beyond the Pentateuch. There is, however, no ancient evidence in the papyri or manuscript traditions that confirms the existence of biblical concordances. Greg Sterling points out to me, however, that Philo may have committed large parts of the Pentateuch, if not the whole, to memory, which he could draw upon when making these verbal analyses.

[31] See below section 7 on §§1–25, 26–66, 67–123.

[32] Cf. "Further Observations," 120. This claim on my part is cited by Gershowitz and Kovelman, "A Symmetrical Teleological Construction," 231, but they do not comment on its validity.

[33] See "Further Observations," 130, where I claim that Philo "possessed a strongly associative mind."

5. *Rhetoric, purple prose and exhortation*

But there is of course much more to Philo's allegorical treatise than just the framework of biblical texts—both primary and secondary—on which the exegesis is draped. We must also look at its prose rhetoric, i.e. those features of Philo's literary style which enable him to elaborate on the exegetical themes that form the treatise's contents. This prose rhetoric is quite varied and operates at different levels.

In the first place we should note the use of introductory and transitional phrases and sentences that give structure to the treatise as a whole and within its parts. The clearest examples are at §26, §67, §124 and §181, where the main parts of the treatise are articulated.[34] The role of these passages is not very different from the way that the Exposition of the Law, which is *not* a running commentary on scripture, is structured. No doubt they are more prominent in *Agr.* precisely because the amount of biblical text on which the running commentary focuses is so limited. But also within the various sections of the commentary many phrases are introduced which give direction to the reader, such as §7 "let us now examine in turn . . .," §22 "how could anyone demonstrate more clearly . . .," §56 "here is proof," §72 "move now . . . to your own soul and examine it if you will," and so on. Careful attention should be given to such phrases when we unpack the structure of the individual parts of the treatise. Philo gives plenty of clues.

It goes without saying that Philo has also made extensive use of the various techniques and tropes of Greek rhetoric, although the treatise has not received much attention from scholars who have studied this aspect of his writing.[35] A striking example is his use of the trope of personification or *prosopopoeia* in §§17–19 when the skill of cultivation is portrayed as proclaiming how it will deal with the various plants that are the focus of its attention. The same trope occurs at §§52–53 when the Bible text Ps 23:1 (LXX 22:1) is placed in the mouth of the entire cosmos and its individual parts. Other examples are the extensive use of tricola in the construction of

---

[34] These passages take the place of chapter headings, which Philo does not use. These were starting to be used in the first cent. c.e., just after Philo's death; see Jaap Mansfeld and David T. Runia, *Aëtiana: The Method and Intellectual Context of a Doxographer. Volume II: Aëtius' Compendium*, 2 parts (PhilAnt 114; Leiden: Brill, 2009), 196–204.

[35] Manuel Alexandre Jr, *Rhetorical Argumentation in Philo of Alexandria* (BJS 322; Studia Philonica Monographs 2; Atlanta: Scholars Press, 1999), does not analyse any passages from *Agr.* But Thomas M. Conley, *Philo's Rhetoric: Studies in Style, Composition and Exegesis* (Center for Hermeneutical Studies Monograph 1; Berkeley: Center for Hermeneutical Studies, 1987), 46–50, gives a valuable analysis of §§26–66 in discussing the role of diaeresis in Philo.

his sentences and the frequent occurrence of synonyms or near synonyms joined by καί.[36]

Our treatise contains many examples of what we might call Philonic purple prose, passages where he pulls out all the stops and writes in an elevated style, with frequent use of complex periods and elaborate and sometimes quite specialized terminology. As befits a conscious literary stylist, the aim appears to be to captivate his readers, leading them along and persuading them of the validity of his interpretations. An early example is the description of the skill of plant cultivation, both in the literal and in the allegorical sense (§§5–11). A subsequent example is the description of the multitude of cattle interpreted as the herd of the senses §§30–40. The depiction of the difference between a horseman and a rider in §§67–77 at both the literal and the allegorical levels is a virtuoso performance. Similarly the portrait of the "ubiquitous crowd of sophists" and other professional educators in §§136–144 is masterly in its examples of fine distinctions that sharpen the mind but do not contribute to *aretê*.[37] The lengthy passages §§149–156 and §§157–168 are of interest because of their strong rhetorical character. Philo demonstrates with a high degree of elaboration that the literal reading of Deut 20:5–7 does not appear to make very good sense, but that an allegorical interpretation applies very well to the beginner on the path to perfection. We should note that part of the rhetoric is to adopt a personal appeal to the reader who might doubt Philo's approach, using the direct vocative with ὦ at the beginning and end of this section (§149, §167).

In the majority of these cases Philo appears to draw inspiration from disagreement. Showing that someone or something is on the wrong track adds intensity to his prose. A number of passages in the treatise can be loosely associated with the diatribe, a much-used method among popularizing philosophers in Philo's time that attacks the futile activities indulged in by the majority of people. Thus §§23–25 highlight the rapacious pursuit of pleasure, §§30–38 the immoderate behaviour of the senses of those people addicted to sensuality, §§110–121 the folly of entering competitions in vice and the challenge of the true Olympic games of moral excellence. Admittedly the diatribe as a genre is a modern concept, but its moralistic emphasis corresponds well to the tenor of the above passages.[38]

---

[36] These will be discussed in our commentary; see for example §3, §17 and §25.

[37] On this passage see B. W. Winter, *Philo and Paul among the Sophists* (SNTSMS 96; Cambridge: Cambridge University Press 1997), 68–71.

[38] The monograph of Paul Wendland, "Philo und die kynisch-stoische Diatribe," in *Beiträge zur Geschichte der griechischen Philosophie und Religion* (eds. Paul Wendland and Otto Kern; Berlin: Georg Reimer, 1895), 1–75, was very influential; see also his *Die*

A further group of passages open up a dialogic relationship with the reader. "Move now," Philo writes in §72, "from the neighing beasts and their riders to your own soul and examine it, if you will, for in its parts you will find horses and reinsman and rider, just as in the external world." We note the use of the second person, directly addressing the reader. Other passages that do the same at greater length are found at §§90–93, §§110–121 (note again the vocatives with ὦ in §111 and §112), and §§178–180 near the end of the treatise. There are, however, no examples in *Agr.* of the practice of addressing the soul or the mind (ὦ ψυχή, ὦ διάνοια), to which Abraham Terian has drawn our attention.[39] In passages like these the commentary develops a method of exhortation that has roots in the protreptic discourse of Greek philosophy,[40] but is also reminiscent of the synagogal sermon.[41] The function of these passages is very important in the context of the treatise as a whole. They bring home the relevance of the allegorical exegesis for the moral and spiritual life of the reader.

6. *The structure of the treatise unpacked*

I turn now to an analysis of the structure of our treatise, using the method developed in my earlier studies.[42] For each section I give first the formal exegetical structure, followed by a brief remark on its content. The sigla

---

hellenistisch-römische Kultur in ihren Beziehungen zu Judentum und Christentum (Handbuch zum Neuen Testament 1, ii–iii; Tübingen: J. C. B. Mohr (Paul Siebeck), 1912), 75–81. Abraham Malherbe, *Moral Exhortation: a Greco-Roman Sourcebook* (Library of Early Christianity; Philadelphia: Westminster, 1987), 129, regards it as just one kind of the broader category of styles of exhortation.

[39] Abraham Terian, "Inspiration and Originality: Philo's Distinctive Exclamations," *SPhA* 7 (1995): 56–84. He argues that these phrases betray passages of Philonic inspiration.

[40] See again Malherbe, *Moral Exhortation*, 122; Klaus Berger, "Hellenistische Gattungen im Neuen Testament," in *Aufstieg und Niedergang des Römischen Welt II Principat* (ed. Werner Haase; Berlin: de Gruyter 1984), 1138–45.

[41] Philo's treatises have often been regarded as being a development of or inspired by the synagogal sermon; see the discussion at Nikiprowetzky, *Le commentaire de l'Écriture*, 174–77. Note the judicious words of William Horbury, "Old Testament Interpretation in the Writings of the Church Fathers," in *Mikra: Text, Translation, Reading and Interpretation of the Hebrew Bible in Ancient Judaism and Early Christianity* (ed. Martin Jan Mulder and Harry Sysling; CRINT 2.1; Assen: Van Gorcum, 1988), 736, on Old Testament interpretation in the Church fathers: "Nevertheless, commentary and homily should not be too sharply distinguished. The commentator can envisage an auditory, his interests are likely to be spiritual and pastoral as well as exegetical, and preachers in turn draw upon commentaries."

[42] See "The Structure of Philo's Allegorical Treatises," 241–44, on *Deus*, "Further Observations," 133–34 on *Gig*.

used are MBL = main biblical lemma, SBL = secondary biblical lemma, MOT = mode of transition.

Philo of Alexandria
De agricultura (On cultivation)
Exegetical structure of the treatise

PART ONE: Noah as cultivator (§§1–123)

Chapter 1: first distinction between cultivator and worker of the earth (§§1–25)
(a) Citation of the MBL: Gen 9:20–21 cited in abbreviated form (§1), followed by a literal explanation of the term γεωργὸς γῆς (§§1–7):
> There is a difference between the skill of cultivation and mere working the earth; in the latter case there is a lack of skill and it is done for the wrong motives.

(b) Explanation of the skill of cultivating the soul = transition to allegorical interpretation of the term γεωργὸς γῆς (§§8–11):
> Soul cultivation involves the teachings of excellence which produce noble deeds as crops, but harmful or non-productive growth must be pruned away and can be used for fencing.

(c) Citation of SBL Deut 20:20 (§12, MOT mainly thematic, but note term καρπόβρωτος and anticipation of χαράκωσιν by χάρακας in §11) = transition to theme of role of auxiliary sciences (§§12–16):
> Allegory in terms of merely theoretical sciences (including logic and dialectic) which prepare and sharpen the mind but do not contribute to a better character.

(d) The soul practising cultivation announces its program (note ἐκκόψω SBL, φυτεύσω MBL, ταμιεύσομαι ~ SBL) (§§17–19):
> Allegory continued through summary of three activities: (i) cutting away vice and passions; (ii) cultivating excellences with aid of general education (ἐγκύκλιος παιδεία); (iii) storing up growth that can serve as protection.

(e) Demonstration of allegory through comparison of Noah and Cain via the distinction between γεωργία and mere ἐργασία γῆς (citation of MBL Gen 9:20 γεωργός and SBL Gen 4:2 ἐργαζόμενος τὴν γῆν, 11–12 ἐργᾷ τὴν γῆν) (§§20–25):
> The allegory is concluded by the explanation of the distinction in terms of faculties of the soul: the unjust person (ἄδικος) and the majority of people are focused on the body and its pleasures in their ignorance of soul cultivation that leads to the εὐδαίμων βίος.

Chapter 2: second distinction between shepherd and cattle-feeder (§§26–66)
(a) Introduction of another terminological distinction between two roles which seem similar but are very different (§§26–29):

> When the leader of the herd of the soul is morally good (σπουδαῖος) he is called ποιμήν (shepherd), when he is morally bad (φαῦλος) he is called κτηνοτρόφος (cattle-feeder).

(b) Elaborate explanation of the allegorical distinction involved (§§30–40):

> The irrational parts of the soul are like cattle; if badly ruled by the mind they will run amuck; they need to be restrained and held together through discipline, as a shepherd does.

(c) Scriptural evidence for the role of shepherd: SBL Gen 30:36 (MOT verbal ποιμαίνει) and SBL Exod 3:1 (MOT verbal ποιμαίνων) (§§41–43):

> Jacob shepherds the sheep of Laban, the soul which regards sense-perceptibles as goods; Moses shepherds the sheep of Jethro, the deluded mind.

(d) Further scriptural evidence: Moses' prayer in SBL Num 27:16–17 (MOT verbal πρόβατα, ποιμήν) cited and explained (§§44–48):

> It is worthwhile to pray that the flock of the soul does not receive a ruler who is either savage or weak like cattle-feeders but a shepherd who chooses what is advantageous for it.

(e) Role of God in SBL Num 27:16 expanded, with transition to another SBL Ps. 22:1 (MOT verbal ποιμαίνει) (§§49–54):

> God is the shepherd both for the cosmos (in which he is assisted by his logos, as evidenced by SBL Exod 23:20, MOT thematic[43]) and the God-loving soul, so that the soul will not be lacking anything it needs.

(f) Proof that God's disciples practise the science of shepherding and not cattle-feeding through the example of Joseph and his brothers, SBL Gen 46:33–34 (MOT verbal) and SBL Gen 47:3 (MOT verbal) (§§55–62):

> Joseph is young and cannot rule, so he tells them to answer the king of Egypt that they are cattle-feeders (κτηνοτρόφοι), but as rulers they answer that they are shepherds (ποιμένες).

(g) Answer to an objection that the brothers did make their way to Egypt through further citation of SBL Gen 47:4 (MOT thematic and following the biblical sequence) (§§63–66):

---

[43] It is probable that this biblical text, which is closer to the proto-rabbinic Καί γε translation than the LXX, is an interpolation in Philo's original text; see Wendland's note in the apparatus of C-W ad loc.; Dominique Barthélemy, "Est-ce Hoshaya Rabba qui censura le 'Commentaire Allégorique'? A partir des retouches faites aux citations bibliques, étude sur la tradition textuelle du Commentaire Allégorique de Philon," in *Philon d'Alexandrie. Lyon 11-15 Septembre 1966: colloques nationaux du Centre National de la Recherche Scientifique* (Paris: Editions de CNRS, 1967), 52.

They came to sojourn, not live, as befits the wise person (σοφός) who lives as a stranger on earth; so the distinction between shepherd and cattle-feeder holds.

Chapter 3: third distinction between horseman and rider (§§67–123)
(a) Introduction of literal distinction between ἀναβάτης and ἱππεύς (§§67–71):
The chief difference is that the rider is carried along, whereas the horseman leads through use of skill.
(b) Same distinction explained allegorically and then linked to SBL Deut 20:1 (MOT verbal, ἵππον καὶ ἀναβάτην) (§§72–78):
The soul is compared to a charioteer and two horses; the fate of the bad reinsman is terrible, but God protects those who disdain spirit and passion.
(c) Illustration by means of the two choirs of virtuous souls under the leadership of Moses and Miriam via quotation of SBL Exod 15:1, 21 (MOT verbal, ἵππον καὶ ἀναβάτην) (§§79–83):
The virtuous souls celebrate the fall of the horse and rider, i.e. the passions and the intellect which is under their sway.
(d) Do not appoint a king who is a horse-feeder (ἱπποτρόφος) via quotation of SBL Deut 17:15–16 (MOT verbal ἵππον) (§§84–93):
This is not so much about a literal cavalry, but rather about the soul, which needs a mind that understands how to control the reins.
(e) Further quotation of prayer of Moses in SBL Gen 49:17–18 (MOT verbal, ἵππου, ἱππεύς) (§§94–105):
Dan as judgment (κρίσις) is a serpent—like Moses' bronze serpent symbolizing endurance (καρτερία), not Eve's representing pleasure—, so Moses' prayer is that he be "on the path" ambushing pleasure.
(f) Continuation of exegesis SBL Gen 49:17–18, with brief reference to contrasting SBL Gen 3:15 (MOT verbal πτέρναν) (§§106–123):
Dan "will bite the horse's heel," i.e. passion and evil, and "the horseman (ἱππεύς) will fall," i.e. he will fall away from evil and by losing the unholy contest will win the truly Olympic contest of excellence and obtain the "Lord's salvation."

PART TWO: Noah begins as a cultivator (§§124–181)

Chapter 1: making the right beginning (§§124–145)
(a) Return to MBL Gen 9:20 with emphasis now on Noah as beginner (§§124–126):

Introductory remarks on the importance of beginning and of reaching the end.

(b) Quotation of SBL Gen 4:7 (MOT thematic, διέλῃς recalls διαίρεσις): (§§127–130):

The account of Cain's attempt at offering sacrifice illustrates the error of not distinguishing correctly, particularly in relation to God.

(c) Introduction of an allegorical example involving division via paraphrase of SBL Lev 11:4 (MOT verbal/thematic διχηλεῖ) (§§131–135):

Dietary precepts interpreted allegorically illustrate the need for both memory and division on the part of the soul of the lover of learning (φιλομαθής).

(d) Excessive and futile division illustrated (§§136–141):

Extensive list of examples of division by sophists, musicians, geometers and philosophers.

(e) Application of example to SBL Lev 11:7 (paraphrased, MOT verbal/ thematic) (§§142–145):

The crowd of sophists are compared by scripture swine who divide the hoof but do not chew the cud; in fact both activities are required for the complete good.

Chapter 2: making progress on the path to perfection (§§146–168)

(a) Transition to citation of new SBL Deut 20:5–7 (MBL verbal/thematic ἐφύτευσεν ἀμπελῶνα, cf. MBL) (§§146–148):

Some are too weak to immediately go into battle and achieve perfection, so those who have begun projects are exempted from military service.

(b) Rejection of the literal meaning (§§149–156):

The prescription of this text does not make sense when taken literally.

(c) Explanation of the allegorical meaning of the SBL Deut 20:5–7 (§§157–168):

First basic concepts set out—the good life occurs through not only acquisition but also enjoyment of excellence, and this is achieved through good beginnings, advancements and completions—, then their application is set out in the struggle against the preying sophists.

Chapter 3: a successful end (§§169–181)

(a) Quotation of new SBL Deut 22:8 (MOT verbal οἰκοδομήσῃς οἰκίαν καινήν, cf. Deut 20:5; στεφάνη anticipating κεφαλή and ἀρχή below) (§§169–173):

Failure to achieve an auspicious completion will occur for those who do not recognize God as the author of good things (illustrated by another SBL Deut 8:18, MOT thematic).

(b) Quotation of another SBL Num 6:9 & 12 (MOT thematic/verbal, κεφαλή = ἀρχή) (§§174–180):

Another group that can fail are those who commit unintentional sins, but these are sins ἄλογοι, i.e. not reckoned to the perpetrators.

(c) Concluding return to the MBL Gen 9:20 (§181):

This is what has been said about the beginning (ἀρχή) and the end (τέλος) in relation to Noah, who begins but is not strong enough reach the goal.

End of treatise

7. *Comments on the treatise's structure*

The structure that has been set out above is of course no more than an outline of the full contents and thematics of the treatise. It cannot now be our task to discuss these in detail. This will have to occur in the Commentary that is under preparation. Nevertheless the structural analysis I have given does give rise to some significant observations and questions.

Firstly, using the empirical approach advocated above, we may conclude that a structural analysis that takes the biblical texts of the treatise as its starting point works, i.e. it furnishes genuine insight into the treatise's structure. The transitions from the one text to the next can be explained, and in many cases (more than half) they involve verbal parallelism. The extent to which texts are cited and explained varies to a considerable degree. Sometimes a single secondary text gives rise to an extended treatment (e.g. in §§146–168). Sometimes they are cited in clusters and treated much more cursorily (e.g. eight texts in §§40–66).[44] It is clear that Philo assumes the Torah to be a unified whole. The biblical texts cited are drawn from many different locations in the Pentateuch (and in one case from outside it). This allows Philo to link up with numerous other exegetical themes from outside the immediate Genesis story in his interpretations. References to Jacob, Laban, Joseph and his brothers, Dan and Eve, Pharaoh and his office bearers, Moses, Miriam and Jethro, as well as various prescriptions of the Law relating to Nazarites, soldiers and house-builders, are woven into the

---

[44] Greg Sterling suggests to me that it might be useful to distinguish between "secondary" texts which get a full treatment and "tertiary" texts that are used chiefly as examples. This suggestion needs to be investigated further.

sequence of his exegesis. The treatise is plainly written for the initiated, who have a good knowledge of the Pentateuch and are well-versed in the methods of literal and allegorical exegesis. But although the exegesis is at times complex and even in the final pages seemingly a bit rushed, its structure is well-signposted and for the most part clear enough for the initiated reader.

We should note at this point that, although as a primarily allegorical treatment of the biblical text, the present treatise is undeniably more complex and recondite than other parts of the Philonic corpus, it does share important common features with Philo's practice elsewhere. A striking feature of *Agr.* is that on no less than four occasions Philo explicitly moves from the literal to the allegorical interpretation of the text:[45] §§1–7 and §§8–11 (the difference between cultivating and merely working the earth); §§67–71 and §§72–78 (the difference between rider and horseman); §§84–87 and §§88–93 (the ruler's cavalry); §§149–156 and §§157–168 (exemption from military service for the recently married). This is exactly the same standard procedure that Philo uses quite rigidly in the *Quaestiones* and more flexibly in the Exposition of the Law.[46] The first pair of these cases involve the primarily biblical text expounded in the treatise, the second pair two secondary texts treated at some length. The method used in both cases is the same. And we should note that in the first two cases Philo is happy enough with the literal explanation, but regards it as not delving deep enough, whereas in the latter two he remarks on the implausibility of the literal meaning and uses that observation as a springboard for a deeper penetration of the meaning of the text.

Next it is worth focusing briefly on the main division of the treatise into two parts. Philo delineates both parts very clearly through his repetition of the main biblical lemma at §125 and §181. As Conley has pointed out,[47] his treatment of the two terms in Gen 9:20, γεωργός and ἤρξατο, actually reverses the order of the biblical text. But it is only logical that the exegete first determines the kind of person who is being referred to and then explains what it means that he is a beginner. The question that is quite intriguing is the extent to which these two parts form a unified whole. It seems to me that at most we can speak of a fairly loose kind of unity. Throughout Part I the key is the distinction between two kinds of people and souls, the good and the bad. It is mainly elaborated in terms of the

[45] This observation was pointed out to me by Greg Sterling.
[46] See for example in *De Abrahamo*, as analysed in my paper, "The Place of *De Abrahamo* in Philo's Œuvre," *SPhA* 20 (2008): 139–40.
[47] Conley, *Philo's Rhetoric*, 78 n. 39; cf. also Cazeaux, *La trame et la chaîne II*, 157.

struggle of the soul or the intellect to rein in the passions and control the senses, with particular emphasis on the destructive role of pleasure. The distinction is black and white, with no shades of grey. It is then quite a surprise when immediately at the outset of Part II Philo announces (§125) that the person who aspires to excellence, i.e. Noah, does not obtain it in a complete form, but is only practising its initial stages. The only other biblical character introduced in this part is Cain, who had already been portrayed in a negative light in §§20–22. Cain's sacrifice is not accepted because he did not distinguish correctly (§127, cf. Gen 4:7). The crowd of sophists make numerous subtle divisions, but these do not contribute to a blameless way of life (§§135–141). How does this theme in Part II relate to the use of correct division between the various skills and occupations in Part I? Philo does not make this clear, and it is perhaps best to regard the two discussions as separate and only loosely related.[48]

This loose unity is bridged, however, by the role of Noah as δίκαιος (the just person, Gen 6:8), who forms a key link between the two parts. In §2 it is emphatically stated the person introduced as cultivator is Noah the δίκαιος and this is repeated in §20. Then at the very end of Part I (§123) Philo states that the horseman who falls to the rear and awaits the salvation of the Lord (cf. Gen 49:18) "can advance in performing just deeds (δικαιοπραγεῖν)." There is clearly a veiled reference to Noah here which rounds off the exegesis in Part I. The final reference to Noah the δίκαιος occurs at the very end of the treatise (§181), where Philo writes that "Noah the just person … acquired the first rudimentary elements of the cultivator's skill but did not have the strength to reach its limits." Cazeaux in his analysis of the treatise has argued that the reader must bear in mind that Noah belongs to the first triad of the Patriarchs.[49] We can compare *Abr.* 31–39, which admittedly gives a literal interpretation only, but interprets the biblical phrase "perfect in his generation" (Gen 6:9) as meaning that Noah was not absolutely good but only in comparison with the men of his time and falls short of the Patriarchs who came later. Cazeaux may be correct, but one does wonder how Philo conveys this point in the absence of any comparison with the other biblical figures (except Cain) in the second part of the treatise.[50]

---

[48] But it is surprising that Irmgard Christiansen, *Die Technik der allegorischen Aus-legungswissenschaft bei Philon von Alexandrien* (Beiträge zur Geschichte der biblischen Hermeneutik 7; Tübingen: J. C. B. Mohr (Paul Siebeck), 1969), who makes huge claims for the process of division in Philo's exegesis, does not discuss the texts in Part II at all.

[49] Cazeaux, *La trame et la chaîne II*, 168–71.

[50] Perhaps he is thinking of Noah's comparative status already at §121 when he speaks about the value of obtaining second or third prizes.

It is clear, therefore, that the theme of Noah the just person is used to link up the two parts of the treatise and its location at the beginning and end give the treatise a degree of symmetry. I have not, however, found any striking examples of teleological structuring in the manner suggested by Gershowitz and Kovelman. Perhaps these remain to be detected. There are some cases of modest anticipation. Thus "stakes" in §11 anticipates the citation of Deut 20:20 in §12. The progression from "crown" in §170 to "head" in §175 to "beginning" in §180 has been planned in advance. In addition, the mention of God's beneficence in §168 is followed through in §173 and §180. Such thematic integration is familiar to all readers of Philo's allegorical treatises.

Finally I wish briefly to look at the concluding sections of the two parts. Endings are often important for Philo and one would certainly expect that to be the case for a treatise that has beginnings and ends as one of its main themes. The final part of Part I is taken up with exegesis of Gen 49:17–18, provoked by its mention of the horseman (ἱππεύς). Paradoxically, we read in §110, there are contests in which it is better to fail. That is why the horseman falls, because he does not wish to win a contest in evil-doing. It is the truly Olympian contest of excellence that he strives to win (§§119–121). The biblical text appropriately says that the horseman will fall backwards, because in a contest in evil-doing it is best to fall behind (§122). For this reason he awaits the Lord's salvation (Gen 49:18), since he can advance in performing just deeds (§123, a reference to Noah as noted above). Implicit in this passage is a double goal, the prize of excellence that the virtuous person gains and the salvation received from God. It is surprising that Philo does not develop these themes further. Perhaps he thought the section on the horseman and the rider was long enough.

Turning to the final part of Part II, we note that the entire section §§169–181 has as its theme the goal of reaching a successful end, which only God can give. But it rarely happens that such a goal is reached without setbacks of various kinds (§180). So in the case of Noah a good start has been made, but he does not have the capacity to reach the limits of the skill of cultivation (§181). The conclusion of the treatise is thus rather muted. Unlike many other treatises, *Agr.* does not end with a fanfare, announcing or praying that the goal of honouring God and living the good life be reached.[51] It is consistent with the interpretation that Philo has given of his main biblical lemma. Noah does not gain the ultimate goal. It should be noted that the emphasis through this last section on divine beneficence is very strong.

---

[51] See esp. the final words at *Ebr.* 224, *Post.* 185, *Somn.* 1.256; note also *Opif.* 172, *Spec.* 1.345, *Contempl.* 90.

God is the giver of strength and the cause of good things (§173, citing Deut 8:18). This theme links up well with the reference to the Lord's salvation at the end of Part I. We recognize the two strands of philosophical and religious thought that are so pervasively entwined in the Allegorical Commentary. The goal of life, not fully reached by Noah, is to achieve complete and perfect excellence and the good life, but it is God who grants the achievement, and the chief part of that life is to honour God and give thanks for what he bestows.

8. *Some consequences for a commentary*

In his announcement of the Philo of Alexandria Commentary series published in 1995, Greg Sterling wrote:[52]

> The commentary proper will work with units of the treatise in agreement with the basic structure of the analysis of the tractate. So, for example, in the case of a commentary on a treatise in the Allegorical Commentary, Philo's use of primary or secondary (and even tertiary) biblical lemmata will determine the extent of the unit. The reason for this structure is that the primary objective of the commentaries is to illuminate the thought of the tractate.

The results of our investigation confirm that this is a practical route to follow in writing a commentary on one of Philo's allegorical treatises.

A difficulty that *Agr.* poses, and it is shared by *Plant.* and *Ebr.*, is that we cannot use the quotations of the main biblical lemma as markers to indicate the extent of "chapters" of exegesis. This was the method that I used in my commentary on *Opif.*, but it would obviously lead to difficulties in the case of *Agr.* In actual fact, if we take the main biblical lemma as our starting point, there are only two chapters in the treatise: §§1–123 discussing Noah's status as cultivator and §§124–181 on the statement that he commenced his role. But it would not be practical to divide the commentary into these chapters only. So we have decided to reformulate this division as the two main parts of the treatise and further subdivide each into a series of three chapters. In Part I these divisions are made very clear in Philo's transitional comments in §26 and §67. In Part II such transitional

---

[52] Gregory E. Sterling, "Announcement: Philo of Alexandria Commentary Series," *SPhA* 7 (1995): 165. In a note he adds that this method had already been used in the commentaries of Winston and Dillon, *Two Treatises of Philo of Alexandria,* and Roberto Radice, "Commentario a La creazione del mondo e a Le allegorie delle Leggi," in *La filosofia mosaica. La creazione del mondo Le allegorie delle Leggi* (ed. Clara Kraus Reggiani, Roberto Radice and Giovanni Reale; I classici del pensiero: Sezione I Filosofia classica e tardo antica; Milan: Rusconi, 1987), 231–533.

remarks are missing. As a result the internal divisions are much less clear and one could argue that the entire Part is a continuous whole that should be treated as such. Nevertheless on pragmatic grounds it seems best to subdivide further. We follow Cazeaux's analysis and divide the second part into three chapters which relate in a rather neat fashion to reflections on commencement, progress and the final goal.

For each chapter a number of further subdivisions can be made which correspond to the progress of Philo's thought. These vary in length from about three to a dozen sections in length.[53] It seems that Philo's thought and writing tends to move in blocks of text of about this length, so there is a happy correspondence between the structure of his thought and the structure we can give our commentary.

A final point I wish to make is that the preliminary analysis that I have given of the treatise confirms the wisdom of Sterling's injunction in the quote above that the commentary should mirror the progression of the biblical lemmata which Philo cites and expounds, whether these be primary or secondary. In our commentary we will pay particular attention to the manner in which Philo uses biblical texts to structure and organize the development of his thought in the treatise. By exposing this "skeleton" of biblical texts the treatise will become much easier to read and understand.

The rich and variegated tapestry of Philo's allegorical treatises will always remain a challenge for the reader. They are an acquired taste and the challenge they pose is not for the faint-hearted. The task of the commentator is not to remove the challenge, but to assist the reader in rising to it. My collaborator and I will continue our labours and we look forward to making this assistance available.[54]

Queen's College
The University of Melbourne

[53] According to the numbering of C-W's text, which has now become standard in Philonic studies. The Commentary series does not use the old Roman numbering.

[54] I would like to express my gratitude to the Chairs of the Philo of Alexandria Group of the Society of Biblical Literature, Sarah Pearce and Ellen Birnbaum, for inviting me to present the original paper, and the Group itself for the stimulating discussion at the meeting. My sincere thanks also to David Winston, Ellen Birnbaum, Greg Sterling and Jim Royse for their careful reading of the paper and for their valuable responses which have allowed me to improve it.

The Studia Philonica Annual 22 (2010) 111–129

SOME OBSERVATIONS ON THE BIBLICAL TEXT
IN PHILO'S *DE AGRICULTURA**

JAMES R. ROYSE

As is usual with Philo's works, the biblical quotations in his *De agricultura* present an interesting set of problems, where the textual histories of the Philonic corpus and the Septuagint intersect. What we find is that Philo, of course, basically follows the Septuagint version. But already at Philo's time variations in the transmission of the LXX existed, and like all manuscripts his scrolls of the various books of the Bible would have contained their own peculiar readings. Indeed, in his citations we sometimes find minor variations as are also found in LXX manuscripts, and at such places it is reasonable to think that Philo is simply copying verbatim the text as found by him in his scrolls of the LXX.

However, Philo's quotations also contain variations that are found nowhere else (or almost nowhere else) in the LXX tradition, and at such places we may be able to detect Philo's own modifications of the biblical text. Within the limited space of this article, I have selected a few of the explicit citations of the Bible that are found in *De agricultura*, and will examine the various discrepancies from the usual LXX. In the following I will typically cite the MT from the Biblia Hebraica Stuttgartensia, the LXX from the Göttingen Septuagint, and Philo's words from the Cohn-Wendland edition.[1] I have included the textual evidence that is cited in PCW, but have been selective about reproducing the evidence for the LXX, although I have tried to include everything that might be relevant to understanding the vicissitudes of the Philonic text.

---

* Presented to the Philo of Alexandria Group at the meeting of the Society of Biblical Literature in New Orleans, November 22, 2009. I occasionally refer to the sample commentary on *Agr.* by David T. Runia and Albert C. Geljon, as presented at the meeting. I would also like to thank David T. Runia, Gregory E. Sterling, and an anonymous reviewer for their helpful corrections and suggestions.

[1] Naturally, the printed text of the MT and of the LXX cannot necessarily be taken as the text at Philo's time.

Agr. 1: The opening Biblical lemma is Gen 9:20–21:

	LXX	Philo
	καὶ ἤρξατο Νῶε ἄνθρωπος γεωργὸς γῆς,	καὶ ἤρξατο Νῶε ἄνθρωπος γεωργὸς γῆς εἶναι,
4	καὶ ἐφύτευσεν ἀμπελῶνα, καὶ ἔπιεν ἐκ τοῦ οἴνου, καὶ ἐμεθύσθη καὶ ἐγυμνώθη	καὶ ἐφύτευσεν ἀμπελῶνα, καὶ ἔπιε τοῦ οἴνου, καὶ ἐμεθύσθη
8	ἐν τῷ οἴκῳ αὐτοῦ.	ἐν τῷ οἴκῳ αὐτοῦ.
	1 post ανθρωπος add. ειναι Bohairic 2 γης om. Arabic Bohairic	1–8 om. UF 2 γης om. H 5 επιε του : επιεν εκ του AH

It is curious that Philo elsewhere also adds εἶναι (which is not in the LXX manuscripts, and not supported by the Hebrew) to the first clause of Gen 9:20, but in a different place. At *Agr.* 1 it comes after γῆς, while at *Agr.* 20, *Agr.* 125, *Plant.* 1, and *Plant.* 140 it comes before γεωργός.[2] The only other place where we have an explicit citation of this clause is at QG 2.66 (preserved in Armenian only). Here the *quaestio* also reads (the equivalent of) εἶναι before γεωργός.[3] And in a partial citation the *solutio* again has (the equivalent of) εἶναι before γεωργός.[4] We should thus suppose that Philo added εἶναι in order to present a smoother construction. Certainly this is a "stylistic addition."[5]

---

[2] At *Agr.* 181 we find ἤρξατο γῆς εἶναι γεωργός. Despite the quotation marks in PCW, PLCL, PCH, and PAPM, I find it difficult to believe that this is meant to be a precise quotation, since it differs so much from his other citations. Rather, the only word that is relevant to Philo's point is ἤρξατο, in contrast to having "reached the furthest limits of full knowledge." So Philo is *quoting* "ἤρξατο" and just adds the other words (including εἶναι) to provide the required context. One should thus print: λέγεται γὰρ ὅτι "ἤρξατο" γῆς εἶναι γεωργός.

[3] Aucher (1826, p. 152) has: *ayr linel mšak erkir*, literally ἄνθρωπος εἶναι γεωργὸς γῆς, or in his Latin "homo agricola esse terrae." I note that Zohrab's edition has the text of Gen 9:20: *ayr hołagorc zerkir gorcel*, which would be literally ἄνθρωπος γεωργὸς γῆν ἐργάζεσθαι.

[4] Aucher has: *sksaw asē linel mšak*, literally ἤρξατο, λέγει, εἶναι γεωργός.

[5] This is the term used in the sample commentary (p. 3).

With respect to the phrase "and he was naked" Heinemann thought that Philo was being inexact.[6] Indeed, we explicitly find ἐγυμνώθη ἐν τῷ οἴκῳ αὐτοῦ at *Leg.* 2.60 and the Armenian equivalent at *QG* 2.69;[7] so Philo certainly knew of ἐγυμνώθη. It is thus tempting to suppose that, as explicitly stated in the Göttingen Septuagint for Genesis, the words καὶ ἐγυμνώθη have been omitted in *Agr.* 1 by homoeoteleuton: εμεθυσθη και εγυμνωθη.[8] According to this hypothesis, Philo wrote the full text as found in the LXX.[9] And we should then, presumably, emend Philo's text by restoring the words καὶ ἐμεθύσθη.[10] However, as we shall see, Philo often makes (as it seems) small adjustments to the text of the LXX to suit his own purposes. So perhaps here it is more likely that he omitted the words καὶ ἐμεθύσθη since they were not relevant to his immediate discussion.

Moreover, Mangey omitted γῆς from his text, following H alone, arguing that Philo had in mind more the cultivation of the soul than of the earth.[11] On the other hand, it seems more likely that the omission of γῆς by H is the result of (more or less) homoeoteleuton: γεωργος γης.[12] And thus PCW correctly prints γῆς.

Finally, we may note the fluctuation between ἔπιε τοῦ οἴνου and ἔπιεν ἐκ τοῦ οἴνου. The LXX certainly contained ἐκ, which is in all manuscripts and reflects מן. (The shift between ἔπιε and ἔπιεν is, of course, simply a result of

---

[6] PCH 4.113 n. 1: "Philo zitiert ungenau; daß er richtig entblößte [i.e., καὶ ἐγυμνώθη after ἐμεθύσθη] las, geht aus All. Erkl. II § 60 und Quaest. in Gen. II § 69 hervor." Similarly, Pouilloux, PAPM 9.23 n. 1 (from 22): "Philon altère légèrement la citation des LXX." Colson and Whitaker, PLCL 3.108 n. a, simply note the difference from the LXX.

[7] Here Aucher's Armenian in the *quaestio* agrees precisely with Zohrab's text.

[8] No LXX manuscript is cited for this omission.

[9] Note that at *Plant.* 140 he simply ends his citation of Gen 9:20–21 with ἐμεθύσθη, since Noah's nudity is not there relevant; it is thus misleading to say (as the commentary, p. 3, does) that "[t]he words are also left out" there. *Agr.* 1 is the only place where Philo would have possibly cited the entire phrase καὶ ἐμεθύσθη καὶ ἐγυμνώθη. Elsewhere (as at *QG* 2.68 and 2.69) he breaks up his discussion of the drunkenness and the nudity.

[10] In the discussion in New Orleans, David T. Runia raised this issue.

[11] Thomas Mangey, Φίλωνος τοῦ Ἰουδαίου τὰ εὑρισκόμενα ἅπαντα. *Philonis Judaei opera quae reperiri potuerunt omnia* (2 vols.; London: William Bowyer, 1742), 1.300 n. a: "MSS. Med. & Vat. addunt γῆς, quibus suffragitur quoque Textus sacer; nec tamen vocem istam addendum censeo; quippe quam Philo de industriâ omisisse videtur, cum non tam telluris quam animi culturam exhibeat." It may be worth noting that Mangey's great work is available as an electronic resource from ECCO, which can be accessed at many research libraries, and can be downloaded (in portions up to 250 pages) as PDFs. Indeed, it is Markland's copy of Mangey's edition (see my "Jeremiah Markland's Contribution to the Textual Criticism of Philo," *SPhA* 16 [2004] 50–60) that is available, so that one can see, more or less clearly, Markland's annotations as well.

[12] Peter Katz, *Philo's Bible* (Cambridge: Cambridge University Press, 1950), 32, says simply that "H amends" the text.

whether a consonant or vowel follows; the presence or absence of ἐκ is the variation here.) But what did Philo have? He cites these words at three places:[13]

Agr. 1   τοῦ οἴνου MG (PCW) : ἐκ τοῦ οἴνου AH (Mangey)
Plant. 140   τοῦ οἴνου MUF (PCW Mangey) : ἐκ τοῦ οἴνου G
QG 2.68 *quaestio*   the Armenian has the equivalent of ἐκ τοῦ οἴνου[14]

Naturally, it is plausible to suppose, as does Katz,[15] that there would be a scribal tendency to conform Philo's citations to the prevailing text of the Septuagint, and so we could reasonably think that the scribes of AH and G (respectively) added ἐκ. And we could similarly think that the Armenian scribes of the *Quaestiones* added the equivalent of ἐκ to conform to the prevailing Armenian text. There seems to be no plausible explanation for the omission of ἐκ if Philo originally wrote it. So it seems that Cohn and Wendland are correct in writing τοῦ οἴνου without the ἐκ.

However, Philo's remarks at the *solutio* of *QG* 2.68 appear to present a problem for this view. There he says: "In the first place, the righteous man did not drink the wine but a portion of wine and not all of it."[16] Marcus comments: "Philo stresses the scriptural wording 'drank *of* the wine.'"[17] It thus seems that Marcus thought that Philo read ἐκ (as in Genesis). Now there is a Greek paraphrase of the relevant lines by Procopius, but, as one can see clearly in Petit's presentation, it cannot be trusted to give Philo's precise words. What Procopius has is: . . . οὐδὲ τὸν οἶνον ὅλον ἀλλ᾽ ἐκ τοῦ οἴνου πίνει κτλ.[18] This would indicate that Philo had ἐκ here, but of course Procopius would have known the ἐκ from Gen 9:21 in any case. Indeed, if we look at the Armenian of the *solutio*, we see that Philo there does not say "from the wine," but rather "a portion of wine" (*zginoyn zmasn*, corresponding, it seems, to τοῦ οἴνου μέρος).

But it seems that Philo's point at *QG* 2.68 would have been equally clear if he had not written ἐκ in the *quaestio*. The genitive τοῦ οἴνου alone would indicate (or at least could indicate) that the drinking was from a part of the wine, and not all the wine. We could thus see all the witnesses that contain

---

[13] Note that the Göttingen Septuagint refers at Gen 9:21 to *Agr.* 1 and *Plant.* 140, although ἐκ is mistakenly said to be omitted in the apparatus of *Plant.* 140 rather than in the text.
[14] It reads *i ginwoyn*, precisely as does Zohrab's text of Gen 9:21.
[15] *Philo's Bible*, 32, citing *Agr.* 1 and *Plant.* 140, but not *QG* 2.68; a reference to Katz is given in the sample commentary (p. 3).
[16] This is Marcus's translation.
[17] PLCL Supp 1.159 n. i.
[18] See Petit, PAPM 33.121.

ἐκ—AH at *Agr.* 1, G at *Plant.* 140, the Armenian *quaestio* at QG 2.68, and Procopius at QG 2.68—as having been influenced by the usual text of Gen 9:21. And thus Katz seems correct in saying: "We have to conclude that the πίνειν ἐκ was awkward Greek to Philo who set it right with a light touch so that its re-introduction [i.e., in AH and G] was at variance with his own tendencies."[19]

We thus see right at the start of the treatise Philo's willingness to revise what he found in his manuscripts of the LXX for stylistic or grammatical reasons. There will be more examples.

Agr. 12: Philo cites Deut 20:20 as: πᾶν ὃ οὐ καρπόβρωτόν ἐστιν, κτλ., where the LXX has: ἀλλὰ ξύλον, ὃ ἐπίστασαι ὅτι οὐ καρπόβρωτόν ἐστιν, κτλ. Here Philo departed more substantially from the LXX.[20] Moreover, we have an interesting textual variation in the Philonic manuscripts UF.[21] But let me here merely observe that it is not clear to me that PCW is correct in placing an opening quotation mark before πᾶν. Indeed, the Göttingen Septuagint cites Philo as reading πᾶν ὅ for the LXX's ὃ ἐπίστασαι ὅτι, although one might well think that πᾶν ὅ corresponds to the entire opening phrase ἀλλὰ ξύλον, ὃ ἐπίστασαι ὅτι. In fact, one could avoid foisting such a thorough rewriting on Philo by simply editing: λέγει γὰρ πᾶν ὃ "οὐ καρπόβρωτόν ἐστιν κτλ.," as Katz suggests.[22] And the implied referent of πᾶν would not be ξύλον, as in the LXX, but presumably δένδρον, which at this point has occurred four times (§§ 6, 8, 10, 11) already in *Agr.*, while ξύλον does not occur in the book at all.[23]

Agr. 94: Here we have a long citation from Gen 49:17–18, beginning: γενέσθω Δαν ὄφις ἐφ᾽ ὁδοῦ ἐγκαθήμενος ἐπὶ τρίβου. The sole discrepancy with the LXX is that Philo has γενέσθω instead of the LXX's γενηθήτω (which translates the MT's יְהִי). Philo quotes the opening words of Gen

[19] *Philo's Bible*, 32.
[20] Heinemann remarks: "Philo zitiert den Vers frei."
[21] See Katz, *Philo's Bible*, 32–33, and John William Wevers, *Text History of the Greek Deuteronomy* (MSU 13; Göttingen: Vandenhoeck and Ruprecht, 1978), 70.
[22] *Philo's Bible*, 32: "the inverted commas should be put with rather more discrimination, to mark more clearly Philo's omissions and paraphrases." Indeed, Katz writes: "ὃ οὐ . . . ἐκκόψεις καὶ" ποιήσεις "χαράκωσιν . . . πόλεμον." This interpretation does avoid making Philo substitute ποιήσεις for οἰκοδομήσεις, but seems to be a drastic remedy, since it supposes that Philo drops out of quoting for just one word. As an alternative I would conjecture that Philo balked at the use of οἰκοδομέω with χαράκωσις (used in the LXX only here [but it is used by Theodotion at Ezek 21:22(27), and 26:8] and in Philo only here).
[23] The Loeb translation has "Every tree," with δένδρον or ξύλον understood, while Heinemann has "Alles," which is a more literal rendering of πᾶν alone.

James R. Royse

49:17 three other times, and at each place the same substitution occurs: at *Agr.* 101, where the first five words of Gen 49:17 are repeated; at *Leg.* 2.94, where Philo cites Gen 49:16–18; and at *Leg.* 2.97, where he repeats the first five words of Gen 49:17.[24] And he makes the same substitution at *Leg.* 2.98, where he allegorically transforms the first three words of Gen 49:17 into γενέσθω οὖν ὁ σωφροσύνης λόγος ὄφις. We thus have five places where Philo writes γενέσθω instead of γενηθήτω in connection with Gen 49:17, and there is no support for Philo's γενέσθω among the LXX witnesses.[25]

Now, this turns out to be a very interesting substitution. Philo uses γενέσθω five other times. At *Sobr.* 59 he quotes Gen 9:27, and has γενέσθω for the LXX's γενηθήτω (again for the MT's יְהִי]), also with no support among the LXX witnesses.[26] At *Conf.* 39 he quotes Ps 30:19 (LXX, 31:19 Hebrew), and has γενέσθω for the LXX's γενηθήτω (where there is no verb in the MT).[27] At *Somn.* 1.75 Philo quotes Gen 1:3, and has γενέσθω for the LXX's γενηθήτω (for the MT's יְהִי]), this time with support from Eusebius.[28] And at the final two times, *Spec.* 3.30 and *Gaium* 236, Philo uses γενέσθω in his own composition.

So, Philo uses γενέσθω a total of ten times, eight of which replace γενηθήτω in the LXX. Furthermore, according to the TLG γενηθήτω does not occur in Philo. So, the inevitable conclusion is that Philo has made these substitutions on his own, preferring for some reason or other to use the aorist middle imperative instead of the aorist passive imperative.

Some light may be shed on what Philo's reason for that choice was by observing that Phrynichus, the second-century proponent of strict

---

[24] The repetitions of γενέσθω at *Agr.* 100 and *Leg.* 2.97 are (uncharacteristically) missed by the Göttingen Septuagint.

[25] The Göttingen Septuagint informs us that ἔσται is read by DialTA 91r Arab Bo, and also that ἐγενήθη τῷ is found in A, many minuscules, Aeth, ᴸᵃᵗAmbr *Patr* 32. The addition of τῷ is, presumably, intended to avoid a possible ambiguity: the Greek of the LXX can be read either as "Let Dan be a serpent on the road" or "Let there be a serpent on the road for Dan," as Philo points out at *Agr.* 99. The latter reading takes Δαν to be in the dative case, as Philo indicates by prefixing τῷ, just as A etc. do. By the way, the same ambiguity seems to be present in the MT (יְהִי־דָן נָחָשׁ עֲלֵי־דֶרֶךְ]).

[26] And we find the alternative readings ἔσται in Dᴳ *b* 59 DialTA 108v, and ἐγεννήθη τῷ in 527.

[27] Here the only variation cited in the LXX is γενηθήτωσαν in B 1219.

[28] Eusebius, *Praep. evang.* 11.25.2 and 13.13.12 (but not 7.11.2). According to LXX ms. 912 (which has Gen 1:1–5 in both the LXX and Aquila), Aquila has γενηθήτω. However, Philoponus (*De opificio mundi libri VII*, ed. Walter Reichardt [Leipzig: B. G. Teubner, 1897] 73–74) cites Aquila for γενέσθω and Symmachus for ἔστω and Theodotion for γενηθήτω. See further below on Gen 1:3.

adherence to Atticism, condemns the use of the passive of γίνομαι.[29] Those who prefer Attic forms should thus use the middle. If we think of γίνομαι in these contexts as basically representing "to be" or "to become," it may indeed seem difficult, if not impossible, to think of a passive construction as appropriate. Certainly in English "to be" does not have a passive, although one can construct various paraphrases, such as "it was caused to be," or even "let it be," which serve something of the same purpose. The usual English "let there be light," which derives from Tyndale, constructs what might be viewed as a causative of "to be." But this does not really capture the passive imperative, since "light" is here the object of "let," rather than the subject as in Greek.[30] However, as part of his commentary on Plato's *Parmenides* 141E1–7, Proclus gives the following clarification of the difference between γενήσεται and γενηθήσεται:

> *will become* [γενήσεται] signifies the timeless indivisible existence in the future, as for instance "there will be a flash of lightning" (*genēsetai*): whereas *will have become* [γενηθήσεται] expresses progression along with extension, as in the case

[29] See *Die Ekloge des Phrynichos*, ed. Eitel Fischer (SGLG 1; Berlin: de Gruyter, 1974), 67 (item 79): Γενηθῆναι· ἀντὶ τοῦ γενέσθω παρὰ Ἐπιχάρμῳ, καὶ ἔστι Δώριον· ἀλλ᾽ ὁ Ἀττικίζων γενέσθαι λεγέτω; and W. Gunion Rutherford, *The New Phrynichus* (London: Macmillan, 1881), 194–95 (item 87): γενηθῆναι παρὰ Ἐπιχάρμῳ καὶ ἐστὶ Δώριον· ἀλλ᾽ ὁ Ἀττικίζων γενέσθαι λεγέτω. Rutherford discusses γενηθήσεται at Plato, *Parm.* 141E1 and E6–7, calling it "simply absurd." And he cites Heindorf as saying that he can see no difference between γενήσεται and γενηθήσεται. On this see Staffan Wahlgren, *Sprachwandel im Griechisch der frühen römischen Kaiserzeit* (Studia Graeca et Latina Gothoborgensia 60; Göteborg: Acta Universitatis Gothoburgensis, 1995), 53 n. 4. The Oxford text of Plato reads: Τί δέ; τὸ ἔσται καὶ τὸ γενήσεται καὶ τὸ γενηθήσεται οὐ τοῦ ἔπειτα [τοῦ μέλλοντος]; . . . τὸ ἕν . . . οὔτ᾽ ἔπειτα γενήσεται οὔτε γενηθήσεται οὔτε ἔσται. F. M. Cornford (*Plato and Parmenides* [London: Kegan Paul, 1939], 129) distinguishes the three verbs as "will be" (ἔσται), "will be becoming" (γενήσεται), and "will become" (γενηθήσεται). Alternatively, the translation by Mary Louise Gill and Paul Ryan (in Plato, *Complete Works*, ed. John M. Cooper [Indianapolis and Cambridge: Hackett, 1997], 375) uses "will be," "will come to be," and "will be coming to be," respectively. Here the distinction between future middle and future passive is expressed by the simple future and the progressive future forms. This distinction in English between the simple and the progressive form seems to be quite a different issue. For example, Herbert Weir Smyth says flatly (*Greek Grammar*, rev. Gordon M. Messing [Cambridge: Harvard University Press, 1956], §1857): "For the 'progressive' tenses of English . . . Greek has no exact equivalent." Of course, at the passage in the *Parmenides* translators were no doubt struggling to make any distinction at all. (These are the only passive forms of γίνομαι in Plato.)

[30] One can, of course, see this by noticing that the English is parallel to, say, "let him go" (not "let he go"). In Greek one says γενηθήτω γῆ, where γῆ is the subject of the verb. Naturally, this is all just to say that English does not really have an imperative passive for the third person.

of "he will have become a man"; in the case of lightning, it would be false to say "it will have become."[31]

Of course, whatever sense the passive may have, the fact seems to be that Philo avoids using it.[32]

The example of Gen 1:3 is especially interesting. Thanks to the TLG one can trace the fate of the phrases γενηθήτω φῶς and γενέσθω φῶς throughout Greek literature. Naturally, the usual phrase for God's creation of light is γενηθήτω φῶς, as was surely the reading of the LXX and was copied repeatedly; the TLG shows 126 occurrences. On the other hand, the phrase γενέσθω φῶς occurs in only six places:

Philo, *Somn.* 1.75
Longinus, *De sublimitate* 9.10
Eusebius, *Praep. evang.* 11.25.2, citing Clement of Alexandria, *Strom.* 5.94.1
Eusebius, *Praep. evang.* 13.13.12, citing Clement of Alexandria, *Strom.* 5.94.1

---

[31] Proclus, *Commentarium in Platonis Parmenidem* (ed. Victor Cousin, Hildesheim: Georg Olms, 1961 [repr. of 1864 edition]), 1237; trans. Glenn R. Morrow and John M. Dillon, *Proclus' Commentary on Plato's "Parmenides"* (Princeton: Princeton University Press, 1987), 576. In fact, Proclus discusses this passage in the *Parmenides* at some length (*Commentarium in Platonis Parmenidem*, 1233–39), and, as A.-Ed. Chaignet (trans., Proclus, *Commentaire sur le Parménide* 3 [Frankfurt: Minerva, 1962 (repr. of 1903 edition)], 77 n. 1) says, shows no indication that the term γενηθήσεται is especially problematic. By the way, although Chaignet says that γενηθήσεται is a *hapax legomenon*, the TLG shows that this form occurs twenty five times, of which two are in Plato and nine are in the commentary by Proclus.

However, Proclus himself turns out to avoid using the passive of γίνομαι apart from this context. As far as the TLG shows, the only other use of a passive form of γίνομαι by Proclus is in his *Theologica Platonica* 5.31, where we find: μεμιγμένη γὰρ ἡ τοῦ παντὸς φύσις ἐκ νοῦ καὶ ἀνάγκης ἐγενήθη, φησὶν ὁ Τίμαιος. (See H. D. Saffrey and L. G. Westerink, eds. and trans., Proclus, *Théologie platonicienne* 5 [Paris: Société d'Édition «Les Belles Lettres», 1987], 113.) Now this is an allusion to Plato, *Timaeus* 47E5–48A2: μεμειγμένη γὰρ οὖν ἡ τοῦδε τοῦ κόσμου γένεσις ἐξ ἀνάγκης τε καὶ νοῦ συστάσεως ἐγεννήθη. For the final word Burnet cites: ἐγεννήθη A F : ἐγενήθη Y et fecit A². So, there seem to be three possibilities for Proclus. Either he read ἐγενήθη in his copy of Plato and so quoted, he read ἐγεννήθη but mistakenly wrote ἐγενήθη, or he read and quoted ἐγεννήθη and his scribes erroneously shifted to ἐγενήθη. However, in any case, we do not have Proclus's own free use of the passive.

[32] In a brief survey using limited material (but including Philo) Wahlgren feels able to assert: "Vermutlich ist es aber korrekt zu behaupten, daß es in der frühen Kaiserzeit allgemein eine größere Tendenz gibt, die passive Form [i.e., of γινέσθαι] zu vermeiden" (*Sprachwandel im Griechisch*, 55 [the evidence is presented on 53–56]). See also Henry St John Thackeray, *A Grammar of the Old Testament in Greek* 1 (Cambridge: Cambridge University Press, 1909), 238–39, on the middle and passive forms of γίνομαι in the LXX.

Philoponus, *De opificio mundi* 2.8, citing Aquila[33]
Papyri magicae 4.970 (Preisendanz)[34]

The last occurrence may not really be a citation of Gen 1:3 at all; at least, if one follows the references in Preisendanz one will come to an article by Eitrem,[35] who compares the use here to a third century C.E. papyrus written in Demotic, which speaks of "a form of inquiry of the sun."[36] Thus, the context is not (it would seem) that of God's creation of light as reported in Genesis, but the presence of light within the mysteries. However, the other five occurrences are clearly meant to be citing Gen 1:3, albeit with the shift in verb form.

The report by Philoponus may rest on some confusion. The LXX manuscript 912 (P.Amh. 1.3, which is known as 𝔓¹² in the New Testament for its citation of Heb 1:1) presents Gen 1:1–5 in both the LXX and Aquila's version, and it reports Aquila as having γενηθήτω with the LXX. And I note that at Jer 38:9 for the ἐγενόμην of the LXX Aquila is reported to have read ἐγενήθη. On the other hand, at Gen 1:14 Aquila is said to have had γενέσθωσαν for the LXX's γενηθήτωσαν. Thus, at Gen 1:3 we find conflicting reports (between 912 and Philoponus), at Jer 38:9 Aquila has the passive where the LXX has the middle, and at Gen 1:14 Aquila has the middle where the LXX has the passive. I will leave the issue with this variety of evidence.

Of course, one could suppose that Longinus, rather than quoting Aquila, is using what might be seen as better Greek.

The citations in Eusebius are especially suggestive. He twice cites the same passage from Clement. Now, Eusebius's own text of Genesis seems to have had the ordinary reading. At least he cites γενηθήτω φῶς on four occasions: *Praep. evang.* 7.11.2, *Ecl. proph.* 4.23,[37] and *Comm. in Ps* 91:2 (LXX)

---

[33] *De opificio mundi libri VII*, ed. Reichardt, 73.

[34] *Papyri magicae graecae, Die griechischen Zauberpapyri*, ed. Karl Preisendanz (2d ed. by Albert Henrichs; Stuttgart: Teubner, 1973), 106.

[35] Samson Eitrem, "Die vier Elemente in der Mysterienweihe," *SO* 4 (1926): 46–47.

[36] F. Ll. Griffith and Herbert Thompson, eds., *The Demotic Magical Papyrus of London and Leiden* (London: H. Grevel, 1904; repr., Milan: Cisalpino La Goliardica, 1976), 165. Thus begins col. 29 of the papyrus, as found on pp. 164–69 (text and translation).

[37] The text is found in Thomas Gaisford, ed., *Eusebii Pamphili episcopi Caesariensis Eclogae propheticae* (Oxford: Oxford University Press, 1842), 206: αὐτὸς δ' ἂν εἴη ᾧ προστάττων ἐν κοσμοποιίᾳ φησὶν ὁ Πατὴρ τὸ, γενηθήτω φῶς, καὶ γενηθήτω τάδε καὶ τάδε· καὶ τὸ, ποιήσωμεν ἄνθρωπον κατ᾽ εἰκόνα ἡμετέραν. (I have retained Gaisford's accentuation.) The same text is found in PG 22.1232B14–C2. It is striking that Eusebius chooses γενηθήτω τάδε καὶ τάδε as the way to say, in effect, that God said "Let other things be." In fact, after Gen 1:3 this locution is found in the Creation story only at Gen 1:6 (γενηθήτω στερέωμα) and 1:14 (γενηθήτωσαν φωστῆρες). The only variation at these two places that is found in

bis.[38] It would thus seem unlikely that he would have altered Clement's citation away from the LXX, and it also seems unlikely that the scribes of Eusebius's work would have altered away from the LXX. In fact, there is a variation in the manuscripts at *Praep. evang.* 11.25.2; there γενέσθω is found in ION, while γενηθήτω is found in B. A little later, at *Praep. evang.* 13.13.12, all the manuscripts have γενέσθω. I thus suppose that Eusebius wrote γενέσθω at both places, and that at the first B replaced it with the usual LXX text, but at the second accepted that it was the correct reading.[39]

But, if Eusebius wrote γενέσθω at both these places, while writing γενηθήτω elsewhere, he must have found γενέσθω in his copy of Clement's *Stromateis*. However, the manuscripts of Clement are reported to be unanimous in reading the usual γενηθήτω at *Strom.* 5.94.1. What I would suggest is that Clement wrote γενέσθω and that the scribes of Clement altered his unusual γενέσθω to conform to the standard LXX text.[40] We can thus use Eusebius to emend Clement. Similarly at *Plant.* 8 and 10 editors have used Eusebius to emend Philo by writing λόγος and λόγου with Eusebius instead of νόμος and νόμου, which are read by all the Philo manuscripts.[41] Naturally, Eusebius is earlier than the manuscripts of Clement and Philo (except for the portions preserved in the Coptos and Oxyrhynchus papyri), although one has to be careful to find the readings of Eusebius himself rather than those of his later manuscripts.

---

the Göttingen Septuagint is that Field reports that Aquila has γενέσθωσαν at the latter place. Yet what we find in support of that reading in Field is merely the note (Frederick Field, *Origenis Hexaplorum quae supersunt* [2 vols.; Oxford: Clarendon, 1875], 1.9 n. 30): "Sic Montef., tacito autore; fortasse ex sola collatione Hexaplorum ad vv. 3, 4."

[38] Found in PG 23.1172.B1 and 23.1173.C14–15.

[39] We thus have an example of what Wordsworth and White perceptively call the true reading's gaining the victory in the end; see John Wordsworth and Henry Julian White, eds., *Novum Testamentum Domini Nostri Iesu Christi Latine* 1 (Oxford: Clarendon, 1889), 727–28.

[40] Unfortunately, it would seem that we would then need to emend Clement at *two* places, since he cites Gen 1:3 at *Strom.* 5.94.1 and also at *Ecl. proph.* 38.1. At neither place does the GCS edition of Clement cite any variation in the manuscripts of Clement (at the first only the discrepancy in Eusebius).

[41] See my discussion of this change in "The Text of Philo's *Legum Allegoriae*," *SPhA* 12 (2000): 20–21. There is a similar change at *Deus* 57 where UFL² read νόμῳ for λόγῳ. (My article has "UFL2.") Barthélemy attributes all three changes to the reviser of Philo's text who created the "aberrant text," although at *Plant.* 8 and 10 this aberrant text has contaminated all the manuscripts. I note that already Mangey says of νόμος at *Plant.* 8: "Euseb. λόγος, & sic omnino rectius. Passim enim Philo rerum tum creationem tum conservationem λόγῳ tribuit." And at *Plant.* 10 he notes on νόμου: "Scribe iterum cum Eusebio λόγου, cui contextus certè fidem facit." At *Deus* 57 Mangey prints λόγῳ, with no report of manuscript variation, but he notes: "λόγον esse rerum conditorem passim docet Philo."

But let us (finally) return to Philo. Apart from the substitution of the aorist middle γενέσθω for the aorist passive γενηθήτω, as cited above, in general passive forms of γίνεσθαι are very rare (at least) in Philo. They are (as reported by the TLG):

γενηθῇ   *Plant.* 175
ἐγενήθησαν   *Mos.* 1.31
γενηθῆναι   *QG* 2.16

For the second Wahlgren suggests that we should in fact read ἐγεννήθησαν, comparing the construction to *Mos.* 1.5.[42] Such forms are commonly confused, and it does seem that the form of γεννάω would actually fit the context better. For the first there is a variant reading, γεννηθῇ, found in F, although there it is not at all clear (to me, at any rate) that a form of γεννάω would make sense.[43] Finally we have *QG* 2.16. Regrettably there seems to be some confusion in the Armenian here, which makes the correspondence with the Greek less than ideal.[44] Nevertheless, it does seem that we have at least two passive forms (both aorist) of γίνομαι in Philo: *Plant.* 175 and *QG* 2.16. However, we can see a tendency to remove such forms by Philo. Perhaps to be consistent we should emend *Plant.* 175 and *QG* 2.16 to the middle forms, i.e., to γένηται and γενέσθαι, respectively, and suppose that Philo's scribes were not as meticulous about Atticism as he was. Of course, in doing so we run the risk of being more meticulous (or perhaps more mechanically consistent) than Philo was.

Agr. 127: The text of Gen 4:7 in the LXX, as usually printed, reads:

οὐκ, ἐὰν ὀρθῶς προσενέγκῃς, ὀρθῶς δὲ μὴ διέλῃς, ἥμαρτες; ἡσύχασον· πρὸς σὲ ἀποστροφὴ αὐτοῦ, καὶ σὺ ἄρξεις αὐτοῦ.

However, Philo evidently read this text as:

οὐκ ἐὰν ὀρθῶς προσενέγκῃς, ὀρθῶς δὲ μὴ διέλῃς· ἥμαρτες, ἡσύχασον· πρὸς σὲ ἀποστροφὴ αὐτοῦ, καὶ σὺ ἄρξεις αὐτοῦ.

At *Agr.* 127 Philo cites the opening words, οὐκ ἐὰν ὀρθῶς προσενέγκῃς, ὀρθῶς δὲ μὴ διέλῃς, taking διέλῃς as the end of the clause. At *Sobr.* 50 and *Mut.* 195 he takes as a separate phrase the following words: ἥμαρτες

---

[42] Wahlgren (*Sprachwandel,* 55–56) notes that γεννάω is often found with τρέφω, e.g., at *Spec.* 1.314 (to which one may add several other examples), and says that at *Mos.* 1.31 ἐγεννήθησαν "semantisch besser paßt."

[43] Wahlgren (*Sprachwandel,* 56) remarks: "Passive Konjunktive kommen, wie schon erwähnt, besonders selten vor, was vielleicht gegen den Text spricht."

[44] See Petit's note in PAPM 33.97, as well as the remarks of Marcus and Mercier.

ἡσύχασον. And at *QG* 1.64–66 Philo cites the entire verse. He discusses the opening clause (ending with διέλῃς) at 1.64,[45] and separately discusses the next two words at 1.65. Then at *QG* 1.66 he cites the further words πρὸς σὲ ἡ ἀποστροφὴ αὐτοῦ (in the *quaestio*), and the final words, [καὶ] σὺ ἄρξεις αὐτοῦ (in the *solutio*).[46]

Colson notes Philo's division of the text, and asserts that, in contrast to Philo's understanding, "[i]n the LXX, as usually and rightly printed, ἥμαρτες is the apodosis" of the preceding clause.[47] We thus find, for example, the recent NETS translation of Gen 4:7: "If you offer correctly but do not divide correctly, have you not sinned? Be still; his recourse is to you, and you will rule over him."[48] However, I fail to see how one can know that this is the *correct* understanding of the words, since the manuscripts of the original translation, the manuscripts of the LXX that Philo used, and the manuscripts for some centuries after him certainly had no punctuation.[49] And of course the Hebrew manuscripts had no punctuation either until well into the Common Era.

[45] However, there is a duplication of the negative (*oč*) in the Armenian, the first part of which Marcus renders as "Not that thou dost not offer rightly." The second "not" here finds no support elsewhere, and I suppose that the obscurity of the text has led to its introduction within the Armenian tradition.

[46] The καί in this final clause is the only word of the verse that Philo does not explicitly cite, at least if we can trust the accuracy of the Armenian on this point (see Marcus's translation, PLCL Supp 2.40). Note that Procopius's rendering does have καί, but this is presumably yet another aspect of his paraphrastic tendency; Petit (PAPM 33.64) correctly notes that it is not represented in the Armenian. But in the French translation of the Armenian Mercier (PAPM 34A.137) nevertheless writes: "Et toi, tu le domineras." I presume that Philo simply omitted the καί because of the context of his quotation; there is no evidence of its omission in the LXX.

[47] PLCL 3.470 n. b, commenting on *Sobr.* 50. Colson refers to this note at PLCL 3.173 n. c, on *Agr.* 127. See also Mercier's note to *QG* 1.64 (PAPM 34A.134 n. 1), as well as Heinemann's note to *Agr.* 127 (PCH 4.136 n. 3).

[48] *A New English Translation of the Septuagint*, ed. Albert Pietersma and Benjamin G. Wright (New York: Oxford University Press, 2007), Genesis translated by Robert J. V. Hiebert. The two older translations may also be cited. Charles Thomson, trans., *The Holy Bible, containing the Old and New Covenants, commonly Called the Old and New Testament* (4 vols.; Philadelphia: Jane Aitken, 1808) has: "Though thou hast offered right, yet if thou hast not rightly divided, hast thou not sinned? Be composed. To thee shall be his recourse, and thou shalt rule over him." And Lancelot Charles Lee Brenton, trans., *The Septuagint Version of the Old Testament* (2 vols.; London: Samuel Bagster and Sons, 1844) renders: "Hast thou not sinned if thou hast brought it rightly, but not rightly divided it? be still, unto thee shall be his submission, and thou shalt rule over him."

[49] Nevertheless, all of the editions of the LXX that I have seen connect ἥμαρτες with what precedes, and place a question mark after ἥμαρτες.

It happens that the relation between the LXX and the MT is especially problematic precisely at the juncture of διέλης and ἥμαρτες.[50] Of course, Philo was blissfully unaware of what the Hebrew might have said. But in fact the exact understanding of Gen 4:7, in whatever language, is very controversial. I will note here merely that, for example, looking at the Hebrew we see that the grammatical relationship of שְׂאֵת (which corresponds to the LXX's προσενέγκης) is cited as one of the five ambiguities in the Torah.[51] Now, the understanding of the Hebrew does not tell us how the Greek should be understood, but it is not clear to me why it should not be possible to start a fresh clause with the reference to sin within the Greek, which is especially obscure.[52] In any case, it seems indisputable that Philo so read the text.

In fact, the interpretation (i.e., what we call punctuation) that Philo chooses is also adopted in the *Apostolic Constitutions* (of perhaps the fourth century C.E.).[53] There we read (2.16.4):

τοιοῦτον γάρ τι ὑπεμφαίνει καὶ τὸ ἐν τῇ Γενέσει εἰρημένον τῷ Κάιν· ἥμαρτες; ἡσύχασον· τοῦτ᾽ ἔστι μὴ προσθῇς.[54]

There can hardly be any doubt that here, whatever the precise understanding of these words might be, we have the separation of ἥμαρτες from the preceding clause in Gen 4:7. Moreover, if we keep in mind that the punctuation here is editorial, it seems perfectly reasonable to take ἥμαρτες not as a question (as in the LXX editions and the Greek above), but as an assertion. (Even viewed as a question, it is clearly a *rhetorical* question, and thus basically a statement in force.) And in fact the translation in the *Ante-Nicene Fathers* volume reads:

[50] See the discussion by Wevers, *Notes on the Greek Text of Genesis* (SBLSCS 35; Atlanta: Scholars Press, 1993), 55.

[51] See *b. Yoma* 52a–b, *Mekilta* 17.9, and *Song of Songs Rabbah* 1.2.1; the five places are not the same everywhere. Of course, whichever ones are chosen, presumably they are considered to be five especially problematic ambiguities.

[52] See the remarks by Marguerite Harl, *La Bible d'Alexandrie* 1: *La Genèse* (2nd ed.; Paris: Éditions du Cerf, 1994), 114–15, who says: "Ce verset est particulièrement difficile." She refers to Philo's comments at *Agr.* 127–30 and *QG* 1.66, but does not discuss his breaking the text before ἥμαρτες.

[53] This is cited by Harl, *La Bible d'Alexandrie*, 1.114.

[54] The Greek text may be found in P. A. de Lagarde, ed., *Constitutiones apostolorum* (Leipzig and London: B. G. Teubner and Williams & Norgate, 1862), 30; Wilhelm Ültzen, ed., *Constitutiones apostolicae* (Schwerin and Rostock: Stiller, 1853), 26; Franz Xaver Funk, ed., *Didascalia et Constitutiones apostolorum* 1 (Paderborn: Ferdinand Schoeningh, 1905), 61 and 63; and Marcel Metzger, ed., *Les Constitutions apostoliques* (SC 320; Paris: Éditions du Cerf, 1985), 186. The editions agree on all essential points.

Of this sort of declaration is that which is said in the book of Genesis to Cain: "Thou hast sinned; be quiet;" that is, do not go on in sin.

After all, the original text of the *Apostolic Constitutions*, wherever and whenever that might have existed, probably did not have punctuation, and in any case the LXX manuscript(s) that are quoted by it would fairly certainly not have had punctuation. We could thus take the comment at *Apos. Con.* 2.16.4 as supporting Philo's understanding of the Greek. And an English translation might run as follows:

> Not, if thou offerest rightly, but dost not rightly distinguish; thou hast sinned, be still; to thee is his return, and thou shalt rule over him.[55]

This is exceptionally difficult, but something more or less like it seems to be required by Philo's citations of the Greek.

Agr. 148: Philo presents here a quotation from Deut 20:5b–7 (Τίς ὁ ἄνθρωπος . . . λήψεται αὐτήν). Philo's citation agrees mostly with the LXX, but there are what appear to be some simplifying alterations.[56]

Deut 20:5b–7

LXX	Philo
Τίς ὁ ἄνθρωπος ὁ οἰκοδομήσας οἰκίαν καινὴν καὶ οὐκ ἐνεκαίνισεν αὐτήν;	Τίς ὁ ἄνθρωπος ὁ οἰκοδομήσας οἰκίαν καινὴν καὶ οὐκ ἐνεκαίνισεν αὐτήν;
. . .	. . .
⁶ καὶ τίς ὁ ἄνθρωπος, ὅστις ἐφύτευσεν ἀμπελῶνα . . .	⁶ καὶ τίς ὃς ἐφύτευσεν ἀμπελῶνα . . .
⁷ καὶ τίς ὁ ἄνθρωπος, ὅστις μεμνήστευται γυναῖκα . . . λήμψεται αὐτήν.	⁷ καὶ τίς ἐμνηστεύσατο γυναῖκα . . . λήψεται αὐτήν.

Philo follows the LXX closely. However, at the beginning of vss. 6 and 7 he simplifies the construction slightly by writing (in vs. 6) ὅς for ὁ ἄνθρωπος ὅστις and (in vs. 7) omitting ὁ ἄνθρωπος ὅστις altogether. The omission at vs. 7 could have been caused by a scribal leap (και τις ο ανθρωπος οστις), but there seems to be no evident cause of the variation at vs. 6. So I am inclined to think that we have Philo's own simplification at both places, which

---

[55] I have here pieced together the translations found in PLCL of the citations from *Agr.* 127, *Sobr.* 50, *Mut.* 195, and *QG* 1.66. The opening "not" is especially obscure. At *Agr.* 127 we find: "<All is> not <well>, if . . . ."

[56] Runia calls this quotation "verbatim" ("Structure," p. 6).

avoids the repetition of ὁ ἄνθρωπος from vs. 5. The writing of λήψεται for λήμψεται at the end of the citation (where most LXX manuscripts agree) probably reflects Philo's preference for Attic forms.[57]

Agr. 172, citing Deut 8:18, which reads: καὶ μνησθήσῃ κυρίου τοῦ θεοῦ σου, ὅτι αὐτός σοι δίδωσιν ἰσχὺν τοῦ ποιῆσαι δύναμιν. Philo paraphrases these words by writing (with a presumably stylistically preferable participle instead of parataxis):

> ἀλλὰ μνησθῆναι θεοῦ τοῦ διδόντος ἰσχὺν ποιῆσαι δύναμιν.

Wendland places the entire phrase after ἀλλά within quotation marks, but it is difficult to imagine that Philo intended this to be a direct quotation. What would seem to be more appropriate would be to edit:

> ἀλλὰ μνησθῆναι θεοῦ τοῦ διδόντος "ἰσχὺν ποιῆσαι δύναμιν."

Now, Philo cites the entire clause more precisely at *Sacr.* 56, beginning with Deut 8:17 and continuing:

> μὴ εἴπῃς, φησίν, ἡ ἰσχύς μου ἢ τὸ κράτος τῆς χειρός μου ἐποίησέ μοι πᾶσαν τὴν δύναμιν ταύτην· ἀλλὰ μνείᾳ μνησθήσῃ κυρίου τοῦ θεοῦ σου τοῦ διδόντος σοι ἰσχὺν ποιῆσαι δύναμιν.

Cohn has all of this except for φησίν within quotation marks. However, Deut 8:17–18a reads:

> μὴ εἴπῃς ἐν τῇ καρδίᾳ σου ἡ ἰσχύς μου καὶ τὸ κράτος τῆς χειρός μου ἐποίησέν μοι τὴν δύναμιν τὴν μεγάλην ταύτην· καὶ μνησθήσῃ κυρίου τοῦ θεοῦ σου, ὅτι αὐτός σοι δίδωσιν ἰσχὺν τοῦ ποιῆσαι δύναμιν.

Now, this is the only citation in Philo of Deut 8:17, and we see that the quotation diverges from the LXX at several places, namely:

ἐν τῇ καρδίᾳ σου	om. Philo (no LXX witness)
καί	ἤ Philo (no LXX witness)
τὴν μεγάλην	om. Philo (LXX 426ᵗˣᵗ 767 321* Arab) = MT

I would ascribe the omission of ἐν τῇ καρδίᾳ σου to Philo's retouching (here omitting) as he begins the quotation; he no doubt saw it as redundant after

[57] See the discussion by Thackeray, *A Grammar of the Old Testament in Greek* 1.108–9, according to which the forms without μ are earliest, the forms with μ dominated during the first four centuries C.E., and the forms without μ then returned. The early LXX majuscules are from the period that preferred the μ. The LXX apparatus reads: λημψεται A B F V 82 56* Wˡ 407´ : ληψεται Fᵇ rell.

μὴ εἴπῃς. The shift from καί to ἤ is either a slip or just another slight rewording. However, the omission of τὴν μεγάλην could have been caused by a scribal leap:

την δυναμιν την μεγαλην ταυτην

At least, this seems more plausible to me than that Philo was correcting toward the MT. Of course, this leap could have been made at any one of several places: in the manuscript of Deuteronomy that Philo had at hand, by Philo (or his amanuensis) when copying that manuscript, or at an early stage within the manuscript tradition of Philo. The scattered support for the omission among LXX witnesses shows, I believe, that such a leap could be made independently by more than one scribe.

The quotation at *Sacr.* 56 deserves a close examination because it shares the discrepancy from the LXX found at *Agr.* 172, namely τοῦ διδόντος for ὅτι αὐτός σοι δίδωσιν. Now, it seems implausible that at *Sacr.* 56 Philo would cite almost precisely (except for two omissions and one very minor shift) all of vs. 17, would cite almost precisely (except for the addition of μνείᾳ) the beginning of vs. 18a, and would cite almost precisely (except for the omission of τοῦ) the end of vs. 18a, but would drastically paraphrase the middle portion of vs. 18a. Yet this is what we see. And this paraphrase is exactly what we find at *Agr.* 172, except that there σοι is also omitted.[58]

It would thus be tempting to think that, contrary to all of the other LXX witnesses, Philo actually found τοῦ διδόντος (σοι) in his copy of the LXX of Deuteronomy. But then we find that he cites a text much closer to the usual LXX at *Virt.* 165, at least in so far as it has δίδωσιν, where he cites the second part of vs. 18a:

οὗτος γάρ σοι, φησί, δίδωσιν ἰσχὺν ποιῆσαι δύναμιν.[59]

Although this may still not be verbatim, Cohn places everything except φησί within quotation marks:[60]

"οὗτος γάρ σοι," φησί, "δίδωσιν ἰσχὺν ποιῆσαι δύναμιν."

But this is not quite correct, I believe. The γάρ is certainly Philo's own addition in order to tie the quotation with what has gone before in Philo's exposition. Thus, one should write:

---

[58] At *Sacr.* 56 G omits σοι; perhaps this is correct, and the other manuscripts have added σοι by assimilation to the LXX.
[59] Here the manuscript S writes οὕτως and transposes to ἰσχὺν δίδωσι.
[60] He also neglects the commas around φησί.

"οὗτος" γάρ "σοι," φησί, "δίδωσιν ἰσχὺν ποιῆσαι δύναμιν."

Here Philo differs from the LXX (i.e., the Göttingen text) in having οὗτος for αὐτός. And again οὗτος has respectable support in the LXX, being read by V O⁻⁴²⁶ *b d* 54ʹ-75ʹ-767 *t* Sa¹ ² Syh ᴸᵃᵗcod 100, as well as by Clement (*Strom.* 2.96.3).⁶¹ Wevers asserts that "ουτος seems to be a Byz [i.e., Byzantine] reading, whereas αὐτός is LXX."⁶² But the fact that the reading is found already in Philo suggests that it was circulating at an early period.

In any event, it is clear from these citations that Philo's text omitted τοῦ before ποιῆσαι (there is no variation in the manuscripts at any of the three places).⁶³ The only support cited in the Göttingen Septuagint for the omission of τοῦ is Clement, *Strom.* 2.96.3.⁶⁴ But the explanation of this agreement as well as the earlier one with οὗτος is that Clement was using Philo's *Virt.*, and did not bother to check the biblical text itself, but simply wrote what Philo wrote.⁶⁵

Finally, we should edit at *Sacr.* 56:

ἀλλὰ μνείᾳ "μνησθήσῃ κυρίου τοῦ θεοῦ σου" τοῦ διδόντος σοι "ἰσχὺν ποιῆσαι δύναμιν."

I have placed the opening two words here outside the quotation marks. There is no support within the LXX tradition for adding μνείᾳ, so this is probably Philo's own paraphrastic addition, perhaps as a recollection of Deut. 7:18 (μνείᾳ μνησθήσῃ),⁶⁶ although here it shows up in the middle of an extended quotation of Deut 8:17–18.

Returning to *Agr.* 172, we may view the transformation of the LXX's μνησθήσῃ into μνησθῆναι as part of Philo's alteration within the context, more specifically in order to form a parallel to the earlier infinitive

---

⁶¹ Two manuscripts (458–767) read ουτως, as does the Philonic manuscript S, and one manuscript (44) has ουτοι. These are all witnesses to the reading ουτος. The Göttingen Septuagint omits reference to *Virt.* 165 at this variation unit.

⁶² *Notes on the Greek Text of Deuteronomy*, 155 (omitting the accent and breathing on ουτος).

⁶³ The absence of the article before the infinitive would thus agree with what is usual in Deuteronomy; see Wevers, *Text History of the Greek Deuteronomy*, 102–3, who cites Philo's omission.

⁶⁴ This is found in the GCS edition at 2.165; the Göttingen Septuagint cites Clement's citation as "III 165."

⁶⁵ On Clement's use of Philo's *Virt.*, see my "The Text of Philo's *De virtutibus*," SPhA 18 (2006): 80–81.

⁶⁶ The MT, with its simple וְזָכַרְתָּ, provides no basis for such an addition.

ἀναγράψαι.[67] Similarly, the change from the indicative δίδωσι (as Philo quotes at *Virt.* 165) to διδόντος shifts from the ὅτι clause of the LXX.

We turn to the final point. Where the LXX has κυρίου τοῦ θεοῦ σου (rendering the MT's יְהוָה אֱלֹהֶיךָ) we find in Philo a variety of readings:

Agr. 172	θεοῦ	omnes codices
Sacr. 56	κυρίου τοῦ θεοῦ σου	Pap HP = LXX rell
	κυρίου	UF
	κυρίου τοῦ θεοῦ	MAG = LXX z⁻⁸³ ⁶³⁰ᶜ

The reading of UF at *Sacr.* 56 is very curious.[68] One thinks of UF as representing an aberrant text that is influenced by Aquila (for whom there is no evidence at Deut 8:18), but here a literal translation (of the MT, at any rate) would surely be κυρίου τοῦ θεοῦ σου, as found in Pap HP. Perhaps one should postulate a scribal leap (κυριου του θεου σου του).[69] The omission of σου may similarly be explained (θεου σου).[70] But then the universally attested reading at *Agr.* 172 is also very puzzling. Presumably this is also Philo's paraphrasing. For his purposes at the moment the phrase "the Lord your God" was of no interest to him, and so he was content simply to refer to "God."

Although we have here only a small sample of Philo's quotation technique, we have perhaps seen enough to draw some conclusions. One must always

[67] For what it is worth, note that Mangey, who indicates biblical quotations not by introducing quotation marks into the Greek but by italicizing the corresponding Latin translation, does not italicize "memores simus" here, but begins the quotation by italicizing "Dei" corresponding to θεοῦ.

[68] The Göttingen Septuagint cites the Arabic version in support of the Greek of UF, and so one wonders if this might be something other than a coincidental agreement. Now, Wevers did extensive investigation into the Arabic manuscripts (see the Göttingen Genesis, 44–46), and I have not tried to check his material. But the printed sources that I did check do not confirm this reading. P. A. Lagarde, *Materialien zur Kritik und Geschichte des Pentateuchs* (Leipzig: Teubner, 1867), 1.201, prints at this place: ʾallaha rabbika, which *very* literally would correspond to θεοῦ τοῦ κυρίου σου. This would not in any case support UF's κυρίου. But in fact this inversion seems to be the regular representation there of the combination κυρίου τοῦ θεοῦ σου. The Arabic text in the Walton Polyglot, i.e., Brian Walton, ed. *Biblia sacra polyglotta* (London: Rycroft, 1653–57), 1.755, has the same reading. (Placing a possessive pronoun after "Allah" in Arabic would be as solecistic as modifying the Tetragrammaton in Hebrew.) However, the American Bible Society's edition of the Arabic Bible (1994) translates ʾarrabba ʾilāhaka, which precisely corresponds to κυρίου τοῦ θεοῦ σου.

[69] Within manuscripts written using *nomina sacra* the leap would be: K̄Ȳ ΤΟΥ Θ̄Ȳ ΣΟΥ ΤΟΥ.

[70] Or again more precisely: Θ̄Ȳ ΣΟΥ.

keep in mind that Philo is reading and writing Greek without accents, breathings, or punctuation marks. Of course, he also does not have quotation marks at his disposal, and so their placement by editors must be carefully checked.[71] Philo basically uses the LXX, but omits words that seem superfluous (e.g., ὁ ἄνθρωπος at Deut 20:5b–7) or irrelevant to his discussion (e.g., καὶ ἐμεθύσθη at Gen 9:21),[72] adds words for clarification of grammar (e.g., εἶναι at Gen 9:20), rewrites constructions (e.g., δίδωσιν to διδόντος at Deut 8:18), and shifts to preferred grammatical forms (e.g., from γενηθήτω to γενέσθω in Gen 1:3 and elsewhere). It may seem puzzling that Philo feels such freedom in dealing with the sacred text. But that is a topic for another occasion.

San Francisco

---

[71] This is a point often made by Peter Katz.
[72] That is, if this is indeed Philo's omission rather than his scribes.

The Studia Philonica Annual 22 (2010) 131–138

OF TWO MINDS: PHILO *ON CULTIVATION*

DAVID KONSTAN

In this paper, I argue that Philo's engagement with the theme of doubling in *De agricultura*, inspired by his close exegesis of passages in Genesis and elsewhere to which he applied the Platonic method of *diairesis* or division, led him to a new conception of the dual nature of the human mind beyond anything that Plato or other classical Greek philosophers had suggested. I begin by tracing Philo's application of the method of division, then note his reservations about taking it to excess (in this respect he is in accord with Stoic thinkers of the Roman period), and finally indicate the novel nature of the conclusions that he reaches.

Farmer vs. Worker of the Land

With his usual acumen, Philo noticed that the word γεωργός occurs for the first time in Gen 9:20, applied to Noah after the flood receded, and he wonders why this should be so, especially since Cain, as he recalled (*Agr.* 20–22; cf. *QG* 2.66), had been described as ἐργαζόμενος τὴν γήν or "working the earth" (Gen 4:2; cf. 4:12). Indeed, the expulsion of man from Eden resulted precisely in the requirement to till the earth (Gen 3:23). To Philo's sharp eye, Noah cannot have been the first human being to work the ground, as the verb ἤρξατο might seem to imply (cf. the RSV translation, "Noah was the first tiller of the soil"), and so there must be another explanation—or in fact, two, as we shall see. His first move, then, is to draw a distinction between working the earth and being a true γεωγός or "farmer."[1]

---

[1] Philo's insertion of εἶναι into the Septuagint text (reading καὶ ἤρξατο Νῶε ἄνθρωπος γεωγός γῆς εἶναι) may conceivably have been motivated by his desire to make clear his own interpretation of the meaning of ἤρξατο here; for full discussion of the textual tradition, see James R. Royse, "The Biblical Text in Philo's *De agricultura*," in this volume. Philo may well have been responding here to critics who pointed up the ostensible inconsistency in calling Noah the first farmer; for the scholarly context in which Philo was writing, with its particular debt to the Alexandrian commentary tradition that developed above all around

Philo's strategy is clear enough. He discriminates between being a mere hired laborer, who works the earth for profit, and a true cultivator of the soil, who serves the art or principle of agriculture and hence looks to improve the land entrusted to his care.[2] This conception of the role of an artisan as expert in an art or τέχνη is an old one, and its explicit articulation goes back at least to Plato, with medicine and the training of horses being good examples: health is the goal or function (ἔργον) of the doctor's art, just as the well-being of the horse is the object of the horse-trainer (cf. *Ap.* 25A–B; *Charm.* 170C; *Gorg.* 503D–E, etc.).[3] The next move is, of course, typical of Philo: rather than see horsemanship or agriculture as arts comparable to that of the lawgiver, he reads mentions of these skills in the Bible as allegories for the care of the spirit.[4] Thus, Noah, as the genuine cultivator, nourishes the fruitbearing plants whose product is the virtues, uproots weeds and noxious plants which give rise to vices, and makes good use of unproductive but harmless growth to build fences (14–19). By a nice coincidence, Philo found in Stoic texts a parallel conceit, according to which the threefold division of Stoic science into physics, ethics, and logic was compared to a field, with logic serving precisely as the hedge that protects the cultivated area.[5] This conception suited Philo's purpose to a tee.

So far, so good: but Philo decided to assign yet another meaning to the distinction that he drew, and this was to have significant consequences. For a true farmer now becomes not only the person who takes good care of the

---

the Homeric epics, see Maren R. Niehoff, "Homeric Scholarship and Bible Exegesis in Ancient Alexandria: Evidence from Philo's 'Quarrelsome' Colleagues," *Classical Quarterly* 57 (2007), 166–182.

[2] See R. G. Hamerton-Kelly, "Some Techniques of Composition in Philo's *Allegorical Commentary* with Special Reference to *De agricultura*: A Study in the Hellenistic Midrash," in R. G. Hamerton-Kelly and R. Scroggs, eds., *Jews, Greeks and Christians: Religious Cultures in Late Antiquity: Essays in Honor of W. D. Davies* (Leiden: Studies in Judaism in Late Antiquity 21, 1976), 45–56, who observes that Philo follows Plato in the art of *diairesis*, but he "understands the art of dividing and distinguishing in a special way" (p. 54).

[3] See in general Anne Balansard, *Techné dans les dialogues de Platon* (Sankt Augustin: Academia Verlag, 2001).

[4] For background on allegory, see Jean Pépin, *Mythe et allégorie: Les origines grecques et les contestations judéo-chrétiennes* 3rd ed. (Paris: Études Augustiniennes, 1981); David Dawson, *Allegorical Readers and Cultural Revision in Ancient Alexandria* (Berkeley: University of California Press, 1992); Ilaria Ramelli, *Allegoria: I, L'età classica*, in collaboration with G. Lucchetta, Introduction by R. Radice (Milan: Vita e Pensiero, 2004); Peter Struck, *Birth of the Symbol: Ancient Readers at the Limits of Their Texts* (Princeton: Princeton University Press; 2004).

[5] For the tripartite division of philosophy into logic, physics, and ethics, see Diogenes Laertius 7.39–40 = *SVF* 2.37; Philo mentions it also at *Leg.* 1.57, *Virt.* 8, and elsewhere. On philosophy conceived more particularly as a field, see Sextus Empiricus *Adv. Math.* 7.17 = *SVF* 2.38; this is clearly the inspiration for Philo's exegesis here.

crops, insuring that nourishing fruit—that is, virtues—are produced, and those in abundance, whereas the mere tiller looks only to his profit; rather, the farmer in this second explanation cultivates the soul, whereas the tiller looks only to the body and its pleasures (20–22)—a distinction motivated by the contrast between Noah and Cain.[6] On this interpretation, the worker of the earth fosters the growth of the pleasures, which are rooted in the body: he is not just artless, as opposed to the true or expert γεωργός, but downright wicked (φαῦλος, 22), a producer of carnal delights rather than spiritual virtues. The difference is important, and the two interpretations cannot, I think, be wholly reconciled. It is one thing to lack science, another to apply it—or a perverse version of it—to the wrong ends. Philo conjures up a picture of two types of craftsman of humanity, as it were: one works to the betterment of the moral self, while the other serves the somatic appetites. Here is prefigured the novel conception of the mind or self that Philo intimates in this treatise.

Herdsman vs. Tender of Sheep

Having drawn this subtle, and complex, distinction between the farmer and the worker of the ground, Philo proceeds to identify other such contrasts, and the next one he develops is that between the mere tender of sheep and the true shepherd or herdsman (26–66). Here too, of course, he had good precedents in the Greek tradition: a shepherd cares for the well-being of the flock, whereas an overseer of sheep has no interest in their well-being, but merely exploits them for his own gain.[7] But once again, Philo complicates the image, by allegorizing the flock not simply as the subjects of a monarch, who is a good king if he looks to their welfare, and a bad one if he exploits them for his own benefit, but also by suggesting that the good pastor keeps his sheep trim and fit, whereas the mere keeper of sheep overindulges them, with the result that they grow fat and cease to heed his bidding.

---

[6] For the contrast between these two figures, see Hindy Najman, "Cain and Abel as Character Traits: A Study in Allegorical Typology of Philo of Alexandria," in Gerard P. Luttikhuizen, *Eve's Children: The Biblical Stories Retold and Interpreted in Jewish and Christian Traditions* (Themes in Biblical Narrative 5; Boston, MA: Brill, 2003).

[7] On the role of the good shepherd in ancient sources generally, see Nicholas Cachia, *The Image of the Good Shepherd as a Source for the Spirituality of the Ministerial Priesthood* (Rome: Pontificia Università Gregoriana, 1997), 27–112, esp. pp. 35–36 on the classical Greek background, and pp. 36–37 on Philo. In Xenophon *Mem.* 3.2, Socrates explains the Homeric formula "shepherd of the people" (ποιμένα λαῶν), applied to Agamemon, as a reference to his duty to care for those he rules the way a shepherd does for his flocks; cf. Xen. *Cyr.* 8.2.14; see also Plato *Resp.* 343–45, *Pol.* 267–68, 275.

These spoiled animals represent the pleasures which the bad herdsman allows to run riot. Insofar as the herdsman, then, stands for the rational part of the soul, in contradistinction to the bodily pleasures or appetites, we have a contrast not simply between reason and passion, but between two kinds or states of reason: one is the intelligence of the wise, who recognize that their relation to the body is temporary, and that they must control its appetites; the other intelligence has surrendered to the body, and ministers to its needs and pleasures. Once again, the keeper of the flocks does not simply lack the skill of the true shepherd, nor does he, strictly speaking, exploit his flock, but he has placed himself in the service of the animals which—in their metaphorical role as the passions—he is supposed to dominate.

Horseman vs. Rider

The final distinction that Philo draws and supports with biblical citations—and this latter, to be sure, is the harder part—is that between the true horseman and the mere rider (67–123). Once more, this can be taken to be a contrast between possessing real skill in regard to horses, which involves the proper care and training of them, and an absence of art, as a result of which the horses run wild and deteriorate. A proper trainer, moreover, looks to the horses' good, whereas the incompetent horseman seeks only his comfort and advantage, we may suppose, and so further damages the beasts in his care. On an allegorical level, it is impossible, of course, not to think of Plato's image, in the *Phaedrus* (256A–254E), of the soul as a charioteer holding the reins on two horses, one representing the appetites, the other the θυμός or spirited element in the soul. The charioteer, in turn, represents reason or λόγος (253E), which must control the steeds. But once again, and perhaps here most clearly, Philo departs from the Platonic model by doubling the riders or charioteers. In Plato's account, reason or the mind either succeeds or fails in reining in the refractory horses, and more particularly the one representing the appetites. Philo, however, though he speaks of the driver without skill (ἄνευ τέχνης, 77), simultaneously equates the poor rider with foolishness (ἀφροσύνη), the opposite of φρόνησις. Foolishness, however, is not simply an absence or deprivation, but a kind of negative or perverted reasoning in its own right. Thus, Philo insists that one must pay no heed to the θυμός and desires and passions, and to the λογισμοί—"reasonings" or "rationalizations"—that ride upon them (78).[8] The corrupted mind is that which has yielded to the passions, and hence hates virtue and delights in pleasure and wrongdoing (83), and this charioteer deserves to be overturned and lose the race, and indeed to be thoroughly extirpated. The problem with the intellect, then, is not simply that it is stronger or weaker, purer or more contaminated by the bodily affections and hence less able to resist and dominate them. It is rather that there are two kinds of intellect, one wise and capable, while the other caters to the passions and appetites, having become their servant rather than their master.

The Art of Making Distinctions

Although Philo's divisions are compatible with a differentiation between greater and lesser skill in husbandry, shepherding, and horsemanship, he has in each case pushed them further, and installed something like a double nature of the mind, one good, the other bad. The good, which looks to the virtues and higher things, is to be preserved, while the bad is to be exterminated. Philo found support for this interpretation in various passages of the Bible, such as Exod 15:1 (cited in 82), where both the horse and the rider are cast into the sea. But the effect is to suggest not only a conflict within the self between the mind and the lower passions and appetites, but a clash between good and evil, the Noahs and the Cains of this world, or their allegorical representatives—hypostasizations of healthy and unhealthy reason within the soul.

In the same spirit of *dédoublement*, Philo introduces yet another distinction between good and bad serpents, the bad being the one that seduced Eve, whereas the good serpent is the bronze one that Moses created. Such divisions are necessary, of course; thus, Philo interprets the name Dan to mean "judgment" or "distinction" (κρίσις, 95), which accurately examines and discriminates the parts of the soul. So, too, Philo explains that "one must not confound and mix everything up," without division and distinction (ἄνευ τομῆς καὶ διαιρέσεως) but one must rather reason by way of separation (διαστολή, 128–29).

Nevertheless, Philo also worries about an excessive passion for logical division, and more particularly a waste of energy on minute distinctions that have no bearing on the virtuous life. In this, he is at one with Stoics such as Epictetus. Thomas Bénatouïl observes that "Epictète n'expose jamais l'utilité de la philosophie théorique sans rappeler ainsi ses dangers:

---

[8] There is a textual problem here, but it does not bear on the present question.

elle constitue un détour nécessaire pour devenir philosophe mais, du même coup, elle détourne très souvent les jeunes philosophes de leur objectif initial, au profit des plaisirs vains de la théorie et au détriment de la mise en oeuvre des principes, seul activité dont on peut à bon droit être fier."[9] Philo had already signalled his suspicion of such useless accuracy near the beginning of the treatise, where he criticized those aspects of dialectics and geometry that make no contribution to moral improvement (13), but he returns to it in earnest in what is generally taken to be the second part of the essay, where he signals a turn from the discussion of horsemen, shepherds, and farmers to something new (124–25).[10]

Philo begins by attending to the significance of the word ἤρξατο, which he interprets as meaning that Noah had made a beginning of his career as a farmer or γεωργός, but did not fully achieve excellence in it. Now, given the distinction that Philo draws between the γεωργός and the tiller of the earth, he could perfectly well have understood the phrase to mean that Noah was indeed the first farmer in the strict sense of the term. Inasmuch, however, as Noah turns at once to the cultivation of the vine, and to getting drunk on its fruits into the bargain, it is clear that he still falls something short of complete virtue, and Philo naturally finds in the text an indication of this deficiency.[11] Philo takes up in the sequel the dangers that beset a novice in the sciences, above all in relation to making distinctions—the core theme of the treatise as a whole. One must, he insists, know how to resolve ambiguities (136), but not in matters that have no bearing on the acquisition of virtue (142), as sophists do, who seek only to display their ingenuity. Those still on the path to wisdom, but who have not yet achieved it, are most vulnerable to this kind of distraction, and likely to fall into error by applying their wits in the wrong way. Here again, Philo is in perfect accord with the Stoic view, as expressed by Epictetus.

Philo offers as an illustration of this danger the interpretation of the injunction, in Deut 20:5–7, not to recruit in battle those men who have embarked upon, but not completed, projects such as building a house or

---

[9] *Les Stoïciens III: Musonius, Épictète, Marc Aurèle* (Paris: Les Belles Lettres, 2009), 137; cf. Epictetus *Disc* 1.7.32–33, 2.1.38, 2.3.3–5. 3.6.3, etc.

[10] For the division of the essay into two principal parts (sections 1–123 and 124–81), see David Runia's article in this volume.

[11] In citing the passage from Genesis, which in the Septuagint reads καὶ ἐμεθύσθη καὶ ἐγυμνώθη ἐν τῷ οἴκῳ αὐτοῦ, Philo omits the words καὶ ἐγυμνώθη. I suspect that he did so in order to keep the focus on Noah's activity as a husbandman, who plants the vine and then gets drunk on the grape; his nakedness, which looks forward to the consequences of his inebriation, are not relevant to the immediate context. But see Royse in this volume for a different view.

planting a vineyard,[12] a passage he comments on also in *De virtutibus*, where he defends Moses' rule as a sign of his brilliance as a strategist on the grounds that such men will have their minds on their pending undertakings back home rather than on battle (27–33).[13] Here in *De agricultura*, however, Philo worries about a too literal interpretation of the exemption, which is exposed to captious interpretations by sophists, and so he takes refuge in the allegorical sense, arguing that what it really means is that one must bring the beginnings of moral endeavor to completion, so as to achieve the happiness that comes with complete virtue (157). What is more, those who are still progressing toward virtue are vulnerable to the sophisms of professional philosophers, and so should avoid debates and confrontations with them—this, Philo says, is precisely Moses' message, in counselling those who are at the beginning of an enterprise to keep away from battle (165–66).

In this way, Philo conveys the lesson that drawing correct distinctions, such as he does in the first part of the treatise, is crucial, but at the same time carries risks and is not an activity for novices, who can easily be deceived by the tricks of practised sophists. Noah himself serves as a case study in the difference between a true farmer and a mere tiller, and simultaneously as an object lesson in why one needs to progress far in order to attain a secure grip on virtue. The mind must indeed be sharpened if it is to know how to deal with specious arguments; but this acuteness is not an end in itself, and can, if not properly directed, serve to justify immoral rather than virtuous behavior. The wisdom of the philosophers alone is not sufficient to avoid this pitfall.

For in fact—and this is the deeper point of the treatise—there is not just art and the lack of it, but two kinds of intelligence, or at least intelligence in the service of opposite ends: the good husbandman or shepherd not only has the proper skill and training, but applies his knowledge to cultivating virtue and not to providing the passions and appetites with all that they might desire, and finding plausible excuses for doing so. But if the intellect can thus be led astray, and if the attainment of virtue is not simply a matter of acquiring more understanding but also of shunning, especially during the process of learning and development, the fallacious distinctions prof-

[12] David Runia, in "The Structure of Philo's Allegorical Treatise *De agricultura*" (this volume), suggests that the passage in Deuteronomy may have occurred to Philo as a result of the exact verbal echo of the phrase ἐφύτευσεν ἀμπελῶνα that is found in the main biblical lemma of Gen 9:20. This would again be evidence of Philo's strict focus on cultivation, which may have induced him to omit the phrase καὶ ἐγυμνώθη in his citation of the lemma.

[13] For discussion, see David Konstan, "Philo's *De virtutibus* in the Perspective of Classical Greek Philosophy," *The Studia Philonica Annual* 18 (2006), 59–72, esp. p. 61.

fered by cunning sophists, then wit alone may not be sufficient to guide a person to virtue. The mere rider, as opposed to the horseman, has his skill as well, and we must hope that he—that is, the wrong intelligence within us—tumbles and is defeated in the race.

The alternative to bad philosophy, as practiced by the sophists and their allies within us, that is, the tiller and the keeper of sheep and the rider, is the careful exegesis of the true meaning of the Scriptures, which is what distinguishes Philo's method from the oversubtle cavils of the philosophers. Or rather, this, and God's assistance. Thus, at the conclusion to the first part of the treatise, Philo affirms (123): "Moses says that he is 'awaiting the salvation which comes from God'" [Gen 49:18]; and at the end of the second section he reminds the reader (180): "It is, therefore, a very rare thing when God gives to any one to keep his life in a steady course from the beginning to the end."

Given the split nature of the self, including the mind, reason alone can carry one just so far in the pursuit of virtue, for it is potentially at the mercy of its Doppelgänger, the mere tiller who is Cain. Here is where Philo parts company with his Platonic and Stoic predecessors, and expresses the need for God's guidance, over and above philosophy, if one is to achieve a good life. If, in *De agricultura*, Philo sketched out a new conception of the radically divided self, it dovetailed perfectly with his vision of God's grace in the attainment of a moral life.[14]

Brown University

---

[14] See David T. Runia, *Philo of Alexandria and the Timaeus of Plato* (Leiden: Brill, 1986), who observes (p. 133) in connection with the Creation: "Plato's doctrine is now explicitly [sc. at *Leg.* 3.78] attributed to Moses, but is at the same time connected with the unPlatonic theme of God's grace. Indeed the goodness and the grace of God are so closely associated in Philo's mind that the word χάρις in the biblical text induces him, without any support from the context, to recollect the creational account." Cf. Peter Frick, *Divine Providence in Philo of Alexandria* (TASJ 77; Tübingen: Mohr Siebeck, 1999).

The Studia Philonica Annual 20 (2008) 139–142

SPECIAL SECTION

THE HYPOTHETICA

INTRODUCTION

GREGORY E. STERLING

The works of Philo circulated in several different regions of the ancient world.[1] The most important region was Philo's native city of Alexandria where many of the treatises passed into Christian hands. Origen took them to Caesarea when he moved to Palestine where they became part of the Episcopal library. Eusebius, a later bishop of Caesarea, gave us a catalogue of the Episcopal library's collection of Philo's works in his *Ecclesiastical History*.[2] Among the single volume works that he listed was a treatise entitled *Concerning the Jews*.[3] The title may not have been the original since the use of περί followed by the name of the people ("concerning x") was a known practice among those who collected works on specific peoples.[4] This probably explains—at least in part—why we do not have an extant work with this title among Philo's treatises.

We may, however, have selections from the work. The treatise is often associated with two fragments that Eusebius preserved and attributed to Philo in his *Preparation for the Gospel*. Eusebius ascribed the first fragment to the first volume of a work of Philo's with the enigmatic title *Hypothetica*. He summarized the fragment by saying that it "argued on behalf of the Jews against their accusers."[5] The text offers a defense of key events (the exodus,

---

[1] For details see David T. Runia, *Philo in Early Christian Literature: A Survey* (CRINT 3.3; Assen: Van Gorcum / Minneapolis: Fortress, 1993), 16–31. He has a useful chart on p. 18 summarizing the basic lines of transmission.

[2] Eusebius, *HE* 2.18.1–8.

[3] Eusebius, *HE* 2.18.6.

[4] E.g., Alexander Polyhistor, *FGrH* 273 frg. 19, named his collection of works that dealt with the Jews Περὶ Ἰουδαίων.

[5] Eusebius, *PE* 8.5.11–7.20.

Moses' qualities as a leader in the wilderness, and the settlement)[6] as well as a summary of the law-code in five sections.[7] The bishop introduced the second fragment as an excerpt "from (Philo's) apology on behalf of the Jews." The fragment sets out the life of the Essenes, a group held out as a model of a virtuous life.[8] The two fragments appear to belong to the same multi-volume work. The content is similar: Eusebius explicitly characterized both as defenses of the Jewish people. He probably substituted "apology on behalf of the Jews" for *Hypothetica* when he introduced the second fragment to highlight its character. He also suggested that the two fragments came from the same work when he divided the Jewish people into two groups in his introduction to the second fragment: those who followed the law literally (an allusion to the summary of the law in frg. 1) and those who advance to a higher level of contemplation (the Essenes of frg. 2). This also gives us an idea of the order of the fragments in the original work.

Should we identify the two fragments in the *Preparation for the Gospel* with the single volume *Concerning the Jews* in the *Ecclesiastical History*? While the difference in the number of the volumes is problematic, it is not unique. Eusebius also placed *On providence* among the one volume treatises in his catalogue,[9] and gave us two fragments in his *Preparation for the Gospel*.[10]

On the basis of the Armenian translation, however, we know that the work originally contained two volumes.[11] It is thus not unreasonable to make the identification, although the differences must be noted.

There are, however, other problems. The nature of the historical treatment of issues in frg. 1 in the *Preparation for the Gospel* is highly unusual. The author played freely with the biblical traditions in offering alternative explanations of events. The author was aware of this freedom and wrote: "I do not think that I should run through the probable events so much on the

---

[6] Euesbius, *PE* 8.6.1–9.

[7] Eusebius, *PE* 8.7.1–20.

[8] Eusebius, *PE* 8.10.19–11.18.

[9] Eusebius, *HE* 2.18.6.

[10] Eusebius, *PE* 7.21; 8.14 (= LCL §§1–72).

[11] J. B. Aucher, *Philonis Judaei Sermones tres hactenus inediti: I. et II. De Providentia et III. De animalibus* (Venice: S. Lazarus, 1822), 1–121. Aucher has been corrected at points in several recent studies: G. Bolognesi, "Problémes d'interprétation de la traduction arménienne du 'De Providentia' de Philon le Juif" in *Armenian Studies: Etudes arméniennes in memoriam Haïg Berbérian* (ed. D. Kouymjian; Lisbon, 1986), 2068–2145 and M. Oliverieri, "Note critico-testuali al *De Providentia* di Filone Alessandrino all luce della traduzione armena," *Eikasmos* 7 (1996): 167–78.

basis of history as on the basis of a certain line of reasoning about them."[12] Similarly, the summary of the laws varies from both the biblical text and Philo's treatments of the same laws in *On Special Laws*. In particular, the summary of the laws in frg. 1 imposed the death penalty in cases where it was not required. The text began ominously with "Is there anything like these or anything similar to these among the former (i.e., Greek laws); anything that seems to be mild and soft; anything that includes argumentation in trials, pleas, delays, assessments, and excuses? None. Everything is clear and straightforward."[13] The severity of the code was uniquely emphasized. These unusual features make it clear that the treatise was not like Philo's three major commentary series: the *Questions and Answers on Genesis and Exodus*, the Allegorical Commentary, or the Exposition of the Law. This has raised the issue of audience. Could this have been addressed to a non-Jewish audience?

The problematic nature of the transmission of the treatise, the highly unusual character of the historical section, the differences in the treatment of the law, the fact that the two fragments are unlike the commentaries are among the factors that have led to doubts about the authenticity of the fragments. Leopold Cohn and Paul Wendland omitted them in their *editio major* of Philo.[14] While F. H. Colson recognized these difficulties, he thought that the Philonic nature of the description of the Sabbath in frg. 1 established the authenticity of the most problematic fragment. He therefore included the work in the Loeb Classical Library edition of Philo.[15] Most scholars have agreed with Colson, although John Barclay has recently challenged its authenticity once again.[16]

The fragmentary nature of the extant work and the unusual character of the specific treatments have contributed to its relative neglect in Philonic scholarship. When Earle Hilgert ran the Philo of Alexandria unit for the Society of Biblical Literature, he made it a practice to devote sessions to relatively neglected treatises of Philo, including a session on the *Hypothetica* at the annual meeting of the society in the fall of 1990. Hilgert presented a paper on the *status quaestionis*, I gave one on the nature and occasion of the

---

[12] Eusebius, *PE* 8.6.5.

[13] Eusebius, *PE* 8.7.1.

[14] Leopold Cohn and Paul Wendland, *Philonis Alexandrini opera quae supersunt* (6 vols.; Berlin: Georg Reimer, 1896–1915).

[15] F.H. Colson, G. H. Whitaker, and R. Marcus, *Philo in Ten Volumes (and Two Supplementary Volumes)* (LCL; Cambridge: Harvard University Press, 1929–62), esp. 9:407–08.

[16] John Barclay, *Against Apion* (Flavius Josephus, Translation and Commentary 10; Leiden: Brill, 2007), 353–55. See my review in *SPhA* 20 (2008): 236–41.

Hypothetica,[17] and George Carras gave one on the nature of the relationship of the law code in Philo and Josephus.[18] I returned to the *Hypothetica* in the spring of 2009 when I taught a doctoral seminar on it at the University of Notre Dame. Among the ten students who participated in the seminar, three addressed issues that help situate the *Hypothetica*. After making the transition from seminar papers to articles suitable for submission, they went through the standard rounds of review. I am grateful to the members of the editorial board who not only accepted the contributions, but more importantly, provided helpful criticisms that improved them. They are presented here in the same spirit that we have routinely presented other special sections based on sessions at meetings of the Society of Biblical Literature. The hope is that they will advance our understanding of the unusual nature of the reasoning in frg. 1 and the setting of this understudied treatise of Philo.

University of Notre Dame

[17] Gregory E. Sterling, "Philo and the Logic of Apologetics: An Analysis of the *Hypothetica*," *SBLSP* 29 (1990): 412–30.

[18] George Carras, "Philo's *Hypothetica*, Josephus' *Contra Apionem* and the Question of Sources," *SBLSP* 29 (1990): 431–50, revised and published as "Dependence or Common Tradition in Philo *Hypothetica* VIII 6.10–7.20 and Josephus *Contra Apionem* 2.190–219," *SPhA* 5 (1993): 24–47.

The Studia Philonica Annual 22 (2010) 143–163

PHILO'S DESCRIPTIONS OF JEWISH SABBATH PRACTICE

DULCINEA BOESENBERG

One of the challenges of studying Philo's immense body of work is the categorization of his corpus. Scholars generally agree on which works belong to his three extensive commentary series, the *Quaestiones et solutiones in Genesim et in Exodum*, the *Allegorical Commentary*, and the 'Exposition of the Law.'[1] More challenging are the texts which do not fit into any of these series, such as the *Hypothetica* and *De vita contemplativa*. Both of these texts have been labeled 'apologetic,' meaning that they function to defend the Jews against their accusers. This paper will test the appropriateness of this label through a comparison of the descriptions of the Sabbath in these two texts in the context of Philo's Sabbath descriptions elsewhere in his corpus. This analysis will demonstrate that the Sabbath description in the *Hypothetica* gives clear indications of its apologetic function, while the Sabbath description in *De vita contemplativa* should raise doubts regarding the appropriateness of describing this text as apologetic.

The Texts

The *Hypothetica* is perhaps the most enigmatic of Philo's preserved writings, due in large part to its fragmentary nature. Two extracts from this text are preserved by Eusebius in his *Praeparatio evangelica*, and we have no way of knowing how much or what Eusebius did not record, nor can we be certain that the two fragments belong to the same work.[2] Nonetheless, the text

---

[1] Jenny Morris, "The Jewish Philosopher Philo," in *The History of the Jewish People in the Age of Jesus Christ* (ed. Emil Schürer; rev. ed. Geza Vermes, Fergus Millar, and Martin Goodman; Edinburgh: T&T Clark, 1987), 809–889, esp. 819–870; James R. Royse, "The Works of Philo," in *The Cambridge Companion to Philo* (ed. Adam Kamesar; Cambridge: Cambridge University Press, 2009), 32–64.

[2] Gregory E. Sterling, "Philo and the Logic of Apologetics: An Analysis of the *Hypothetica*," *SBLSP* 29 (1990): 412–30, esp. 413–418.

appears to be a defense of the Jews against various pagan criticisms. It includes a brief history of the Exodus, a summary of Jewish law, a more detailed treatment of the Sabbath and the sabbatical year, and a brief discourse on the Essenes.

In *De vita contemplativa* Philo describes the Therapeutae, a group of Jews who have separated themselves from society and who devote themselves continually to the study of their ancestral philosophy. At the beginning of the treatise, Philo contrasts the Therapeutae, the exemplars of the contemplative life, with the Essenes, who are devoted to the active life. Philo briefly describes their living conditions and how their days are structured. A large part of this treatise is devoted to a contrast between luxurious Greek banquets and the simple and frugal gatherings of the Therapeutae.

While most scholars identify the *Hypothetica* as apologetic, there is less consensus regarding *De vita contemplativa*. In 1965 Victor Tcherikover challenged the claim that Jewish Alexandrian literature was "mostly a literature of self-defence, polemics and propaganda . . . directed not inwards but outwards."[3] Yet, he maintains that the *Hypothetica*, which he calls "The Apology of the Jews," is apologetic literature directed toward non-Jews, but does not list *De vita contemplativa* among Philo's apologetic works.[4] Similarly, Jenny Morris claims that the *Hypothetica* is "essentially apologetic . . . a defense of the Jews against slanders and unfavourable criticism,"[5] but that it "is, in fact, the *only* work of Philo's which could be described as apologetic."[6] On the other hand, James R. Royse includes both the *Hypothetica* and *De vita contemplativa* in his list of apologetic works.[7] Others also describe *De vita contemplativa* as apologetic. According to David T. Runia, the "aim of the treatise is plainly apologetic," since Philo uses the framework of Greek philosophy to extol the Therapeutae.[8] David M. Hay emphasizes that Philo aims both "to portray [the Therapeutae] in a highly favorable light" and to ridicule paganism by "arguing the moral and religious superiority of Judaism." [9] Joan Taylor places *De vita contemplativa* with *Legatio ad Gaium* in the five volume work *De virtutibus*, and thus assigns *De vita contemplativa* to the "period of political unrest" beginning

[3] "Jewish Apologetic Literature Reconsidered," *Eos* 48/3 (1956): 169–193, esp. 171.
[4] "Jewish Apologetic Literature," 182.
[5] "The Jewish Philosopher Philo," 867.
[6] "The Jewish Philosopher Philo," 867 n. 231. Italics mine.
[7] "The Works of Philo," 34.
[8] "The Reward for Goodness: Philo, *De vita contemplativa* 90," *SPhA* 9 (1997): 3–18, esp. 16.
[9] "Things Philo Said and Did Not Say About the Therapeutae," *SBLSP* 31 (1992): 673–683, esp. 677.

with the Alexandrian riots in 38 c.e. and described in *Legatio ad Gaium*.[10] She understands *De virtutibus* as Philo's preparation for the embassy to Claudius in 41;[11] thus Philo wrote *De vita contemplativa* "as if he is speaking aloud on the virtue of his subjects to an audience not entirely on his side."[12]

Philo's Regular Pattern in his Sabbath Descriptions

In seven of his works, Philo describes Jewish Sabbath practice as he knows it. Some of these descriptions are longer and fuller than others, but all provide a general outline of what the Jews do on the Sabbath. Two of the works, *De vita contemplativa* and the *Hypothetica* have been described above. The other five works are *De vita Mosis*, *De specialibus legibus*, *De decalogo*, *Quod omnis probus liber sit*, and *Legatio ad Gaium*.

De vita Mosis is a two-volume work which includes both stories from Moses' life (biblical and extra-biblical) and some discussion of the Mosaic law. It is commonly thought to have some connection to the "Exposition," but is not properly included in it.[13] Philo likely intended this work as an introduction to the "Exposition."[14] *De decalogo* and *De specialibus legibus* are

---

[10] *Jewish Women Philosophers of First-Century Alexandria: Philo's 'Therapeutae' Reconsidered* (Oxford: Oxford University Press, 2003), 34–38. The identification of the five treatises in Philo's *De virtutibus* is a matter of scholarly debate. Jenny Morris reconstructs the five volume work *De virtutibus* as follows: (1) a general introduction, now lost, (2) a work on Sejanus and Pilate, now lost, (3) *In Flaccum*, (4) *Legatio ad Gaium*, and (5) the Palinode, now lost ("The Jewish Philosopher Philo," 862–863). Pieter W. van der Horst suggests this reconstruction: (1) a work on Pilate, (2) a work on Sejanus, (3) *In Flaccum*, (4) *Legatio ad Gaium*, and (5) the Palinode, though he acknowledges that Morris' suggestion is also a reasonable possibility and that certainty cannot be reached (*Philo's* Flaccus: *The First Pogrom* [Leiden: Brill, 2003], 5–6). Against this, Taylor argues that "*Flacc.* is fundamentally different in theme to *Legat.*," and therefore is not part of *De virtutibus* (*Jewish Women Philosophers*, 37). However, Maren R. Niehoff finds the same theme in both *In Flaccum* and *Legatio ad Gaium* (together with its Palinode)—that God will bring about the downfall of the ruler who treats the Jews poorly (*Philo on Jewish Identity and Culture* [TSAJ 86; Tübingen: Mohr Siebeck, 2001], 39–42).

[11] *Jewish Women Philosophers*, 37.

[12] *Jewish Women Philosophers*, 42.

[13] Morris, "The Jewish Philosopher Philo," 855; Royse, "The Works of Philo," 47; Albert C. Geljon, *Philonic Exegesis in Gregory of Nyssa's* De Vita Moysis (BJS 333; Providence, R.I.: Brown Judaic Studies, 2002), 13–30.

[14] One primary indication of this is that the structure of the Pentateuch which Philo lays out in *De vita Mosis* is very similar to what he describes in *De Abrahamo* and in *De praemiis et poenis*, both of which are certainly included in the 'Exposition.' This point is well supported by Gregory E. Sterling in "'Prolific in Expression and Broad in Thought': An Introduction to the Writing of Philo of Alexandria" (paper presented at the University of Lisbon, May 2009), 17–19, 26–27. See also Morris, "The Jewish Philosopher," 855. Geljon

both part of the "Exposition."[15] The former focuses on the ten command-ments, and the latter discusses all of the laws which fall under these ten heads. *Quod omnis probus liber sit* is a philosophical treatise on the Stoic principle that freedom is not influenced by external circumstances.[16] In it Philo presents the Essenes as an example of truly free people. Lastly, in *Legatio ad Gaium* Philo tells the story of the Jewish embassy from Alexandria which went to present its case before Gaius following the Alexandrian pogrom of 38 c.e., as well as the surrounding events including Gaius' decision to erect a golden statue of himself in the Temple in Jerusalem.[17]

Though the seven works under consideration vary greatly in length, topic, and purpose, as will be demonstrated below, Philo's way of describ-ing the Sabbath in them is relatively consistent. He regularly includes certain elements, often using the same vocabulary. Additionally, these elements are generally presented in the same order. Each of the following characteristics or practices shows up in at least three of Philo's seven Sabbath descriptions.[18]

First, Philo refers to the Sabbath as the sacred seventh day (*Mos.* 2.209, 263; *Spec.* 2.56; *Decal.* 96; *Legat.* 156, 158), where "sacred" modifies the substantive "seventh." He also calls the day "the seventh" (*Mos.* 2.215; *Spec.* 2.41, 62; *Prob.* 81; *Contempl.* 30, 36; *Hypoth.* 7.12) or refers to it as holy (*Prob.* 81) apart from this specific construction. Philo uses "seventh" as a substantive in all instances but one; only in the *Hypothetica* does it modify the noun "days" (7.12).[19]

---

argues for an alternate view. He understands *De vita Mosis* as an introductory philoso-phical bios and thus imagines that the work functions as an introduction not only to the "Exposition" but to the whole of Philo's exegetical series, including the *Allegorical Commen-tary*, the "Exposition," and the *Quaestiones et solutiones* (*Philonic Exegesis*, 7–46).

[15] Royse, "The Works of Philo," 45–50.

[16] Morris, "The Jewish Philosopher Philo," 856; Royse, "The Works of Philo," 55–56.

[17] The content of this work limits the time period in which it could have been written, but there is debate over the nature and audience of this text. Recently Niehoff has argued against a Roman and in favor of a Jewish audience (*Philo on Jewish Identity*, 39–43).

[18] See the chart at the end of the article. Included in the chart are all elements occurring in at least three of the seven Sabbath descriptions. The chart includes both instances of parallels in vocabulary and places where similar ideas are expressed with different words. The Greek is given so that the reader can distinguish between the two types of parallels.

[19] In these seven descriptions, Philo uses "Sabbath" only once. In *De specialibus legibus* he says that the seventh day is "called by the Hebrews in their native tongue Sabbath" (σάββατον [2.41]). (All translations of Philo are from the LCL.) According to Jutta Leonhardt, Philo prefers the Greek "seventh" to the Hebrew "Sabbath" partly because "the Hebrew term has been deliberately misinterpreted by anti-Jewish propaganda, while the number seven is more neutral" (*Jewish Worship in Philo of Alexandria* [TSAJ 84; Tübingen: Mohr Siebeck, 2001], 54).

In *De vita Mosis*, *De specialibus legibus*, and *De decalogo*, Philo includes a discussion of the number seven in his Sabbath description. Philo's interest in numbers is well known, and in these three accounts he goes on at some length regarding the honor of the number seven. Two items appear in all three accounts. Seven is motherless (ἀμήτωρ [*Mos.* 2.210; *Spec.* 2.56; *Decal.* 102]), which Philo explains by saying that seven is "exempt from female parentage, begotten by the Father alone" (*Mos.* 2.210). Additionally, seven is ever virgin (παρθένος [*Mos.* 2.210; *Spec.* 2.56; *Decal.* 102]), thus "neither born of a mother nor a mother herself, neither bred from corruption nor doomed to suffer corruption" (*Mos.* 2.210).

Philo explains that the Jews abstain (ἀνέχειν) from work (ἔργων) on these seventh days. In five of the seven Sabbath descriptions, Philo includes both of these terms. In four places the terms appear near one another and ἔργων is the object of ἀνέχειν (*Mos.* 2.211; *Spec.* 2.60; *Prob.* 81; *Hypoth.* 7.11). In *De decalogo* Philo uses a different construction. He says that God commanded that the Jews "apply themselves to work (ἔργα) for six days but rest (ἀνέχοντας) on the seventh" (98). In *Legatio ad Gaium* neither of these words appears, but Philo conveys a similar meaning by saying that "no one is permitted to receive or give anything or to transact any part of the business of ordinary life" (158).

In four Sabbath descriptions, Philo specifies that the Jews are not inactive on the Sabbath. Having stated that the Jews abstain from work, he wants to ensure that he does not leave the impression that they sit idle. In *De vita Mosis*, Philo describes at length what the Jews do not do on the Sabbath. They do not waste their time "in bursts of laughter or sports or shows of mimes and dancers on which stage-struck fools waste away their strength" (2.211). Philo seems to be suggesting that this is how others squander their leisure time; the Jews, on the other hand, devote their Sabbaths only to the study of wisdom (μόνῳ τῷ φιλοσοφεῖν [2.211]).

In *De specialibus legibus*, Philo immediately follows his statement that the Jews rest from work on the Sabbath with the clarification that the law does not teach laziness. Philo writes, "On this day we are commanded to abstain from all work, not because the law inculcates slackness" (2.60). Rather, the Jews are encouraged to work six full days each week. The Sabbath allows rest for the body, but the mind is to be active (2.64), as the Jews study philosophy and the virtues (2.61–63).

This same combination of an affirmation of six days of work and the seventh day devoted to the study of wisdom also appears in *De decalogo*. Here Philo emphasizes that because each person needs "a vast multitude of things to supply the necessaries of life" (99), each must work six days a week to meet these needs. The seventh day should be devoted to the study of wisdom and the truths of nature, as well as examination of one's own soul (98).

In the *Hypothetica*, Philo gives his most explicit argument that the Jews are not inactive on the Sabbath. Having described what the Jews do on these seventh days and how they devote their time to learning their laws, he asks, "Do you think that this marks them as idlers or that any work is equally vital to them?" (7.14). Note here that the order of the elements in the *Hypothetica* is different from the other Sabbath descriptions. In the other accounts, the claim against inactivity precedes the description of what happens on the Sabbath.

In three accounts Philo specifies that the Jews gather together on the Sabbath. In *De vita contemplativa* the Therapeutae "meet together (συνέρχον-ται) as for a general assembly" (30). In the *Hypothetica* Moses requires that the Jews "assemble (συνάγεσθαι) in the same place" (7.12). Philo repeats that "they do always assemble (συνέρχονται)" (7.13). In the *Legatio ad Gaium* Philo explains that Augustus knew that the Jews "have houses of prayer and meet together (συνιόντας) in them, particularly on the sacred Sabbaths" (156). Philo then praises Augustus because he did not prevent the Jews "from meeting (συνάγεσθαι) to receive instructions in the laws" (157). That the Jews meet together on the Sabbath is also implied in three other accounts. In *De vita Mosis* the people must gather together so that the ruler can instruct them (2.215). In *De specialibus legibus* the Jews must come together in the "schools" where they sit and listen to the teacher (2.62). In *Quod omnis probus liber sit* since the Essenes go to synagogues and sit in rows, it is clear that they gather (81).

Philo next describes what the Jews do in their Sabbath gatherings. Having gathered together, the Jews (1) sit (2) in order and (3) quietly while (4) one person expounds and (5) they all study wisdom. In four texts Philo specifies that the Jews sit, using a form of καθέζομαι in every instance (*Spec.* 2.62; *Prob.* 81; *Contempl.* 30; *Hypoth.* 7.12). In these four texts Philo describes their sitting as being orderly, though with various formulations. They sit ἐν κόσμῳ (*Spec.* 2.62), μετὰ κόσμου (*Prob.* 81), ἑξῆς (*Contempl.* 30), or σὺν . . . κόσμῳ (*Hypoth.* 7.12). Again in these four texts Philo comments on the silence or near silence of those gathered to learn. They sit together σὺν ἡσυχίᾳ (*Spec.* 2.62), ἔχοντες ἀκροατικῶς (*Prob.* 81), καθ' ἡσυχίαν (*Contempl.* 31), or σιωπῇ (*Hypoth.* 7.13). That someone of special importance expounds is specified in these four texts as well as in *De vita Mosis*. In *De vita Mosis* the ruler expounds and teaches (ὑφηγουμένου καὶ διδάσκοντος [2.215]). In *De specialibus legibus* a teacher with special experience ὑφηγεῖται (2.62). In *Quod omnis probus liber sit* a learned member ἀναδιδάσκει (82). In *De vita contemplativa* an elder διαλέγεται (31). In the *Hypothetica* a priest or elder ἐξηγεῖται (7.13). Finally, all of the Sabbath descriptions with the exception of the *Hypothetica* specify that what the Jews study is wisdom, most often expressed with the infinitive φιλοσοφεῖν (*Mos.* 2.211, 212, 215; *Spec.* 2.61; *Decal.* 100; *Contempl.* 34).[20]

In a few accounts, Philo states that what the Jews study has been passed down to them from their ancestors. In two accounts Philo describes the object of the Jews' studies as "their ancestral philosophy" (τὴν πάτριον φιλοσοφίαν [*Mos.* 2.216]; τὴν πάτριον . . . φιλοσοφίαν [*Legat.* 156]). In the *Hypothetica* Philo says first that the Jews study "their ancestral laws and customs" (τῶν πατρίων νόμων καὶ ἐθῶν [7.11]) and second that they all know τῶν πατρίων (7.14), where the adjective is substantive and should call to mind the aforementioned laws and customs.

In three accounts Philo gives a list of virtues which the Jews learn in their Sabbath study (*Mos.* 2.216; *Spec.* 2.63; *Prob.* 83).[21] Only three virtues (εὐσεβείας, ὁσιότητος, and δικαιοσύνης) appear in all three of these accounts. In each instance they are presented as part of the curriculum for the Jews at their Sabbath gatherings. Additionally, in the *Hypothetica* Philo claims that the Jews' Sabbath study results not only in their knowledge of their laws, but also in their "advance in piety" (εὐσέβειαν [7.13]), though no other virtues are mentioned.

Deviations from this Pattern

While each of Philo's seven Sabbath descriptions contains much of this basic pattern, each Sabbath description also contains elements unique to itself and lacks at least a few of the common elements. For the most part, these additions and omissions can be explained by the character of each individual work.

Of these seven Sabbath descriptions, those in *De vita contemplativa* and *Quod omnis probus liber sit* are the most similar to one another. Both of these accounts are located within a description of the lifestyle of a group of Jews who have separated themselves from society and devoted themselves to a

---

[20] Within the Sabbath accounts themselves, Philo only claims that the Jews study their laws in the *Hypothetica* (7.11, 13) and *Legatio ad Gaium* (157). However, this is not to say that Philo completely avoids mentioning the laws in the other texts under consideration. In *Contempl.* 25 the Therapeutae spend their days studying "laws (νόμους) and oracles." In *Prob.* 80 the Essenes study ethics, "taking for their trainers the laws (νόμοις) of their fathers."

[21] Leonhardt notes that the virtues listed in *Spec.* 2.62 "are the virtues central to Greek philosophy" (*Jewish Worship*, 81).

communal existence. This likely explains why in these two places Philo's description is almost entirely limited to the activities of the Sabbath day and how they are carried out. Philo is particularly attentive to how the Jews sit in their gathering, adding that these Jews sit "according to their age" (*Contempl.* 30; *Prob.* 81). In *De vita contemplativa* Philo also describes the sanctuary in which they meet, how it is divided by gender, and the common, frugal meal which is eaten each Sabbath. Here Philo cannot specify that the Therapeutae work six full days because all their days are devoted to study. However, he does note that even the cattle who do work six days are released "from their continuous labor" on the Sabbath (36). It is clear that the emphasis in these two accounts is on the *practice* of these particular communities of Jews, and this explains the absence of elements such as a discourse on the number seven or a Scriptural reason for the Sabbath day, though this latter might also be intentionally omitted if Philo primarily has a non-Jewish audience in mind.[22]

De vita Mosis and *De specialibus legibus* contain the two longest Sabbath accounts, which is unsurprising given the length of these works. In both of these accounts, Philo relates the story of the man from Num 15:32–36 who is found gathering sticks on the Sabbath day (*Mos.* 2.213–217; *Spec.* 2.250–251). In connection with this story, Philo reports that it is forbidden to light a fire on the Sabbath (*Mos.* 2.219; *Spec.* 2.65, 251), and that the penalty for breaking the Sabbath is death (*Mos.* 2.217–218; *Spec.* 2.249). Given that *De vita Mosis* addresses the events of Moses' life and *De specialibus legibus* is an exegetical work concerned with the various laws in the Pentateuch, it is quite reasonable that Philo would include this particular Scriptural incident, one of the few dealing with the Sabbath, in these Sabbath accounts. Similarly, it is understandable that Philo would draw a connection between the announcement of the Sabbath and the shower of manna in *De vita Mosis* (2.264), and that Philo would call upon the account of creation as the reason for celebrating the Sabbath at seven day intervals in the exegetical work *De decalogo* (97, 100). It is natural to find Scriptural references in these works which have a direct connection to Scripture.

---

[22] Ellen Birnbaum discusses the challenge of determining Philo's intended audience. Philo gives little explicit indication of his audience, but the internal characteristics of his writings "suggest that they are composed with different purposes for individuals who differ in their spiritual sensibilities and in their familiarity with Jewish beliefs, practices, and people" (*The Place of Judaism in Philo's Thought: Israel, Jews, and Proselytes* [BJS 290; Atlanta: Scholars Press, 1996], 18). That *De vita contemplativa* requires no prior knowledge of Scripture or Judaism allows for the possibility that it is directed toward non-Jews, but does not eliminate the possibility of a Jewish audience.

Structural Deviation

In the five Sabbath accounts just mentioned, *De vita Mosis, De specialibus legibus, De decalogo, De vita contemplativa,* and *Quod omnis probus liber sit,* the deviations from Philo's regular pattern are best understood as additions or omissions which can be explained in terms of the content, length, and intent of the larger work in which they are located. In spite of the differences between these accounts, all five relay details of Sabbath observance in the same basic order for the purpose of explaining the Jews' Sabbath practice and presenting it in a positive light. In the *Hypothetica,* and in *Legatio ad Gaium* to a lesser extent, Philo does not describe the Sabbath merely to inform and subtly seek to enhance the reputation of the Jews, but rather he puts his regular Sabbath discussion to the service of arguing a specific point. That this is the case is demonstrated by the structure of these two accounts.

In the section of the *Legatio ad Gaium* in which the Sabbath description appears, Philo is concerned with demonstrating that Augustus was a superior emperor to Gaius. Philo mentions the Sabbath here only because Augustus allowed the Jews to continue observing the Sabbath and to Philo this demonstrates that Augustus was "a character truly imperial" (*Legat.* 157). Though the actual description of the Sabbath day is quite brief, Philo does include here many of the elements of his regular description of the Sabbath, as can be seen in the chart at the end of the article. However, the elements are not in the regular order. Whereas Philo generally explains that the Jews abstain from work prior to describing how they meet together for instruction, in *Legatio ad Gaium* this information only comes to light at the very end of the account as Philo explains why the Jews could not receive the monthly allotments of money or corn on the Sabbath. Philo's primary aim is not to give a clear description; rather, he makes note of the elements of the Sabbath which are relevant when arguing for Augustus' superiority in dealing with the Jews.

That Philo puts his description of the Sabbath to the service of a larger agenda is even clearer in the *Hypothetica.* Here Philo's account is structured around a series of questions, as though he is directly addressing an interlocutor.[23] Philo begins by asking, "Is it not a marvel that for a whole day they should have kept from transgressing on any occasion any of the ordinances...?" (7.10). He presents the Sabbath as a challenging law to keep and commends the Jews for their ability to do so. He next asks, "Is not this merely a case of practicing self-control...?" (7.11). In this way he not only

---

[23] Sterling, "Philo and the Logic of Apologetics," 424.

emphasizes that the Jews demonstrate self-control, a quality highly admired in the Roman world, but he also creates an opportunity to present the lawgiver's brilliance. The Sabbath is not *merely* an opportunity for practicing self-control; rather, Moses ingeniously determined that the Jews should devote every seventh day to the study of their ancestral laws (7.11). Within this context of lauding Moses' ingenuity, Philo presents the description of what the Jews do on the Sabbath day. Note on the chart that most of the elements of Philo's regular pattern occur in *Hypoth.* 7.12–7.13. Following this descriptive section, Philo asks another question, which appears to be the focal point: "Do you think that this marks them as idlers or that any work is equally vital to them?" (7.14). His description serves the purpose of showing that the Jews are not idle on the Sabbath. Philo ends this account by claiming that all the Jews know all their laws and have no need to consult experts, which further demonstrates that the Jews have used their Sabbath study time well (7.14).

The structure of this description of the Sabbath is determined by Philo's goal of responding to particular charges. Most explicit is his response to the charge that by observing the Sabbath the Jews show themselves to be idlers.[24] He emphasizes this response by placing it near the middle of his discussion, building up to it with an account of what the Jews study, and following it with evidence that their studying is not in vain. Additionally, Philo extols the Jews by emphasizing the challenge of keeping the Sabbath commandments and the self-control demonstrated in doing so. These points also argue against the Jews' idleness.

Pagan Comments Regarding the Sabbath

In the Sabbath description in his *Hypothetica* as well as in the other works under consideration, Philo gives evidence that he is aware of certain pagan accusations against Jewish Sabbath practice and against Jews in general. Philo is clearly responding to the charge of idleness in the *Hypothetica*, and he seems to be responding to this charge as well as to accusations of foolish superstition and misanthropy in his other Sabbath descriptions.

One of the earliest accusations against Jewish Sabbath practice is that it is foolish, especially when the Jews do not defend themselves. This accusation appears first in the writings of the peripatetic Agatharchides of Cnidus (second century B.C.E.) who spent some time in Alexandria, where

---

[24] Louis H. Feldman, *Jew and Gentile in the Ancient World: Attitudes and Interactions from Alexander to Justinian* (Princeton: Princeton University Press, 1993), 166; Gregory E. Sterling, "The *Hypothetica*," in *The Lost Bible* (forthcoming), 34.

he likely encountered Jews.[25] Agatharchides' comments on the Jews are preserved by Josephus in his *Contra Apionem*. Josephus introduces this pagan author by saying, "There is another writer whom I shall name without hesitation, although he mentions us only to ridicule our folly."[26] Agatharchides knows that the Jews abstain (ἀργεῖν) from work every seventh day.[27] Note that his verb has a more negative connotation than Philo's neutral ἀνέχειν ἔργων. Agatharchides knows that they spend the day in prayer and avoid both agricultural and military activities. As an example he cites the time Ptolemy brought in his army and the Jews did not defend their city because they "persevered in their folly."[28] He continues, "That experience has taught the whole world, except that nation, the lesson not to resort to dreams and traditional fancies about the law,"[29] which demonstrates the negative tone of his comments.[30] The whole world has learned from such experiences except the Jews who continue their foolish practices.

Plutarch (forties of the first century to twenties of the second century c.e.) speaks contemptuously against the Jews' superstitious Sabbath observance.[31] He includes "keeping of the Sabbath (σαββατισμούς)"[32] in a list of barbarian superstitions. In the same work he expounds further on this foolishness: "But the Jews, because it was the Sabbath day, sat in their places immovable, while the enemy were planting ladders against the walls and capturing the defences, and they did not get up, but remained there, fast bound in the toils of superstition as in one great net."[33] Plutarch condemns not only the Jews but also other "barbarians"[34] for their superstitious practices.[35] However, Peter Schäfer is right in pointing out "the tone of contempt which pervades the list of barbarian customs."[36] Plutarch's negative attitude toward Sabbath observance is not lessened simply because of his contempt for other non-Greek customs.[37]

---

[25] Menahem Stern, *Greek and Latin Authors on Jews and Judaism* (3 vols.; Jerusalem: Israel Academy of Sciences and Humanities, 1974), 1:104.

[26] *C. Ap.* 1.205 = *GLAJJ*, vol. 1, no. 30a.

[27] *C. Ap.* 1.209 = *GLAJJ*, vol. 1, no. 30a.

[28] *C. Ap.* 1.210 = *GLAJJ*, vol. 1, no. 30a.

[29] *C. Ap.* 1.211 = *GLAJJ*, vol. 1, no. 30a.

[30] Peter Schäfer, *Judeophobia: Attitudes toward the Jews in the Ancient World* (Cambridge: Harvard University Press, 1997), 83–84.

[31] Stern, *GLAJJ*, 1:545–547; Schäfer, *Judeophobia*, 88–89.

[32] *De superstitione* 3 = *GLAJJ*, vol. 1, no. 255.

[33] *De superstitione* 8 = *GLAJJ*, vol. 1, no. 256.

[34] *De superstitione* 3 = *GLAJJ*, vol. 1, no. 255.

[35] Stern, *GLAJJ*, 1:547.

[36] *Judeophobia*, 89.

[37] There are others who know that the Jews do not defend themselves on the Sabbath, but whose remarks are neutral. Cassius Dio (ca. 160–230 c.e.) simply states that the Jews

The charge of Jewish Sabbath observance as idleness appears to be unique to Roman authors. According to Schäfer, "The Romans with their sense of efficiency and industry obviously had no sympathy for a day every week with no work."[38] The first to make this accusation is Seneca (end of the first century B.C.E. to 65 C.E.).[39] In a passage preserved by Augustine, Seneca "declares that their practice is inexpedient, because by introducing one day of rest in every seven they lose in idleness almost a seventh of their life, and by failing to act in times of urgency they often suffer loss."[40] Seneca not only accuses the Jews of being lazy, but he also specifically connects this laziness with their failure to act in emergencies. This distinguishes Seneca's charge from those of Agatharchides and Plutarch who blame the Jews' failure to act on their foolishness. Schäfer observes that according to Seneca, it is not a divine law but rather the Jews' laziness which prevents them from acting to save themselves.[41] Note that the first preserved pagan accusation of idleness comes from Seneca, who is a younger contemporary of Philo. Yet, since Philo responds to the charge of idleness, this accusation must have preceded Seneca. In fact, Philo appears to be our earliest evidence for this particular charge.

Tacitus (ca. 56–120 C.E.) continues this Roman condemnation.[42] He connects the Sabbath with the end of the Jews' journey from Egypt to their own land. Tacitus writes, "They say that they first chose to rest on the seventh day because that day ended their toils; but after a time they were led by the charms of indolence to give over the seventh year as well to inactivity."[43] Tacitus, similar to Seneca, accuses the Jews of observing the sabbatical year out of laziness rather than in obedience to divine law.

Juvenal (ca. 60–130 C.E.), a contemporary of Tacitus, laments the "intrusion of foreign elements into the capital of imperial Rome,"[44] including the influence and spread of Judaism. In *Saturae* 14, Juvenal satirizes that a father who reveres the Sabbath produces a son who adopts more of the Jewish

---

"made an exception of what are called the days of Saturn, and by doing no work at all on those days afforded the Romans an opportunity in this interval to batter down the wall" (*Historia Romana* 36.16.2 = *GLAJJ*, vol. 2, no. 406). Frontius (ca. 40–104 C.E.), too, merely reports, "The deified Augustus Vespasian attacked the Jews on the day of Saturn, a day on which it is sinful for them to do any business, and defeated them" (*Strategemata* 2.1.17 = *GLAJJ*, vol. 1, no. 229).

[38] *Judeophobia*, 86.
[39] Stern, *GLAJJ*, 1:429.
[40] *De superstitione* in *De civitate Dei* 6.11 = *GLAJJ*, vol. 1, no. 186.
[41] *Judeophobia*, 87.
[42] Stern, *GLAJJ*, 2:1.
[43] *Historiae* 5.4.3 = *GLAJJ*, vol. 2, no. 281.
[44] Stern, *GLAJJ*, 2:94.

law, going as far as circumcision and obeying Jewish law in place of Roman law, and for this deterioration "the father was to blame, who gave up every seventh day to idleness, keeping it apart from all the concerns of life."[45] It is the lure of laziness which attracts a person to this barbarian custom.[46]

This Roman accusation proves to be enduring. As late at the fifth century C.E. Rutilius Namatianus, who was "probably the last non-Christian Latin writer to give vent to antipathy to Judaism," maintains the charge of laziness.[47] He calls the Jews a "filthy race that infamously practises circumcision; a root of silliness they are."[48] Regarding the Sabbath he asserts that "Each seventh day is condemned to ignoble sloth, as 'twere an effeminate picture of the god fatigued."[49] Rutilius Namatianus goes further than accusing the Jews of laziness; he claims that their God stands as the model for such contemptuous behavior.[50]

Philo's writings also bear witness to his knowledge of pagan accusations of Jewish misanthropy. The charge of misanthropy is not directly related to Sabbath observance. Rather, pagans charge that Jews live an antisocial lifestyle, often claiming that Moses commanded this behavior during the Jews' exodus from Egypt. One way Philo argues against this accusation is by presenting the Mosaic law as comprised of duties to God and duties to people (e.g. *Mos.* 2.216; *Spec.* 2.63). Since such discussions of the Mosaic law are found within Philo's descriptions of what the Jews study on the Sabbath, it is appropriate to recognize that Philo responds to the charge of misanthropy in his Sabbath descriptions.

Hecataeus of Abdera (ca. 300 B.C.E.)[51] includes in his tale of the Jews being expelled from Egypt a reference to the Jews' resultant misanthropy:[52] "The sacrifices that [Moses] established differ from those of other nations, as does their way of living, for as a result of their own expulsion from Egypt he introduced an unsocial and intolerant mode of life."[53] Similarly, Manetho (third century B.C.E.)[54] reports that Osarseph, who later changed his name to Moses, commanded that the people "should have intercourse with none save those of their own confederacy,"[55] and that those he led, the

---

[45] *Saturae* 14.105 = *GLAJJ*, vol. 2, no. 301.
[46] Schäfer, *Judeophobia*, 87.
[47] Stern, *GLAJJ*, 2:660.
[48] *De reditu suo* 1.387–388 = *GLAJJ*, vol. 2, no. 542.
[49] *De reditu suo* 1.391–392 = *GLAJJ*, vol. 2, no. 542.
[50] Schäfer, *Judeophobia*, 87.
[51] Stern, *GLAJJ*, 1:20.
[52] Schäfer, *Judeophobia*, 16.
[53] *Aegyptiaca* in Diodorus Siculus, *Bibliotheca Historica* 40.3.4 = *GLAJJ*, vol. 1, no. 11.
[54] Stern, *GLAJJ*, 1:62.
[55] *Aegyptiaca*, in Josephus, *C. Ap.* 1.239 = *GLAJJ*, vol. 1, no. 21.

Jews, treated others "impiously and savagely."[56] According to Josephus, Apollonius Molon (first century B.C.E.)[57] condemns the Jews "for refusing admission to persons with other preconceived ideas about God, and for declining to associate with those who have chosen to adopt a different mode of life."[58] Diodorus (first century B.C.E.)[59] reports that the Jews "alone of all nations avoided dealings with any other people and looked upon all men as their enemies."[60] Finally, Juvenal, in the same passage mentioned above, claims that the Jewish law does not allow its adherents "to point out the way to any not worshipping the same rites."[61]

The pagan writer who perhaps spoke most vehemently against the Jews was the Egyptian Apion (first half of the first century C.E.),[62] whose remarks are preserved by Josephus in the work named after the pagan author. According to Apion, the etymology of the word "Sabbath" is related to the Jews' exodus from Egypt. In six days the Jews marched from Egypt to Judea, and during this time they developed "tumours in the groin," because of which they were forced to rest on the seventh day from the pain, and they "called that day *sabbaton*, preserving the Egyptian terminology; for disease of the groin in Egypt is called sabbatosis."[63] This is a particularly derogatory etymology, for, as Schäfer has pointed out, it insinuates that "this disease, not a divine law, forced them to rest."[64] Apion's polemical comments against the Jews are unlike those above which charge the Jews with a specific fault. This purely malevolent report of the origins of the Sabbath by Philo's own Alexandrian contemporary suggests the high degree of tension in Philo's city.

Philo's Implicit Responses to Pagan Accusations

Five of the accounts, *De vita Mosis*, *De specialibus legibus*, *De decalogo*, *De vita contemplativa*, and *Quod omnis probus liber sit*, betray implicit responses to these pagan charges. In these cases, with knowledge of pagan accusations against the Sabbath, one can determine that Philo likely had such charges in mind as he constructed his Sabbath descriptions. However, were the pagan

---

[56] *Aegyptiaca*, in Josephus, *C. Ap.* 1.248 = *GLAJJ*, vol. 1, no. 21.

[57] Stern, *GLAJJ*, 1:148.

[58] *C. Ap.* 2.258 = *GLAJJ*, vol. 1, no.50.

[59] Stern, *GLAJJ*, 1:167.

[60] *Bibliotheca Historica* 34–35, 1.1 = *GLAJJ*, vol. 1, no. 63.

[61] *Saturae* 14.103–104 = *GLAJJ*, vol. 2, no. 301.

[62] Stern, *GLAJJ*, 1:389.

[63] *C. Ap.* 2.21 = *GLAJJ*, vol.1, no. 165.

[64] *Judeophobia*, 86.

charges not preserved, it would probably not be possible to deduce them from these particular Philonic sources.

In *De vita Mosis*, Philo seems to be responding to charges of foolishness, idleness, and misanthropy. First, having stated that the Jews abstain from work, Philo immediately clarifies that this leisure is not spent "as by some in bursts of laughter or sports or shows of mimes and dancers," but rather "by the pursuit of wisdom only" (2.211). Additionally Philo lists multiple virtues which the Jews learn as a result of studying their ancestral philosophy (2.216). Thus the Jews are not idle on the Sabbath, but rather spend the time in serious study. Giving the day over to such activity is not foolish, for it results in the acquisition of virtue. Philo articulates that it is through these virtues that the Jews discern and perform "duties to God and men" (τά τε ἀνθρώπεια καὶ θεῖα [2.216]). Surely, then, the Jews are not misanthropic.

Similarly, in *De specialibus legibus* Philo responds to the same three charges. He immediately follows the statement that the Jews abstain from work with a clarification that this is "not because the law inculcates slackness" (2.60).[65] Rather, the law directs the Jews to work on the other six days and "spurns those who would idle (ἀργεῖν) their time away" (2.60). This is the same verb Philo uses in the *Hypothetica* when he asks whether the Jews' Sabbath practice "marks them as idlers" (7.14). Here in *De specialibus legibus* Philo further argues that regular rest allows one to regain strength and thus return to work with greater force.[66] By resting every seventh day, the Jews are even more productive than those who work every day. Additionally, while the body rests on the Sabbath, the soul is working (2.64). As in *De vita Mosis*, Philo mentions all the virtues which the Jews learn in their Sabbath study, and here specifies that the two main categories of their studies are duty to God and duty to people (τὸ πρὸς ἀνθρώπους [2.63]). The virtues of humanity (φιλανθρωπίας) and justice (δικαιοσύνης) demonstrate that the Jews are not misanthropic (2.63).

The Sabbath description in *De decalogo* lacks the response to misanthropy[67] but again emphasizes that the Jews are not idle on the Sabbath. In stating the law, Philo says Moses "commanded that they should apply themselves to work for six days but rest on the seventh and turn to the study of wisdom" (98). Even before mentioning the command to rest, Philo claims that the law itself tells the Jews to work. Philo further explains that

---

[65] Feldman, *Jew and Gentile*, 166; Leonhardt, *Jewish Worship*, 67.

[66] Philo uses the same argument in support of the sabbatical year in *Hypoth.* 7.15–16.

[67] While Philo does not specifically respond to the accusation of misanthropy in his Sabbath description in *De decalogo*, the whole treatise is shaped by Philo's understanding of the ten commandments as divided into two tables, the first concerning duties to God and the second concerning duties to other people (50–51, 106).

people must work throughout their whole lives to "supply the necessaries of life" (99). Even the Jews' rest is well-spent; they examine their souls, repenting of and taking precaution against sin (98).

In *De vita contemplativa*, the response to pagan charges is far more subtle than in the three works already discussed. Here Philo emphasizes that the discourse given by the elder "does not lodge just outside the ears of the audience but passes through the hearing into the soul and there stays securely" (31), demonstrating that the listeners grow in knowledge of their ancestral philosophy (28). Given that the Therapeutae spend all of their days in study, it is not possible to claim that they work the full six days. Rather, Philo seeks to show that the study of their ancestral philosophy is a noble pursuit.

Finally, *Quod omnis probus liber sit*, like *De vita contemplativa*, contains only subtle responses to pagan accusations. Here Philo extols the Essenes for spending the day in philosophical study (82) and learning various virtues (83). Also, his mention of "love of people" (φιλανθρώπῳ [83]) is likely a response to pagan charges of misanthropy.

Philo's Explicit Response to Pagan Charges in Historical Context

As we have seen, it is common for Philo to respond to various pagan charges in the context of his Sabbath descriptions. In the five cases just discussed, these responses are implicit and have little if any effect on the structure of Philo's accounts. However, as mentioned above, in the *Hypothetica* the response to pagan charges is explicit and the whole account is structured around responding to these charges. Unlike in the five accounts just discussed, scholars could with confidence identify idleness as a pagan charge by looking at the *Hypothetica* even without any pagan writings. That it is the charge of idleness, the accusation unique to Roman writers and not preserved prior to Philo, with which Philo is most concerned, suggests he has a Roman audience in mind.[68]

In addition to these two differences (structure and explicit response to pagan charges) between the Sabbath description in the *Hypothetica* and those in Philo's other works, one difference in content should be noted. In the *Hypothetica*, the Jews devote the day to learning "their ancestral laws and customs" (τῶν πατρίων νόμων καὶ ἐθῶν [7.11]). Jutta Leonhardt notes that, "it is unquestionable that the 'laws and customs' refer to the written

---

[68] This does not mean that it is possible to exclude Greeks from Philo's intended audience.

Law and the other ritual orders of Judaism, not to Greek philosophy."[69] The only other Sabbath description in which Philo uses the word "laws" is *Legatio ad Gaium*, where the Jews meet "to receive instructions in the laws" (τῶν νόμων [157]). Elsewhere, the Jews study philosophy (φιλοσοφεῖν) and often a whole list of virtues including σωφροσύνης, δικαιοσύνης, εὐσεβείας, and ὁσιότητος (e.g. *Mos.* 2.216). It appears as though in the *Hypothetica* and *Legatio ad Gaium* Philo finds it in the Jews' best interest to emphasize the study of "law" rather than "philosophy" on the Sabbath. Perhaps Philo perceives the Romans as less philosophically inclined than the Greeks, or perhaps he imagines himself on surer ground by presenting the Mosaic law as law rather than as philosophy.

These three differences between the account in the *Hypothetica* and Philo's regular pattern of Sabbath description can best be explained by the historical context in which Philo most likely composed the *Hypothetica*. Gregory E. Sterling has already suggested the time between the Alexandrian pogrom of 38 C.E. and Philo's subsequent departure as part of the Jewish embassy to Gaius as the *Sitz im Leben* of this text.[70] The emergence of a new and threatening situation for the Jews in Alexandria is a logical impetus for a change in Philo's literary approach.

When rule of Alexandria passed from the hands of the Ptolemies to the Romans, there was a heightened level of tension among the Greeks, Jews, and Egyptians.[71] In 38 C.E. this tension escalated into physical violence and brutality against the Jews. The precise reasons for this rioting are uncertain. It appears as though at least some Alexandrian Greeks, having scared the prefect Flaccus into joining their efforts against the Jews, seized upon Agrippa I's visit to Alexandria in August of 38 C.E. and his perhaps pretentious parade as an opportunity for violence against the Jews.[72] The Jews may not have been innocent in these events,[73] but the resultant treatment

[69] *Jewish Worship*, 84.

[70] "Philo and the Logic of Apologetics," 429.

[71] Joseph Modrzejewski, *The Jews of Egypt: From Rameses II to Emperor Hadrian* (trans. Robert Cornman; Philadelphia: Jewish Publication Society, 1995), 161–163.

[72] For possible reconstructions of the cause of the riots in 38 C.E., see Hans Conzelmann, *Gentiles, Jews, Christians: Polemics and Apologetics in the Greco-Roman Era* (trans. M. Eugene Boring; Minneapolis: Fortress, 1992), 7–43; Sandra Gambetti, *The Alexandrian Riots of 38 CE and the Persecution of the Jews: A Historical Reconstruction* (Leiden: Brill, 2009), 239–252; Aryeh Kasher, *The Jews in Hellenistic and Roman Egypt: The Struggle for Equal Rights* (Tübingen: Mohr [Siebeck], 1985), 18–24; Modrzejewski, *The Jews of Egypt*, 161–183; E. Mary Smallwood, *The Jews under Roman Rule: From Pompey to Diocletian: A Study in Political Relations* (Leiden: Brill, 1981), 220–255.

[73] Allen Kerkeslager, "Agrippa and the Mourning Rites for Drusilla in Alexandria," *JSJ* 37.3 (2006): 367–400; Smallwood, *The Jews under Roman Rule*, 240–241.

by the Greeks can only be described as vicious.[74] Flaccus proclaimed the Jews "foreigners," which deprived them of their right of domicile.[75] They were forced into one of the city's five quarters. Severe overcrowding and violence against those who ventured out for food or supplies mark the world's "first known ghetto."[76] The civic rights of the Jews were on the line.[77]

In *Spec.* 3.1–6 Philo fondly recalls the early part of his life when he could devote himself fully to his studies, in contrast to his subsequent entrance into public affairs. In this period when tension explodes into violence, Philo's writing takes on a new quality. Prior to 38 C.E., and perhaps also following this period of heightened tension, his Sabbath descriptions certainly sought to present the Jews in a positive light, even implicitly responding to common pagan accusations. However, in response to the threatened position of his kin, Philo adopts a new method. Now that the stakes are so high, Philo structures his Sabbath descriptions to accommodate arguments for the benefit of the Jews. In the *Hypothetica* he responds directly to pagan, and particularly Roman, accusations against the Jews. In *Legatio ad Gaium*, he puts his description of the Sabbath to the service of arguing for the Jews' status under Augustus.

The Hypothetica *and* De vita contemplativa

As stated at the beginning of this essay, some scholars maintain that *De vita contemplativa* is an apologetic text. It is certainly the case that in this work Philo intends to present the Therapeutae in a very positive light and thus to raise the esteem of all Jews by association. We have seen above that Philo even includes subtle responses to pagan accusations in this Sabbath description. Also, there are reasons to imagine that *De vita contemplativa* is at least partly intended for a non-Jewish audience.[78] Thus, Philo likely intends his non-Jewish readers to view Jews in a more positive light.

[74] Smallwood, *The Jews under Roman Rule*, 241.

[75] Kasher, *The Jews in Hellenistic and Roman Egypt*, 21; Modrzejewski, *The Jews of Egypt*, 169.

[76] Feldman, *Jew and Gentile*, 115; Smallwood, *The Jews under Roman Rule*, 240.

[77] It is unlikely that more than a few of the Jews possessed citizenship, as strongly suggested by the *Letter of Claudius to the Alexandrians* (P. Lond. 1912). However, the Alexandrian Greeks likely wanted to reduce the rights which the Jews did have as a *politeuma* (Smallwood, *The Jews under Roman Rule*, 235–237).

[78] Runia argues that Philo intentionally uses a philosophical framework "that Alexandrian intellectuals would understand" ("The Reward for Goodness," 15–16). However,

However, there are two serious reasons to question whether the label "apologetic" is appropriate for *De vita contemplativa* based on the way that Philo discusses the Sabbath therein. First, the description of the Sabbath in *De vita contemplativa* is more like that in *Quod omnis probus liber sit* than any of Philo's other descriptions. *Quod omnis probus liber sit* is generally recognized as a philosophical treatise, lacking any apologetic intent. This is merely how Philo describes the Sabbath *practice* of a group of ascetic Jews.

Second, while *De vita contemplativa* does subtly respond to pagan charges, *De vita Mosis*, *De specialibus legibus*, and *De decalogo* all display more obvious responses. In those cases, it is clearer that Philo wants to emphasize that the Jews both work six full days and spend the "leisure" of the Sabbath studying philosophy and acquiring virtue. Additionally, in two of these texts Philo asserts the Jews' love for people, thus arguing against their misanthropy. This argument is absent from *De vita contemplativa*. Though some scholars have argued for the apologetic nature of *De vita Mosis*,[79] it is quite difficult to imagine that the exegetical works *De specialibus legibus* and *De decalogo* have such intent. Thus, the Sabbath description in *De vita contemplativa* is even less apologetic than the Sabbath descriptions in Philo's exegetical works.

Though *De vita contemplativa* and the *Hypothetica* have both been labeled apologetic, it is necessary to distinguish between the functions of these two texts based on the way Philo discusses the Sabbath in each. The *Hypothetica* is clearly apologetic. While its Sabbath description includes the elements Philo commonly presents in describing the Sabbath, the structure of the pericope is determined by the explicit aim of responding to accusations against the Jews. This text defends the Jews against their accusers. While *De vita contemplativa* certainly does aim to present the Jews in a positive light and may be implicitly responding to pagan charges, the way in which Philo describes the Sabbath here raises doubts about describing its function as apologetic. This Sabbath description follows Philo's regular pattern in terms of both content and order. It gives even fewer signs of defending the Jews against their accusers than the Sabbath descriptions in the exegetical works *De specialibus legibus* and *De decalogo*. There is nothing to suggest that here Philo intends to move beyond his regular practice of praising the Jews to the different task of defending them against accusations.

University of Notre Dame

Philo does not assume that his readers will know what "nomes" are, implying a non-Egyptian audience (Taylor, *Jewish Women Philosophers*, 43).

[79] For example, Royse categorizes *De vita Mosis* with Philo's apologetic works ("The Works of Philo," 34, 50–51).

Philo's Regular Pattern in His Sabbath Descriptions

	De vita Mosis	*De specialibus legibus*	*De decalogo*
sacred	2.209, τὴν ἱερὰν ἑβδόμην 2.263, τῆς ἱερᾶς ἑβδόμης	2.56, ἡ … ἱερὰ ἑβδόμη	96, τῆς ἱερᾶς ἑβδόμης
seventh	2.209, τὴν ἱερὰν ἑβδόμην 2.215, ταῖς ἑβδόμαις 2.263, τῆς ἱερᾶς ἑβδόμης	2.41, ἡ … ἑβδόμη 2.56, ἡ … ἱερὰ ἑβδόμη 2.62, ταῖς ἑβδόμαις	96, τῆς ἱερᾶς ἑβδόμης
motherless	2.210, ἀμήτωρ	2.56, ἀμήτορα	102, ἀμήτωρ
virgin	2.210, ἀειπάρθενος	2.56, παρθένον	102, παρθένος
abstain from work	2.211, ἀνέχοντας μὲν ἔργων	2.60, ἀνέχειν ἔργων	98, πρὸς μὲν ἔργα τρεπομένους ἐφ᾿ ἡμέρας ἕξ, ἀνέχοντας δὲ τῇ ἑβδόμῃ
not inactive	2.211, extended description	2.60, extended description	99, extended description
gather together	2.215, extended description	2.62, extended description	
sit		2.62, καθέζονται	
in order		2.62, ἐν κόσμῳ	
quietly		2.62, σὺν ἡσυχίᾳ	
one expounds	2.215, ὑφηγουμένου καὶ διδάσκοντος	2.62, ὑφηγεῖται	
study wisdom	2.211, φιλοσοφεῖν 2.212, φιλοσοφεῖν 2.215, φιλοσοφεῖν 2.216, τὴν πάτριον φιλοσοφίαν	2.61, φιλοσοφεῖν	98, φιλοσοφοῦντας 100, φιλοσοφεῖν
ancestral	2.216, τὴν πάτριον φιλοσοφίαν		
list of virtues	2.216, extended description	2.63, extended description	
piety	2.216, εὐσεβείας	2.63, εὐσεβείας	
holiness	2.216, ὁσιότητος	2.63, ὁσιότητος	
justice	2.216, δικαιοσύνης	2.63, δικαιοσύνης	

Philo's Regular Pattern in His Sabbath Descriptions

Quod omnis probus liber sit	*De vita contemplativa*	*Hypothetica*	*Legatio ad Gaium*
81, ἱερὰ			156, ταῖς ἱεραῖς ἑβδόμαις
			158, τῆς ἱερᾶς ἑβδόμης
81, ταῖς ἑβδόμαις	30, ταῖς δὲ ἑβδόμαις	7.12, ταῖς ἑβδόμαις	156, ταῖς ἱεραῖς ἑβδόμαις
81, ἡ ἑβδόμη	36, τὴν δὲ ἑβδόμην		158, τῆς ἱερᾶς ἑβδόμης
81, ἀνέχοντες ἔργων		7.11, ἀνέχειν ... ἀπὸ	158, extended description
		τῶν ἔργων	
		7.14, ἆρά σοι δοκεῖ ταῦτα	
		ἀργούντων	
81, extended description	30, συνέρχονται	7.12, συνάγεσθαι	156, συνιόντας
		7.13, συνέρχονται	157, συνάγεσθαι
81, καθέζονται	30, καθέζονται	7.12, καθεζομένους	
81, μετὰ κόσμου	30, ἑξῆς	7.12, σὺν ... κόσμῳ	
81, ἔχοντες ἀκροατικῶς	31, καθ᾽ ἡσυχίαν	7.13, σιωπῇ	
82, ἀναδιδάσκει	31, διαλέγεται	7.13, ἐξηγεῖται	
82, φιλοσοφεῖται	34, φιλοσοφεῖν		156, τὴν πάτριον ...
			φιλοσοφίαν
		7.11, τῶν πατρίων νόμων	156, τὴν πάτριον ...
		7.14, τῶν πατρίων	φιλοσοφίαν
83, extended description			
83, εὐσέβειαν		7.13, εὐσέβειαν	
83, ὁσιότητα			
83, δικαιοσύνην			

The Studia Philonica Annual 22 (2010) 165–182

PHILO AND THE LOGIC OF HISTORY

HORACIO VELA

Introduction

Among the most neglected and misunderstood texts traditionally listed in the Philonic corpus is the fragmentary treatise *Hypothetica*. While the meaning of the title has puzzled many scholars, more controversial is the treatise's approach to Judean history.[1] John M. G. Barclay recently argued that Philo of Alexandria was not the author of the *Hypothetica*.[2] Though Barclay cites the text's "poorly arranged" exposition of the law and numerous *hapax legomena* as evidence against authenticity, most importantly, he characterizes the exposition of biblical history as un-Philonic. Barclay claims, "Nothing we know of Philo's style elsewhere prepares us for this approach to such central issues in Judean history, and it is hard to believe that he would suspend his own convictions so fully, even in the genre of apologetic."[3]

The treatment of biblical history in the *Hypothetica* deserves reevaluation. Several important studies clearly demonstrate that Philo himself and other Greek-speaking Jewish authors took great liberties with the interpretation of biblical history. For instance, Madeleine Petit examined how many Jewish authors, often in apologetic contexts, frequently departed from the biblical text in order to gloss over potentially troublesome passages.[4] Furthermore, Katell Berthelot has demonstrated that Philo allegorized, reinterpreted, and even omitted the conquest of Canaan throughout

---

[1] For the history of scholarship on the *Hypothetica*, see Earle Hilgert, "A Survey of Previous Studies on Philo's *Hypothetica*" (paper presented at the annual meeting of the SBL, New Orleans, 1990). Scholars have proposed legal, apologetic, and paraenetic contexts for the interpretation of the treatise and its title.

[2] John M. G. Barclay, *Against Apion* (vol. 10 of *Flavius Josephus, Translation and Commentary*; ed. Steve Mason; Leiden: Brill, 2007), 354.

[3] Ibid.

[4] Madeleine Petit, "A propos d'une traversée du Sinai selon Philon (*Hypothetica* VI, 2–3.8): Texte biblique et apologetique concernant Moise chez quelques ecrivain Juifs," *Sem* 26 (1976): 137–142.

his writings.[5] Given the fact that Philo and other Hellenistic Jews utilized a variety of approaches to interpret biblical history, it seems premature to dismiss the *Hypothetica* as un-Philonic.[6] Though Berthelot and Petit note Philo's appeal to reason in *Hypoth.* 8.6.5, they do not fully elucidate this methodology. It is this mode of reasoning that I consider to be of central importance for the question of authenticity and the nature of the historical section of the *Hypothetica*.

In this paper, I will reexamine the nature of Philo's reasoning and approach to biblical history in the *Hypothetica*. Drawing on the foundational work of Gregory E. Sterling on Philo's use of Stoic logic in *Hypoth.* 8.6.4–9, I will suggest that the text can be illuminated by further study of Stoic logic and the ancient form of logical and rhetorical argumentation known as the dilemma.[7] I will argue that Philo utilized elements of Stoic logic and the rhetoric of dilemmatic arguments to reason with his opponents and subvert their anti-Jewish slanders. Through this rhetorical approach, Philo moved his adversaries beyond the conflicting records of written sources, Jewish and pagan, and trapped them in a positive and reasonable understanding of Jewish history and culture. This conclusion illuminates Philo's apologetic technique and strengthens the case for the authenticity of the *Hypothetica*.

1. *Reassessing The Logic of Apologetics*

Before reexamining crucial aspects of Stoic logic, first I will survey briefly the historical section of *Hypoth.* 8.6.1–9. Barclay claims that the "author adopts a style expressly non-committal towards the biblical account of the exodus and the Judean evaluation of Moses."[8] What Barclay finds problematic is the way the text presents multiple options and probabilities for the audience to decide upon rather than an authoritative, biblical presentation of Judean history.

---

[5] Katell Berthelot, "Philo of Alexandria and the Conquest of Canaan," *JSJ* 38 (2007): 39–56.

[6] For the reinterpretation of the promise of the land and God's covenant with Israel during Second Temple Judaism, see Betsy Halpern Amaru, *Rewriting the Bible: Land and Covenant in Post-Biblical Jewish Literature* (Valley Forge, Pa.: Trinity Press International, 1994).

[7] Gregory E. Sterling, "Philo and the Logic of Apologetics: An Analysis of the *Hypothetica*," *SBLSP* 29 (1990): 412–30. Sterling analyzes the genre, context, and contents of the *Hypothetica* and suggests that Philo, using Lysimachus's anti-Jewish writings as a model, responded directly to many anti-Jewish charges in preparation for the delegation to Gaius by using principles of Stoic logic.

[8] Barclay, *Against Apion*, 354.

In section 8.6.1, the author lists several circumstances that gave rise to the exodus. Against Barclay, Philo does not present his audience with contradictory options.[9] Rather, Philo positively characterizes the exodus and implicitly rejects contemporary Greco-Egyptian allegations that the gods had cursed the Israelites with a disease and that the pharaoh exiled them.[10] Philo explicitly counters in 8.6.2 charges against Moses that he was a trickster or magician, claims extant in authors such as Lysimachus and Apollonius and directly challenged by Josephus in *C. Ap.* 2.145.[11] Philo sarcastically notes that Moses' "fine trickery" (*Hypoth.* 8.6.2) gained the total obedience of the people and preserved their welfare during the harsh conditions of the wilderness. According to Sterling, Philo then juxtaposes three options: "Either Moses was great or the people were or God demonstrated favor by leading them."[12] Sterling suggests that this is an example of the Stoic inclusive disjunction; the options are inclusive insofar as they lead to a positive portrayal of the Jews.

The third section treats one of the more sensitive points of Jewish history, the conquest of Canaan. Lysimachus and Tacitus both accused the Jews of violently taking the land, burning its temples, and mistreating its residents.[13] In *Hypoth.* 8.6.5, Philo deems it better to discuss the settlement by means of a certain kind of reasoning rather than by means of history (οὐ μὴν ἔγωγε δικαιῶ μᾶλλον καθ᾽ ἱστορίαν ἢ κατά τινα λογισμὸν περὶ αὐτῶν τὰ εἰκότα ἐπεξελθεῖν). Sterling contends that Philo then examines the events of the conquest through one of the undemonstrated arguments of Stoic logic.[14] This argument rules out the possibility of a violent conquest and favors a peaceful settlement. Section 8.6.8 includes another inclusive disjunction; Philo considers obedience to the Jewish law to be compatible with piety and holiness. Though unmentioned by Sterling, section 8.6.9 also presents options. Philo states that whether the law came from Moses's own reasoning or from the inspiration of a daemon, the Israelites attributed it all to God and dedicated themselves to it.

[9] Ibid.

[10] These claims can be found among authors such as Manetho, Lysimachus, and Chaeremon. See Menachem Stern, *Greek and Latin Authors on Jews and Judaism* (3 vols.; Jerusalem: Israel Academy of Sciences and Humanities, 1974).

[11] For positive and negative assessments of Moses in the ancient world, see John G. Gager, *Moses in Greco-Roman Paganism* (Nashville: Abingdon Press, 1972).

[12] Sterling, "Logic of Apologetics," 421.

[13] Ibid., 425. See Lysimachus in *C. Ap.* 1.309 and Tacitus, *Hist.* 5.3.2.

[14] Sterling identifies it as an example of the fourth undemonstrated argument: Either A or B; A; therefore, not B. Sterling, "Logic of Apologetics," 421.

Sterling's persuasive evaluation of the historical section makes sense of passages that Barclay too quickly dismisses as un-Philonic. According to Sterling, the title *Hypothetica* may refer to the "hypothetical syllogisms" of Stoic logic; therefore, the title might mean something like "Hypothetical Propositions."[15] The fact that Philo knew Stoic philosophy and specifically referred to logical concepts throughout his writings reinforces Sterling's thesis.[16] However, Philo's potential use of Stoic inclusive and exclusive disjunctions can be reevaluated, especially in light of recent advances in the study of Stoic logic and rhetorical features of dilemmatic argumentation.

Exclusive and Inclusive Disjunctions

First, it is necessary to examine the Stoic understanding of disjunctions and then evaluate their possible presence in the *Hypothetica*. Sterling identifies Stoic inclusive disjunctions in *Hypoth.* 8.6.4 and 8.6.8. As noted above, Sterling finds three inclusive options in 8.6.4: "Either Moses was great or the people were or God demonstrated favor by leading them."[17] Whether the Israelites were obedient or disobedient, Philo argues that a positive view of Moses and the Israelites naturally emerges. In describing the options as an inclusive disjunction, Sterling writes, "Philo does not intend for these to be mutually exclusive alternatives as his conclusion shows. The Stoics dubbed such reasoning παραδιεζευγμένον, 'inclusive disjunction': they recognized both exclusive and inclusive disjunctions."[18] However, it may be possible to interpret Philo's options as an example of the exclusive disjunction, especially if we examine the contrast between the obedience and disobedience of the Israelites. What makes a disjunction inclusive or exclusive is the natural relationship between the disjuncts themselves rather than their relationship to a particular conclusion. The concept and function of Stoic disjunctions deserve closer attention.

A disjunction is made up of two simple assertibles/propositions (ἀξιώματα) joined by the particle ἤ or ἤτοι.[19] The exclusive disjunction (διεζευγμένον) was the most common form mentioned in Stoic writings. To be a true exclusive disjunction, the disjuncts must be in conflict with each

---

[15] Ibid.

[16] See *Agr.* 118, 140–41, *Prob.* 80, and *Spec.* 1.336. For an overview of Philo's knowledge of Stoic logic, see John Dillon, *The Middle Platonists 80 B.C. to A.D. 220* (Ithaca, N. Y.: Cornell University Press, 1977), 178–82.

[17] Sterling, "Logic of Apologetics," 421.

[18] Ibid.

[19] Diogenes Laertius, *Vit.* 7.72; Galen, *Institutio Logica* 3.3.

other.[20] In the typical example "either it is day or it is night," one of the disjuncts must be true and the other must be false. Philo himself provides an example of an exclusive disjunction and tries to persuade his audience to choose one alternative over the other (*Agr.* 118).[21] In this remarkable parallel, Philo interacts with his audience in a manner that coheres with his method in the *Hypothetica*. Gellius offers evidence for an additional, but perhaps optional, condition which states that the contraries of the disjuncts must be in conflict as well.[22] Susanne Bobzien explains, "the contradictories of the disjuncts must all be contrary to each other; this ensures that not all of the contradictories are true, and hence at least one of the disjuncts is true."[23] An example of a disjunction that includes this extra condition would be "either wealth is bad or good, or it is neither bad nor good." Both Philo and Sextus Empiricus are witnesses to this form of the exclusive disjunction.[24] While exclusive disjunctions could be used in Stoic undemonstrated arguments, inclusive disjunctions were never used.[25]

The non-Stoic authors Gellius and Galen each provide evidence for the inclusive disjunction (παραδιεζευγμένον). This less common form of the disjunction is comprised of disjuncts that are not fully at odds with each other. Galen writes, "in some propositions it is possible for more than one or for all the members to be true, and necessary for one to be true; some call propositions of this sort 'paradisjunctives,' since the disjunctives have one member only true, whether they be composed of two simple propositions or of more than two."[26] An example of an inclusive disjunction can be found in a scholium to Ammonius: either Socrates walks or Socrates

---

[20] Diogenes Laertius, *Vit.* 7.72.

[21] For if two things, contrary the one to the other, have been determined against one person or one action, one or the other must of necessity be right and the other wrong; for it is out of the question that they should both be right or both wrong. Which then, rightly, would you praise? Would you not approve the punishment of those who are guilty of unprovoked violence and wrong? In that case you would censure, as a matter of course, the opposite treatment of them, the showing of honor to them. (Philo, *Agr.* 118, Colson, LCL).

[22] Aulus Gellius, *Noct. att.* 16.8.13.

[23] Susanne Bobzien, "Stoic Logic," in *The Cambridge Companion to the Stoics* (ed. Brad Inwood; New York: Cambridge University Press, 2003), 85–123.

[24] Both cite the example of the hound that must choose which path to take. The hound must choose between either right or left, or neither right nor left (that is, by proceeding through the middle). Philo, *Anim.* 45, 84; Sextus Empiricus, *Pyr.* 1.69, *M.* 8.434.

[25] Benson Mates, *Stoic Logic* (Berkeley: University of California Press, 1961), 51. See also Bobzien, "Stoic Logic," 96.

[26] Galen, *Institutio Logica* 5.1. Translation from J.S. Kieffer, *Galen's* Institutio Logica: *English Translation, Introduction, and Commentary* (Baltimore: The Johns Hopkins Press, 1964).

converses.[27] Neither disjunct truly conflicts with the other; though at least one must be true, both can be true at the same time. Gellius provided a useful example of an inclusive disjunction in which neither the disjuncts nor their contraries contradicted each other:

> For instance, this case, in which the things which are opposed are not contraries: "Either you run or you walk or you stand." These acts are indeed contrasted, but when opposed they are not contrary; for "not to walk" and "not to stand" and "not to run" are not contrary to one another, since those things are called contraries which cannot be true at the same time. But you may at once and at the same time neither walk, stand, nor run.[28]

Galen provides a similar example of an inclusive disjunction with three members:

> The distribution of nourishment from the belly to the whole body occurs, either by the food being carried along of its own motion, or by being digested by the stomach, or by being attracted by the parts of the body, or by being conducted by veins. Let it be granted that all these actions could occur together; for in fact, this is possible, and the paradisjunctive differed from the disjunctive in just this respect; in the latter, one member was always true and none of the others, but in the former, one member always is true, but one of the others, or even all of those comprehended, may be true at the same time.[29]

Galen and Gellius thus present interesting parallels for Sterling's assessment of *Hypoth.* 8.6.4 where, in his view, Philo's three options form an inclusive disjunction. However, it seems that there is a sharp contrast between the purported obedience and disobedience of the Israelites. Philo does not indicate that these options can be simultaneously true; instead, he invites his audience to choose one of the options. Even if we grant that the question of Moses's ability is one of the options at stake, Philo's challenge to his audience remains the same; they must account for the survival of the Israelites in the wilderness. Whichever option they choose, they must admit something positive about Israel's past. This is a crucial feature absent from the examples found in Galen and Gellius. They do not tie each disjunct to a particular conclusion; they merely note that certain acts can occur at the same time and are not naturally contradictory. Thus, I am inclined to see *Hypoth.* 8.6.4 as an instance of the exclusive disjunction.

[27] Mates, *Stoic Logic*, 53.
[28] Aulus Gellius, *Noct. att.* 16.18.14 (Rolfe, LCL).
[29] *Institutio Logica* 15 (J.S. Kieffer). Concerning the definition of the inclusive disjunction, Kieffer observes that since Gellius "is discussing Stoic terminology in this chapter and seems to be quoting a Stoic source, it is evident that Galen is giving a different and possibly non-Stoic sense to the word." In fact, Galen might be synthesizing Stoic thought with Aristotelian or Peripatetic principles. See Kieffer, *Galen*, 25–7, 85–7.

In summary, the inclusive disjunction takes the same linguistic form as an exclusive disjunction, but it is true "either when its subdisjuncts do not conflict with each other or when the contradictories of its subdisjuncts are not mutually incompatible."[30] Furthermore, it must be noted that disjunctions are merely propositions, they are not argument schemes. To determine whether a disjunction is inclusive or exclusive, one must examine the relationship between the disjuncts themselves, not their relationship to a conclusion. The terms "inclusive" and "exclusive" are descriptive of the inherent relationship between two or more disjuncts. The inclusivity Sterling finds in the disjunction of 8.6.4 is in fact a property not of the disjunction itself but rather of a broader argument scheme that came to be known as the dilemma. Philo's insistence that various options lead inevitably to the same conclusion has close parallels with dilemmatic arguments.

2. *Dilemmatic Argumentation*

Having discussed the Stoic understanding of exclusive and inclusive disjunctions, I will turn now to the ancient logical and rhetorical device known as the dilemma. Gabriel Nuchelmans explains that, in logical terms, a dilemma "refers to a type of argument whose premises are a combination of conditional and disjunctive propositions."[31] That is, it consists of "if, then" clauses and exclusive disjunctions. The word dilemma (διλήμματον) appears in Gregory of Nyssa's *Contra Eunomium* 2.6, an important parallel to *Hypoth.* 8.6.4 that I will discuss below. Like Philo, Gregory proposes for his opponent alternatives that lead to the same conclusion.

The Stoics are a witness to this kind of argumentation. The dilemma takes the form of one of the lesser known Stoic non-indemonstrable syllogisms, that is, a syllogism based on more than two premises.[32] One example takes the following form: If p, p; if not p, p; either p or not p; therefore p. A concrete example of a Stoic non-indemonstrable syllogism used within the

[30] Katerina Ierodiakonou, "Stoic Logic," in *Blackwell Companion to Philosophy: A Companion to Ancient Philosophy* (eds. M.L. Gill and P.P. Pellegrin; Malden, Mass.: Blackwell, 2006), 513.

[31] Gabriel Nuchelmans, *Dilemmatic Arguments: Towards a History of their Logic and Rhetoric* (Amsterdam: North Holland, 1991), 139.

[32] For examples of other non-indemonstrable syllogisms, see Susanne Bobzien, "Logic II-III.7," in *The Cambridge History of Hellenistic Philosophy* (eds. K. Alegra, J. Barnes, J. Mansfeld, and M. Schofield; Cambridge: Cambridge University Press, 2008), 83–157; cited here 136–39. The Stoics even had rules for reducing these non-indemonstrable syllogisms down to the standard five undemonstrated syllogisms. See Bobzien, "Logic II-III.7," 139–57.

context of a debate over logic can be found in Sextus Empiricus *Math.* 8.281–84 (cf. 466–69): (1) if a sign exists, a sign exists; (2) If a sign does not exist, a sign exists; (3) But a sign either exists not or exists; (4) Therefore a sign exists. There are many other places in Sextus Empiricus where the same argument scheme is used to defend the existence of proof, criteria, and causes.[33] While the word διλήμματον is not used in these cases, the word περιτροπή (turning an argument against an opponent) is used frequently.[34] Sextus Empiricus notes two important things about these arguments: the disjunction in each argument is exclusive (*Math.* 2.282), and the arguments were used by dogmatists (Stoics) against skeptics. Regarding these forms of argument, Susanne Bobzien notes, "Generally, such syllogisms may have been of the kind: if p, q; if r, q; either p or r; therefore q. This is a simple constructive dilemma, which was used, for example, in paradoxes. The examples in Sextus would then be a special case of this kind."[35]

This by no means indicates that the Stoics created the idea of the dilemma or that it was a purely logical phenomenon.[36] According to Nuchelmans, the dilemma could be used for purely rhetorical purposes without concern for logical precision and form or for specific issues of logic. From a rhetorical standpoint, a dilemma may be characterized as "a form of argument that involves an adversary in the choice of two alternatives either of which is equally unpalatable to him."[37] The first attested use of the word dilemma (διλήμματον) is found among Greek rhetoricians (Hermogenes, *De Inventione* 4.6). An example of a rhetorical dilemma concerns advice against marriage: Whether you married a fair woman or an ugly one, you should not have married. Marrying a fair one entails sharing her with others while marrying an ugly one is a punishment.[38] The fact that no intermediate

---

[33] Signs: *Pyr.* 2.130–3; Proof: *Pyr.* 2.185–186; Criteria: *Math.* 7.440; Causes: *Pyr* 3.19, *Math.* 9.204–206.

[34] Nuchelmans, *Dilemmatic Arguments*, 19.

[35] Bobzien, "Stoic Logic II–III.7," 137. It is interesting to note that the dilemma could be used in paradoxes. Famous examples of paradoxes include the Liar, the Crocodile, the Sorites, and the Horned Man. On the Horned Man, see Nuchelmans, *Dilemmatic Arguments*, 51–57. Chrysippus wrote several books on paradoxes and paid particular attention to arguments (such as the Idle Argument) that were leveled against Stoic philosophy. See Susanne Bobzien, *Determinism and Freedom in Stoic Philosophy* (Oxford: Clarendon, 1998).

[36] A non-Stoic example can be found in Aristotle's *Protrepticus*: Whether one must philosophize or not, one must philosophize. Either one must philosophize or not. Therefore, one must philosophize. William Kneale, "Aristotle and the Consequentia Mirabilis," *JHS* 77:1 (1957): 62–66.

[37] Nuchelmans, *Dilemmatic Arguments*, 139.

[38] Ibid., 30.

option exists, such as a woman of average looks, keeps one from escaping the two alternatives that lead to the warning against marriage. Nuchelmans intriguingly suggests that other examples of dilemmatic schemes formulated to pin down one's opponent in defeat can be found in the gospels. Jesus poses a dilemma for his opponents in Mark 11:30 (and parallels) concerning the origin, divine or human, of John's baptism. In Mark 12:13 (and parallels), the Pharisees try to trap Jesus by asking him about paying or not paying taxes to Caesar.[39] These argument schemes, though unrelated to specific issues of logic, utilize exclusive disjunctions that can trap an opponent with options that lead to unfavorable conclusions.

It is difficult to distinguish between purely logical and purely rhetorical uses of the dilemma. Though Nuchelmans characterizes the Stoic examples found in Sextus Empiricus as rhetorical, he maps out the argument according to Stoic patterns.[40] While someone like Hermogenes might not have worried about constructing a logically airtight argument, this does not mean his arguments could not be analyzed and criticized. Gellius himself criticized the argument against marriage mentioned above because, in his view, it did not include a true disjunction. To be a true and complete disjunction (at least according to one ancient definition), the argument should have included "either beautify or ugly" with the contrary "or neither beautiful nor ugly."[41] Furthermore, the Stoic examples themselves could be overturned by their skeptic opponents.[42] Gregory of Nyssa's use of the dilemma in *Contra Eunomium* 2.6, even though Nuchelmans characterizes it as rhetorical, can be mapped out as follows:

If Eunomius denies the Son's divinity, then he promotes impiety.
If Eunomius proposes that the Son is divine but not equal to the Father, then he promotes impiety.
Either Eunomius denies the Son's divinity, or he proposes that the Son is divine but not equal to the Father.
Therefore, Eunomius promotes impiety.[43]
If A then C

---

[39] Ibid., 33.

[40] Ibid., 18–26.

[41] Aulus Gellius, *Att. noct.* 5.11.

[42] Nuchelmans, *Dilemmatic Arguments*, 24–7. See *Pyr.* 2.132–33, 2.188–92 and *Math.* 8.293–96.

[43] Gregory insists that Eunomius's position, however formulated, led inevitably to idolatry or polytheism. Assuming that Eunomius worshipped the Son, he either worshipped a non-divine being or a semi-divine being. Gregory believed that his own Christology maintained both the divinity of the Son and monotheism.

If B then C
Either A or B
Therefore, C

There may be an important connection between dilemmatic arguments (which take the form of non-indemonstrable syllogisms) and Stoic "hypothetical arguments."[44] One of the most intriguing developments in the field of Stoic logic has been the attempt to reconstruct Stoic "hypothetical arguments."[45] Susanne Bobzien argues that hypothetical arguments filled in a gap in Stoic inference by including what standard syllogisms could not include, that is, the hypothesis (ὑπόθεσις or τό ὑποθετικόν).[46] The canonical form of the hypothesis may have been "let it be supposed" (ὑποκείσθω) or "let it be" (ἔστω). When used in an argument, the hypothesis turns the argument into a kind of thought experiment.[47] In Stoic hypothetical arguments, "the interlocutors agree—as it were—to enter a non-actual 'world' built on the respective assumption; but they remain aware of the fact that this assumption and, presumably, any conclusions drawn from it hold only relative to the fact that this assumption has been made."[48]

On several occasions noted above, Stoics made use of exclusive disjunctions and a form of non-indemonstrable syllogisms (the logical backbone of dilemmatic argumentation) to engage in philosophical debate. Bobzien notes that Sextus Empiricus made use of hypothetical argumentation to analyze and break down the non-indemonstrable syllogism into one of the

---

[44] On Stoic hypothetical arguments, see Susanne Bobzien, "The Stoics on Hypotheses and Hypothetical Arguments," *Phronesis* 42 (1997): 299-312.

[45] The five undemonstrated syllogisms are frequently called "hypothetical syllogisms." But the Stoics themselves never referred to them as hypothetical syllogisms. See Susanne Bobzien, "The Development of Modus Ponens in Antiquity from Aristotle to the 2nd Century AD," *Phronesis* 47 (2002): 359-394. Syllogisms based on a hypothesis can be found in Aristotelian and Peripatetic traditions. "Hypothetical syllogism" is a misnomer applied to Stoic logic at a later time via the influence of other schools of logic. This long-standing influence can be seen in many translations. For instance, we often find the translation "hypothetical proposition" for συνημμένον ἀξίωμα. Literally, the phrase merely means conjoined propositions, and it is used for propositions joined by the connectors if, then (see Diogenes Laertuysm, *Vit.* 7.71, 73).

[46] Evidence for hypotheses and hypothetical arguments may be found in Epictetus (*Diatr.* 1.7.1, 1.25.11–13; 3.2.6, 3.17, 3.24.80).

[47] Bobzien, "Stoics on Hypotheses," 305. Bobzien proposes a reconstructed version of what a hypothetical argument might have looked like in Epictetus: If it is night, it is dark; Now, let it be that it is night; Hence—on the assumption that it is night—it is dark.

[48] Ibid., 305.

standard undemonstrated arguments.[49] The argument can be mapped out as follows:

If p, p Let it be that p Hence, on the hypothesis of p, p	If not p, p Let it be that not p Hence, on the hypothesis of not p, p

This provides an interesting connection between hypothetical arguments and the dilemma. Several words derived from ὑπόκειμαι and ὑποτίθημι are scattered throughout *Math.* 8.468, 8.284; *Pyr.* 189–90, and other passages in the writings of Sextus Empiricus. As Bobzien explains, "here all (that is both) possibilities given by the exclusive and exhaustive disjunction have been hypothesized separately, and the same conclusion follows each time."[50] It is intriguing that Philo himself uses a form of the word ὑποτίθημι in *Hypoth.* 8.6.6 and that the very title of the treatise is *Hypothetica*. Though the evidence for Stoic hypothetical arguments is limited, it may be possible to speculate that Philo's adversaries used this methodology to engage in a thought experiment to assess the options whose truth values they did not know. The dilemma itself, however, is much more widely attested in the ancient world, and the comparison between Philo and dilemmatic arguments stands on firmer ground than comparisons with hypothetical arguments.

3. *Dilemmatic Argumentation and the Hypothetica*

In light of the preceding discussion, we can now turn to the text of Philo's *Hypothetica* and reconsider its connections with principles of Stoic logic and dilemmatic arguments. I will limit my discussion to *Hypoth.* 8.6.4–9.[51] Philo's proposal of options and alternatives, one of the main reasons Barclay doubts the authenticity of the *Hypothetica*, can be seen as an exercise in dilemmatic argumentation.

The first of these arguments is in section 8.6.4. Having argued against the charge that Moses was a charlatan and trickster, Philo implies instead that he was a capable leader who successfully led his people in spite of so many hardships in the desert (famine, thirst, starvation, uncertainty).

---

[49] Ibid., 311.

[50] Ibid.

[51] As noted above, though 8.6.1 lists various reasons about the exodus, Philo does not present them as contradictory alternatives.

Revising the biblical account of discord and dissent, he claims that the Israelites never rebelled against Moses during the journey. He asks his audience, "What do you think of these things?" After asking whether one should attribute great skill to Moses, Philo then proposes an exclusive disjunction:

ἢ γὰρ τὰς φύσεις τῶν ὑπ᾽ αὐτὸν ἀνθρώπων οὐκ ἀμαθῶς οὐδὲ δυσκόλως, ἀλλ᾽ εὐπειθῶς καὶ τοῦ μέλλοντος οὐκ ἀπρονοήτως ἔχειν.

ἢ τούτους μὲν ὡς μάλιστα κακοὺς εἶναι, τὸν δὲ θεὸν τὰς δυσκολίας αὐτῶν πραΰνειν καὶ τοῦ παρόντος καὶ τοῦ μέλλοντος ὥσπερ ἐπιστατεῖν.

For either the natures of the people under him were not unlearned and stubborn but rather obedient and forward-looking, or they were extremely base but God tamed their stubbornness and it was as if he took over the present and future.

Philo uses the canonical particle ἤ/ἤ that we expect in a disjunction. As noted earlier in the paper, this disjunction should be considered exclusive; natural obedience is contrasted with disobedience changed by God. One could include Moses's abilities in the disjunction. It would remain an exclusive disjunction because Philo attributes the success of the migration either to Moses, the people, or to God. In any case, whether Moses excelled as a leader or the people were naturally obedient or God took charge of the situation, in *Hypoth.* 8.6.4 Philo declares that one cannot help but marvel at how the entire people made it through such dire circumstances: ὅπερ γάρ σοι μάλιστα ἂν ἐκ τούτων ἀληθὲς εἶναι δόξῃ, πρὸς ἐπαίνου καὶ τιμῆς καὶ ζήλου περὶ αὐτῶν συμπάντων ἰσχύειν φαίνεται (For whichever of these seems most true to you, it appears to strengthen the praise, honor, and zeal for them all). While his audience might not have wanted to concede that there was anything virtuous about the Israelites or Moses, Philo tries to catch his opponents in a dilemma.

Philo does not tell his audience which option to choose. Though he allows them to decide what seems most likely, he does dictate the conclusion each option entails. Strictly speaking, a full, logical argument is not constructed. It has the appearance of a rhetorical scheme in which conflicting options all lead to a conclusion that the audience may dislike. This does not mean that the argument cannot be analyzed logically. It is the audience that creates the logical outline. The exclusive disjunction could be considered the third premise in a non-indemonstrable syllogism:

If the people were obedient they are worthy of praise.
If the people were disobedient, but God took charge of them, they are worthy of praise.
Either the people were obedient or disobedient.
Therefore, they are worthy of praise.[52]

If his opponents knew Stoic logic, they could have reasoned through the dilemma by means of hypothetical argumentation. We have seen this practice already in Sextus Empiricus. Philo has invited his audience to weigh the logical possibilities, and, regardless of what they think really happened, he has trapped them into concluding that the exodus was in fact an admirable event. While Philo has stretched the biblical account by claiming that they were all obedient to Moses, the disjunction somehow leaves open the possibility that they were disobedient. Even his most vitriolic opponents who claimed that the Israelites were cursed fools who wandered in the desert had to accept the possibility that their journey was successful and that the anti-Jewish versions of the exodus were not logical.

The dilemma may also be at work in section 8.6.5 where Philo actually declares his intention to analyze the settlement by means of reason rather than history (οὐ μὴν ἔγωγε δικαιῶ μᾶλλον καθ᾽ ἱστορίαν ἢ κατά τινα λογισμὸν περὶ αὐτῶν τὰ εἰκότα ἐπεξελθεῖν). Philo, aware of the fact that the narrative is described in scripture (ἐν ταῖς ἱεραῖς ἀναγραφαῖς δηλοῦται), decides to depart from both scripture and pagan ethnographies.[53] Thus, reason rather than scripture or any other written account takes center stage.[54] Even though this appeal to a certain kind of reasoning is only mentioned explicitly in this passage, it is probably the guiding principle throughout his entire exposition of Judean history. Philo formulates another exclusive disjunction in *Hypoth.* 8.6.6 in the case of the conquest of Canaan:

---

[52] This argument fits well with the formula mentioned in the previous section:
   If A then C
   If B then C
   Either A or B
   Therefore C

[53] In the Philonic corpus, ἱστορία and related words refer to ancient historical writings and events (*Cher.* 1:105; *Congr.* 1.15; *Abr.* 1.65; *Aet.* 1.139, 1.146; *Somn.* 1.205, 2.302). Philo also uses the word group to characterize the sacred writings of his own tradition (*Spec.* 2.146; *Mos.* 2.46–7, 2.59, 2.143; *Praem.* 1.1, 1.2; *Somn.* 1.52; *Congr.* 1.44). Thus, Philo's appeal to reason indicates a departure from the written record of the Jews as well as those of his Egyptian and Roman opponents.

[54] Flavius Josephus himself uses this phrase κατά λογισμὸν in his account of the young men in the fiery furnace (*A.J.* 10.215). Josephus rationalizes the story and claims that the fire was not strong enough to harm the men and that God had prepared their bodies to be resistant to the fire.

πότερον γάρ ποτε βούλει; τῷ πλήθει τῶν σωμάτων ἔτι περιόντας, καίπερ
εἰς τέλος κεκακωμένους, ὅμως δ᾽ ἰσχύοντας καὶ τὰ ὅπλα ἐν χερσὶν
ἔχοντας, εἶτα κατὰ κράτος ἑλεῖν τὴν χώραν, Σύρους τε ὁμοῦ καὶ
Φοίνικας ἐν αὐτῇ τῇ ἐκείνων γῇ μαχομένους νικῶντας,

ἢ τοὺς μὲν ἀπολέμους καὶ ἀνάνδρους εἶναι καὶ παντελῶς ὀλίγους
ὑποθώμεθα καὶ τῶν εἰς πόλεμον παρασκευῶν ἀπόρους, αἰδέσεως δὲ
τυχεῖν παρὰ τούτοις καὶ τὴν γῆν λαβεῖν παρ᾽ ἑκόντων, ἔπειτα δ᾽ εὐθὺς
οὐκ εἰς μακρὰν τόν τε νεὼν οἰκοδομῆσαι καὶ τἆλλα εἰς εὐσέβειαν καὶ
ἁγιστείαν καταστήσασθαι;

For which do you prefer? Were they still flourishing in numbers, even
though they had been thoroughly defeated, yet still powerful and
armed that they took the land by force and defeated the Syrians and
Phoenicians who were fighting in their own land?

Or, should we suppose that they were not adept at war, weak, few in
number, and lacking weapons, but nevertheless won respect and
received the land from the willing inhabitants and shortly thereafter
built both the temple and established everything needed for religion
and ritual?

Again, the disjunctive connective ἤ is employed. The disjunction must
be considered exclusive in Stoic terms because a warlike settlement is juxta-
posed with a peaceful one. Both cannot be true at the same time, and the
audience must choose one or the other. Unambiguously religious language
highlights the second, peaceful option. As noted earlier in this paper, Philo
clearly responded to the charge of a violent, sacrilegious conquest of the
land. Thus, he plays with the accusations known to his opponents that the
Israelites were warlike and sacrilegious people who conquered, mistreated
the people, and built their own temple. The other option is that Israelites
were few in number, weak, and dedicated to religion alone; this may allude
to the accusations that they wandered aimlessly and suffered in the desert.
Thus, Philo invites his audience to examine their own conflicting presuppositions and accusations about the Jewish people. They would have had to
determine whether a destitute people that had wandered foolishly in the
desert would have been capable of engaging in a violent struggle for the
land. He concludes that the Syrians and Phoenicians recognized the
Israelites as beloved by God and willingly gave up their land in accordance
with the divine plan: δηλοῖ γάρ, ὡς ἔοικε, ταῦτα καὶ θεοφιλεστάτους αὐτοὺς
ἀνωμολογῆσθαι καὶ παρὰ τοῖς ἐχθροῖς (For it is clear, it seems, that they were
considered by their enemies to be loved by God).

Philo seems to prefer the possibility of a peaceful settlement. Sterling has argued that Philo uses a version of the fourth undemonstrated syllogism:[55]

> Either they took the land by force or they won the land peacefully
> They won the land peacefully
> Therefore, they did not take the land by force
>
> Either A or B
> B
> Therefore, not A

This does not follow the strict canonical formula, but the undemonstrated syllogisms could take on slightly different forms.[56] According to this perspective, Philo uses Stoic logic to rule out the possibility of a violent conquest and to exalt the Israelites as peaceful and dedicated to religion.

Though she cites Sterling's analysis of the *Hypothetica*, Berthelot does not mention any specific features of Stoic logic. Instead, she argues that Philo takes a rationalizing approach to scripture. Berthelot claims that in *QE* 2.22 Philo reinterpreted Exod 23:27 in a peaceful, moral sense.[57] According to Berthelot, Philo attributes the acquisition of the land to the power of the unsurpassed virtue and morality of the Israelites, not the power of their military forces. Berthelot suggests that Philo may have been aware of the traditions attested in Strabo's *Geography* which claimed that the Hebrews won the land peacefully and that Moses gained the admiration and support of the natives. *Hypoth.* 8.6.6 would thus represent a rational interpretation of scripture which downplays the literal meaning of the conquest and emphasizes both the willing transferal of the land and the conversion of the native people to the morally superior Jewish law.

I am inclined, however, to interpret Philo's argument not as a mere rationalization of scripture but rather as another instance of the dilemma. In a certain sense, Philo's conclusion that the Israelites won the respect of their enemies is ambiguous. It does not necessarily rule out the possibility that the Israelites were indeed adept at war and earned the fearful respect of their enemies through a military victory that clearly demonstrated God's favor for the Israelites. Philo does not explicitly judge whether the settlement was peaceful or violent; he merely concludes that the enemies of the Israelites willingly gave up the land and granted them respect. With

[55] Sterling, "Logic of Apologetics," 421.
[56] See Bobzien, "Stoic Logic," 106.
[57] See Berthelot, "Conquest of Canaan," 52-6.

this interpretation in mind, the two members of the exclusive disjunction lead to the same conclusion: either through conflict or peaceful means, the Israelites won the admiration of their enemies as well as their land. Thus, if Philo's opponents wish to brand the Israelites as either warlike or as feeble in their emergence from the desert, they have to conclude in the end that God was on their side.

I do not deny Berthelot's proposal that Philo may be aware of traditions of a peaceful settlement found in ethnographic writings, nor do I deny the possibility that Philo rationalized scripture and preferred a moral interpretation of the conquest. Nevertheless, the actual form of the argument found in this particular text resonates with the tradition of dilemmatic arguments.

I agree with Sterling that Philo proposed an exclusive disjunction, but I suggest that his argument took the form of the dilemma rather than one of the undemonstrated syllogisms. We can map out his argument in terms of the non-indemonstrable syllogism:[58]

> If the Israelites took the land by force, they won the respect and land of the people.
> If the Israelites were peaceful, they won the respect and the land of the people.
> Either the Israelites took the land by force or were peaceful.
> Therefore, they won the respect and land of the people.

If Philo intended to create a dilemma here, then his audience may have sorted through the options by means of hypothetical argumentation. The use of ὑποθώμεθα in 8.6.6 points intriguingly in this direction.[59] Philo gives his audience two options from which to choose by incorporating traditions they would have been familiar with (wandering in the wilderness and reports of a violent conquest). Even if his opponents chose the potentially more negative option, that the Israelites took the land by force, Philo hoped they would interpret the conquest as divinely sanctioned and positive. On the other hand, if they deemed the Israelites as foolish and feeble, they were still favored by God and won the land from a willing people persuaded by their piety. Either way, Philo does not mention the burning of temples or impiety against foreign gods. Instead, he indicates that the settlement

---

[58] If A then C
If B then C
Either A or B
Therefore C.

[59] As mentioned earlier, ὑπόκειμαι and ὑποτίθημι were both used by Sextus Empiricus in hypothetical argumentation. See *Math.* 8.468.

results in the building of the temple and Israel's extraordinary piety (εὐσέβεια).

This emphasis on the foundation of the temple and its rituals segues thematically into a brief discussion of the law and its origins. Philo appears to be concerned about pagan conceptions of the Jewish law. We know that Jewish law was seen as misanthropic and incompatible with Egyptian and Roman sensibilities. Critics of the Jewish law may have speculated that Moses the trickster and charlatan invented the entire law code. Philo declares that the fact that the Israelites won respect and honor among the people shows that they have surpassed all others in excellence. Philo asks his audience what else could be said in praise of the Jews, their loyalty to the law or their holiness, righteousness, and piety. It is possible that Philo constructs here an inclusive disjunction out of what would almost certainly be an exclusive disjunction for his audience: either obedience to the Jewish law or religious piety. These are equivalent concepts for Philo.

This leads to a brief discussion of the origin of the law. There is another possible use of the dilemma in section 8.6.9. As has been the case in the other arguments, Philo takes a noncommittal stance toward scripture. He does not insist that the law came from God on Mt. Sinai or Mt. Horeb. Instead, in *Hypoth.* 8.6.9 he declares that whether it came from Moses's own reasoning or whether he obtained it through a daemon, the people ultimately attributed it to God:

εἴτε οὖν λελογισμένος αὐτὸς εἴτε ἀκούων
παρὰ δαίμονος ἔφρασε, τοῦτο ἅπαν εἰς τὸν θεὸν ἀνάγειν,

Therefore, whether he had reasoned or spoke while listening to a daimon, all attributed it to God.

Here we have another exclusive disjunction, although the connective used is εἴτε. The canonical connective is not used here, but εἴτε/εἴτε could be considered the functional equivalent. The disjunction is exclusive because the options presented cannot both be true at the same time. Philo does not indicate that some of the laws came from Moses and some from a daemon. He merely asserts that in each scenario the people accepted the law and were willing to perish for it. If this is a use of the dilemma, we may analyze the argument according to this scheme:

If Moses developed the law on his own, the people accepted it and attributed it to God.
If Moses received the law from a daemon, the people accepted it and attributed it to God.

Either Moses developed the law on his own or he received it from a daemon
The people accepted it and attributed it to God

Whatever his audience thinks of the origins of the law (either Moses made it up or he received it from a daemon), the conclusion is that the Jews ultimately attributed it to God. Their ultimate loyalty and dedication to the law, even to the point of death, evinces the divine origin and rationality of the law itself. Whichever option his audience chooses, the law ultimately has its origins in God and is worthy of respect.

Conclusion

This paper has attempted to illuminate and clarify certain aspects of the purpose and strategy of the fragmentary text known as the *Hypothetica*. Specifically, I reexamined Sterling's thesis in light of further study of Stoic disjunctions and recent advances in the field of Stoic logic. I concur with Sterling that Philo appealed to Stoic logic, although in a slightly different manner. Rather than inclusive disjunctions, I propose that Philo set up exclusive disjunctions in order to create dilemmatic arguments (that is, the non-indemonstrable syllogism). This strategy countered conflicting reports about the Jews and trapped his audience in a positive understanding of Judean history and culture. As noted earlier, Berthelot has established that Philo previously allegorized or contradicted the story of the conquest of Canaan. In the *Hypothetica*, Philo took a different approach. Aware of various negative portrayals that distorted the biblical account, Philo appealed to reason and rhetoric to force his audience to admire the Jewish past. Whatever his audience might have heard about the exodus, settlement, and Jewish law, they could not help but admit that the Jews were favored by God's providence. This strategy allowed Philo to operate on a level playing field with critics of Jewish history for whom the scriptures had no authority. It is reasonable to assume that Philo was aware of this line of argumentation through his knowledge of Stoicism and ancient rhetoric and that he could have incorporated it in an apologetic context. Though other assessments of ancient logic and rhetoric may alter the interpretation of the author's strategy in *Hypoth.* 8.6.4–8.6.9, it is safe to conclude that this section need not trouble interpreters any longer. The approach to biblical history in the *Hypothetica* is both Philonic and intelligible in light of ancient modes of argumentation.

University of Notre Dame

The Studia Philonica Annual 22 (2010) 183–207

RECONCEPTUALIZING CONQUEST: COLONIAL NARRATIVES AND PHILO'S ROMAN ACCUSER IN THE *HYPOTHETICA*

MICHAEL COVER

Introduction

In the eighth book of his *Praeparatio evangelica*, Eusebius begins a discussion of the state (*politeuma*) established by Moses with the first of two fragments[1] from Philo of Alexandria's otherwise lost apologetic work, the *Hypothetica*. As a preface to this first fragment Eusebius says that he will quote:

ἀπὸ τοῦ πρώτου συγγράμματος ὧν ἐπέγραψεν Ὑποθετικῶν, ἔνθα τὸν ὑπὲρ Ἰουδαίων, ὡς πρὸς κατηγόρους αὐτῶν, ποιούμενος λόγον ταῦτά φησιν·

> from the first book of the work which [Philo] entitled the *Hypothetica*, where he makes his defense on behalf of the Jews, as against their accusers, saying the following things. . . (*Praep. ev.* 8.5.11).

Although Eusebius died almost three centuries after Philo,[2] his introductory remarks here, undoubtedly influenced by knowledge of a fuller version of the text,[3] pose important questions about the place of the *Hypothetica* within the Philonic corpus and about the nature of Philo's self-presentation as a Jew on the Greco-Roman stage. In particular, Eusebius invites us to ask who Philo's accusers were, what accusations they made, and how these accusations shaped the content and rhetoric of Philo's response.

---

[1] Eusebius divides this first fragment into four pericopes with some material omitted. See John Barclay, "The Sources of the Apologetic Encomium," in *Against Apion* (ed. Steve Mason; vol. 10 of *Flavius Josephus, Translation and Commentary*; Leiden: Brill, 2007), 353–361, esp. 353.

[2] Henry Chadwick, *The Early Church* (Pelican History of the Church 1; Baltimore: Penguin Books, 1967), 304.

[3] So the editorial refrain, καὶ μετὰ βραχέα φησίν (*Praep. ev.* 5.6.2). For an in-depth study of Eusebius's method of citation, see Sabrina Inowlocki, *Eusebius and the Jewish Authors: His Citation Technique in an Apologetic Context* (AGJU 64; Leiden: Brill, 2006), esp. 179–180.

This essay will venture to answer these questions by situating Philo's *Hypothetica* within the imperial Roman context. In particular, I will defend the thesis that the *Hypothetica* was composed by Philo in preparation for the Jewish embassy to the emperor Gaius, which Philo led in 39/40 C.E. in the wake of the political persecution of the Alexandrian Jews under the Roman prefect of Egypt Avillius Flaccus.

The question of audience in Jewish apologetic literature from the Hellenistic and Roman periods needs to be undertaken carefully for several reasons. Firstly, the *Hypothetica* itself gives no explicit indicators of its *Sitz im Leben*. Secondly, in a now-foundational essay,[4] Victor Tcherikover warns strongly against an overly facile identification of the form and function of early Christian and Jewish apologetic literature. Jewish apologetic should not be construed as having a primarily proselytizing function aimed at a general Gentile audience. Rather, writes Tcherikover, "we may . . . conclude that every passage in Alexandrian literature which shows a special interest in the prescriptions of the Torah, one in which some biblical events are mentioned, was meant not for the Gentiles, but for the Jews."[5] At first blush, the *Hypothetica*, with its concern for scriptural narrative and law, seems to fit this description.

Taking a cue from Tcherikover, some recent scholarship on Philo's apologetic corpus has sought to read these texts with the presumption of a Jewish audience. Maren Niehoff, for instance, has argued that the *Legatio ad Gaium* and *In Flaccum* had in mind a Jewish rather than a Gentile audience. The aim of these texts was not the external defense of Jewish beliefs but the internal construction of Hellenistic Jewish identity. Niehoff writes:

> Both the *Legatio* and *In Flaccum* aimed at defending Philo's pro-Roman politics. He wished to convince his Jewish readers back home that the more radical positions . . . were unwise and doomed to failure . . . It is generally acknowledged now that the *Legatio* and *In Flaccum* were never designed as pieces of detached historiography. Nor were they intended for a Roman audience, as Goodenough and others following him have assumed.[6]

---

[4] Victor Tcherikover, "Jewish Apologetic Literature Reconsidered," *Eos* 48 (1956): 169–193.

[5] Tcherikover, "Jewish Apologetic," 179.

[6] Maren Niehoff, *Philo on Jewish Identity and Culture* (TSAJ 86; Tübingen: Mohr Siebeck, 2001), 39. For the view that *In Flaccum* would have been presented to the new Alexandrian prefect and *Legatio ad Gaium* to the new Roman emperor, see Erwin R. Goodenough, *The Politics of Philo Judaeus: Practice and Theory* (New Haven: Yale University Press, 1938; repr. Hildesheim: Georg Olms Verlagsbuchshandlung, 1967), 19.

Niehoff's critical reassessment of these two apologetic works naturally leads to the question of whether the *Hypothetica*, too, was intended for a Jewish audience.

On one hand, it is certainly plausible that, in the years following the embassy, many Jews read and learned from Philo's apologetic method in the *Hypothetica*. It could have provided a rich sourcebook for defenses of the faith and the formation of Alexandrian Jewish identity. However, the evidence cannot fully support the claim that Philo composed the *Hypothetica* initially for a Jewish audience, and in fact sometimes seems to discourage this conclusion. In all fairness, Niehoff herself does not include the *Hypothetica* among the apologetic texts which she reorients toward a Jewish audience. Moreover, Niehoff's reassessment of the audience of *Legatio ad Gaium* and *In Flaccum* hardly represents the majority opinion. For example, John Barclay holds that *In Flaccum* still represents an external apologetic effort.[7] Tcherikover himself maintained that the *Hypothetica, Legatio ad Gaium,* and *In Flaccum* were all intended for Gentile audiences, "sent by the author directly to the Government [*sic*] representatives in Rome and in Alexandria."[8]

Because of the variety of scholarly speculation about Philo's audience, any attempt to situate the *Hypothetica* in the context of the embassy must not arise from presuppositions about apologetic treatises but from the text of the *Hypothetica* itself. The first step in making my argument will be to reconstruct some of the charges and concerns implicit in Philo's apologetic encomium and to look for specifically Roman parallels. Only after traces of Roman concern surface in the *Hypothetica* will I turn to other Philonic and Greco-Roman texts to try to reconstruct the Roman audience Philo might have expected in the embassy.

To delimit the rather large scope of the proposed investigation, this essay will focus on Philo's remarks on one particular subject of accusation in the first fragment of the *Hypothetica* (8.6.1–8.7.20): Jewish ethnic origins and the conquest of Canaan. It will proceed in three stages.

First, one must carefully distinguish between first and twenty-first century concerns regarding the Israelite settlement of Canaan. The various conquest narratives of Joshua and Judges have raised ethical questions and produced voluminous debate among modern biblical scholars. Even when one brackets the question of historicity, the biblical narratives themselves

---

[7] John Barclay, *Jews in the Mediterranean Diaspora: From Alexander to Trajan (323 BCE–117 CE)* (Edinburgh: T&T Clark, 1996), 422. For a list of other dissenters, see Niehoff, *Identity*, 118.

[8] Tcherikover, "Jewish Apologetic," 182.

continue to pose potential problems for some. John J. Collins writes,
"Whether we see these texts as reflecting expansionistic policies of King
Josiah or as mere fantasies of powerless Judeans after the exile, they project
a model of the ways in which Israel should relate to its neighbors."[9]

Modern ethics, however, do not reflect the concerns of Philo's day.
Roman consular and imperial culture certainly had no reticence about the
valorization of martial success, and the displacement of indigenous peoples
and previous settlers was almost a type scene in classical Greek colonization narratives.[10] It is all the more surprising, then, to find that Philo's
reconceptualization of the conquest in the *Hypothetica* seems to have a
certain affinity with modern concerns. As we shall see in the first section of
this essay, the traditions about the Hebrew conquest of Canaan (even
without direct dependence on the biblical narratives) provided fodder for
anti-Jewish writers in the Ptolemaic and early Roman periods. As Collins's
observation intimates, neighbors (and, I might add, rulers) of the Judeans
and Diasporan Jews did in fact look uneasily at the record of the conquest.
Greco-Roman leaders and Alexandrian locals might have recalled the wave
of uprisings in Jerusalem under the Macabees or the uneasy transfer of
power after the death of Herod the Great,[11] as well as the recent pogrom
against the Jews in 38 C.E. during the prefecture of Flaccus.[12]

If certain Hellenistic and Roman opponents of Judaism were wont to
draw a connection between the Israelite conquest narrative and contemporaneous Jewish uprisings, the poets and historians of Augustan Rome
likewise understood their own bloody rise to civic stability and international *imperium* as foreshadowed by Aeneas's violent expulsion of the
Aborigines when he first set foot in Italy. One can hear in Virgil's prophecy,
set in the mouth of the Cumaean Sibyl, *bella, horrida bella*,[13] the fatigue of the

---

[9] John J. Collins, *Does the Bible Justify Violence?* (Minneapolis: Fortress Press, 2004), 15.

[10] See, for instance, Thucydides, *History of the Peloponnesian War* 6.1 on the colonization of Sicily. For a general introduction to Greek colonization, see Alexander J. Graham,
Colony and Mother City in Ancient Greece (Chicago: Ares, 1983), 1–22.

[11] Tacitus, *Hist.* 5.9.

[12] See Joan E. Taylor, *Jewish Women Philosophers of First-Century Alexandria: Philo's
'Therapeutae' Reconsidered* (Oxford: Oxford University Press, 2003), 29, who notes, "From
Josephus' use of the word *stasis* ('civil dissension') we may suppose that the Jews did not
remain entirely passive victims." See Josephus, *A.J.* 18.257. Philo himself notes that in the
face of cultural violence, the Jews justifiably fought for their ethnic customs (*Flacc.* 48). The
evidence which reveals the most about Roman perceptions of the pogrom and subsequent
Jewish riot in 41 C.E. is Claudius's own description of the situation in his "Letter to the
Alexandrians," *CPJ* 2.153: τῆς δὲ πρὸς Ἰουδαίους ταραχῆς καὶ στάσεως, μᾶλλον δ' εἰ χρὴ τὸ
ἀληθὲς εἰπεῖν τοῦ πολέμου.

[13] Virgil, *Aen.* 6.86.

decades of civil war and colonization that had brought Rome to the *Pax Augusta* and domination of the Mediterranean (and beyond). The question of ethnogenesis had acquired new vogue among several Greco-Roman historians of Augustus's principate, notably Livy and Dionysius of Halicarnassus.[14] In the second section of this essay, I will argue that Philo's reconceptualization of the conquest not only takes into account the charges made against the Jews, but also reflects Greco-Roman portrayals of Rome's own origins, in an attempt both to gain sympathy from his chief Roman accuser and also to present Jerusalem and all the citizens of her *politeuma* as worthy peers in Rome's historical drama.

Having shown the potential Roman accusations against the Jews in the first section and the influences of Greco-Roman historiography on Philo's argumentation in the second section, in the third part of this essay I will attempt to sketch the Roman court scenario Philo might have envisaged while preparing his remarks, drawing on the *Legatio ad Gaium*, *In Flaccum*, and the Egyptian papyrological evidence.

1. *Roman Accusations: The Conquest of Canaan in Greco-Roman Historiography*

As a first order of business, however, I must demonstrate (1) that the narrative of the conquest was known in Greco-Egyptian and Roman antiquity and (2) that it provided grounds for moral and political accusations against the *politeuma* established by Moses.[15] The earliest Egyptian histories to mention the story of the founding of Jerusalem in their Jewish ethnographies, however, do not sufficiently meet both of these criteria. Hecataeus of Abdera and Manetho both wrote under Ptolemy I Soter (367–282 B.C.E.) and, perhaps in the case of Manetho, under Ptolemy II Philadelphus (308–246 B.C.E.).[16] They deserve mention here largely because of how different their writings are from the later Alexandrian accounts. As John J. Collins

---

[14] See Emilio Gabba, *Dionysius and The History of Archaic Rome* (Berkeley: University of California Press, 1991), 97, who speaks of "the burgeoning antiquarianism at Rome in the first century B.C."

[15] I am using *politeuma* here in Eusebius's general sense to mean "state" or "polity." The presence of an actual Jewish *politeuma* in Alexandria, suggested by the *Letter of Aristeas* 310, is defended by Aryeh Kasher and gains support from the papyrological evidence for *politeumata* in and around Ptolemaic Herakleopolis. See Kasher's important review of the Herakleopolis papyri in Aryeh Kasher, *JQR* 93 (2002): 257–268. For the view that there was no Jewish *politeuma* in Alexandria, cf. Constantine Zückerman, "Hellenistic *politeumata* and the Jews: A Reconsideration," *Scripta Classica Israelica* 8–9 (1988): 171–85.

[16] Dorothy J. Thompson, "Ptolemy (1)" *OCD* 1271–1272 (eds. Simon Hornblower and Anthony Spawforth; 3rd ed.; Oxford: Clarendon, 2003).

has argued, neither description of the conquest is based on the biblical narrative; both arise from Egyptian tradition.[17] Hecataeus's account involves no conquest; the land is simply not inhabited. Manetho's *Aigyptiaka* contains the first extant anti-Jewish ethnography composed by an Egyptian; despite the arguments of Erich Gruen to the contrary, the hostile identification of the Jews with the Hyksoi was likely original to Manetho.[18] Manetho's account of the settlement, however, is entirely detached from Moses (whose identification with Osarseph is likely an interpolation).[19] It is rather the Jewish ancestors (Hyksoi) who found Jerusalem in Syria out of fear of the Assyrians.[20] Manetho's account, like that of Hecataeus, stems from Egyptian cultural memory and Greek historiographical tradition, not from the biblical account.

Thus, while Manetho may have been in the background of Philo's mind, the primary Egyptian accusations that would have concerned him came from later Alexandrian ethnographers. These more contemporaneous histories, composed in a period of heightened Gentile animosity toward Judaism during the first centuries B.C.E. and C.E., provided many accusations that the members of the Alexandrian embassy could bring before Caligula in making their case against the Jews. In particular, Gregory Sterling has proposed that the *Aigyptiaka* of the Alexandrian author Lysimachus (ca. second-first centuries B.C.E.) "became the battle ground for argumentation" between the Jewish and Alexandrian embassies.[21] Lysimachus's history, preserved by Josephus, includes the following account of the conquest:

ἱκανῶς δὲ ὀχληθέντας ἐλθεῖν εἰς τὴν οἰκουμένην χώραν, καὶ τούς τε ἀνθρώπους ὑβρίζοντας καὶ τὰ ἱερὰ συλῶντας καὶ ἐμπρήσαντας ἐλθεῖν εἰς τὴν νῦν Ἰουδαίαν προσαγορευομένην, κτίσαντας δὲ πόλιν ἐνταῦθα κατοικεῖν. Τὸ δὲ ἄστυ τοῦτο Ἱερόσυλα ἀπὸ τῆς ἐκείνων διαθέσεως ὠνομάσθαι.

And having had sufficient hardship [in the wilderness] they came to inhabited country: once they had abused the population and robbed and burned their temples, they entered the land which is now called Judea, and having built a city they settled there. And this town was named Hierosyla, because of their disposition to rob temples. (*C. Ap.* 1.310–11)

---

[17] John J. Collins, "Reinventing Exodus: Exegesis and Legend in Hellenistic Egypt," in *Jewish Cult and Hellenistic Culture: Essays on the Jewish Encounter with Hellenism and Roman Rule* (JSJSup 100; Leiden: Brill, 2001), 44–57.

[18] Collins, "Reinventing," 55. Cf. Erich Gruen, *Heritage and Hellenism: The Reinvention of Jewish Tradition* (Berkeley: University of California Press, 1998), 61–63.

[19] Collins, "Reinventing," 50.

[20] Josephus, *C.Ap.* 1.90.

[21] Gregory E. Sterling, "Philo and the Logic of Apologetics: An Analysis of the *Hypothetica*," *SBL Seminar Papers, 1990* (SBLSP 29; Chico, Calif.: Scholars Press, 1990), 429. For Sterling's list of structural similarities, see Ibid., 428.

.re, unlike in Hecataeus and Manetho, the land is inhabited (εἰς τὴν οἰκουμένην χώραν). Colonization was accomplished by violence (τούς τε ἀνθρώπους ὑβρίζοντας) in the destruction of indigenous religious and civic infrastructure. Lysimachus's depiction of Jewish hostility toward the religions of other nations reflects a suspicion of Jewish colonization history and Mosaic government and meets the two criteria I set out to demonstrate above: that Jewish opponents in antiquity knew and used the conquest narrative.

It is impossible to say for certain how well known Lysimachus's ethnography of the Jews would have been in Rome at the time of Philo's embassy. By the end of the first century, however, we see clear evidence of its reception in the *Historiae* of Cornelius Tacitus.[22] Although Tacitus composed the *Historiae* in the wake of the turbulent events of the year 97 C.E.,[23] more than forty years after the death of Philo,[24] at least several of the critiques of the Jews compiled by the historian were known at the beginning of the first century C.E. or earlier.[25] Tacitus thus provides critical evidence for reconstructing the Roman reception of Lysimachus's charges, which might have influenced Philo in his composition of the *Hypothetica*.

Tacitus's depiction of the Jewish *ethnos* in *Hist.* 5.2 catalogues five potential origins of the race. The Jews are said to stem from Cretan (Idaean), Egyptian, Ethiopian or Assyrian stock, or perhaps, most fantastically, they are Homer's famous *Solymi*, a *celebrata gens*.[26] His aim here is not so much to accuse as to cloak the nation that Titus is about to conquer in a mantle of mythic antiquity. It will be recalled that to defeat the *Solymi* was the second trial which the king of Lycia commanded the hero Bellerophon, "the hardest battle with men that he ever entered."[27]

Tacitus's mention of a possible Mesopotamian origin for the Jews merits attention:

> *Sunt qui tradant Assyrios convenas, indigum agrorum populum, parte Aegypti potitos, mox proprias urbis Hebraeasque terras et propiora Syriae coluisse.*

[22] Heinz Heubner, *P. Cornelius Tacitus: Die Historien* (Wissenschaftliche Kommentare zu griechischen und lateinischen Schriftstellern; Heidelberg: C. Winter, 1982), 30.

[23] Ronald Syme, *Ten Studies in Tacitus* (Oxford: Clarendon, 1970), 3.

[24] Gregory E. Sterling, *The Jewish Plato* (forthcoming), 51.

[25] Sterling, "Logic," 428. For negative Roman stereotypes of the Jews in the first century B.C.E., see Cicero, *Flac.* 66–68 and the discussion in Harry J. Leon, *The Jews of Ancient Rome* (Philadelphia: Jewish Publication Society of America, 1960; repr. Peabody, Mass.: Hendrickson, 1995), 5–8.

[26] Σολύμοισι . . . κυδαλίμοισι: Homer, *Il.* 6.184; cf. Homer, *Od.* 5.238.

[27] Homer, *Il.* 6.184 in Martin Hammond, trans., *The Iliad: A New Prose Translation* (London: Penguin, 1987).

There are some who report that they were Assyrian refugees, a landless people, who first got control of a part of Egypt and then later inhabited their own cities in the Hebrew country and the nearer parts of Syria. (*Hist.* 5.2 [Moore, LCL], lightly adapted)

This version of Jewish origins follows roughly the biblical emigration pattern, and in its major points resembles Philo's description in *Hypoth.* 8.6.1. It bears witness to the Roman reception of Jewish ethnographies and its characteristic interest in ethnogenesis. Lysimachus the Alexandrian, at least in the fragments preserved by Josephus in *Contra Apionem*, does not mention ethnic origins at all but begins his polemical history with the events of the Exodus, which are considered by Tacitus in *Hist.* 5.3.[28] Given Tacitus's apparent knowledge of some features of the biblical account (e.g. unleavened bread in the Exodus),[29] it seems likely that he knew a (Roman?) tradition of Jewish ethnogenesis which did not emphasize the Patriarchs' previous settlement in Canaan but, rather, their various migrations after leaving Mesopotamia. The Jews are, for Tacitus, "a landless people" (*indigum agrorum populum*) until they attain "their own cities" (*propias urbis*) after the conquest.[30]

After discussing ethnic origins, Tacitus moves on in *Hist.* 5.3 to a discussion of the exodus itself, which he places, with Lysimachus, during the reign of King Bocchoris. The many similarities between Lysimachus and Tacitus in this story, including the name of the King, the Jewish plague, the consultation of Ammon's oracle, and the prescribed cure of banishment of the polluted people,[31] support the conclusion that Tacitus was dependent on Lysimachus.[32] Philo's account of the Exodus—that the Jews emigrated because of their large numbers, the insufficient size of their land, their youthful spirit, and their desire for their fatherland[33]—can be viewed in part as a reaction to Lysimachus's account, which may have been known in Rome. It is likely, however, that Philo's account was also shaped positively on the model of Greek colonization narratives.[34]

---

28 Josephus, *C. Ap.* 1.304.

29 Tacitus, *Hist.* 5.4, *panis Iudaicus nullo fermento detinetur*. Cf. Exod 12:15–20.

30 Tacitus, *Hist.* 5.2.

31 Josephus, *C. Ap.* 1.305; Tacitus, *Hist.* 5.3.

32 Sterling "Logic," 429, n. 75; Stern, *GLAJJ*, 2:35, remains skeptical. However, the near echoes of Lysimachus in Tacitus, discernable despite their different languages, make the position of Sterling, who follows Heubner more likely.

33 Philo, *Hypoth.* 8.6.1.

34 Philo and Dionysius of Halicarnassus respectively portray Jerusalem and Rome as cities founded because of population overflow, again borrowing a convention from Greek colonization narrative. See Graham, *Colony*, 5. Philo, in his description of the Exodus, mentions that a possible explanation for the departure was that τῆς γῆς οὐκ οὔσης ἱκανῆς,

Tacitus presents the conquest in one compact phrase:

> *et continuum sex dierum iter emensi septimo <u>pulsis cultoribus obtinuere terras</u>, in quis urbs et templum dicata.*

> And after they had marched continuously for six days, on the seventh day they expelled the inhabitants and seized the land, in which a city and temple were dedicated. (*Hist.* 5.3)

Tacitus's depiction, which involves a violent conquest, departs from Lysimachus's account in an important way. Tacitus reports that the Jews founded both city and temple, whereas Lysimachus reports only the building of a city. Tacitus likely knew a tradition similar to Manetho's as preserved in *C. Ap.* 1.228, "[they] founded Jerusalem, and built the temple." Tacitus and Manetho preserve the base story; Lysimachus either knows a different version of the settlement narrative or (if he had read Manetho) omits the temple foundation in order to underscore instead Moses' propensity for temple robbery and to depict the Jews as an intrinsically impious people. In sum, Tacitus's awareness of Lysimachus and his preservation of a second account of Jewish origins and the conquest demonstrate that Romans likely would have known many of the charges brought by the Alexandrian delegation and might have had their own variations of these charges. Tacitus's fivefold account of national origins shows that Jewish ethnogenesis had become a topic of Roman interest by the end of the first century. This depiction, although admittedly late, may thus be seen as providing some preliminary evidence that Philo's "response" to Lysimachus in the *Hypothetica* was intended to reply to Roman as well as Greek concerns about Jewish history.

2. *Colonial Narratives: Philo's* Hypothetica *and Livy's* Ab Urbe Condita

If Philo did indeed have the Roman court in mind, he would have shaped the *Hypothetica* accordingly. Thus, while his apology may have been formally framed on the basis of the Alexandrian and Roman charges he intended to refute, Philo very plausibly also incorporated into his presentation of Jewish history features from Roman historiography. In particular, in this section I will advance the thesis that Philo's discussion of the Jewish

---

"the land was not sufficient [for their number]" (*Hypoth.* 8.6.1). This language echoes Dionysius's description of the immigration of the Aborigines, who came to Italy with ὅσοι χώραν εἶχον ἐλάττω τῆς ἱκανῆς, "as many other Greeks as did not have sufficient land" (*Ant. rom.* 1.9).

conquest narrative is colored by contemporaneous historical accounts of the arrival of Aeneas in Italy and the founding of Rome. But before moving ahead to this part of the argument, Philo's presentation of the conquest in the *Hypothetica* needs to be presented. It runs as follows:

ἐπειδὴ δὲ εἰς τὴν γῆν ταύτην ἦλθον, ὅπως μὲν ποτε ἄρα ἱδρύθησαν καὶ τὴν χώραν ἔσχον, ἐν ταῖς ἱεραῖς ἀναγραφαῖς <u>δηλοῦται</u>· οὐ μὴν ἔγωγε δικαιῶ μᾶλλον καθ' ἱστορίαν ἢ κατά τινα λογισμὸν περὶ αὐτῶν τὰ εἰκότα ἐπεξελθεῖν. πότερον γὰρ ποτε βούλει τῷ πλήθει τῷ κατὰ τῶν σωμάτων ἔτι περιόντας καίπερ εἰς τέλος κεκακωμένους, ὅμως δ' ἰσχύοντας καὶ τὰ ὅπλα ἐν χερσὶν ἔχοντας εἶτα <u>κατὰ</u> <u>κράτος ἑλεῖν τὴν χώραν</u>, Σύρους τε ὁμοῦ καὶ Φοίνικας ἐν αὐτῇ τῇ ἐκείνων γῇ μαχομένους νικῶντας; ἢ τοὺς μὲν ἀπολέμους καὶ ἀνάνδρους εἶναι καὶ παντελῶς ὀλίγους ὑποθώμεθα καὶ τῶν εἰς πόλεμον παρασκευῶν ἀπόρους, <u>αἰδέσεως δὲ τυχεῖν</u> <u>παρὰ τούτοις καὶ τὴν γῆν λαβεῖν παρ' ἑκόντων</u>, ἔπειτα δ' εὐθὺς οὐκ εἰς μακρὸν τόν τε νεὼν οἰκοδομῆσαι καὶ τἆλλα εἰς εὐσέβειαν καὶ ἁγιστείαν καταστήσασθαι; <u>δηλοῖ γάρ</u>, ὡς ἔοικε, ταῦτα γε καὶ θεοφιλεστάτους αὐτοὺς ἀνωμολογῆσθαι καὶ παρὰ τοῖς ἐχθροῖς· ἐχθροὶ γὰρ ἦσαν ἐξ ἀνάγκης ὧν ἐπὶ τὴν γῆν ἐξαίφνης ἦλθον <u>ὡς</u> <u>ἀφαιρησόμενοι</u>. <u>παρὰ τούτοις δ' οὖν αἰδέσεως καὶ τιμῆς τυγχάνοντες</u> πῶς οὐκ ὑπερβάλλειν εὐτυχίᾳ τοὺς ἄλλους φαίνονται;

But when they entered into this land, the manner in which they settled and occupied the country <u>is set out clearly</u> in the holy scriptures. But I do not think it better to proceed according to history than to discuss what is probable concerning these events according to a certain kind of reasoning. Which option do you prefer? That still being preeminent in sheer mass of bodies, although having fared very badly [during the wilderness years], they nevertheless, retaining strength and with weapons in their hands, then <u>took the land by</u> <u>force</u>, and were victorious in battle with the Syrians and Phoenicians on their own soil? Or are we to suppose that although they were unwarlike and without courage and entirely depleted in number, and likewise untrained in implements of war, <u>they nonetheless gained reverence in the eyes of their opponents</u> <u>and received the land from them who willingly handed it over</u>, and then immediately without delay, built the temple and established the other things necessary for *pietas* and religion? <u>For even these things make clear</u>, as it seems, that they were acknowledged as very beloved by God, even by their enemies. For they were their enemies by necessity, whose land they had suddenly come upon <u>in order to seize it</u>. <u>And so, when they received reverence and honor from</u> <u>them</u>, how do they not seem to surpass others in good fortune? (*Hypoth.* 8.6.5–8.6.8a)

In *Hypoth.* 8.6.6, Philo poses two possible scenarios in which the Jews acquired the land of Canaan. Either they "took the land by force, and were victorious in battle with the Syrians and Phoenicians on their own soil" or "although they were unwarlike and without courage and entirely depleted in number, and likewise untrained in implements of war, they nonetheless gained reverence (αἴδεσις) in the eyes of their opponents and received the land from them who willingly handed it over."

To the biblically literate reader, Philo's bifurcated conquest account seems preposterous: it clearly transgresses the plain sense of the narratives of Joshua and Judges.[35] Moreover, the second peaceable option does not match Philo's own retelling of Israel's early military efforts in *De vita Mosis*, in which he ascribes the Israelite defeat of king Cananēs (Num 21:1–3), the first-fruits of the conquest,[36] to Israelite courage.[37] Neither does Philo employ here his allegorical method, as he does elsewhere[38] and as his Alexandrian exegetical heir, Origen, would likewise do in his *Homilies on Joshua*.[39] Rather, he adopts a strategy of argumentation in which the historical dimension of the conquest is eclipsed by philosophical reasoning about the situation. Although Philo applies this "hypothetical" method to several other issues in the *Hypothetica*,[40] his explanation of the method here suggests its close connection with this case in particular.

Philo may have created his bifurcated conquest narrative purely in response to Lysimachus's charge that the Jews colonized Jerusalem in the most shameful of ways. Instead of simply contradicting Lysimachus, Philo invents two general counter-narratives, which rhetorically embrace the totality of historical possibility. However, to the reader of Roman history, something more seems to be at work. Philo's two tales of the acquisition of a land by a colonizing people—the first warlike, the second peaceable— bear a strikingly resemblance to Livy's account in *Ab urbe condita* 1, when

---

[35] So Madeleine Petit, "À propos d'une traversée exemplaire du désert du Sinaï selon Philon (*Hypothetica* VI, 2–3.8): texte biblique et apolgétique concernant Moïse chez quelques écrivains Juifs," *Sem* 26 (1976): 137–42, writes of the reader's astonishment at "le travestissement du texte biblique." For a possible basis for Philo's peaceful settlement account, however, cf. Josh 9:3–15.

[36] Philo, *Mos.* 1.254.

[37] Philo, *Mos.* 1.251, εὐτολμία, θαρρέω. Cf. Philo, *Virt.* 22–33 on ἀνδρεία as the quintessential wartime Mosaic virtue. See Katell Berthelot, "Philo of Alexandria and the Conquest of Canaan, *JSJ* 38 (2007): 39–56, for a comprehensive discussion of Philo's non-allegorical approaches to the conquest narrative.

[38] See Berthelot, "Conquest," 40–41, who rightly notes: "At first sight, it seems Philo's favourite reading of the conquest narrative is allegorical." Philo often gives Israel's enemies symbolic meaning in the Allegorical Commentary. The Egyptians are identified with the body (*Leg.* 2.59, 77; 3.37, 212, 242) or the passions (*Leg.* 2.84; 3.13, 37, 81, 87, 94). In *De posteritate Caini* (*Post.* 122), referring to Num 14:9, Philo implicitly identifies "the people of the land" (ὁ λαὸς τῆς γῆς) with "the opposing doctrines" (αἱ ἐναντίαι δόξαι) against which the ethical person wages war (πολεμεῖν).

[39] Origin, *Homilies on Joshua* (trans. Barbara J. Bruce; Washington, D.C.: Catholic University of America Press, 2002), *Homily* 1, 33–34, gives an allegorical and ethical reading of the nations conquered by Joshua: "There are certain diabolical races of powerful adversaries against whom we wage battle and against whom we struggle in this life . . . Within us, indeed, are all those breeds of vices that continually and incessantly attack the soul. Within us are the Canaanites; within us are the Perizzites; here are the Jebusites."

[40] Cf. *Hypoth.* 8.6.4, where Philo gives two options for explaining Moses' successful leadership of the people in the wilderness and *Hypoth.* 8.6.9, where he provides two options for the source of Moses' wisdom.

Aeneas and the Trojans first come to acquire land in Italy and found the town of Lavinium. After their defeat and expulsion from Troy, Aeneas and the Trojans arrive in Italy by way of a long sea voyage, having stopped in Macedonia and Sicily. Arrayed on the Laurentine field, the Trojans are met by King Latinus and the Aborigines; both armies stand poised for war. Then Livy continues:

> *Duplex inde fama est. Alii proelio victum Latinum pacem cum Aenea, deinde adfinitatem iunxisse tradunt: alii, cum instructae acies constitissent, priusquam signa canerent, processisse Latinum inter primores ducemque advenarum evocasse ad conloquium . . . postquam audierit multitudinem Troianos esse, ducem Aenean filium Anchisae et Veneris, cremata patria domo profugos, sedem condendaeque urbi locum quaerere, et nobilitatem admiratum gentis virique et animum vel bello vel paci paratum, dextra data fidem futurae amicitiae sanxisse.*

> From this point, the story is twofold. Some people recount that Latinus, after he had been conquered in battle made peace with Aeneas, and then joined in kinship by marriage. Others say that when the battle lines had been drawn up and stood in position, before the trumpets could be sounded, Latinus came forward among his chieftains and called forth the leader of the foreigners to a private meeting . . . and after he had heard that they were a Trojan bunch, that their leader was Aeneas, the son of Anchises and Venus, and that they were refugees from their home after their fatherland had been burned and were seeking a settlement and place to found a city; moreover, because [Latinus] admired the nobility of the race and the man and their spirit ready for war or peace, he gave [Aeneas] his right hand and made a pledge for a future alliance. (*Ab urbe condita* 1.1.6–1.1.8)

Before diving headlong into a discussion of the fascinating parallels between Livy and Philo, an important *caveat* is in order. Despite the many similarities which I will note, one must always hold in mind a fundamental difference: the difference between history and hypothetical argumentation. Livy, like Tacitus in his pluriform ethnography of the Jews, presents a labyrinthine history;[41] his two versions of the story, while mutually exclusive, retain relatively equal truth value. Philo, on the other hand, is careful not to rewrite the narrative of the conquest, well known to him and his fellow Alexandrian Jews in the scriptural account (ἐν ταῖς ἱεραῖς ἀναγραφαῖς δηλοῦται). Philo decides to proceed not so much according to history but according to a certain reasoning (οὐ μὴν μᾶλλον . . . καθ' ἱστορίαν ἢ κατά τινα λογισμόν). For Philo the proposition of multiple accounts of the

---

[41] For the labyrinth as a guiding heuristic image for reading Livy, as well as the category of the *bivia* as a feature of his historiographical architecture, I am indebted to the work of Mary Jaeger, "Guiding Metaphor and Narrative Point of View in Livy's *Ab Urbe Condita*," in *The Limits of Historiography: Genre and Narrative in Ancient Historical Texts* (ed. Christina S. Kraus; Leiden: Brill, 1999), 169–195.

conquest is emphatically *not* a historiographical project.[42] The history, fixed in scripture, is unicursal in contrast to Livy's historical *biviae*. Philo is not searching through various Jewish annals. His hypothetical procedure here, as Sterling has insightfully suggested, may stem from his use of Stoic propositional logic, which develops truth claims from merely possible premises.[43] For this reason in particular, one must admit a real difference between Philo's and Livy's work.

Nonetheless, the parallels between these two passages are too striking to pass over and in comparing them several key similarities emerge. Firstly, like Philo, Livy tells the story of a colonizing conquest of seminal national significance. That story can take two forms. In both Livy and Philo, the first account is violent and somewhat more believable. The peaceable second account appears to be the political preference of both authors, especially of Livy.[44] For Philo, either narrative could effectively corroborate his argument of Jewish εὐτυχία.[45] Philo illustrates this rhetorically by echoing language from *both* narrative paths in his conclusion about Jewish good fortune (ἑλεῖν τὴν χώραν [*Hypoth.* 8.6.6]: ὡς ἀφαιρησόμενοι, [*Hypoth.* 8.6.7]; αἰδέσεως δὲ τυχεῖν παρὰ τούτοις [*Hypoth.* 8.6.6]: παρὰ τούτοις δ' οὖν αἰδέσεως καὶ τιμῆς τυγχάνοντες [*Hypoth.* 8.6.8]). In fact, the quality of Aeneas which so impresses Latinus in Livy's second peaceful account—that he possesses an *animum vel bello vel paci paratum*—has similar force to the logical conclusion that Philo draws in *Hypoth.* 8.6.7–8.6.8a from *both* of his narrative options: in either war or peace, the Jews emerge favorably.[46] Still, Philo seems to show some preference for the peaceful settlement by placing

---

[42] My understanding of Philo's method thus stands in contrast to that of Berthelot, "Conquest," 52, who considers the account of the conquest in the *Hypothetica* to be an instance of Philo's "creative rewriting of the biblical account." This is not to deny that Philo rewrites biblical material elsewhere in his literary corpus.

[43] Sterling, "Logic," 429.

[44] So Robert M. Ogilvie, *A Commentary on Livy: Books 1–5* (Oxford: Clarendon, 1965), 38: "The second version, which spares the Latins the humiliation of defeat and the Romans the infamy of aggression, doubtless gained currency from the late fourth century when the foundation legend was invoked to improve relations with the Latins . . . The first version, which makes Aeneas the aggressor is . . . anti-dynastic." Likewise, Gary Miles, *Livy: Reconstructing Early Rome* (Ithaca: Cornell University Press, 1995), 30, notes that the "relative position and length [of the two versions] form a consistent pattern of emphasis that clearly privileges one of the two alternatives reported."

[45] *Pace* Berthelot, "Conquest," 53, who writes that "Philo's question to his reader is rhetorical, and he obviously believes that the second solution is more likely."

[46] The referent of the demonstrative ταῦτά in *Hypoth.* 8.6.7 is ambiguous, but in my estimation it likely resumes *both* of the settlement narratives which Philo has presented. Cf. Philo, *Hypoth.* 8.6.4, Colson, "Whichever of these views you consider to be the truth it appears to redound mightily to his praise and honour and zeal for them all."

it second, thereby rendering it final in the experience of the hearer. Like-wise, he has carefully changed the definitive "seizure" of the land in the first narrative path, signified by the aorist aspect of ἐλεῖν, to the mere inten-tion to seize it, signified by the future participle of purpose ὡς ἀφαιρησό-μενοι in his concluding argument. The latter circumstantial construction need not imply that any conquest actually took place, but it does suggest that the settlers were armed to do so.[47]

Secondly, Latinus's admiration is clearly based on Aeneas's descent (and quasi-divinity), his leadership, and his people; Philo likewise praises Moses, his leadership, and the Jews.[48] Thirdly, each author, in his narration of civic foundation, reflects in mythic and symbolic ways on recent political history—Philo on the status of the Jewish *politeuma* amid the various regions of the Empire and Livy on Rome's self-perception after its emer-gence from decades of civil war and imperialism.

Besides these thematic parallels, Livy and Philo also share a deep rhetorical continuity in their presentation of multiple conquest narratives, despite the important generic distinction mentioned above. I claimed in my *caveat* that the difference between Philo and Livy was a difference between (a) hypothetical argumentation about history and (b) historiography proper. While this claim holds generally (and generically), it needs to be nuanced here. For the fork in Aeneas's narrative is not properly speaking a fork in *historia*, but, *per* Livy's own vocabulary, a fork in *fama*, i.e. "rumor" or "tradition." As Gary Miles notes, Livy states in the preface of his history that "he has no intention either 'to refute or to affirm' an unreliable tradi-tion." Thus, neither account of the conquest of Italy bears Livy's full stamp of "historical reliability."[49] Like Philo, then, Livy retreats from history into the realm of unreal accounts (if I may borrow a phrase from Emilio Gabba's discussion of Dionysius) "insofar as the obscure and uncertain archaic

---

[47] It is worth noting that negative features from the second (peaceful) hypothetical narrative (e.g. the description of the Israelites as ἀνάνδρους) likewise disappear when Philo starts drawing conclusions.

[48] The Roman counterpart to Moses in his legislative role is Romulus, the eponymous lawgiver of Rome. See Gabba, *Dionysius*, 215, who notes the similarities between Moses and Romulus in Josephus, *Contra Apionem*, and Dionysius, *Antiquitates romanae*. The paral-lel between Moses and Aeneas arises primarily from Moses' role in the Exodus and Aeneas's leadership in the great national wandering after Troy. Note that the biblical story of Moses' death before crossing the Jordan is absent from the *Hypothetica*. Especially given Tacitus's chronology of a six day journey between Egypt and the Hebrew territory, the logical conclusion of the biblically illiterate reader of these epitomes would be that Moses, like Aeneas, entered the land.

[49] Miles, *Reconstructing*, 29–31.

history was richer in essentially true moral exempla."[50] Although these legends remain a part of Livy's multi-source historical work, Livy intentionally obscures their "reliability" by more Polybian standards.

Conversely, I would suggest that Philo's palinode against history in *Hypoth.* 8.6.5 in some sense entails his use of it. History is the literary genre from which he draws his hypothetical propositions. In giving himself the freedom to sidestep the literal account in the scriptures (thereby preserving it intact), he opens the possibility of using historiographical material previously inaccessible to him. The colonial origins of Rome come to color his depiction of the Israelite conquest despite the clear impossibility of certain parallels between them. (It would be historically and legally impossible for the Jews to intermarry with the Phoenicians and the Syrians as the Romans did with the Aborigines; but this is not hypothetically impossible in Philo's imagined scenarios.)[51] Even more remarkable in Philo's account is the rhetorical unity between history on the one hand and logical conclusions drawn from hypothetical reasoning on the other. What is clear to Philo from scripture (δηλοῦται)[52] about the historical (biblical) conquest need not inhibit him from clearly demonstrating (δηλοῖ),[53] by way of hypothetical propositions, the pious, virtuous, and ultimately socially harmonious character of the Jewish *ethnos*.

Philo's adoption of a "both/and" narration of the conquest, which neither denies the biblical account nor entirely eschews the need to reconceptualize it for the embassy to Gaius, contributes significantly to our understanding of the range of Jewish self-presentations during the Hellenistic and Roman eras. Philo stands at the nexus of two poles of Jewish exegetical relation to scripture. John Collins helpfully summarizes:

> On the one hand, James Kugel has argued that the return of the Jewish exiles in the Persian period ushered in "the age of interpretation," which came to full bloom in the Hellenistic and Roman periods . . . On the other hand, Erich Gruen has noted the frequency with which Hellenistic-Jewish authors "simply rewrote scriptural narratives, inventing facts and attaching fanciful tales."[54]

Philo's account of the conquest in the *Hypothetica* is remarkable in that it represents a *tertium quid* between these two extremes. Philo clearly holds to

---

[50] Gabba, *Dionysius*, 95.

[51] Josephus goes even further at times and seemingly rewrites Moses in Aeneas's image. See *A.J.* 2.252–253 where Moses conquers Ethiopia and marries the daughter of the enemy king.

[52] Philo, *Hypoth.* 8.6.5.

[53] Philo, *Hypoth.* 8.6.7.

[54] Collins, "Reinventing," 44.

the authority of the scriptural narrative (which is not *fama*), while recon-ceptualizing its meaning for the current political situation.[55]

In light of these foregoing similarities, I have suggested that Philo based his hypothetical scenarios for the conquest of Canaan on the model of the double tradition associated with Aeneas's colonization of Italy. While such a "Roman" depiction of Jewish origins may have corresponded with Philo's own conception of his Judaism,[56] this seems far from certain. I have argued here that Philo exploits this similarity in the *Hypothetica* primarily for political ends. Any stigma that his accusers might have attached to the conquest of Canaan would, in light of the parallel with Aeneas, amount to an accusation against Rome's early history as well. To disperse any concerns about the conquest narrative, Philo paints the Jewish *ethnos* in Roman epic proportions, depicting them as a people who could contribute greatly to the virtue and cultural capital of the Empire.

Of course, some may object that the similarities between Philo and Livy are merely formal or rhetorical. Philo adapts the historiographical motif of forked-narrative to fit his Jewish situation, but does not explicitly intend to draw parallels with early Roman history. This objection, however, over-looks two important points of the previous argument. Firstly, Philo argues several times on the basis of hypothetical premises. If Philo is drawing on a model of logical premises (Stoic or otherwise) to construct his historical argument, then his literary form did not begin as an adaptation of the historiographical *bivia*. Secondly, what Philo does share with Livy, though in part rhetorical as I have argued, is primarily content: the juxtaposition of *two colonization campaigns, one violent, the other peaceful*. It is highly plausible, especially given Livy's use of the word *fama*, that Philo drew upon the well-known and popular narratives about Aeneas's colonization when constructing his own hypothetical conquest scenarios.

Philo could have become aware of these traditions in several ways. Most plausibly, Philo encountered the double colonization legend through Greek annalists such as Q. Fabius Pictor[57] and other sources consulted by

---

[55] My position, again, stands in contrast to Petit, "Traversée Exemplaire," 139, who like Berthelot considers Philo's method in the *Hypothetica* to be identical to the rewritten Bible of Josephus and Artapanus: "Le procédé est très commun . . . mais il est remarquable qu'il soit employé par des Juifs si respectueux du texte sacré."

[56] For the argument that at times "features of Rome's position in the empire were assimilated by Philo and transposed to Jerusalem," see Niehoff, *Identity*, 37.

[57] That the Greek *Annales* of Fabius Pictor included Aeneas (*Aeneae somnium*) is confirmed by Cicero, *Div.* 1.21.43. Cf. Hermann Peter, ed., *Historicorum romanorum reliquiae* (2 vols.; Stuttgart: Teubner, 1967) 1:5, fr. 3, and 1:5–7, fr. 4. No specifics regarding the battle with Latinus are preserved.

Livy and Dionysius of Halicarnassus.[58] While Dionysius does not explicitly present the same two options as Livy, he does admit that he knows multiple traditions about Aeneas's arrival and notes that he himself had to sift through many Greek and Latin sources.[59] In Dionysius's narration of Aeneas's arrival, although the Latin and the Trojan armies do meet upon the plain in *Ant. rom.* 1.57–58, the transfer of land happens peacefully, in a way that is echoed by Philo's second option:

λαβόντες δὲ παρὰ τῶν Ἀβοριγίνων χωρίον εἰς οἴκησιν καὶ ὅσα ἠξίουν, πολίζονται .
. .

And receiving land from the Aborigines for settlement and whatever else they thought necessary, they built a town . . . (*Ant. rom.* 1.45)[60]

Whereas Livy and Philo offer two options, as far as their respective literary conventions and theological traditions permit them, Dionysius offers only one. This should not, however, lead us to conclude that Dionysius was not aware of Livy's *duplex fama* or the historiographical traditions which underpinned them. On the contrary, as Gabba writes, "One may . . . readily suppose that in many instances where Dionysius differs from Livy, despite, in the last analysis, their mutual dependence on the same sources in the annals, the difference is intentional."[61] Dionysius's aim is to extol Rome. He relates a story of Roman origins in which "there were no subjugations or conquests among the five waves of Greek emigration that came to Italy, and hence no violent cultural transformations."[62] Livy's history, on the other hand, is far from encomiastic; as he says in his *Praefatio*, his aim is to trace the gradual decline of Rome from its mythic origins to the present times, "in which we are able to endure neither our vices nor their

[58] Presuming that Philo knew no Latin, another alternative would be that Philo had secondary access to the narratives passed down in Livy's history through oral tradition (*fama*) or through his connection with the Roman literary elite, e.g. his friendship with Seneca the Elder. For Philo's Roman connections, see Niehoff, *Identity*, 9.

[59] Dionysius, *Ant. rom.* 1.45 (Cary, LCL): "But also concerning the arrival of Aeneas in Italy, since some historians have been ignorant of it *and others have related it in a different manner*, I wish to give more than a cursory account, having compared the histories of those writers, both Greek and Roman, who are the best accredited. The stories concerning him are as follows . . . " [emphasis is mine]. Moreover, Dionysius does at times actually present conflicting Aenean traditions side by side without adjudicating between them. For example, see Dionysius, *Ant. rom.* 1.55, for the question of whether Aeneas's edible tables were made of parsley or cakes.

[60] Cf. Dionysius, *Ant. rom.* 1.63.

[61] Gabba, *Dionysius*, 95. Cf. Gabba, *Dionysius*, 20: "Both Livy and Dionysius rework the same materials for the archaic period that were furnished to them by the earlier annalists . . . "

[62] Gabba, *Dionysius*, 106.

remedies."[63] Livy has no interest in bowdlerizing the early tradition of potentially problematic material.[64] The onset of this moral decline, however, was in Livy's eyes relatively recent.[65] His double colonization account, despite its veiled premonitions of civic violence, nonetheless accomplishes for Rome what he intends to do in his preface: *consecrare origines suas et ad deos referre auctores*, "to consecrate one's own origins and to trace one's founders back to the gods." Dionysius's omission of Livy's first colonization account, in turn, should be seen as a deliberate suppression of this "anti-dynastic" option, which likely existed in his as well as Livy's sources.

Like Livy and Dionysius, Philo wrestles with how best to present a people's conquest narrative. Unlike Livy and Dionysius, Philo had the difficult task of defending the conquest of a political minority. His reasoning about the conquest, nonetheless, shows a striking resemblance in content and rhetoric to Livy's presentation of Aeneas's conquest of Italy. By reconceptualizing the Jewish conquest narrative in these terms, Philo is preparing to diffuse Roman suspicions and the Greco-Egyptian accusations which would be presented afresh by Apion in the embassy to Caligula.

3. *Roman Audience: Reconstructing Philo's Preconceptions of the Imperial Court*

In the previous section, I argued from the text of the *Hypothetica* that Philo shapes his defense of the Jewish conquest narrative on the basis of Roman narratives of the colonization of Italy. Such an apologetic move makes the most sense in the context of Philo's embassy to Gaius, when Philo went to plead for the Jewish *politeuma* before a Roman.[66] The task of this final

---

[63] Livy, *Ab urbe condita*, *Praefatio* 9: *donec ad haec tempora quibus nec vitia nostra nec remedia pati possumus.*

[64] The antiquity of the peaceful settlement account is assured by its multiple attestation in Livy and Dionysius. The origin of the warlike account, despite its being somewhat more realistic, is harder to trace. By the fourth century C.E., one sees evidence in Ps.-Aurelius Victor, *Origo Gentis Romanae*, that the peaceful account had become dominant. The warlike conquest was attributed to M. Porcius Cato by the Virgilian commentator Servius: *Aeneam cum patre ad Italiam venisse et propter invasos agros contra Latinum Turnumque pugnasse in quo proelio periit Latinus.* See Martine Chassignet, *Caton: Les Origines (fragments)* (Paris: Belles Lettres, 1986), 4, fr. 9a. Even if this version is erroneously attributed to Cato, as Chassignet cautions (*Les Origines*, 4, n.2), it differs from both Virgil and Livy in its explicit inclusion of Anchises (*cum patre*) in the Italian conquest, and thus very plausibly preserves an early annalist.

[65] Gabba, *Dionysius*, 95.

[66] The *Hypothetica* admittedly makes no direct allusion to the events reported in *In Flaccum* or *Legatio ad Gaium*. Although the imperial court setting thus remains speculative, in my view it is highly plausible. As I mentioned earlier, Greco-Roman concerns regarding

section is to reconstruct what kind of judicial setting Philo might have anticipated as he prepared his remarks in defense of the Jews. The primary evidence for illustrating the *Sitz im Leben* of the *Hypothetica* will be drawn from two of Philo's other apologetic works, his own account of the embassy, the *Legatio ad Gaium*, and his account of the Alexandrian pogrom against the Jews, *In Flaccum*. Secondary support will be drawn from the *Acta Alexandrinorum*.

3.1 *The* Legatio ad Gaium *and* In Flaccum

The dramatic situation depicted in the *Legatio ad Gaium* jibes well with the Roman setting suggested by the rhetoric of the *Hypothetica*. Philo refers to the members of the Alexandrian embassy as οἱ δὲ κατήγοροι.[67] It is reasonable to conclude that the members of the Alexandrian embassy were one of the sets of accusers that Philo had in mind while composing the *Hypothetica*.[68] By his own admission, however, Philo had another and in fact greater accuser in Caligula himself:

εἰσελθόντες γὰρ εὐθὺς ἐγνώμεν . . . ὅτι οὐ πρὸς δικαστὴν ἀλλὰ κατήγορον ἀφίγμεθα . . .

For when we entered, immediately we knew . . . that we had come not before a judge but before an accuser. (*Legat.* 349)

If Philo and the Jewish embassy were disappointed by Gaius's treatment, they were certainly not surprised. *Legatio ad Gaium* 182 indicates that Philo

---

the conquest narrative were certainly relevant to the political instability in Alexandria which prompted Philo's embassy in the first place. Moreover, it would have made sense for Philo to begin by addressing deeply-held prejudices against the Jews before turning to the more contemporary accusations. Plato's *Apology*, although clearly situated in a personal court case, provides a precedent. Socrates begins his defense in *Apol.* 18a not with the current charges, but by attempting to diffuse the old prejudices against himself: ἐμοῦ γὰρ πολλοὶ κατήγοροι γεγόνασι πρὸς ὑμᾶς καὶ πάλαι πολλὰ ἤδη ἔτη καὶ οὐδὲν ἀληθὲς λέγοντες.

[67] Philo, *Legat.* 359.

[68] The exact composition of the Alexandrian embassy is not known. Josephus, *A.J.* 18.257–260, mentions only three ambassadors, whereas Philo, *Legat.* 370, seems to indicate no fewer than five. Aside from Apion and Isidorus, who are mentioned in the foregoing texts, E. Mary Smallwood, *The Jews Under Roman Rule* (Leiden: Brill, 1976), 242, suggests Lampo as a possibility. Sterling, "Logic," 429, suggests Chaeremon, the Egyptian priest and Stoic philosopher. *CPJ* 2.153 apparently lists the members of a second Alexandrian embassy that included Chaeremon. Andrew Harker, *Loyalty and Dissidence in Roman Egypt* (Cambridge: Cambridge University Press, 2008), 15, suggests Lampo, Dionysius, and Theon (the exegete). However, his subsequent dismissal of Chaeremon (Harker, *Loyalty*, 20) as a potential Alexandrian delegate to Gaius rests on an argument from silence.

had premonitions of Gaius's hostility to the Jewish cause the minute he laid eyes on the emperor at their arrival on the banks of the Tiber. During the time between this first meeting and the final hearing, Philo would have had ample opportunity to converse with the well-established Jewish community in Rome, as well as with his other Roman friends, and hone his understanding of local Roman impressions about Jews.[69] Moreover, Philo's familial connection with Rome,[70] as well as the likelihood of his Roman citizenship and his political involvement prior to the embassy, suggests that Philo was aware of his Roman accusers long before he sailed from Alexandria for Rome in 39 C.E. [71]

In light of these observations, I have followed Sterling in suggesting that the *Hypothetica* was composed in preparation for the embassy in 39/40.[72] I have further suggested that Philo had an imperial Roman audience in mind. Philo notes in the *Legatio ad Gaium* that the Jewish embassy "determined to give Gaius a document presenting in a summarized form the story of our sufferings and our claims. This document was practically an epitome of a longer supplication which we had sent to him a short time before through the hands of Agrippa."[73] The *Hypothetica* was perhaps originally part of one of these written drafts or, as I have suggested, an edition of Philo's oratorical case (ὑπόθεσις)[74] reworked in Rome with a focus on Jerusalem after the news of Gaius's intended "gift" to the temple.

Philo did not anticipate making his case before the Roman emperor alone. Several texts from his apologetic treatises make clear the kind of audience he envisioned. Firstly, in describing how Gaius should have behaved at the hearing, Philo gives the following retrospect:

> For these would have been the works of a judge: he would sit with the counselors (σύνεδροι) selected for their merit . . . while the opposing parties would stand on each side with their advocates (συναγορεύσοντες), he would hear in turn the accusation and the defense, in accordance with the time [lit.

---

[69] My thanks are due to Joshua Yoder, my colleague at the University of Notre Dame, for bringing this possibility to my attention.

[70] The ties between Philo's brother Alexander and Agrippa I, who had close connections with the Julio-Claudians, date back at least to 36 C.E. Philo's nephew Tiberius Julius Alexander, who denounced his Jewish faith, was procurator of Judea and later appointed Roman prefect of Egypt in 66 C.E. See Smallwood, *Jews*, 258.

[71] For a summary of Philo's familial and political connections, see Daniel R. Schwartz, "Philo, His Family, and His Times," in *The Cambridge Companion to Philo* (Adam Kamesar, ed.; Cambridge: Cambridge University Press, 2009), 9–31.

[72] Sterling, "Logic," 429. Harker, *Loyalty*, 14, specifies a departure in 38/39 rather than 39/40. Philo only tells us that the ambassadors left in winter.

[73] Philo, *Legat.* 178–179 (Colson, LCL).

[74] Philo, *Legat.* 181, 186.

water] allotted; then rising he would consult with the counselors what ought to be publicly declared by most just opinion. (*Legat.* 350)

Although this scene is clearly idealized, it provides an outline of the kind of judicial setting that Philo had anticipated. It depicts what Philo thought Gaius ought to have done in this specific situation, given that "the case under scrutiny was very great and had not been heard of for four-hundred years,"[75] i.e. for the entirety of Alexandria's existence (331 B.C.E.–39/40 C.E.).

Philo also provides a literal description of the trials of provincial governors under Augustus and Tiberius in *Flacc.* 105–106. Although these cases would not be identical to those of the embassy in 39/40, they do provide a very close analogue, especially since Philo tells us that they occurred most frequently when "the wronged cities sent embassies"[76] to complain about a former governor:

For on these occasions the emperors showed themselves impartial judges; they listened equally to both the accusers (τῶν κατηγόρων) and the defenders (τῶν ἀπολογουμένων), making it a rule to condemn no one offhand without a trial, and awarded what they thought to be just, influenced neither by hostility nor favour but by what actually was the truth. (Philo, *Flacc.* 106 [Colson, adapted])

This passage clearly mirrors the description in *Legat.* 350, although not much more about the actual procedure can be gleaned. To fill in the details of these outlines, I turn to the evidence of the *Acta Alexandrinorum*.

3.2 *The Acta Alexandrinorum*

The *Acta Alexandrinorum*, although primarily literary rather than documentary, provide an important window into the procedure of civil and criminal cases before the Roman emperor from a non-Jewish perspective. These fragmentary texts portray, in literary or semi-literary fashion, the misadventures of Dionysius, Isidorus, and Lampo, three Alexandrian demagogues with anti-Jewish leanings who frequently appeared in embassies before the imperial Roman court.[77] These accounts were apparently meant to commend their Alexandrian protagonists as civic martyrs with

---

[75] Philo, *Legat.* 350.
[76] Philo, *Flacc.* 105, καὶ μάλισθ' ὁπότε πρεσβεύσαιντο αἱ ἀδικηθεῖσαι πόλεις.
[77] Herbert Musurillo, *The Acts of the Pagan Martyrs* (Oxford: Clarendon, 1954), 125. All three appear with derogatory epithets in Philo, *Flacc.* 20. Isidorus, as mentioned above, appears in Rome in 39/40 as a member of Apion's embassy. For Isidorus and Lampo as accusers of Flaccus in Rome, see Philo, *Flacc.* 125–145.

something of the satire and color of a tragic historical romance.[78] In his recent monograph, Andrew Harker argues that the *"Acta Alexandrinorum* literature . . . began as a reaction to Alexandrian embassies sent to Gaius and Claudius in the first century AD."[79] Thus while all the narratives may not pertain directly to the "Jewish question" *per se*, they undoubtedly bear witness to how the embassies were remembered in subsequent decades.

Two papyri regarding Isidorus bear special relevance to our reconstructions of Philo's expectations. The first, P.bibl.univ.Giss. 46 (*CPJ* 2.155), recounts the acquittal of Isidorus after accusations were made against him by an anonymous "accuser" before Gaius Caesar in 37 c.e.[80] His accuser (κατήγορος), apparently a non-Alexandrian citizen,[81] is condemned to burning at the stake or branding. This account, though highly fragmentary, further establishes the term κατήγορος, found also in the *Legatio ad Gaium*, *In Flaccum,* and Eusebius's introduction to the *Hypothetica,* fragment 1, as the *terminus technicus* for a plaintiff in an imperial court narrative. It thus seems very likely that Eusebius himself means to link the *Hypothetica* to a court narrative scenario.

A more detailed picture of the imperial court procedure is preserved in the *Acta Isidori*. This text, likely composed no earlier than Hadrian's reign,[82] records the final condemnation of Isidorus and Lampo before Claudius *ca.* 52/53 c.e.[83] The story is preserved in three versions, but the narrative shape of the first will suffice to give an overall picture of the trial proceedings.[84] The first column is damaged but mentions several Roman senators speaking. Toward the end, the unnamed Alexandrian ambassadors (πρέσβεις) are summoned, and Claudius decides to hear their case on the following day. The second column begins with a statement that Claudius Caesar is now to hear the case of Isidorus, gymnasiarch of Alexandria, against King Agrippa (presumably Agrippa II)[85] in some imperial gardens (whose identity remains disputed). We then learn that in addition to being heard before the Emperor, Isidorus made his accusations before twenty senators,

---

[78] So Smallwood, *Jews*, 250: "[The Acts of the Alexandrian Martyrs] bear more resemblance to historical novels than to sober historical record . . . The narratives are highly-coloured."

[79] Harker, *Loyalty,* 8.

[80] P.Bibl.Univ.Giss. 46, col. 3, 24; Musurillo, *Acts*, 111.

[81] P.Bibl.Univ.Giss. 46, col. 3, 21, λαβὼν πολίτειαν ἀναπόγραφον.

[82] Musurillo, *Acts*, 132.

[83] Musurillo, *Acts*, 123; Harker, *Loyalty,* 24, prefers the date 41 c.e. on the basis of the "content of the trial."

[84] Musurillo, *Acts*, 18–20; *CPJ* 2.156a, 156d (= BGU 511 + P.CairoInv. 10448).

[85] Musurillo, *Acts*, 123. Agrippa I is meant if Harker's dating is to be preferred.

sixteen *consulares*, and some significant Roman *matronae*.[86] Isidorus begins by asking Caesar to hear the afflictions of his country and Claudius grants him the day to do so, with the approving nod (συνεπένευσαν) of the senators sitting with him.[87] This seemingly auspicious beginning to the hearing is followed closely by a stern imperial warning that Isidorus say nothing against Claudius's friend (Agrippa II). Claudius then charges Isidorus with already having gotten rid of two of his friends, Theon and Naevius. The appended third column[88] begins with Claudius making the same accusation. Isidorus replies that he was simply following orders. From this point onward, civility devolves: Claudius calls Isidorus the son of a girl musician (μουσική);[89] Isidorus retorts that the Emperor is the son of the Jewess Salome; Lampo tells Isidorus that the king is mad; and Claudius, with all the tyrannical efficiency of Lewis Carroll's Queen of Hearts, orders the executioners to dispose of the unfortunate pair.

Admittedly, the two trials discussed above—that of Isidorus before Gaius and that of Isidorus and Lampo before Claudius—involve individual rather than communal cases. They are unabashedly literary narratives intended for entertainment, not documentary courtroom minutes. Nonetheless, they do offer some insights into the situation Philo might have anticipated when preparing his remarks in the *Hypothetica*. Firstly, they confirm that Philo might have expected the emperor not to hear the case alone but in the company of a *consilium principis*.[90] That *consilium* could play some role in affirming or protesting the judicial decisions made by the emperor. Such an expectation resonates with Philo's description of the ideal imperial judge who "sits with the councilors selected for their merit" (καθίσαι μετὰ συνέδρων ἀριστίνδην ἐπιλελεγμένων) and consults with them (βουλεύσασθαι) once both sides of the case have been heard.[91]

Secondly, both of these accounts suggest that the outcome of any imperial hearing could largely depend upon the whim of the emperor. In

---

[86] BGU 511, col. 2.5–8.

[87] BGU 511, col. 2.13–14.

[88] P.CairoInv. 10448.

[89] Or "son of an actress" in Musurillo, *Acts*, 25.

[90] John Percy, Vyvian Dacre Balsdon and Barbara M. Levick, *"consilium principis"*, *OCD* 377: "A Roman magistrate was always at liberty to summon advisers in deliberation or on the bench. The fluctuating body of advisers summoned to the Roman emperors retained this semi-unofficial character." Cf. Smallwood, *Jews*, 251, and the standard full-length treatment by John A. Crook, *Consilium Principis* (Cambridge: Cambridge University Press, 1955).

[91] Compare σύνεδροι in Philo, *Legat.* 350 with *P.Oxy.* XLII.3021 (published in 1974), which mentions both the Alexandrian and Jewish ambassadors as well as the imperial "assessors" συ[ν]καθημε-. See Harker, *Loyalty*, 30, for further discussion.

the case of Isidorus and Agrippa II, this meant a pro-Jewish verdict. Additionally, as in the *Acta Isidori*, the emperor himself might have some accusations to raise. Thus, while it would have made sense for Philo to prepare the *Hypothetica* on the basic outline of the Alexandrian accusations he anticipated, his expectation of a court setting would have compelled him to fine-tune his remarks for the tastes and prejudices of an educated Roman audience.

Finally, the vast differences in tone and form between the *Hypothetica* and the *Acta Alexandrinorum* help in determining the audience of the former. The *Acta Alexandrinorum* are widely accepted as being composed for a popular Alexandrian audience, written to valorize the demagogues who defended the city's "pure Greek" citizenship. They are marked by a dramatic form and punctuated with pithy repartees aimed at rousing popular sympathy for the local heroes. The *Hypothetica*, in contrast, with its detailed and sophisticated arguments, bears all the marks of a serious apologetic oratory, aimed not to entertain but to persuade. Its modest dialectical elements (e.g. the occasional second person singular) reflect the context of an anticipated oratory before an emperor, not staged arguments between dramatic characters.

The End of the Embassy

Philo's *Hypothetica*, with its intertextual echoes of and allusions to Roman colonization narratives, would have presented a strong case for the restoration of the Jewish *politeuma* had it been spoken before the imperial *consilium*.[92] The peaceful allegiance of these two peoples required one primary concession: that the Jerusalem temple and Diasporan *proseuchai* remain free of imperial images. This was one concession that Gaius could not gladly admit. Only under Claudius was the Jewish *politeuma* reinstated with the legal standing it had enjoyed under Augustus.[93]

One cannot help wondering why such a carefully reasoned apology ultimately failed on the Roman stage. In asking this question, too, one does well to consider audience. When Philo led the embassy before Gaius, he found not a judge but an accuser. It is telling that the emissary who had the most success at curbing Gaius's disrespect for Jewish cult and culture seems to have been Agrippa I, who in the narration of the *Legatio* success-

---

[92] In all likelihood, Gaius never afforded Philo the chance to make his speech. See Philo, *Legat.* 364 and Josephus, *A.J.* 18.259–60.

[93] *CPJ* 2.153; Sterling, *Jewish Plato*, 23–24; Smallwood, *Jews*, 242.

fully forestalls Gaius's plan to dedicate a colossus of himself in the Jerusalem temple. Agrippa presented Gaius with a δέησις, a plea or a prayer, which argued οὐ λογισμῷ μᾶλλον ἢ τῷ τῆς εὐνοίας πάθει,[94] "not according to reason, but according to the feeling of good will," an instinctual preference for one's ancestral ways. Such self-abasing supplication ultimately reached the ego of Caligula; Agrippa's prayer bent the ear of the self-designated god.

Philo, by contrast, presented Gaius with an ὑπόθεσις, a legal case.[95] Unlike Agrippa I, he proceeded οὐ μὴν μᾶλλον . . . καθ' ἱστορίαν ἢ κατά τινα λογισμὸν.[96] In the end neither reason nor history ultimately served him well. It was the very *acumen* of Philo's mind which made him both a formidable opponent to his Alexandrian accusers and, in the final assessment, a failure before Gaius.

University of Notre Dame

---

[94] Philo, *Legat.* 277.
[95] Philo, *Legat.* 350.
[96] Philo, *Hypoth.* 8.6.5.

The Studia Philonica Annual 22 (2010) 209–256

BIBLIOGRAPHY SECTION

PHILO OF ALEXANDRIA
AN ANNOTATED BIBLIOGRAPHY 2007

D. T. Runia, K. Berthelot, E. Birnbaum, A. C. Geljon, H. M. Keizer,
J. Leonhardt-Balzer, J. P. Martín, M. R. Niehoff, T. Seland

2007*

T. Alekniene, 'L'enigme de la 'patrie' dans le Traite 1 de Plotin: heritage de l'exégèse philonienne?,' *Recherches augustiniennes et patristiques* 35 (2007) 1–46.

---

* This bibliography has been prepared by the members of the International Philo Bibliography Project, under the leadership of D. T. Runia (Melbourne). The principles on which the annotated bibliography is based have been outlined in *SPhA* 2 (1990) 141–142, and are largely based on those used to compile the 'mother works', R-R and RRS. There are two changes this year in the team that has prepared the bibliography: Katell Berthelot has taken over the works in French from Jean Riaud; Jutta Leonhardt-Balzer has taken over the works in German from Gottfried Schimanowski. Both scholars are to be thanked for their contributions over a large number of years, Riaud from 1997 to 2009, Schimanowski from 2004 to 2009. The division of the work this year is thus as follows: material in English (and Dutch) by D. T. Runia (DTR), E. Birnbaum (EB), A. C. Geljon (ACG); in French by K. Berthelot (KB); in Italian by H. M. Keizer (HMK); in German by Jutta Leonhardt-Balzer (JLB); in Spanish and Portuguese by J. P. Martín (JPM); in Scandinavian languages (and by Scandinavian scholars) by T. Seland (TS); in Hebrew (and by Israeli scholars) by Maren Niehoff (MRN). Once again this year much benefit has been derived from the related bibliographical labours of L. Perrone (Bologna) and his team in the journal *Adamantius* (Origen studies). Other scholars formally not part of the team who have given assistance this year are Giovanni Benedetto, Marie-Luise Lakmann, Jean Riaud (JR), Olga Vardazaryan, Sze-Kar Wan. My research assistant in Melbourne, Tamar Primoratz, again helped me with various tasks. This year, too, I am most grateful to my former Leiden colleague M. R. J. Hofstede for laying a secure foundation for the bibliography through his extremely thorough electronic searches. However, the bibliography remains inevitably incomplete, because much work on Philo is tucked away in monographs and articles, the titles of which do not mention his name. Scholars are encouraged to get in touch with members of the team if they spot omissions (addresses below in 'Notes on Contributors'). In order to preserve continuity with previous years, the bibliography retains its own customary stylistic conventions and has not changed to those of the Society of Biblical Literature used in the remainder of the Annual. It is envisaged that a sequel to RRS for the years 1997–2006 will be published by Brill in the near future. Investigations are also proceeding in relation

Plotinus rarely indulges in a commentary on the Homeric myths. In the 8th chapter of the first treatise [I, 6], however, he analyzes Odysseus' escape from the houses of Circe and Calypso, and the words 'let us flee to our dear *patris*,' as referring to the soul that has become lost in the world as perceived by the senses and has to go back to the world of the intelligible, which is its true *patris*. This happens through a transformation of one's vision. According to the Epistle to the Hebrews (11:13–16), the believer, too, longs for his celestial homeland (πάτρις). But in that context the soul does not *return* to its homeland, whereas the idea of return is central in Plotinus' exegesis of the *Odyssey*. The theme of the celestial *patris*, closely linked to virtue or wisdom, and of the flight of the soul, is crucial in Philo, particularly in his exegesis of the life of Abraham, who represents the archetype of the soul. Philo seems to be the first author to have based a whole history of the soul upon the allegorical exegesis of a text. The similarities between Philo and Plotinus are numerous and striking. They both write about the flight to the celestial *patris* in the context of an allegorical exegesis. In addition, their notions of a heavenly, transcendent and metaphysical homeland, which can be reached through a transformation of one's vision, are very close. It has been argued that Philo had some knowledge of a Middle Platonic tradition of allegorical interpretation of the *Odyssey*. However, such a tradition is attested only from the second century c.e. onwards, with Numenius. Moreover, in that respect the similarities between Philo and Plotinus are more striking than those between Numenius and Plotinus. Therefore, the similarities between Philo and Plotinus could be explained by an indirect influence of Philo's writings upon Plotinus, maybe through Gnostic intermediaries. (KB)

M. ALESSO, 'Qué es una madre judía según Filón,' *Circe* 11 (2007) 11–25.

The author proposes a reading of Philo's works from the point of view of social identity. The article understands identity as a position that a writer takes in relation to a system of social categories, that is to say, how he defines what belongs to a group and how the relationship is with other groups that could strengthen the positive aspects of his social place. The article investigates what it means to be a Jew for Philo and what is feminine for him, understanding that any bond of filiation, far from being bilateral (genitor-progeny), is subjected to collective constraints and to certain reference signals from the environment. Philo does not specifically address the issue of matrilineage, and it is never possible to assert that in the texts of Philo a Jewish mother gives identity to her children at the expense of the paternal line. (JPM)

M. ALEXANDRE, 'Les études philoniennes et le renouveau patristique,' in Y.-M. BLANCHARD *et al.* (eds.), *"De commencement en commencement". Le renouveau patristique dans la théologie contemporaine*, (Paris 2007) 141–179.

This article recounts the history of research on Philo in the French context, the development of the collection 'Les oeuvres de Philon d'Alexandrie' (OPA) directed by C. Mondésert, J. Pouilloux and R. Arnaldez, and examines the place dedicated to the reception of Philo's work by Patristic authors in the OPA series and in research on Philo in general. It recalls the conferences of Lyon in 1966 and Créteil in 1995, and the important work of V. Nikiprowetzky. M. Alexandre then evokes the development of Philonic studies worldwide, referring particularly to the work of D. T. Runia, A. van den Hoek (on Clement of

to the possibility of making an online version of the Bibliography which will cover the entire history of Philonic scholarship, including the material included in G-G.

Alexandria and Origen), A. C. Geljon (on Gregory of Nyssa), and H. Savon (on Ambrose). She summarizes the reasons why Christian authors were interested in Philo, such as exegesis, apologetics, or Christian admiration for the Essenes and the Therapeutae. But some Christian authors were also critical of Philo's writings, for instance of his allegorical reading of Scriptures. (KB)

A. ANGEL, 'From Wild Men to Wise and Wicked Women: an Investigation into Male Heterosexuality in Second Temple Interpretations of the Ladies Wisdom and Folly,' in D. W. ROOKE (ed.), *A Question of Sex? Gender and Difference in the Hebrew Bible and Beyond*, Hebrew Bible Monographs 14 (Sheffield 2007) 145–161, esp. 148–149.

This article studies the interpretation of the figures of Woman Wisdom and Woman Folly from Proverbs 1–9 in three Second Temple texts: Philo's *Sacr.* 21–28, 4Q184 and Sirach 51:13–21. In Proverbs 1–9 the two women are depicted as sexually attractive. Philo desexualizes Woman Wisdom and oversexes Woman Folly to promote his own view that one should seek wisdom and avoid physical and emotional sensations. In contrast to the author of Proverbs, Philo shows a strongly negative attitude towards male heterosexuality. (ACG)

S. BADILITA, *Recherches sur la prophétie chez Philon d'Alexandrie* (diss. Université de Paris IV–Sorbonne 2007).

The thesis examines various aspects of the theme of prophecy in Philo, such as: the vocabulary of prophecy, the prophetic figure of Abraham, the relation between Moses' prophetic role and the three other roles he receives in *Mos.* (as king, legislator and priest), the question of divine inspiration and the classification of Mosaic oracles, the relation between prophecy and inspiration against the background of the relation between Moses and Aaron, prophetic dreams and their classification, Philo's criticism of divination in the case of the seer Balaam, and the role of early and later prophets in the Alexandrian's writings. A new approach to the subject is put forward in the fact that the study focuses above all on prophetic figures, whereas most previous studies have concentrated on the theoretical aspects of prophecy. (JR)

J. M. G. BARCLAY, *Flavius Josephus: Translation and Commentary, Volume 10 Against Apion: Translation and Commentary* (Leiden–Boston 2007), esp. 353–361.

This volume, published as part of the Brill Josephus project, contains a new English translation of Josephus' apologetic treatise, based on the new critical text established by H. Schreckenberg. It also provides the first English commentary on this treatise, written from a 'postcolonial' perspective and giving a comprehensive treatment of the historical, literary, and rhetorical features of the work. Comparative evidence from Philo is used throughout; see the index of passages on pp. 415–417. But of greatest interest to Philo scholars is the Appendix entitled 'The sources of the apologetic encomium' (2.145–286). Barclay argues that the Eusebian attribution of this text should be called into question. Many aspects of the text, both in terms of style and content, differ from what we know about Philo, though it is conceded that the description of the Sabbath in 7.10–14 does contain strong Philonic echoes. It is possible that this section is influenced by Philo. Further parallels between the two works and the text in Ps.Phocylides are examined and it is concluded that there is insufficient evidence for a direct literary relationship between the three texts. Barclay also notes some general similarities between Josephus' discussion of ritual practices in 2.190–218 and Philo and suggests that Philo and Josephus may have drawn independently from a common tradition. See also the review by Gregory E. Sterling in *SPhA* 20 (2008) 236–241. (DTR)

C. T. BEGG, 'Josephus' and Philo's Retelling of Numbers 31 Compared,' *Ephemerides theologicae Lovanienses* 83 (2007) 81–106.

Both Josephus (*Ant.* 4.159–163) and Philo (*Mos.* 1.305–318) retell the story of the Israel-ites' war against the Midianites as told in Num 31. The author compares both rewritings with each other and with the biblical account. Josephus and Philo have a number of com-mon features: both give, for instance, a motivation for Moses' choice of Phineas as military leader. But there are also several differences, among which the most striking is that Josephus presents a more reduced story, whereas Philo gives a more elaborated narrative. (ACG)

C. T. BEGG, 'Balaam's Talking Ass (Num 22,21–35): Three Retellings of her Story Compared,' *Annali di Storia dell'Esegesi* 24 (2007) 207–228, esp. 211–216, 223–224.

Differences and similarities are presented between the retellings of the story about Balaam's talking ass in Pseudo-Philo (*LAB* 18.9—very succinct), Philo (*Mos.* 1.269–74) and Josephus (*Ant.* 4.108–11). In addition the treatment of the story in targumic and midrashic commentary is briefly reviewed. (HMK)

C. T. BEGG, 'Israel's Confrontation with Edom (Num 20,14–21) according to Josephus and Philo,' *Revista Catalana de Teología* 32 (2007) 1–18.

Analyzes three extensive passages of Greek Judaism that quote Num 20:14–21, where Edom denies Israel's request to pass through its territory. The first text belongs to Josephus, *AJ* 4.76–77, who, in accordance with Deut 2:3–6 and Targum Neofiti, emphasizes the inquiry of God by Moses and the withdrawal of Israel's forces in obedience to the divine oracle. The first text of Philo, *Mos.* 1.239–249, rewrites the story by emphasizing the qualities of Moses as leader and presents a sharp contrast between two peoples who are both the progeny of Isaac. In *Deus* 144–180, Philo writes an extended allegory on the Septuagint text, describing the passage of Israel on the royal road between two opposite forces, the guide of the Logos and the resistance of Edom, symbol of the earthly attraction. The author notes that a minor incident without long-term consequences for the study of history offers the opportunity for Josephus and Philo to enlarge the symbolic fecundity of this Bible passage. (JPM)

C. T. BEGG, 'The Rephidim Episode according to Josephus and Philo,' *Ephemerides theologicae Lovanienses* 83 (2007) 367–383.

The author examines the way in which Josephus in *Ant.* 3.33–38 and Philo in *Mos.* 1.210–213 rewrite the story of the miracle of the rock as told in Exod 17:1–7. Both Philo and Josephus omit some elements, such as Moses' answer to the people who quarrel with him.

Likewise, both make explicit mention of Moses' actual striking of the rock. Josephus offers several 'non-biblical' elements in his reading. In Philo the focus is on theological and psychological reflections that he makes on the miracle. (ACG)

C. T. BEGG, 'Two Ancient Rewritings of Numbers 11,' *Revista Catalana de Teología* 32 (2007) 299–317.

The article examines two rewritings of the biblical quail story of Num. 11, one by Josephus in *AJ* 3.296–299, the other by Philo in *Spec.* 4.126–131. Both authors present an abridged rendering of the text, limiting it essentially to the quail story. Both accentuate the people's verbal assault on their leader and eliminate the speaking role attributed to God. Josephus extends and underlines the interaction between Moses and the people. Philo focuses all his attention on the covetousness and punishment of the people. In addition, as a framework to his presentation, he composes his own preface and postscript, which draw out the theological and moral lessons implicit in the scriptural narrative. (JPM)

P. J. BEKKEN, *The Word is Near You. A Study of Deuteronomy 30:12–14 in Paul's Letter to the Romans in a Jewish Context*, Beihefte zur Zeitschrift für die neutestamentliche Wissenschaft und die Kunde der älteren Kirche 144 (Berlin–New York 2007).

A slightly revised version of the author's 1998 dissertation from the University of Trondheim written under the supervision of Professor Peder Borgen. See the summary at *SPhA* vol. 13, p. 253. The English text has been copy-edited, and there is an updated bibliography. The present volume also includes indexes of modern authors and of references. (TS)

K. BERTHELOT, 'Philo of Alexandria and the Conquest of Canaan,' *Journal for the Study of Judaism* 38 (2007) 39–56.

According to the Torah, the Hebrews were commanded either to expel or to exterminate the Canaanites who were living in Canaan at the time of the conquest. Philo seems to feel rather ill at ease about the literal meaning of these biblical passages. Besides allegory, he uses four hermeneutical strategies to deal with them. First, he sometimes passes over the problematic texts in silence, as in *Virt.* 109, when dealing with Deut 20:15–18. Second, he plays with the meaning of certain Greek words, like *anathema*, which he uses in the way classical Greek authors did and not with the meaning of 'destruction' involved in many passages of the Septuagint. Third, Philo also tries to justify the destruction of the Canaanites from a moral point of view, either by connecting their fate to the story of Ham and Canaan in Genesis 9 and by considering Canaan himself guilty, or by emphasizing the abominations of the Canaanites and in particular their inhuman practice of sacrificing their own children (as in Deut 12:31). Finally, in one case, *Hypoth.* 6.5–7, Philo freely rewrites the biblical account and departs from the literal meaning of the text by suggesting that the conquest did not happen as such, but that the Canaanites voluntarily surrendered the Land to Moses and his followers out of admiration for his wisdom and recognition of God's love towards Israel. (KB)

K. BERTHELOT, 'Zeal for God and Divine Law in Philo and the Dead Sea Scrolls,' *The Studia Philonica Annual* 19 (2007) 113–129.

The two paramount examples of zeal for God in the Bible are Phineas, who killed the impious Jew who had betrayed the covenant (Num 25), and Elijah, who slaughtered the priests of Baal. Their zeal is similar to God's zeal or jealousy for his people. In the *Community Rule*, the zeal shown by the Instructor or by the members of the community is essentially the same as that of Phineas, but since the 'day of revenge' is eschatological, they must refrain from taking the initiative of the punishment and leave everything in God's hands. Thus, the lack of explicit reference to Phineas in the Qumran texts probably follows from the way his zeal led to actual violence and punitive action. Conversely, Philo's works contain several explicit references to Phineas, whose violence against Zimri and Cozbi is praised in *Mos.* 1.300–304 and *Spec.* 1.54–57. In Philo's perspective, zeal for virtue can justify homicide, when virtue is synonymous with obedience to the Law and homicide is motivated by 'hatred for evil,' namely hatred for apostasy and idolatry. However, it is difficult to determine whether in a concrete situation Philo would have gone so far as to advocate the killing of a Jew caught worshipping a foreign god or blaspheming. In any case, one should not conclude that the Qumran texts reflect a more lenient approach than Philo's works. Beyond their common positive appreciation of zeal for the Law, their religious agendas are very different. (KB)

P. BILDE, 'Filon som polemiker og politisk apologet. En undersøgelse af de to historiske skrifter *Mod Flaccum* (*In Flaccum*) og *Om delegationen til Gaius De legatione ad Gaium* [Philo as polemicist and political apologete. An investigation of the two historical works *In Flacccum* and *De legatione ad Gaium*],' in A. KLOSTERGAARD PETERSEN, J. HYLDAHL and K. S. FUGLSETH (eds.), *Perspektiver på jødisk apologetik*, Antikken og kristendommen 4 (Copenhagen 2007) 155–180.

The author here investigates Philo's role as a polemicist and political apologist in *In Flaccum* and in *De legatione ad Gaium*. He first provides a reconstruction of the most important events in Alexandria and Palestine in 38–41 C.E. Then he reads and analyzes the two historical works of Philo, i.e. he provides an investigation of their literary character, genre, purpose, date and audience, especially focusing the term παλινῳδία in *Legat* 137. The conclusion is reached that both works can be said to be political-apologetic as well as theological-apologetic. He then discusses whether Philo can be said to threaten Rome either explicitly or implicitly. Goodenough's suggestion that Philo here presents some hidden warnings to the Roman elites is given support. (TS)

P. BOBICHON, 'Comment Justin a-t-il acquis sa connaissance exception-nelle des exégèses juives?,' *Revue de théologie et de philosophie* 139 (2007) 101–126, 192.

In his *Dialogue with Trypho*, Justin refers 34 times explicitly to Jewish interpretations of Scripture and 15 times to Jewish beliefs and practices which he describes as contemporary. Scholars have generally thought that he drew his information from previous writings that were known to him: either the lost *Dialogue of Jason and Papiscus*, or some Jewish-Christian sources, or even a Jewish polemical work. But the truth probably lies elsewhere. A comparison between Justin's treatise and the writings of Philo, the apocrypha, the Dead Sea scrolls, the New Testament, early Christian literature, and rabbinic literature, shows that there are nearly no examples of a specific tradition shared by both Justin and another source, except in the case of rabbinic texts (generally midrashic texts). Moreover, the exegetical traditions referred to by Justin are attributed in rabbinic literature to Tannaitic sages who lived between the end of the first century and the third cent c.e., mainly in Palestine, and who are often described as involved in polemical dialogues with *minim* or pagans. Although the attribution of a tradition to a specific rabbi is in itself insufficient to determine the dating of this tradition with certainty, one may conclude from the comparison between the *Dialogue* and rabbinic literature that Justin probably had direct contacts with contemporary Jews and used first-hand information. (KB)

E. Bona, 'Echi di Filone nella Vita Syncleticae (BHG 1694)?,' *Revista de Filologia e di Istruzione Classica* 135 (2007) 220–230.

The author identifies two Philonic 'echoes' in the hagiography about the Alexandrian saint Syncletica (of an unknown author, between the end of the fourth and the middle of the sixth century), *Mos.* 1.25 and 1.27, which makes it all the more reasonable to think that the hagiographer may have lived in Alexandria. (HMK)

A. P. Bos, 'Is God 'Maker' of 'Vader' van de kosmos? Het debat tussen Plato en Aristoteles en de voortzetting ervan bij Philo [Is God 'maker' or 'father' of the cosmos? The debate between Plato and Aristotle and its continuation by Philo],' in K. Spronk and R. Roukema (eds.), *Over God [On God]*, (Zoetermeer 2007) 47–71, 188–191, esp. 63–71.

The main theme in this wide-ranging popularizing article is the difference between Plato and Aristotle in their understanding of the origin of the cosmos as ordered physical reality. Philo and many later Christian authors regarded Plato's demiurge as the creator god similar to the biblical conception, but this view is fundamentally wrong (p. 51). Plato's view privileges the role of thinking, whereas in the Bible God is the creator of all reality. In the final part of the article Bos explains more fully why he believes that Philo's view on creation is not faithful to the biblical account. By introducing the divine Logos as a figure intermediate between God and the cosmos, Philo shows that he is following not the Platonic conception of the process of creation but the Aristotelian conception. Nine reasons are given for this conclusion, including the fact that Philo calls God Nous and Being, and that the Logos and not God is presented as the 'maker' of the cosmos. Bos ends by asking whether Philo could have developed these ideas independently or whether he might be dependent on Aristotelian theology as it is presented in the work *De mundo* (which Bos regards as genuinely Aristotelian). He opts for the latter alternative. (DTR)

A. Botica, *The Concept of Intention in the Bible, Philo of Alexandria, and the Early Rabbinic Literature* (diss. Hebrew Union College – Jewish Institute of Religion 2007).

The dissertation examines the concept of intention in the Biblical, Philonic and Rabbinic traditions of Judaism. The fifth chapter focuses on Philo's understanding of intent in criminal and cultic law, and also in the areas of ethics and piety. It also seeks to account for the differences that Greek thought, the milieu of Hellenistic Judaism, and the inheritance of the Law, made to the way Philo thought about intent. (DTR; based on the author's summary)

D. Boyarin, 'Philo, Origen, and the Rabbis on Divine Speech and Inter-
pretation,' in J. E. Goehring and J. Timbie (eds.), *The World of Early Egyptian
Christianity: Language, Literature, and Social Context: Essays in Honor of David
W. Johnson* (Washington DC 2007) 113–129.

The notion of Logos implies both revealer and the meaning that is revealed. In using
allegorical interpretation, Philo has as his aim to uncover the 'clear and determinate
message' (p. 115) in the language of Scripture, but Boyarin finds it difficult to understand
how Philo can justify his ability as an interpreter to 'accomplish that which Moses himself
could not' (p. 116). By contrast, for Origen this ability can be explained by the presence of
the incarnate Logos, which offers direct access to the true interpretation. Yet another
contrast is provided by rabbinic midrash, which envisions 'no transcendental signified,' or
one, true interpretation, but rather 'a multiplicity of interpretations' and 'finally a rabbinic
ascesis that virtually eliminates the practice of interpretation entirely' (pp. 123–124). To
illustrate this last observation, Boyarin focuses on the understanding of Song of Songs by
Origen and the rabbis and argues that they differ not only in interpretation but also in the
underlying theory of language. Unlike Philo, Origen, and other practitioners of allegorical
interpretation who see a Platonic dichotomy between body and spirit, the rabbis make the
physical 'tangible even more strongly than does the biblical text itself' (p. 129). (EB)

R. Brague, *The Law of God. The Philosophical History of an Idea*, Translated
by L. G. Cochrane (Chicago 2007), esp. 101–104.

Although the section devoted explicitly to Philo is brief, it deserves attention because it
forms part of a comprehensive examination of the theme of divine law from Egypt and
Greece to the present, presented as a 'neutral, philosophical reading' (p. 4). In Greece
divine law is a metaphor for natural law. In Israel the concept of the Law of God receives
new meaning, expressed in a contractual relationship between God and his people. Philo
has a conception of the divinity of the law that is just as 'Greek' as it is 'Jewish'. He
recognizes that laws are oracles from God, with Moses as intermediary, but this conception
does not fill him with enthusiasm. For Philo divine law is above all natural law and
unwritten. The divinity of the law resides above all in its intrinsic worth. As for the actual
authorship of the Law, he leaves this question open. It should be noted that Philo does not
attribute to God any particular article of Mosaic law. (DTR)

F. Calabi, 'Tra Atene e Gerusalemme: anima e parola in Filone di
Alessandria,' in R. Bruschi (ed.), *Gli irraggiungibili confini. Percorsi della
psyche nell'età della Grecia classica* (Pisa 2007) 217–236.

This article argues and illustrates how the encounter of notions expressed by the Greek
terms ψυχή and λόγος with those expressed by the Hebrew terms *nefesh* and *davar* has
caused a mutual enrichment of Hebrew and Greek thought in the Hellenistic period. The
meaning of *nefesh* and of a concept of 'soul' or psychical faculties in the Hebrew Bible is
confronted with the meaning of ψυχή and the developing concept of soul—whether or not
immortal—in Greek thought. The article culminates in a discussion of ψυχή and λόγος in
Philo, where the latter term on the one hand comprises meanings (viz. 'thought', i.e. the
rational faculty of the soul, and 'word') not rendered by one single Hebrew word, but on
the other hand is enriched with notions—namely of word as command and/or act, notably
of creation—conveyed by *davar* (translated λόγος and ῥῆμα in the LXX). (HMK)

F. CALABI, 'Filone di Alessandria e Ecfanto. Un confronto possibile,' in M. BONAZZI, C. LÉVY and C. STEEL (eds.), *A Platonic Pythagoras. Platonism and Pythagoreanism in the Imperial Age*, Monothéismes et Philosophie 10 (Turnhout 2007) 11–28.

The pseudo-Pythagoreans, among whom is Ecphantus, are a category of authors difficult to date (hypotheses ranging from the third century B.C.E. to the third century C.E.), to localize and to interpret. This article through a comparison of positions taken by Philo and by the *Peri Basileias* of Ecphantus leads to the conclusion that the two authors show affinities, that Philo can help to explain Ecphantus, and that the latter seems to fit in a Neoplatonic context. The themes reviewed in both authors include *homoiôsis theôi*, knowledge of God, God as king of the universe, order and harmony in the universe, the king as intermediary between God and man, and the function and meaning of contemplation/ imitation and persuasion. Throughout the article the author devotes critical remarks to interpretations developed by Delatte in his 1942 Liège monograph (= R-R 4201). An English translation has been published as an appendix to the author's more recent study, *God's Acting, Man's Acting* (Leiden 2008). (HMK)

J. CHERIAN, *Toward a Commonwealth of Grace. A Plutocritical Reading of Grace and Equality in Second Corinthians 8:1–15* (diss. Princeton Theological Seminary 2007).

This study in Pauline theology and ethics builds on Paul's understanding of God's disruptive and subversive grace and a new ethical paradigm revealed in the Christ event. Paul demands a distributive ethic that radically cuts across the dominant socio-economic system of patronage and expects gracious equality within the commonwealth of grace. Chapter 3 studies the uses of the term 'equality' in Philo, Dio Chrysostom, and Plutarch and shows how common and yet uniquely nuanced Paul's words would have sounded in the church at Corinth. (DTR; based on the author's abstract)

H. CLIFFORD, 'Moses as Philosopher-sage in Philo,' in A. GRAUPNER and M. WOLTER (eds.), *Moses in Biblical and Extra-biblical Traditions*, Beihefte zur Zeitschrift für die alttestamentliche Wissenschaft 372 (Berlin 2007) 151–167.

For Philo virtue is the hallmark of all true philosophy and wisdom, and therefore he portrays Moses as the virtuous philosopher-sage. The climax of Moses' virtuous life is his contemplation of God at Sinai. The method of allegorical interpretation enables him to transform Moses into the ideal philosopher-sage in terms familiar to intellectual Greeks and Romans. His motivation is apologetic: the need to defend the reputation of Moses, who had become a contested figure in Jewish and non-Jewish circles. See also a review of the whole volume in which the article is presented by G. E. Sterling, *SPhA* 21 (2009) 127–130. (ACG)

N. G. COHEN, *Philo's Scriptures: Citations from the Prophets and Writings: Evidence for a Haftarah Cycle in Second Temple Judaism*, Supplements to the Journal for the Study of Judaism 123 (Leiden 2007).

The book addresses Philo's approach to non-Pentateuchal texts. It begins with a chapter on Philo and his time, then it includes reworked versions of two previously published articles, one on the names of the individual books of the Pentateuch (summary *SPhA* vol. 12, p 152) and one relating Philo's prophetic quotations to a later Haftarah Cycle (summary *SPhA* vol. 12, p 153). Further chapters explore the introductions to the other non-Pentateuchal quotations, those of the Latter Prophets, the Former Prophets and Chronicles, the Psalms, Proverbs and Job in varying detail. These chapters serve to underline the claim that Philo's non-Pentateuchal quotations are based on either texts known to his audience from their regular worship, or taken from midrashic or allegorical sources or exegetical aids such as a scriptural concordance and a homiletic lexicon of proper names, all translated into Greek. Cohen ends with a chapter arguing on the basis of the order of the Philonic writings in the Loeb edition that at one time Philo was a member of an 'allegorical circle of Moses', a group of extreme Alexandrian allegorists, but that he later distanced himself from too strong an allegorical approach. See further the review of J. Leonhardt-Balzer, *SPhA* 20 (2008) 221–224. (JLB)

J. J. COLLINS, 'Philo and the Dead Sea Scrolls: Introduction,' *The Studia Philonica Annual* 19 (2007) 81–83.

This article introduces the four articles that follow it, which compare different aspects of Philo's thought to the Dead Sea Scrolls. While the author stresses that Philo and the Scrolls represent the opposite extremes of ancient Judaism, he also believes that it is meaningful to compare them, because both are part of Judaism by virtue of grounding their identity and religion in the Mosaic Scriptures. A summary of each article as well as some constructive criticism is subsequently offered. The author concludes that 'while the findings of these essays are modest, they are certainly sufficient to suggest that the possibility of further affinities between the sectarians ... and the philosopher of Alexandria is well worth exploring.' (MRN)

R. R. COX, *By the Same Word: Creation and Salvation in Hellenistic Judaism and Early Christianity*, Beihefte zur Zeitschrift für die neutestamentliche Wissenschaft und die Kunde der älteren Kirche 145 (Berlin–New York 2007), esp. 87–140.

Middle Platonism explained how a transcendent principle could relate to the material world by positing an intermediary, modeled after the Stoic active cause, that mediated the supreme principle's influence to the world while preserving its transcendence. The monograph examines how having similar concerns as Middle Platonism, Hellenistic Jewish sapientialism, early Christianity, and Gnosticism appropriated this intermediary doctrine as a means for understanding their relationship to God and to the cosmos, though varying in their adaptation of this teaching due to their distinctive understanding of creation and humanity's place therein. Both Philo and the Wisdom of Solomon espouse a holistic ontology, combining a Platonic appreciation for noetic reality with an ultimately positive view of creation and its place in human fulfilment. The lengthy chapter on Philo focuses primarily on the doctrine of the Logos, taking *Sacr.* 8 as its starting-point. The Logos must be seen as an entity between God and matter, bringing the divine image to bear on matter and thus producing and sustaining the physical world. The doctrine of the Logos also plays a significant role in Philo's anthropology. The final part of the chapter examines how in Philo's view the Logos brings the human mind into existence. The author concludes

(p. 140): 'Anthropology and cosmology are of a piece in Philo of Alexandria and that piece is the all-encompassing Logos.' (DTR)

M. R. D'ANGELO, 'Gender and Geopolitics in the Work of Philo of Alexandria: Jewish Piety and Imperial Family Values,' in T. PENNER and C. VANDER STICHELE (eds.), *Mapping Gender in Ancient Religious Discourses*, Biblical Interpretation Series 84 (Leiden–Boston 2007) 63–88.

This article engages the work of Maren R. Niehoff, arguing that Philo's gender categories reflect the contemporary Roman discourse to an extent hitherto unnoticed. Unlike Niehoff in her 2001 monograph (see *SPh* vol. 16, p. 249), the author identifies this discursive strategy as part of Philo's apologetics on behalf of Judaism. The article focuses on four themes, namely, Jewish *eusebeia* as Roman *pietas*, the laws of Moses and Roman laws, Roman sexual politics and Philo's interpretation of the creation. In Philo's apologetic works, such as the *Legatio* and *De Decalogo*, he no longer uses the notion of *eusebeia* in its classical Greek sense of devotion to the gods, but rather in the distinctly Roman sense, which combines manly devotion with familial love and public display of the appropriate disposition. In Philo's discussion of Mosaic Law disproportionate attention is given to adultery and family values. This emphasis becomes understandable in light of imperial family politics. Finally, Philo's interpretation of Eve as sense-perception and thus subordinate to the rational male conforms to the Roman view of women as ruled by their husbands and represented by male members of the family in legal affairs. (MRN)

K. P. DE LONG, *Surprised by God: Praise Responses in the Narrative of Luke-Acts* (diss. University of Notre Dame 2007).

This dissertation investigates twenty-eight instances of praise of God in Luke-Acts by combining a close, intrinsic reading with extrinsic, comparative study. Part one overviews praise of God in selected early Jewish literature (including Philo) and Greek texts and analyzes it as a narrative motif in Tobit and Joseph and Aseneth. Part two focuses on Luke-Acts, in comparison with the findings of part one. (DTR; based on author's summary)

D. DEL BELLO, *Forgotten Paths. Etymology and the Allegorical Mindset* (Washington DC 2007), esp. 66–71.

Acknowledging that etymology is currently not highly regarded as a science, Del Bello selectively examines the role throughout history of etymology as a way of thinking and knowing. He focuses especially on the relationship between etymology and allegory and employs the term ἐτυμηγορία, coined by Proclus, to underscore and illuminate the connection. In his view etymology and allegory share much in common because they pertain to the relationship between language, meaning, and reality. A chapter entitled 'The names of heroes: Greek and Alexandrian etymologizing' begins with a consideration of etymologizing in Plato's *Cratylus* and among the Stoics, and Del Bello discusses the related role of eponyms in both describing and determining characteristics of the name-bearer. A distinctive aspect of Philo's etymologies is that they are part of a larger allegorization that extends beyond the etymologies themselves. Thus, Adam, or 'perishable earth,' does not simply refer to created beings but also symbolizes 'earthly and perishable mind.' Likewise Cain, derived from the Hebrew word meaning to acquire or possess, describes not only the character of the biblical figure Cain but also represents the "self-loving principle' which recognizes the mind as its only master' (p. 85). Other chapters explore the use of etymology diachronically from Rome through to the science of etymology in the nineteenth and twentieth centuries. An earlier version of the same book was published in Bergamo in 2005. (EB)

S. Di Mattei, 'Quelques précisions sur la φυσιολογία et l'emploi de φυσικῶς dans la méthode exégétique de Philon d'Alexandrie,' *Revue des Études Juives* 166 (2007) 45–74.

Contrary to what has been commonly argued, in Philo the term φυσικῶς does not mean 'physical allegory' as in Stoicism; neither does φυσιολογία mean 'allegorical interpretation,' as in Heraclitus for instance. For Philo, who can in this respect be compared to Plutarch, φυσιολογία is a φυσικὸς λόγος, which in fact coincides with the biblical text in Genesis about the creation of the world and with knowledge about God obtained through the allegorical interpretation of the text. In Philonic texts, the adverb φυσικῶς is used to show that the Book of Genesis teaches philosophical truths pertaining to physics. This applies, for instance, to the organisation of the soul or its processes; but physics also includes the study of the cosmos and discourses on the divine. Thus the expression φυσικῶς ἀλληγορεῖ in *Leg.* 2.5 does not refer to a physical allegory, but to an allegorical discourse that conveys some philosophical teaching about physics. Moreover, in several instances where φυσικῶς is used, Philo is in agreement with the Stoic doctrine of the soul. (KB)

A. Dinan, 'The Mystery of Play: Clement of Alexandria's Appropriation of Philo in the *Paedagogus* (1.5.21.3–22.1),' *The Studia Philonica Annual* 19 (2007) 59–80.

The article gives a close reading of a passage in Clement of Alexandria's *Paedagogus* in which he makes creative use of Philo's allegorical exegesis of Gen 26:8, in which King Abimelech is said to have looked through a window and seen Isaac 'playing with his wife Rebecca.' Scholars have long recognized that Clement adapted a text in *Plant.* 169–170. The author compares the two texts and shows that both appropriation and adaptation of Philonic material occurs. But he goes on to argue that there is also significant influence from another passage at *QG* 4.188. Indeed Philo's reference to the theme of God's play is what has prompted Clement to quote on the philosopher Heraclitus' most famous and most cryptic pronouncements (22A52 DK). He concludes that, although Clement took much from Philo, he 'significantly reworked what he found in order to develop a christological reading of the Genesis passage, to corroborate his understanding of childhood, and to hint at one of the most mysterious claims in his extant works—that God plays' (p. 80). (DTR)

T. L. Donaldson, *Judaism and the Gentiles: Jewish Patterns of Universalism (to 135 CE)* (Waco TX 2007), esp. 217–278.

To show that Judaism during the Second Temple period was 'in its own ways just as 'universalistic' as was Christianity' (and perhaps ever more so) (p. 1), Donaldson considers 222 texts and classifies them according to one or more 'patterns of universalism.' These patterns include sympathization, whereby Gentiles show sympathy for Jews and Judaism through, e.g., worshipping at the Temple or associating with Jews; conversion, whereby Gentiles completely adopt a Jewish way of life and join the Jewish community; ethical monotheism, whereby the Torah is seen 'as a particular expression of a natural law accessible to everyone through reason' or Judaism and philosophy are seen 'as parallel paths to the same goal' (p. 11); and eschatological participation, whereby the Gentiles have a positive role as end-time beneficiaries alongside Israel. Texts are drawn from Scripture, Septuagint and Apocrypha, Qumran, Philo, Josephus, Greco-Roman literature, early Christian literature, and inscriptions. In the section on Philo, Donaldson offers a detailed discussion of 23 texts, some of which he classifies in more than one category: conversion (16 texts), sympathization (5), ethical monotheism (4), and eschatological participation (1). Although Philo evinces 'two quite distinct patterns of universalism—one by means of proselytism and the law of Moses, the other by means of philosophy and reason' (275), Donaldson believes that Philo would counsel a sympathetic Gentile to convert to Judaism rather than pursue philosophy as a Gentile. See further the review by E. Birnbaum in *SPhA* 20 (2008) 213–221. (EB)

M. Ebner, 'Mahl und Gruppenidentität. Philos Schrift De Vita Contemplativa als Paradigma,' in M. Ebner (ed.), *Herrenmahl und Gruppenidentität, Quaestiones disputatae* 221 (Freiburg 2007) 64–90.

Philo's *De vita contemplativa* is studied paradigmatically as an example of inclusion and separation by means of participation in meals. An overview of the literary conventions in the ancient symposia literature leads to the conclusion that Philo deliberately juxtaposes the Therapeutae to the meal conventions in Greco-Roman culture and their literary representation in order to achieve a more pronounced self-definition. Particularly the position of the young men during the meal of the Therapeutae is a case of clear polemic against Greek pederastic practices. The socio-historical context of Philo's argument is the Jewish situation in first-century Alexandria as a community caught between attempts to obtain the citizenship and persecution. In this context the Therapeutae represent the faithful adherence to the Jewish customs as a superior way of life. (JLB)

C. Escudé, *La Guerra de los Dioses: los Mandatos Bíblicos frente a la Política Mundial* (Buenos Aires 2007), esp. 91–96.

The author, diplomat and professor of political science, wants to apply to the current situation of the Western nations a general division between those who support pacifist ideals and those who take literally the Biblical order to destroy their enemies. The political weakness of the Western nations, according to Escudé, is due to the fact that they have forgotten this Biblical order. This negligence has been caused especially by the allegorical reading of the Bible and by Gnostic tendencies, which conceive the Demiurge as a secondary god. In this context, Philo is presented as an initiator of the weakening process through his allegory and for his theory according to which angels or *dynameis* take part in the creation of man. A proof of Philo's influence in this process is the medieval sect of Magharians, which the author knows from an article of H. A. Wolfson (*JQR* 1960–61, 89–106). (JPM)

L. H. Feldman, 'Moses the General and the Battle Against Midian in Philo,' *Jewish Studies Quarterly* 14 (2007) 1–18.

Frequently in *Mos.* Philo refers to Moses as leader or general, and he underlines Philo's capacity as military leader. In the description of the war against Amalek, it is Moses who is the highest commander, whereas in the Biblical account Joshua is told to be the general. In Philo's retelling of the war against the Midianites (Num 31) in *Mos.* 1.305–318, Moses plays a very active and prominent role. Moses himself appoints Phineas as commander-in-chief and chooses the soldiers, as well as encouraging the people in a speech. Philo emphasizes that God Himself is the chief combatant in the war, which gives the Israelites the zeal to fight. He omits the scene in which Moses rebukes the commanders for showing mercy towards women and children, but explains Moses' command that anyone who has killed a person must purify himself by referring to the common kinship of the human race. Finally, he also gives an explanation for the distribution of spoils. (ACG)

L. H. FELDMAN, *Philo's Portrayal of Moses in the Context of Ancient Judaism* (Notre Dame IN 2007).

This extensive monograph discusses Philo's presentation of Moses within the broader context of ancient Judaism. It is divided into four parts. In Part I Feldman brings up some general issues relating to Philo's *Mos.*, for instance, its audience and its genre. Feldman qualifies *Mos.* as an aretology and as an encomium which glorifies the birth, education, and virtues of Moses. It is directed towards a non-Jewish audience. Philo's relationship with the midrash is also discussed. In Part II Feldman deals with Philo's presentation of Moses' life in a chronological way from his birth to his death. Moses' life is divided into short episodes. In analysing an episode, Feldman indicates in each case deviations from and additions to the biblical narrative. *Mos.* plays an important role, but passages from other treatises are also included in the discussion. References are also made to Greco-Roman authors such as Eupolemus, Aristobulus, Artapanus, Ezekiel Tragicus, and Josephus. The Pseudepigrapha, the Apocrypha and the Dead Sea Scrolls are also included. Besides this, Greek and Roman writers are quoted as well. Part III is devoted to the virtues of Moses. Moses is the epitome of virtue, possessing wisdom, courage, temperance, justice, and piety. Through piety he gains the offices of king, legislator, prophet and high priest. Attention is also paid to Moses as mediator, inventor, performer of miracles and as magician. The question whether Moses is a divine man is dealt with extensively. Part IV presents the conclusions. Philo's *Mos.* is an aretology, one of the goals of which was to catch the attention of non-Jews for the greatness of the Mosaic law. In dealing with the Bible Philo's purpose is to present not a paraphrase but rather an analysis. When he changes the biblical narrative, he does so to answer objections that readers might have. Like Ezekiel, he rationalizes the miraculous elements in the story of Moses' birth. In his description of Moses' education he deviates from the biblical narrative to a considerable extent. Like Josephus, he omits the incident of Moses' failure to circumcise his son. Philo tries to explain the ten plagues scientifically. The manifestation of God at mount Sinai is omitted in *Mos.* Philo uses the episode of the golden calf to condemn Jews of his own day who were attracted to the Egyptian way of life. He gives less attention to the revolt of Korah than Josephus does and emphasizes Moses' mildness. Unlike Josephus, Philo presents a negative portrait of Balaam as a soothsayer and mercenary technician at unusual length in order to contrast him with Moses, the true prophet. Philo regards Moses as a creative lawgiver rather than a mere transmitter of God's laws. Concerning the question of Moses' divinity, Philo rejects the view that a human being can be deified (p. 375): 'Philo's Moses is the Jewish equivalent of Plato's philosopher-king, the greatest of lawgivers, more than a mere transcriber of G-d's decrees, the model high priest, and the prophet who had a unique relationship with G-d.' See further the review by A. C. Geljon at *SPhA* 21 (2009) 125–127. (ACG)

L. H. FELDMAN, 'The Case of the Blasphemer (Lev. 24:10–16) according to Philo and Josephus,' in L. LiDONNICI and A. LIEBER (eds.), *Heavenly Tablets: Interpretation, Identity and Tradition in Ancient Judaism,* Supplements to the Journal for the Study of Judaism 119 (Leiden 2007) 213–226.

While Josephus omits the account of the blasphemer (Lev. 24:10–16), perhaps to avoid portraying the Jews as quarrelsome, Philo elaborates on this incident in *Mos.* 2. Like the Rabbis, he distinguishes between general cursing of God and, worse, specific cursing with use of the Tetragrammaton. Emphasizing that the blasphemer was the child of a mixed marriage between a Jew and an Egyptian, Philo also associates the sin of the golden calf with Egyptian worship of the bull Apis, perhaps to counter Jews' attraction to the Egyptian cult. Of particular concern to Philo is the possibility that proselytes might feel free to blaspheme the gods and that the blasphemer's disrespect of the Deity might suggest a similar refusal to respect parents, country, and benefactors. One could think that Moses' not knowing how to punish the blasphemer might place him, as lawgiver, in a bad light, but Philo underscores that because this and other cases had no precedents. Moses, as prophet, had to communicate directly with God. Both Philo and Josephus emphasize that the blasphemy of other gods is also not allowed. (EB)

P. Frick, 'The Means and Mode of Salvation: A Hermeneutical Proposal for Clarifying Pauline Soteriology,' *Horizons in Biblical Theology* 29 (2007) 203–222.

The objective of this study is to answer the question 'what is the cause of salvation according to Paul?' The argument put forward is that just as Philo understood cause in an Aristotelian sense of the multiplicity of causes (formal, material, efficient and final) constituting one overarching cause—what is here called the 'means' of salvation—so Paul, too, implicitly assumes that the one cause or 'means' of salvation consists in various causes. A second step shows how the 'means' of salvation corresponds to faith as the 'mode' of salvation. In *nuce*, the 'means' of salvation is the initiative of God and the 'mode' of salvation is the human response to that divine initiative. (TS, based on the author's abstract)

P. Frick, 'Johannine Soteriology and Aristotelian Philosophy: a Hermeneutical Suggestion on Reading John 3,16 and 1 John 4,9,' *Biblica* 88 (2007) 415–421.

The aim of this short study is to propose a hermeneutical reading of Johannine soteriology based on John 3:16 and 1 John 4:9 in order to clarify in what sense Jesus was 'the cause' of salvation. The author first presents the Aristotelian categorization of the various causes, followed by Philo's application of these causes in his explanation of the creation of the cosmos. This scheme is then applied to the Johannine texts. The result is (1) a specific definition of what constitutes the cause of salvation and (2) the important distinction between the means (understood as the four conjoint Aristotelian causes) and the mode (understood as faith) of salvation. (DTR; based on the author's summary)

E. Früchtel, 'Philon und die Vorbereitung der christlichen Paideia und Seelenleitung,' in F. R. Prostmeier (ed.), *Frühchristentum und Kultur*, Kommentar zu frühchristlichen Apologeten. Ergänzungsband 2 (Freiburg 2007) 19–33.

The article studies various aspects of Philo's approach to the guidance of the soul and its education. The principle that like can only be recognized by like is at the root of the idea of the three different levels of human insight. Philo frequently uses the terminology of the Greek mystery religions and Logos speculation to describe the human epistemological ascent. The distinction between Greek education, represented by the slave Hagar, and the study of the Law of Moses, represented by the free woman Sarah, highlights different aspect of human knowledge. Philo is presented as a forerunner of Christian approaches to education and guidance of the soul. (JLB)

K. S. Fuglseth, 'Filons forhold til tempelet i Jerusalem i eit apologetisk perspektiv [Philo's relationship to the Jerusalem Temple in an apologetic perspective],' in A. Klostergaard Petersen, J. Hyldahl and K. S. Fuglseth (eds.), *Perspektiver på jødisk apologetik*, Antikken og kristendommen 4 (Copenhagen 2007) 263–282.

Was Philo an apologist? How did he consider the Jerusalem Temple? Does he describe it as an apologist? First, Fuglseth argues that in Philo we can find both a strict apology, intended as a defense against criticism, and a softer attitude, useful for the exchange of opinions between different cultures and milieux. In relation to Philo's view of the Jerusalem Temple, some read Philo as uninterested in that temple; others, however, regard him as not only not breaking away from the Temple, but also defending it—in his own way. This view can be seen as complementary. Fuglseth then tries to demonstrate this by having a closer look at how Philo describes 'temple' in four ways: he describes the concrete Temple in Jerusalem, he describes its functions and other aspects as the High Priests ornaments, he describes other non-Jewish temples and their sacrifices, and finally, he understands 'temple' symbolically as humans, nation, kosmos, soul etc. But these should not be read as contradictory; Philo's attitude to the Jerusalem Temple is both loyalist and apologetic. (TS)

S. Gambetti, 'A Brief Note on Agrippa I's Trip to Alexandria in the Summer of 38 CE,' *Journal of Jewish Studies* 58 (2007) 33–38.

On the basis of Philo's *Flacc.* it is generally assumed that going to his kingdom king Agrippa visited Alexandria at the end of July/beginning of August of 38 c.e. This date has been rejected by Alla Kushnir-Stein who, discussing cultural and numismatic evidence, argues that Agrippa was in Alexandria a month earlier in June. In this article Gambetti examines the same evidence and concludes that Philo's account is valid: Agrippa visited Alexandria in July/August 38 c.e. (ACG)

F. García Martínez, 'Divine Sonship at Qumran and in Philo,' *The Studia Philonica Annual* 19 (2007) 85–99.

This article underlines the differences between the notions held at Qumran and Philo. In the Dead Sea Scrolls the notion of divine sonship has strong messianic connotations, being applied primarily to the sect itself as well as a future king. Philo, by contrast, engages Greek philosophical ideas, especially Plato, and conceives of Abraham as God's adopted son and the cosmos as God's created offspring. (MRN)

A. C. Geljon, 'Didymus the Blind's Use of Philo in his Exegesis of Cain and Abel,' *Vigiliae Christianae* 61 (2007) 282–312.

This article investigates the influence of Philo on the exegesis of Cain and Abel presented by Didymus the Blind in his Commentary on Genesis. Didymus makes extensive use of Philo, to whom he refers a few times by name. Both exegetes regard Cain and Abel as representing two different world-views which are in conflict with each other. Cain is the wicked person who does not show respect for God, whereas Abel represents the virtuous person who loves God. Philo bases his exegesis on etymologies of the names Cain and Abel which are absent in Didymus. Didymus' interpretation of Abel as shepherding the senses is also Philonic. (ACG)

A. C. GELJON, 'God in de duisternis: een Alexandijnse uitleg van Exodus 20:21 [God in the darkness: an Alexandrian exposition of Exodus 20:21],' *Hermeneus* 79 (2007) 184–190.

This brief article discusses two Philonic texts, *Post.* 12–15 and *Mut.* 8–15, as part of an overview of Alexandrian interpretations of Moses entering the darkness on Mount Sinai as described in Exod 20:21. Clement, Origen and Gregory of Nyssa all follow Philo's interpretation but add their own individual emphases. All three Church fathers combine biblical exegesis with themes derived from Platonic philosophy. Their interpretations are thus good examples of the Hellenization of the Christian faith. (ACG)

M. E. GORDLEY, *The Colossian Hymn in Context: An Exegesis in Light of Jewish and Greco-Roman Hymnic and Epistolary Conventions*, Wissenschaftliche Untersuchungen zum Neuen Testament 2.Reihe 228 (Tübingen 2007), esp. 105–109, 162–164, 208–212, 218–219, 224–225.

Philo's references to and use of hymns are studied as background to the Colossian hymn. Philo uses Greco-Roman musical categories and the term ὕμνος, not ψαλμός. The Therapeutae are the most prominent example of hymn composition and singing in Philo, but his other references to hymnody follow along the same lines, particularly the account of the Jewish praise after the downfall of Flaccus (*Flacc.* 121). In the context of the interpretation of Colossians Gordley also refers to Philo's Logos doctrine as intermediary, instrument of creation and image of God. (JLB)

M. GRAVER, *Stocism and Emotion* (Chicago–London 2007), esp. 102–105.

In this monograph on the Stoic conception of the emotions Philo and his Alexandrian Christian successors are studied for the evidence they can give on the *propatheiai*, 'pre-emotions' or involuntary feelings which are not to be counted as true 'emotions' because assent is not given to the relevant impressions. This conception most likely goes back to the early Stoa. The chief Philonic texts on this subject are problematic because they occur in the *Quaestiones*, the original Greek text of which is not extant, but the original terminology can be discerned through the Armenian translation. See further the 1999 article summarized in *SPhA* vol. 14, p. 149. (DTR)

J. P. HERING, *The Colossian and Ephesian* Haustafeln *in Theological Context: an Analysis of their Origins, Relationship, and Message*, American University Studies Series 7, Theology and Religion 260 (New York 2007).

The *Haustafeln* (HT), or 'household codes', in Col 3:18–4:1 and Eph 5:22–6:9 reflect commonalities with household codes in other literature but are also shaped somewhat by the theological approach of each letter. In the past, HT were studied independently of their contexts within specific New Testament works and were considered incompatible with Christian ethics because they prescribe submission of husband to wife and slave to master, in contrast to the Christian emphasis on egalitarianism. Philo is one of six sources—including Plato, Aristotle, Pseudo-Aristotle, Musonius Rufus, and Plutarch—that provide points of comparison in ancient treatments and writings contemporary to New Testament times. Although Philo does not present a single HT treatment, he does address relationships between husband and wife, parents and children, and masters and slaves, especially in his discussions of Jewish law. Particularly striking is Philo's presentation of reciprocal duties between master and slave, since this reciprocity is lacking in his discussion of the other two relationships: his criticism of harsh masters, and his view that slaves are 'ontologically equal to their masters' (p. 241), a view strongly influenced by the concept of Sabbath rest that applies to masters and slaves alike. (EB)

M. Hirschberger, 'Fremdbilder und Selbstbilder der Juden und des Judentums in der griechischen Literatur des Hellenismus und der frühen Kaiserzeit,' *Würzburger Jahrbücher für die Altertumswissenschaft* N.F. 31 (2007) 55–106, esp. 89–92.

Philo is mentioned in the context of the refutation of the claim that the Jews are intent on destroying other nations' cultures and religion and that they are misanthropic. Philo argues in contrast that the Mosaic law is the most humane law in existence and that it leads to virtue. The Jewish Temple and worship have a universal relevance, and the Jewish people has the role of being priests for the nations. The accusation that the Sabbath is a sign of laziness is countered by the argument that it serves the acquisition of virtue. The Jews are the philosopher nation *par excellence*, for their law corresponds to the universal law of nature. (JLB)

G. Holtz, *Damit Gott sei alles in allem: Studien zum paulinischen und frühjüdischen Universalismus* (Berlin–New York 2007), esp. 139–167, 379–504.

Holtz examines the relationship of universalism and particularism in early Judaism and in Paul. Both Philo's particularistic expectations for a human future determined by Jewish influences and his universalizing interpretation of Judaism are studied in detail. Philo's particularistic expectations focus on the expectation of universal peace between man and animal, the eschatological wealth of nature, the healing of the body at the end of time and the eschatological renewal of the land (*Praem.* 85–158). This is the expectation of the return of the golden age, but the ultimate victory of the Jewish people, their renewal and their rule over the nations through the Law of Moses is never in doubt. Philo's universal interpretation of Judaism extends to the Law and the opening of the Jewish nation to non-Jews. The universal meaning of the Torah is based on the one hand on an individualizing interpretation to the soul, on the other on its relevance for the whole cosmos. The Torah has universal relevance because it comes from God and it corresponds to the natural law, which makes it superior to the laws of other nations, not only in principle but also in its details. The Jewish Temple service and Jewish worship as a whole have a special universal relevance. This universal relevance enables Philo to extend membership of the elite of virtue not only to the Jews but also to proselytes, a *politeia* based on the constitution of Moses. Thus the unique character of the Jewish people serves to draw borders internally and externally. Philo's universality is always tied to the observance of the particular Law. (JLB)

J. HYLDAHL, 'Mellem ny og gammel kultur: Allegori i apologetisk per-spektiv i aleksandrinsk jødedom [Between new and old cultures: allegory in apologetic perspective in Alexandrian Judaism],' in A. KLOSTERGAARD PETERSEN, J. HYLDAHL AND K. S. FUGLSETH (eds.), *Perspektiver på Jødisk Apologetik,* Antikken og kristendommen 4 (Copenhagen 2007) 181–206.

The author, after having discussed the nature of ancient apologetics, accepts the view that Philo's apologetic works are primarily meant for his fellow Jews in order to confirm their own identity. Thus Philo's intention is not to conquer and 'Judaize' the Greek-Hellenistic culture, but to convince his Jewish readers that they can live with confidence in this culture because it is in fact indebted to and congruent with the wisdom of Moses, that is, Judaism. The author then tries to support this view by arguing that Philo's theology is defined by Platonic conceptions and that his allegories are influenced by Stoic theory of language and hermeneutics. By giving allegorical readings it can be shown that biblical texts conceal what is now found in contemporary philosophies. Philo's readers are thus encouraged to uphold their Jewish identity, and there is no need to be in opposition to the Greco-Roman culture, since this is—after all—Mosaic. (TS)

S. INOWLOCKI, 'Un 'mélange de langues' dans la tour de Babel?: le choix du terme sugkhusis pour traduire la 'confusion' des langues (Genèse 11:1–9),' *Revue de philosophie ancienne* 25 (2007) 61–79.

The Septuagint translators chose to render the word play in Genesis 11:9 between Babel and the verb *balal,* by using the name Σύγχυσις (confusion) and the verb συνέχεεν. In both Hebrew and Greek, the story is puzzling because, whereas it tells the reader about the appearance of several languages, it speaks about confusion, which rather implies the idea of merging together different languages, peoples, etc. However, the term σύγχυσις also implies the idea of destruction and of political unrest or chaos, an aspect underlined by both Philo and Josephus. As the Hebrew *balal,* the Greek terms may also have contained some underlying echoes of the story of the Flood, which is closely connected with that of the Tower. Other Jewish texts written either in Hebrew or Greek—the fragments attributed to Pseudo-Eupolemus, the *Book of Jubilees,* the *Sibylline Oracles,* the *LAB,* and *3 Baruch*—, show a great deal of interpretative freedom in their rewriting of the episode, and do not seem to have used the LXX translation. (KB)

S. K. JIN, *Doxa and Related Concepts in the Fourth Gospel: An Inquiry into the Manifestation of Doxa in Jesus' Cross* (diss. University of Pretoria (South Africa) 2007).

The dissertation focuses on the meaning of the term δόξα (glory) in the Gospel of John as manifested in the description of the events of the cross. Since NT usage usually follows that of the LXX, a survey of the lexicographical background of δόξα focuses on its use in the LXX. The concept of δόξα in the LXX, however, is derived from its meaning in extra-biblical Greek coupled with the concepts of the Hebrew words translated as δόξα in the LXX. This investigation is supplemented by an inquiry into its use in extra-biblical litera-ture, particularly the writings of Philo and Josephus. (DTR; based on author's abstract)

O. Kaiser, *Des Menschen Glück und Gottes Gerechtigkeit. Studien zur biblischen Überlieferung im Kontext hellenistischer Philosophie*, Tria corda 1 (Tübingen 2007), esp. 207–230.

In a chapter on the Stoic paradoxes Cicero's *Paradoxa Stoicorum* and Philo's *Prob.* are compared. After an introduction on Philo and his setting the book is placed in its intellectual context and its structure and argument are described. Here Kaiser finds a parallel between Philo and Cicero in the way they emphasize the good natural law, which is reason and should be the basis of all human behaviour. For Philo, however, the natural law and the Torah are the same and the Essenes are an example of those people who prefer the contemplation of nature and pray that others might attain the same virtue. By trusting in virtue the wise can overcome all vicissitudes of fate and achieve true freedom. (JLB)

M. B. Kartzow, *Gossip and Gender: Othering of Speech in the Pastoral Epistles* (diss. University of Oslo 2007), esp. 112–114.

The focus of this study is the Pastoral Epistles' employment of the notion that gossip is gendered speech. Furthermore, it is investigated how opponents are labeled as gossipers as a rhetorical device in order to construct them as others ('othering') and what role gender plays in this process of naming and blaming. In the chapters entitled Method and Theory, and on Identifying the Ancient Gossip Discourse, there follows a chapter on Ancient Figurations of Female Gossipers. In a section on female gossipers in Jewish texts, Philo is briefly dealt with. The author focuses on *Spec.* 3.169–171, in which Philo forbids a woman to be a busybody. Though this text has little to do directly with gossiping, Philo does argue that a woman should not meddle with matters outside her household, as if that prevented her from being a busybody. The study has now been published in a revised edition under the same title in the series Beihefte zur Zeitschrift für die neutestamentliche Wissenschaft und die Kunde der älteren Kirche, vol. 164 (2009). (TS)

S. W. Keough, *Exegesis Worthy of God: the Development of Biblical Interpretation in Alexandria* (diss. University of Toronto 2007), esp. chap. 3.

Late antique Jews and Christians were at least as troubled by anthropomorphic depictions of the deity as their pagan counterparts, and descriptions of divine wrath and vengeance presented exegetical difficulties. It was necessary to provide a response to these exegetical difficulties that reconciled the sacred texts with the received fundamentals of theology, that is, with appropriate notions of divinity. The need for exegesis worthy of God thus became the fundamental interpretive motivation and criterion of Jews and Christians. The results of exegesis were examined against this fundamental criterion, and rival exegetical claims were staked on this principle, a principle of basic theological convictions regarding the nature, identity, and character of the deity. The manner in which this principle develops in Philo, Clement and Origen is examined, with a chapter being devoted to each thinker. The investigation yields results which display not only continuity but also considerable diversity, as well as specifically biblical concerns to preserve the specific and nontransferable identity of the God whose character is narrated in scripture. (DTR; based on author's abstract)

A. Klostergaard Petersen, 'Filon som apologet—en læsning af *De migratione Abrahami* [Philo as an apologete—a reading of *De Migratione rahami*],' in A. KLOSTERGAARD PETERSEN, J. HYLDAHL and K. S. FUGLSETH (eds.), *Perspektiver på Jødisk Apologetik,* Antikken og kristendommen 4 (Copenhagen 2007) 233–262.

The author first discusses the nature of ancient Jewish apologetics, emphasizing that it was never meant only—if at all—for outsiders, but rather for those on the inside, serving to consolidate their identity in view of attacks from the outside. Discussing Philo's interpretations of Scripture, the author views them as Philo's attempt to rewrite and integrate Greco-Roman culture within a Jewish horizon of understanding. This is done by way of allegory. Classical meaning and texts are thus subordinated to Scripture. Petersen then provides some brief comments on *Migr.* as an example of Philo's attempt to defend his Judaism by means of an allegorical reading of Gen 12:1–4, 6. (TS)

A. KLOSTERGAARD PETERSEN, J. HYLDAHL, and K. S. FUGLSETH, *Perspektiver på Jødisk Apologetik [Perspectives on Jewish apologetics],* Antikken og kristendommen 4 (Copenhagen 2007).

In a total of eleven articles, a broad spectrum of Jewish writers and texts from the second century B.C.E. to the first century C.E. are investigated. The contributions comprise various perspectives, throwing light upon Judaism at the end of the Second Temple Period. A common denominator in all the articles is the focus on the various texts as apologetic texts. Major questions are to what extent one may talk about a Jewish apologetic tradition and to what extent it is profitable to understand some authorships as apologetic. Both questions are considered as associated with a more comprehensive attitude to Judaism's relation to the Hellenistic culture at large. (TS)

A. KOVELMAN, 'Jeremiah 9:22–23 in Philo and Paul,' *Review of Rabbinic Judaism* 10 (2007) 162–175.

The author identifies allusions to Jer 9:22–23 in both Philo and Paul, even though neither of them explicitly refers to that passage. This is done on the basis of some common vocabulary as well as explicit medieval interpretations of Jeremiah, which show similar philosophical tendencies. Whether or not one accepts this reconstruction, the article is worth reading for its analysis of Philo's and Paul's engagement with Platonic and Aristotelian ideas. (MRN)

S. KRAUTER, 'Die Beteiligung von Nicht-juden am Jerusalemer Tempelkult,' in J. FREY, D. R. SCHWARTZ and S. GRIPENTROG (eds.), *Jewish Identity in the Greco-Roman World,* Ancient Judaism and Early Christianity 71 (Leiden–Boston 2007) 55–74.

Philo provides evidence regarding the question of the participation of non-Jews in the Jerusalem Temple cult. Thus he describes in detail the visit of Augustus' son-in-law, M. Vipsanius Agrippa, who adhered to the rules and did not enter further than the first court and on leaving left a large number of votive offerings (*Legat.* 295–297). Information is also provided about regular sacrifices for the emperors (*Legat.* 157, 317). Finally Philo does not support the idea that non-priests (and non-Jews) could perform the sacrifices, but they could bring the animal to the priests and have them sacrifice it (*Spec* 1.198f., 2.145).

Altogether the evidence points to the conclusion that pagan participation in the Temple cult was more widespread than commonly assumed. (JLB)

M. LANDFESTER, and B. EGGER (eds.), *Geschichte der antiken Texte. Autoren– und Werklexicon*, Der Neue Pauly Supplemente Band 2 (Stuttgart 2007).

The aim of this ambitious work, a supplement to the *Neue Pauly Encyclopedia of Antiquity*, is to illustrate how the principal works of Greek and Latin literature have been transmitted in the cultural memory of Europe. For each author, where applicable, it records the main stages of the history of each work, i.e. papyri, scholia, manuscripts, early and modern editions, translations and commentaries. In the case of Philo we are presented with the following: name; brief division of works; very brief overview of history of textual transmission; very brief overview of editions and translations; listing of works (only eleven listed); listing of seven chief manuscripts; listing of six early editions; listing of modern editions, translations and commentaries. Although much information is packed in four pages, the treatment is not satisfactory. See further the review by J. R. Royse in this Journal. An English translation was published in 2009. (DTR)

P. LANFRANCHI, 'Reminiscences of Ezekiel's *Exagoge* in Philo's *De vita Mosis*,' in A. GRAUPNER and M. WOLTER (eds.), *Moses in Biblical and Extra-Biblical Traditions*, Beihefte zur Zeitschrift für die alttestamentliche Wissenschaft 372 (Berlin–New York 2007) 144–150.

In this article the author lists a great number of lexical similarities between Philo's *Mos.* and Ezekiel's tragedy *Exagoge*. They occur, for example, in Philo's description of Moses' birth and childhood, his stay in Midian, the episode of the burning bush, and the narrative of the ten plagues. Exegetical parallels are also pointed out. It is particularly striking that Philo and Ezekiel both mention the pagan education of Moses. Despite these lexical and exegetical similarities, many differences between the two works remain. Nevertheless, Philo's emphasis on the role of Moses as leader of the Jewish people reflects the presentation of Moses in Ezekiel. (ACG)

K. D. LAVERY, *Abraham's Dialogue with God over the Destruction of Sodom: Chapters in the History of the Interpretation of Genesis 18* (diss. Harvard University 2007).

The dissertation analyses the early history of the interpretation of Genesis 18:16–33. Chapter 3 is devoted to Philo's interpretation of Gen 18. His allegorical reading also exercised influence on Christian readers, and particularly Origen. The author concludes that the history of the interpretation of Gen 18 yields a representative view of the development of the history of ideas. (DTR; based on author's summary)

J. LEONHARDT-BALZER, 'Jewish Worship and Universal Identity in Philo of Alexandria,' in J. FREY, D. R. SCHWARTZ and S. GRIPENTROG (eds.), *Jewish Identity in the Greco-Roman World*, Ancient Judaism and Early Christianity 71 (Leiden–Boston 2007) 29–54.

Worship is an important aspect of Jewish identity. Philo uses the term λατρεία to describe the specific aspects of Jewish festival observance, prayers and Temple service, which are all specifically ordained by the Torah but all have universal relevance, because of the correspondence of the Mosaic Law to the cosmic law. Philo supports this conclusion by describing aspects of worship in terms similar to Plato's Laws, thus turning the Jewish worship into that which would occur in the ideal state. Instead of interpreting the rites allegorically, *Migr.* 89–93 emphasizes the social importance of the actual observance of the laws. Two Jewish institutions serve as test cases: the Temple and the synagogue, which, far from being rivals, are interlinked in a chiastic net of references to universal relevance and particular observance. Each particular aspect of Jewish worship contains a universal relevance, but the universal interpretation of Jewish worship cannot be thought without the actual observance. (JLB)

C. Lévy, 'La question de la dyade chez Philon d'Alexandrie,' in M. Bonazzi, C. Lévy and C. Steel (eds.), *A Platonic Pythagoras. Platonism and Pythagoreanism in the Imperial Age,* Monothéismes et Philosophie 10 (Turnhout 2007) 11–28.

The paper presented at a conference on 'Platonism and Pythagoreanism in the Imperial Age' held near Lake Garda in 2005 first examines Philo's references to the Pythagoreans. These are quite extensive, and more numerous than references to other schools, particularly when one takes into account Philo's fondness for arithmology (it is noted that the explicit references to the Pythagoreans in an arithmological context are all found in the *Quaestiones*). The bulk of the paper focuses on the question of the dyad in Philo's thought. Here it is important to note when Philo refers to the dyad (and the monad) and when he does not. In his account of creation in *Opif.* the dyad is strikingly absent. This is because from a cosmological viewpoint it is a secondary concept. In fact, the concept is primarily used as an exegetical tool. The chief reason that Philo's thoughts on the dyad are hard to determine is because the treatment of the role of matter in creation is much more problematic for him than his views on the role of the creator. The article concludes with a brief observation on *Fug.* 8, where the reference to those who divinize substance deprived of quality may well have the philosopher Strato of Lampsacus in mind. For a review of the entire volume in which the paper is published see *SPhA* vol. 20 pp. 242–244 (by D. T. Runia). (DTR)

A. Lieber, 'Between Motherland and Fatherland: Diaspora, Pilgrimage and Spiritualization of Sacrifice in Philo of Alexandria,' in L. LiDonnici and A. Lieber (eds.), *Heavenly Tablets: Interpretation, Identity and Tradition in Ancient Judaism,* Supplements to the Journal for the Study of Judaism 119 (Leiden 2007) 193–210.

Contrary to modern and ancient views of 'diaspora' as negative or non-normative, Philo exemplifies a positive attitude, expressed through his use of Greek colonial language to legitimate diaspora life and his high evaluation of pilgrimage and spiritualization of sacrifice, which both suggest and facilitate a higher level of observance in the diaspora. In this characterization, Jews' settlement abroad is thus a sign of strength rather than disempowerment. Moreover, Philo's description of Jerusalem as mother city and the diaspora country as fatherland reverses a gender association with the diaspora as feminized and weaker. Philo's depiction of pilgrimage, in which he emphasizes the difficulty of leaving home, has eschatological overtones, and his focus on the importance of centralized worship may have been influenced by Deuteronomy and Chronicles but also by Book 10 of Plato's *Laws*. Despite the importance of the Temple to Philo, his 'extreme 'spiritualization'' and interiorization of the sacrificial cult allow for 'a truer form of cultic worship to be practiced in a diaspora setting' (202, 204). Although the Temple was active in Jerusalem, then, for Philo Jerusalem was a 'spiritual condition' attainable in the diaspora, and his general approach to the diaspora reflects the ideals of Greek colonization (209). (EB)

T. H. Lim, 'Deuteronomy in the Judaism of the Second Temple Period,' in S. Moyise and M. J. J. Menken (eds.), *Deuteronomy in the New Testament*, Library of New Testament Studies (Edinburgh 2007) 6–26.

This is the first in a collection of essays, the rest of which focus on Deuteronomy in the NT. The author surveys the transmission history of Deuteronomy, particularly in light of manuscripts from Qumran, and underscores the range of textual variants. Deuteronomy was excerpted for various purposes that include devotion and liturgy, as reflected in excerpts used for *mezuzot* and phylacteries. The rest of the essay turns to interpretations of Deuteronomy in the Septuagint (based on a proto-Masoretic text), sectarian scrolls, the Temple Scroll, Philo, and Josephus. Depending on what he wishes to highlight, Philo refers to the book with different titles: *deuteronomion*, to introduce biblical verses; *protreptikoi* (*logoi*) and *paraineseis*, to stress admonition; and *epinomis*, 'to emphasize the book's summative character' (p. 23). Among the themes from Deuteronomy on which Philo comments are its blessings and curses, the ten commandments, particular laws, the sovereignty of God, the exemplary character of Moses, and the need for humans to choose 'the true life as the Levites have done' (p. 24). (EB)

N. E. Livesey, *Circumcision as a Malleable Symbol: Treatments of Circumcision in Philo, Paul, and Justin Martyr* (diss. Southern Methodist University 2007).

The scholarship on the meaning of circumcision in the first and second centuries c.e. often ascribes a single meaning for this rite. The dissertation demonstrates through a method of contextual analysis of the treatments of circumcision of this time period, however, that circumcision in fact has a wide range of meanings. The authors used to prove this thesis are Philo, Paul and Justin Martyr. Philo treats the subject of circumcision in some detail three times within his lengthy corpus of writings, and in each occurrence the dominant sense of circumcision changes. In *Migr.* 89–93, where Philo expresses his frustration with Jews who neglect circumcision in favor of a purely cognitive recognition of this rite as a benefit for the mind alone, circumcision garners the respect of one's fellow Jews. In contrast, in *Spec.* 1.1–11, where Philo challenges ridicule of this rite from outsiders, circumcision acquires benefits for health, fertility, and general well-being, characteristics that would appeal not only to Jews but to outsiders as well. A similar pattern of variety in the meanings of circumcision occur in the writings of Paul and Justin Martyr, who, along with Philo, are our primary interpreters of this rite during the first two centuries. (DTR; based on the author's summary)

J. P. Lotz, *Ignatius and Concord: the Background and Use of the Language of Concord in the Letters of Ignatius of Antioch*, Patristic Studies 8 (New York 2007), esp. 96–102.

Chapter 5 of the monograph investigates the use of the term ὁμόνοια in the literature of early Judaism, namely Philo, Josephus and 4 Maccabees. It is remarkable that the word ὁμόνοια does not occur in *Flacc.* or in *Legat.* In these treatises Philo uses the vocabulary that is related to the Pax Romana of emperor Augustus, for instance εἰρήνη. Probably he avoids the term ὁμόνοια because it has Greek civic overtones. In his other writings Philo does employ the term, frequently combining it with the synonym κοινωνία. It is a human virtue and is claimed to be a feature of the Jewish people. Philo regards the Law as the source of the concord that exists among the Jews. (ACG)

S. D. MACKIE, *Eschatology and Exhortation in the Epistle to the Hebrews,* Wissenschaftliche Untersuchungen zum Neuen Testament 2. Reihe 223 (Tübingen 2007), esp. 105–124.

In this study, a revised version of a doctoral dissertation prepared at Fuller Theological Seminary under the supervision of Donald A. Hagner, Philo is primarily investigated in relation to Hebrews 10:1–18, especially 10:1, where the Law is said to possess only a shadow of the good things to come, and 10:9. On pp. 105–124 the author investigates the term εἰκών (partly together with σκία and ὑπόδειγμα) as possible evidence for a Platonic and Middle Platonic mindset. Focusing on Philo (pp. 108-112), he reads *Opif.* 68–71 as a minority voice within the Philonic corpus, *Opif.* 25 being more typical. For Philo εἰκών is read as representing a reflection or copy in a lower realm of something belonging to a higher realm (p. 111). Σκία, on the other hand, represents physical objects in the sense-perceptible realm. Mackie seems to consider the accusation that the author of Hebrews failed to understand Platonic and Middle Platonic cosmology as perhaps attributable to an inadequate assessment of the breadth of meaning possessed by εἰκών in the first century (p. 114). He himself regards the use of this term in Hebrews to be clearly within the limit of Middle Platonic conventions. But the employment of terms like σκία, εἰκών and πρᾶγμα occurs within an essentially Jewish framework, thus representing a deliberate hybridization of Middle Platonism and Jewish eschatology. As such it might even be read as a deliberate critique of the Philonic view of the Mosaic law. (TS)

J. MAIER, 'Bezeugung der Bibel,' in A. GRABNER-HAIDER (ed.), *Kulturgeschichte der Bibel,* (Göttingen 2007) 181–211.

The article looks at ancient bible quotations and references. Philo is given a separate section, in which the predominance of his quotations from the Pentateuch is emphasized. The Pentateuch is seen as holy, but there is evidence that he also valued the other writings, if not quite to the same degree as the Torah. *Contempl.* 25 on the use of writings among the Therapeutae is mentioned, but interpreted not as reference to three different text corpora but as different types of literature. (JLB)

J. P. MARTÍN, 'Il primo convegno italiano su Filone di Alessandria,' *Adamantius* 13 (2007) 276–281.

Extended review of the proceedings of the Italian conference on Philo held in Bologna in September 2003 published by A. M. Mazzanti and F. Calabi in 2004 (see summaries in vol. 19 of this Journal). The author concludes that hitherto Philo has been studied in many scattered 'palazzi', but now through the efforts of these Italian scholars a 'house of Philo' is being constructed in which such centrifugal tendencies are overcome. In Italy the lead is being taken by the 'palazzi' of letters and philosophy. Many different approaches can visit the 'house', but attention to the Jewish-Alexandrian text has rightly been placed at the centre. (DTR)

A. M. Mazzanti, 'Filone di Alssandria,' in U. Mattioli, A. Cacciari and V. Neri (eds.), *Senectus. La vecchiaia nell'antichità ebraica e cristiana. Vol. III Ebraismo e cristianesimo,* (Bologna 2007) 99–109.

This brief study of Philo's interpretations of old age starts from the presupposition, fundamental for Philo, that an earlier origin implies a higher ontological position. Adam as the first created human being is considered to have had a perfection that could only diminish in those who, as copies of a copy, came after him. The pre-existence of the soul in comparison with the body corresponds with the former's higher status. 'Elder' (πρεσβύτε-ρος) in the real sense is synonymous with 'wise' (*Abr.* 271–272); Scripture can call old one who is still young in years but merits honour and veneration. The concept of youth, however, can be employed also to express a positive, laudatory condition. In contrast to πρεσβύτερος, the term πολιός refers to old age in a negative sense, the result of degeneration caused by time. Physical decline, on the other hand, is a condition for generation (cf. Gen 21:7). Old age is the time for reflection and contemplation, when the passions have calmed down, although for some it is the time in which passions and vices may attain complete dominion. We thus find in Philo multiple aspects and meanings of old age. The most elevated, ethical interpretation of old age, however, ultimately points to the precedence and pre-eminence of God. (HMK)

T. A. Miller, 'Liturgy and Communal Identity: Hellenistic Synagogal Prayer 5 and the Character of Early Syrian Christianity,' in D. B. Capes, A. D. DeConick, H. K. Bond and T. A. Miller (eds.), *Israel's God and Rebecca's Children: Christology and Community in Early Judaism and Christianity. Essays in Honor of Larry W. Hurtado and Alan F. Segal,* (Waco Tex. 2007) 345–358.

In contrast to Helmut Koester, who sees Gnosticism as central to understanding Syrian Christianity, Miller believes that Judaism was the primary formative influence. To support this contention he shows a number of parallels between the *Hellenistic Synagogal Prayer 5* (*HSP5*), one of several such prayers preserved in the *Apostolic Constitutions*. Among the parallels between *HSP5* and Jewish sources are similarities in *HSP5* to one of the Seven Benedictions for Sabbath and for festivals or holy days; the Prayer's narrative remembrance of Passover, Sukkot, and Pentecost; and several parallels with Philonic thought, even though Philo probably did not influence the *Prayer* directly. The parallels with Philo's thought include the reference in *HSP5* to the 'true Israel' as 'one who sees God,' and Miller views Philo's understanding of Israel as an assertion of unique identity in contrast to other Jews rather than to outsiders. Another parallel is the emphasis in both sources on the number seven, even though *HSP5* does not allegorize in relation to this number as much as Philo does. Miller argues further, against Stephen Wilson, that Christian additions to *HSP5* not only do not distance Christians from Judaism but instead reflect a wish to represent them as connected with 'overt Jewish traditions, themes, and practices' (358). (EB)

M. Mira, 'Art.' Filone di Alessandria, in L. F. Mateo-Seco and G. Maspero (eds.), *Gregorio di Nissa. Dizionario,* (Rome 2007) 287–289.

Brief survey of topics in which Gregory of Nyssa has been influenced by or shows contact with Philo, as identified by Aubineau, Runia, and especially Daniélou. The issues dealt with focus particularly on the place of the human being in creation (between *kosmos* and *logos*) and that status of being *methorios* (a borderline creature between spirit and passions, good and evil). It also highlights where Gregory's position is different from Philo's. (HMK)

H. NAJMAN, 'Philosophical Contemplation and Revelatory Inspiration in Ancient Judean Traditions,' *The Studia Philonica Annual* 19 (2007) 101–111.

This article points to an important similarity between the Dead Sea Scrolls and Philo: both assume that the locus of revelation, even in their own time, is the desert. Philo makes this point in his discussion of the Decalogue, where he stresses that only in the wilderness is man able to cleanse himself of his impure thoughts, thus preparing for divine revelation. A similar image of the desert emerges in Philo's description of the contemporary Therapeutae. In the Land of Israel parallel ideas are expressed in the Dead Sea Scrolls, where the Damascus Document depicts the desert as a place where the law can be properly observed. Both communities moreover strive to overcome the gap between exile and imperfection, on the one hand, and perfection and spiritual ascent, on the other. (MRN)

M. R. NIEHOFF, 'Homeric Scholarship and Bible Exegesis in Ancient Alexandria: Evidence from Philo's 'Quarrelsome' Colleagues,' *Classical Quarterly* 57 (2007) 166–182.

This article provides a pioneering case study of the connections between Jewish Bible interpretation and Homeric scholarship in Alexandria. It is argued that Philo's polemics against other interpreters to Scriptures refer to Jewish readers, who engaged the critical methods of Homeric scholarship developed at the Alexandrian Museum. The article focuses on a close reading of *Mut.* 60–65 (pp. 7–17), arguing that some Jews in Alexandria suggested an emendation of the Biblical text in line with the Greek practice of *athetesis* (marking a verse as spurious). (MRN)

M. R. NIEHOFF, 'Did the *Timaeus* Create a Textual Community?,' *Greek, Roman, and Byzantine Studies* 47 (2007) 161–191, esp. 170–177.

This article investigates the status of Plato's *Timaeus* from its early interpretations up to Celsus' use of it in his attack on Christianity. It is argued that this dialogue became a marker of group identity only at a relatively late stage, while in the centuries immediately after Plato's death both Platonists and Aristotelians interpreted it in a similar allegorical fashion. Philo played a central role in this process, attributing to the *Timaeus* the kind of sacred authority associated among Jews with Moses' Bible. Moreover, he is the first known writer in the Hellenistic period who advocated the literal interpretation as the authentic meaning of the text, which in his view had been falsified by the allegorical readers. Philo thus distinguished Plato's assumption of a literal creation from the Aristotelian notion of an eternal world. Celsus in the mid-second century C.E. marks another important step in the interpretation of the *Timaeus*. Fighting the increasing influence of Christianity, he is the first writer who refers to this dialogue as a reflection of Greek identity as such. (MRN)

F. Oertelt, 'Vom Nutzen der Musik. Ein Blick auf die Funktion der musikalischen Ausbildung bei Philo von Alexandrien,' in A. Standhar-tinger, H. Schwebel and F. Oertelt (eds.), *Kunst der Deutung—Deutung der Kunst: Beiträge zu Bibel, Antike und Gegenwartsliteratur. FS Sieghild von Blumenthal,* Ästhetik – Theologie – Liturgik 45 (Münster 2007) 51–62.

The article begins by looking at the importance of musical education in ancient Greece, where not only musical practice, metre and rhythm but also musical theory was studied intensively. Philo follows in this tradition when he distinguishes between beneficial and harmful types of music. The strong effect of music is the reason why a thorough education is needed. Thus the theme of music plays a part in the interpretation of Abraham, Sarah and Hagar. Like arithmetic and geometry, music is one of the important areas of know-ledge needed on Abraham's path to virtue in order to establish harmony. Music is not an end in itself, and exclusive study of it must be regarded as sophistry and a distraction from philosophy. Music does not lead to any single virtue but is a step on the way towards the good. The parallel between earthly music and heavenly harmony is important, and Philo also applies the musical metaphor to the human soul as a harmonious mixture of human and divine nature. Harmony as the right mixture of intervals is also the structure of creation in *Opif.* Thus it must be concluded that the contemplation of the importance of harmony and musical theory is more important for Philo than the actual practice of the art. (JLB)

S. J. K. Pearce, *The Land of the Body: Studies in Philo's Representation of Egypt,* Wissenschaftliche Untersuchungen zum Neuem Testament 204 (Tübingen 2007).

This important monograph presents a comprehensive analysis of the representation of Egypt in Philo's writings and thought. In the Pentateuch, Egypt is at first in the book of Genesis a place of refuge. But from the book of Exodus onwards it is the land that the children of Israel must leave behind as they return to the promised land. Many of the readers of the Greek Bible lived in Egypt, or the gateway to Egypt, as Alexandria was regarded. How did they view the biblical depiction of Egypt? Philo is the only substantial witness of Hellenistic Judaism. His extensive body of writings is the only source from which an answer to the above question can be gained. In a series of eight chapters Pearce investigates every aspect of her theme, whether theoretical or ideological or political. In chapter 1 she sets out both the historical and intellectual context of Philo's work, with emphasis on the role of allegory in his writings. Chapter 2, entitled Egyptians in Philo's World, focuses on how Philo presents Egyptians in the context of contemporary Alexan-drian politics. He repeatedly emphasizes their tendency to sedition and envy, and claims that as such they are a dangerous force which can deceive and ultimately destroy Roman leaders. The next chapter discusses Egypt as it is presented in the Pentateuch. In allegorical terms it is the 'land of the body', a potent symbol of all that it opposed to spiritual ascent. Migration to and from Egypt is read in terms of the moral and spiritual progress of the soul in relation to the corporeal. The various biblical figures involved—Abraham, Isaac, Jacob, Joseph, Moses and Israel—are discussed in turn. At best Egypt can symbolize the goods of the body, but almost always the negative symbolism of the body, passions and the senses prevail. Chapter 4 looks at Egyptians as symbols. Here the biblical figures of Pharaoh, the Egyptian overseers, the sophists and Hagar are analysed. What Egyptians symbolize above all is the failure to see God, making them the opposite of Israel who does see God. Chapter 5, entitled Wicked Hosts and Perfect Guests, examines the theme of hospitality. Philo observes a sharp contrast between the hospitality shown by the Hebrew ancestors and the inhospitality of the Egyptians. The purpose here may have been to refute accusations against Jews that they are hostile to strangers. The final three chapters deal with the theme of Egyptian religion. Chapter 6 examines the river Nile as potent symbol of Egyptian atheism. Chapter 7 moves to Egyptian animal worship as viewed by contemporary Greeks, Romans and Jews. Chapter 8 then presents Philo's own attitude to animal worship. It emerges that Philo not only belongs to the negative tradition regarding animal worship, but is in fact 'its most severe opponent' (p. 308). Animal worship is rooted in a theology of a disordered world and is a concrete expression of what it means to be 'in Egypt', i.e. a state of spiritual or intellectual blindness. (DTR)

S. J. K. PEARCE, 'Philo on the Nile,' in J. FREY, D. R. SCHWARTZ and S. GRIPENTROG (eds.), *Jewish Identity in the Greco-Roman World*, Ancient Judaism and Early Christianity 71 (Leiden 2007) 137–157.

Philo's generally negative discussion of the Nile must be seen within the context of his negative interpretation of Egypt generally. For Philo, Egypt signifies both the 'ultimate other' of Judaism and values opposite to Mosaic teachings. Most prominently, Egypt represents the land of the body and the failure to see God. Likewise the river of Egypt (Gen 15:18) signifies the river's starting point in the life of the body from which to migrate away toward wisdom. In the Nile's manner of flooding the earth so that the land is watered from the ground rather than the heavens, Philo sees the river as an *antimimos*, or counter-model, of heaven. This 'preference for earth over heaven' leads Philo to understand the Egyptian *tropos* as atheist. In his account of the half-Jewish, half-Egyptian blasphemer (Lev 24:10–11) in *Mos.* 2, Philo associates the river specifically with 'Egyptian atheism,' a term that encompasses worship of material, created objects instead of the true God. Under the Ptolemies the Nile itself inspired cultic worship and in Roman times was accorded divine status in association with such ancient traditions as those of Osiris. Philo appears to be the first thinker to denounce reverence for the Nile, and later parallels can be found in Plutarch and Origen. Emphasizing God's sovereignty in the universe, Philo observes that the plagues began with the river so that God could punish its worshippers, an interpretation perhaps linked to Exod 12:12, in which God declares that He will execute judgment on all Egypt's gods. In Philo's symbolic understanding Egypt represents materialist worship, and one's identity as an Egyptian is determined by 'a philosophical choice' (p. 156). (EB)

B. PEARSON, 'Earliest Christianity in Egypt: Further Observations,' in J. E. GOEHRING and J. TIMBIE (eds.), *The World of Early Egyptian Christianity: Language, Literature, and Social Context: Essays in Honor of David W. Johnson* (Washington DC 2007).

Following up on an earlier paper on the same topic, this paper focuses on the Jewish origins of Egyptian Christianity, varieties of early Egyptian Christianity, and Alexandrian precursors of Egyptian monasticism. Contrary to arguments that Christianity in Egypt had Gnostic origins, Pearson sees it as firmly rooted in Judaism, and contrary to arguments that envision a break between Alexandrian Christianity and Judaism after the 117 C.E. revolt, he sees a continuity between the two traditions. This continuity is reflected in Christian use of the Septuagint, in the dissemination of Philo's works, and in the *Epistle of Barnabas* and *Teachings of Silvanus*, the latter of which preserves wisdom speculation 'probably mediated by the Alexandrian Jewish teacher Apollos,' who may have been of pupil of Philo (p. 101). Various Christian sources offer evidence of messianism, Gnosticism that may have dominated Christianity in different forms until the late second century, asceticism, Platonism, and the organized presbyterate. Later Egyptian monasticism has precursors in second century Alexandria and may even have some Jewish roots as reflected in Philo's account of the Therapeutae. In an appendix, Pearson argues that the *Epistula Apostolorum* has an Asian provenance and therefore does not provide evidence about Christianity in Egypt. (EB)

A. Piñero, *Literatura judía de época helenística en lengua griega. Desde la versión de la biblia al griego hasta el Nuevo Testamento* (Madrid 2007), esp. 123–132.

In a wide-ranging presentation of Jewish literature written in the Greek language, from the Septuagint up to the first Christian writings, the author dedicates a chapter to Philo of Alexandria. Exhibiting a good knowledge of problems and bibliography, this contribution contains a valuable synthesis of the current knowledge on Philo's life, on his work and the diverse series of the Corpus philonicum, on his methods and styles, on the recipients and the purpose of the work, and finally on the *Wirkungsgeschichte* of his books, especially in the Christian domain. (JPM)

P. K. Pohjala, *Divination by Bowls in Bible, Septuagint, Qumran Texts, Philo and Matthew 13:1–12: Magnified Visions from Glass Bowls in Bible Interpretation,* Verre et Bible 2 (place of publication not known, 2007).

The study focuses on lecanomancy, the practice of divination by looking at water in bowls. In five sections of the study Philonic evidence purportedly relating to this theme is discussed: Philo's interpretation of the story of Hannah in *Ebr.* 143ff. (2.5.2); his account of magnified fish in a bowl at *Ebr.* 182 (2.5.5); other interpretation of the story of Judah and in particular the Tamar episode (2.5.5); the parable of the sower in Matt 13:1ff. and its Philonic parallels in *Contempl.* 57ff. and *Spec.* 3.32ff. (4.1); Philonic interpretation of Haran, the place of seeing and the cavities of vision. (DTR; based on a table of contents sent by the author)

I. Ramelli and D. Konstan, *Terms for Eternity:* Aiônios *and* Aïdios *in Classical and Christian Texts* (Piscataway N.J. 2007), esp. 51–57.

The authors' interest in the Christian doctrine of apocatastasis (universal restoration and salvation of all people at the end of times) has led them to embark on a wide-ranging analysis of terms used for eternity in ancient Greek (and especially Patristic) literature. Included is a survey of the use of αἰώνιος and ἀΐδιος in Philo. It is concluded that there is a notable lexical overlap between the two terms, but that αἰώνιος represents more the Biblical tradition and ἀΐδιος more the Greek philosophical (esp. Platonic) heritage. (HMK)

E. Regev, *Sectarianism in Qumran: a Cross-cultural Perspective,* Religion and Society 45 (Berlin 2007), esp. 243–266.

This study investigates the people of the Dead Sea scrolls viewed through the concept of sectarianism. With the help of this concept—regarded as an 'organization principle'—it is possible to understand many aspects of the religious ideas and the social system of the

Qumran sectarians. Philo and Josephus are used as sources for our knowledge of the Essenes. Regev examines the ideology of the Essenes from a sectarian perspective and then compares the Essenes with Qumran sectarians. The author regards the Essenes as a later development of the Qumran movement, because they appear to be a more complex social phenomenon. The Essenes were very similar to the Qumran branches but in contrast to the Qumran sects, they renounce marriage and sexuality. They were an extremely introverted sect. (ACG)

D. ROBERTSON, *Word and Meaning in Ancient Alexandria: Theories of Language from Philo to Plotinus* (Aldershot 2007).

This monograph examines theory of mind and language in the period of the first century B.C.E. to the third century C.E. The author focuses on four philosophers and theologians: Philo, Clement, Origen and Plotinus. The chapter devoted to Philo is a lightly revised version of Robertson's article first published in 2006; see *SPhA* vol. 21, p. 94. One of the general conclusions is that for Philo, Clement and Origen meanings are thoughts. They do not explain schematically how language relates to immaterial entities. (ACG)

D. T. RUNIA, 'Philo in the Reformational Tradition,' in R. SWEETMAN (ed.), *In the Phrygian Mode: Neocalvinism, Antiquity and the Lamentations of Reformed Philosophy*, Christian Perspectives Today (Lanham MD etc. 2007) 195–212.

The article forms part of the long-delayed publication of the papers of a conference on 'Antiquity and the Reformed tradition' held in Toronto in June 1995. It investigates a little-known aspect of Philonic scholarship, namely how Philo was studied and interpreted by scholars working in the Reformational tradition, the movement of neo-Calvinistic protestant theology and philosophy initiated by Abraham Kuyper in the last decades of the nineteenth century and closely associated at first with the Free University, Amsterdam, which was founded in 1880. The first scholar to be studied is J. Woltjer, who follows Calvin in developing a logos-theory of human knowledge. Although Philo is not mentioned by him, this view clearly develops ideas from Philo and the Church fathers. This approach was rejected by H. Dooyeweerd and N. J. Hommes (cf. R-R 3709) who argue that Philo and the early Church fathers should be read from the viewpoint of the religious antithesis that rejects all forms of synthesis between non-biblical and biblical thought. This line of criticism was continued by H. Vollenhoven and K. J. Popma (cf. R-R 4405, 7336), who both reject the Philonic attempt to explain scripture with categories of thought taken from Greek philosophy. Next the more recent critiques of A. P. Bos (cf. RRS 9109, 9618), A. Wolters (cf. RRS 9480), W. Helleman (cf. RRS 9428) and J. Klapwijk are discussed. All four discuss the question of synthesis versus antithesis, with some variation in their views on the extent to which the concept of synthesis should be applied to Philo's method. Some evaluative remarks follow. It is argued that the root problem for Philo is the failure to make a proper distinction between religion and philosophy. However, the attempt by Dooyeweerd and Wolters to apply the concept of a form/matter ground motive is questionable. Finally, by way of an epilogue, an intriguing Philonic text in *Spec.* 1.324–345 is examined. Philo here gives a religious critique of human thought with a surprisingly warm description of humanistic thought. There is not much wrong with Philo's religious critique. It is in the area of philosophy that problems arise. But historians of philosophy need to ask what different path, other than Platonism, he could have taken in his intellectual context. (DTR)

D. T. Runia, 'The Rehabilitation of the Jackdaw: Philo of Alexandria and Ancient Philosophy,' in R. Sorabji and R. W. Sharples (eds.), *Greek and Roman Philosophy 100 BC–200 AD*, (London 2007) 483–500.

The article is the published version of the Sheila Kassman Memorial Lecture held at the University of London in 2004 as part of a conference that aimed to give an overview of recent developments in the study of Greek and Roman philosophy from 100 B.C.E. to 200 C.E. The starting-point of the paper is the famous article of E. R. Dodds on 'The *Parmenides* of Plato and the origin of the Neoplatonic One' published in 1928, in which some quite negative remarks are made on Philo, including that 'his eclecticism is that of the jackdaw rather than the philosopher.' Yet 75 years later Philo is regarded as sufficiently important to have a lecture devoted to him. The question posed in the paper is why he is a thinker and a writer worth paying attention to. It is first noted that Philo is much used as a resource for our knowledge of ancient philosophy. A second reason why there is a greater interest in Philo is because a gradual broadening of interest in the study of ancient philosophy has taken place since Dodds' day. Moreover, the methodology of studying ancient philosophers has also changed. There is much less emphasis on systematic presentations of philosophers' thought and more emphasis on contextual readings. Fourthly it is argued that Philo is now much better understood than he was in Dodds' time. Philo must be understood as he saw himself, namely as an exegete or interpreter of the books of Moses. In this he agrees with a tendency of imperial philosophy, in which philosophy is practised through the interpretation of great figures in the past. The final part of the paper returns to the theme that Dodds discussed in his article, Philo's Relation to Neopythagoreanism. Various texts are examined in which Philo relates the monad to God and affirms God's transcendence. These must be understood in terms of a radical negative theology, which prefigures developments in the mainstream of imperial philosophy. The article concludes with the view that Philo is not a true-blood Hellenist, but is nevertheless deserving of attention for those interested in the history of ancient philosophy. (DTR)

D. T. Runia, Art. 'Philo [12] Philo of Alexandria (Philo Iudaeus),' in H. Cancik and H. Schneider (eds.), *Brill's New Pauly: Encyclopaedia of the Ancient World* (Leiden 2007) 11.55–61 (columns).

English translation of the article prepared for the original German version of the work. See below under Extra Items. (DTR)

D. T. Runia, E. Birnbaum, K. A. Fox, A. C. Geljon, H. M. Keizer, J. P. Martín, R. Radice, J. Riaud, D. Satran, G. Schimanowski and T. Seland, 'Philo of Alexandria: an Annotated Bibliography 2004,' *The Studia Philonica Annual* 19 (2007) 143–204.

The yearly annotated bibliography of Philonic studies prepared by the members of the International Philo Bibliography Project covers the year 2004 (144 items), with addenda for the years 1996–2003 (11 items), and provisional lists for the years 2005–07. (DTR)

D. T. Runia and G. E. Sterling (eds.), *The Studia Philonica Annual*, Vol. 19 (Atlanta 2007).

This volume of the journal dedicated to the thought of Philo contains three general articles, a special section entitled on Philo and the Dead Sea Scrolls with an introduction and four articles, the usual bibliography section (see summary above), and eight book reviews. These are followed by the annual News and Notes section, Notes on Contributors and Instructions for Contributors. The various articles are summarized elsewhere in this bibliography. (DTR)

L. SAUDELLI, 'La *hodos anô kai katô* d'Héraclite (Fragment 22 B 60 DK/33 M) dans le *De Aeternitate Mundi* de Philon d'Alexandrie,' *The Studia Philonica Annual* 19 (2007) 29–58.

This thoroughly researched and richly documented study represents the first instalment of a comprehensive study of Philo's use of the treatise of Heraclitus which the author has now completed (see supplementary bibliography for 2008). Saudelli introduces her subject with a brief overview (§1) of scholarly contributions on the subject of Heraclitus and Philo, highlighting the work of J. Mansfeld and D. Zeller. She then turns (§2) to the text of *Aet.* 104–112 and analyses its contents in a number of steps. A considerable number of Heraclitan sayings are utilized in this section. Thus in §109 he alludes to fr. 60 DK on elemental change as 'the road up and down' (the main focus of the article), and this saying is connected in §111 to Heraclitus' psychology as expressed in fr. 36 DK. Philo defends the indestructibility of the cosmos by drawing an analogy between the life of the universe and the fate of the soul. He also attacks the Stoic doctrine of the *ekpurôsis*, implicitly refuting their interpretation of Heraclitus in terms of this doctrine. In the following section (§3) the pre-Philonic evidence on the interpretation of fr. 60 DK is presented. The only witness before Philo is Theophrastus in his *Physikai doxai*, who contrary to Philo and anticipating the Stoics interprets it in terms of a cosmic conflagration. But also the broader pre-Philonic interpretation needs to be taken into account (§4), and in particular the contribution of Aristotle, who recognizes the analogy that Heraclitus draws between the cosmos and human life and also links it to the philosopher's theory of elemental exhalations. Aristotle's interpretations are further developed and modified by the Stoics. The final piece of the puzzle (§5) is supplied by pre-Philonic texts which treat similar themes to those in Philo but do not make explicit reference to Heraclitus. In this section texts from Ps.Aristotle *De Mundo*, Ps.Ocellus and Cicero are discussed. On the basis of all this material Saudelli draws her conclusions on the Philonic passage in *Aet.* Philo is an important witness because he stands in between the earlier interpretations in Aristotle, the Stoa and the first century B.C.E. revival of Pythagoreanism on the one hand and the extensive later usage of the fragment by the Neoplatonists and the Church fathers on the other. He reflects the philosophical interpretation of the fragment—no doubt to be associated with the rise of Middle Platonism—in which cosmology, psychology and theology are fused together in a theory of the cosmic cycle in which the 'death' of the one element in being transformed into the next, guaranteeing the life of the whole. The article concludes by affirming that the use of fr. 60 DK in the remainder of Philo's writings needs to be further studied. (DTR)

K. SCHENCK, *Cosmology and Eschatology in Hebrews*, Society for New Testament Studies. Monograph Series 143 (Cambridge 2007), esp. 118–121.

In a section entitled 'Hebrews and Platonism' the author refers to the much discussed issue of Platonic influence in Hebrews, particularly in relation to the notion that the law is a shadow of good things to come. The author is rather skeptical about a Platonic or

Philonic reading of Hebrews. A Philonic aspect can, however, be seen in the image that the literal interpretation of a biblical text is a shadow of a deeper, allegorical meaning. (ACG)

G. Schimanowski, 'Die jüdische Integration in die Oberschicht Alexandriens und die angebliche Apostasie des Tiberius Julius Alexander,' in J. Frey, D. R. Schwartz and S. Gripentrog (eds.), *Jewish Identity in the Greco-Roman World*, Ancient Judaism and Early Christianity 71 (Leiden–Boston 2007) 111–135.

Most information on Philo's nephew Tiberius Julius Alexander is taken from Josephus, but Philo provides background information about Alexandrian Judaism, the spread of the Jews over the city, their representation before the emperor, the diversity of the Alexandrian population and the conflict with the pagan population. Possibly the dialogue *Anim.* is testimony to internal discussions among Philo's family. Altogether, Alexander seems to have followed a normal career, and even taking Josephus' information into account, the evidence for any genuine apostasy is slim. (JLB)

B. Schliesser, *Abraham's Faith in Romans 4*, Wissenschaftliche Untersuchungen zum Neuen Testament 2.Reihe 224 (Tübingen 2007), esp. 203–210.

To better understand Paul's concept of faith, the author focuses in this revised dissertation prepared at Fuller Theological Seminary on the reception history of Gen 15:6. Chapters are devoted to a history of scholarship on the Pauline understanding of faith, the variety of problems presented by the passage, its treatment in Jewish sources (including Philo), and its treatment in Paul. In the discussion of Philo, the author quotes—in English translation and Greek—from passages related to the verse, and addresses how, according to Philo, faith is attained, what it is, what it is not, and what it entails. Philo has great respect for Abraham's faith, as expressed both in Gen 15:6 and Gen 22. The latter provides an account of the patriarch's readiness to sacrifice Isaac. The linking of these two biblical texts is common in Jewish sources, but Philo 'adds another nuance' by retaining 'a clear borderline between the inner, psychological function of faith and the outward proof of faithfulness...' (p. 211). See also the summary of the dissertation in *SPhA* vol. 21, p. 96. (EB)

V. E. Schmitt, *Contemplatio: die Mystik des Karmel aus den Quellen frühchristlicher Kontemplation* (Würzburg 2007).

In this superficial treatment Philo is described as the origin of Christian mysticism, particularly in his allegory of the soul. Moses is seen as an example of the spiritual person, who can overcome the fundamental impossibility to see God. Another such model is the High Priest. The vision of God can also be described as ecstasy, as complete departure from and negation of the self, the handover to God. The Therapeutae in *Contempl.* are examples of Philo's idea of ecstatic vision of God and their practices are described by the author as predecessors of Carmelite mysticism. (JLB)

M. Shi, *Lun Moxi de sheng ping [On the Life of Moses]* (Beijing 2007).

This publication translates the English of Volume VI of the Loeb Philo that includes *Abr.*, *Ios.* and the two books of *Mos.* It is part of the Two Xi Civilization Philosophical Translated Classics series, 'Two Xi' being *Xila* (Hellenistic) and *Xibolai* (Hebrew). That the series is published by the prestigious National Academy of Social Sciences of Beijing is indicative of the seriousness with which Chinese scholars intend to study Hellenistic-Jewish writings, in particular the writings of Philo Judaeus. Thanks to Shi Minmin (translator of this volume) and her husband Zhang Xuefu, both of Zhejiang University, who have produced a number of critical and translated works on Philo, Philonic studies have gained a foothold in China. Look for more volumes from the same series. (DTR; based on a submission by Sze-kar Wan)

M. Simon-Shoshan, 'The Tasks of the Translators: the Rabbis, the Septuagint, and the Cultural Politics of Translation,' *Prooftexts* 27 (2007) 1–39.

Rabbinic references to the Septuagint legend and even to the Septuagint itself offer a rare example of rabbinic allusions to outside literature and demonstrate a range of concerns about biblical translation and the relationship between the dominant, gentile culture and the subservient, Jewish one. One can identify two trends—the 'changes' and the 'catastrophe' traditions—each reflecting differences between the treatment of the legend in *The Letter of Aristeas* and that in Philo (*Mos.* 2.25–44). For *Aristeas*, influenced by Alexandrian textual scholarship on Homer, translation is a matter of careful philological study, carried out by a committee; the translation project is 'an even exchange' between Ptolemy and the Jews in that both benefit equally (p. 5). Influenced by Platonic scepticism about the power of words to express ideas, Philo views the translation as impossible and attributes its success to divine inspiration. Although both sources regard the translation as perfect and on the same level as the original, Philo, unlike *Aristeas*, sees the translation as a means whereby 'the subservient culture influences the dominant one' (p. 9), since now Jewish wisdom might influence non-Jews. By contrast, the Rabbis see the translation as reflecting tension between Jews and the dominant culture—whether represented by Ptolemy, who forces the Jewish sages to write a translation, or by Christians, who claim to be Israel. The 'changes' tradition understands differences between the Greek and Hebrew to reflect translators' conscious changes because of political and theological issues but nonetheless envisions a kinship between the Rabbis and Alexandrian Jews. By contrast the 'catastrophe' tradition considers translation impossible, deems the endeavour a disaster, and creates an anti-Christian counter-narrative to the earlier positive views of both *Aristeas* and Philo. (EB)

G. E. Sterling, 'The First Theologian: The Originality of Philo of Alexandria,' in D. Hein and T. H. Olbricht (eds.), *Renewing Tradition: Studies in Texts and Contexts in Honor of James W. Thompson*, Princeton Theological Monograph Series 65 (Eugene, Oregon 2007) 145–162.

Although scholars debate which of Philo's ideas are original, Sterling believes 'his greatest contribution to lie in the sphere of theology' (p. 147). Citing Bousset's description of Philo as 'the first theologian of faith,' Sterling explores in what ways this description is true. Philo's thought is founded upon a belief in 'the ontological priority of God' (p. 149), which gives rise to a negative theology and carries additional implications for Philo's understanding of Scripture. Thus, Philo explains that God's declaration 'I am the Self-Existent' (Exod 3:14) signifies that He is unnamable, inconceivable, and incomprehensible. Moreover, Philo understands the ideas as thoughts of God and does not accord them independent status as Plato had. Unlike other thinkers who considered piety merely a secondary virtue, Philo also understands piety to be the greatest virtue. Finally, Philo's 'commitment to Scripture as the primary source for his reflections' (p. 157) further distinguishes him as a theologian rather than a philosopher. His allegorization of Sarah and Hagar as virtue or wisdom and the encyclical studies, respectively, directly influenced the medieval saying that 'philosophy is the handmaid of theology' (p. 158). Compared with Paul, a missionary, and Origen, a systematic theologian, Philo was more like Origen, and the influence of Philo's way of thinking on Christian theology is his 'greatest legacy' (p. 162). (EB)

L. T. STUCKENBRUCK, 'To What Extent did Philo's Treatment of Enoch and the Giants Presuppose a Knowledge of the Enochic and Other Sources Preserved in the Dead Sea Scrolls?,' *The Studia Philonica Annual* 19 (2007) 131–142.

While the author initially stresses the fundamental differences between the apocalyptic literature of the Land of Israel and Philo's allegorical interpretations of the Enoch story, he wonders whether some references to Abraham in the context of the giants may be interpreted as a critical reaction on the part of Philo to such earlier literature. Abraham's idealized description as 'heaven-born' is thus hesitantly identified as a negation of this patriarch's connection to the giants, which is, however, only attested in Ps.Eupolemus. (MRN)

J. E. TAYLOR, 'Philo of Alexandria on the Essenes: a Case Study on the Use of Classical Sources in Discussions of the Qumran-Essene Hypothesis,' *The Studia Philonica Annual* 19 (2007) 1–28.

The broader context of the article is the long-standing controversy on the location of the Essenes, which already preceded the discovery of the Dead Sea scrolls and the archaeological remains at Qumran, but naturally intensified after it. The author focuses on the two accounts of the Essene community given by Philo in *Prob.* and *Hypoth.*, discussing the main features of his presentation and emphasizing the need to *understand* Philo's rhetorical strategy in writing them. For example, given Philo's rhetorical aims, it is unlikely that his statement at *Prob.* 75 should be taken to mean that the Essenes rejected the entire sacrificial system of the Jerusalem temple. The passage in *Hypoth.* is more difficult to interpret because its rhetorical context can only be imperfectly understood. His paradigm of Essenes as 'entirely mature male celibates' is not a complete picture and has to be complemented with what we can learn from Josephus. Taylor concludes that Philo 'used the Essenes as a rhetorical tool' (p. 27). He did not necessarily have access to accurate details about every aspect of their identity, so the modern reader can probably do no more than glean a few details about the historical Essenes, details that relate primarily to how they behaved rather than to what they actually believed. The evidence he gives can be used in the above-mentioned Essene–Qumran controversy, but it needs to be done with greater care. (DTR)

C. TERMINI, 'La Scrittura nei tre grandi commenti di Filone di Alessandria: forme e metodi esegetici,' *Ricerche Storico-Bibliche* 19 (2007) 47–73.

After a general introduction on the commentary as an exegetical format in antiquity in general, the author discusses the three major types of Philonic commentary: the *Quaestiones*, the Allegorical Commentary, and the Exposition of the Law. A lucid analysis of Philo's interpretative method then distinguishes five characteristics: (1) the Pentateuch is considered to be written as an allegorical text; (2) virtually everything in it is allegory; (3)

the deeper meaning, however, does not eliminate the literal one; (4) Philo's allegoresis is a complex whole of various networks of symbolic meaning; (5) the exegete does not 'create' meaning but discovers the original meaning of the text. Sometimes Philo's allegoresis has an apologetic purpose. Prevalent is the meaning of Scripture as instruction for an ethical, spiritual life. (HMK)

C. Termini, 'Isacco, ovvero la dinamica del riso in Filone di Alessandria,' in C. Mazzucco (ed.), *Riso e comicità nel cristianesimo antico. Atti del convegno di Torino, 14–16 febbraio 2005, e altri studi*, (Alessandria 2007) 123–160.

This article leads to the conclusion that Philo shows awareness of the 'playful' dimension of laughter (γέλως) in both anthropological and theological contexts. The author presents a thorough discussion of Philo's exegesis of four Genesis passages in particular, in which laughter and Isaac (whose name signifies as much) play a prominent role: Gen 17:17 (Abram's laughter—the human being recognizing its limits with regard to its Creator); Gen 18:12–15 (Sarah's laughter—human happiness mixed with fear and sorrow); Gen 21:6 (birth of Isaac—the heterogeneity of human happiness as a gift of God); and Gen 26:8 (Isaac 'playing with' his wife Rebecca—an allegory of cosmic joyfulness as found also in Prov 8:30–31, where Wisdom is God's delight). Joy and laughter are part of divine beatitude, to which God's benevolent 'play' with his creation also belongs. (HMK)

J. W. Thompson, 'EPHAPAX: The One and the Many in Hebrews,' *New Testament Studies* 53 (2007) 566–581.

The author of Hebrews consistently makes use of a distinction between the one and the many which is unique in the New Testament, using the terminology of ἅπαξ and ἐφάπαξ. The many priests and sacrifices belong to the created order. The final 'once-for-all' moment is the singular saving event of the sacrifice and exultation of Christ, who becomes the priest εἰς τὸν αἰῶνα. Thompson argues that this theme is indebted to Middle Platonism, as is shown by comparison with the author's contemporaries Philo and Plutarch, even if he does not share their philosophical sophistication and consistency. A section is devoted to Philo, who is shown to make frequent use of the contrast between the one and the many in both his theology and his cosmology, particularly in his opposition between the immutability of God and the instability of the created order. Important passages discussed are *Opif.* 8, 100, *Abr.* 122, *Spec.* 3.180, *Leg.* 2.2, *Deus* 82. (DTR)

M. M. Thompson, 'Jesus: 'The One Who Sees God',' in D. B. Capes, A. D. DeConick, H. K. Bond and T. A. Miller (eds.), *Israel's God and Rebecca's Children: Christology and Community in Early Judaism and Christianity. Essays in Honor of Larry W. Hurtado and Alan F. Segal*, (Waco Tex. 2007) 215–226.

Despite Rudolf Bultmann's claim that hearing is preferred to seeing as a path to Jesus, Thompson argues that in the Gospel of John seeing has primacy. Here Jesus, 'as the sole eyewitness of God' (p. 217), has a unique status in apprehending God differently from everyone else. Metaphorically this apprehension also carries the sense of physical sight. Jesus' seeing God implies too that he has been in God's presence. The uniqueness of Jesus' visual apprehension of God can be viewed against a background tension in biblical and Jewish texts about the possibility—usually qualified—of seeing God. God can be seen, but He hides himself and 'no one can see God and live' (p. 221). The author surveys some passages from the OT, Targums, and Philo. Philo distinguishes between physical and noetic sight and links the possibility of seeing God with the virtue of the seer. Moses was able to apprehend God in a mystical vision, because he himself had become godlike (*Mos.* 1.158–159). (EB)

C. Tibbs, *Religious Experience of the Pneuma: Communication with the Spirit World in 1 Corinthians 12 and 14*, Wissenschaftliche Untersuchungen zum Neuen Testament 2.Reihe 230 (Tübingen 2007), esp. 123–131.

This study, a revised version of a Catholic University of America dissertation (see the summary in *SPhA* vol. 18, p. 99), deals with the theme of communication with the Spirit in 1 Corinthians 12 and 14. The author treats Philo as part of a 'background chapter' (pp. 113–146), which surveys evidence on the communication with the spirit world in the first-century Greco-Roman world and Jewish literature. In the section on Philo (pp. 123–131) he especially focuses on *Her.* 259, 265–66; *Mos.* 1.274, 277, 283 and *Spec.* 4.49. In his view Philo here interprets prophetic experience as a trance in which the prophet became a passive instrument in the hands of a divine spirit. While a medium the prophet is unconscious, but the spirit is communicated intelligibly and with intent by means of the vocal organs, not through erratic behavior or wild, senseless exhibitionism. (TS)

P. J. Tomson, 'Blessing in Disguise: εὐλογέω and εὐχαριστέω between 'Biblical' and Everyday Greek Usage,' in J. Joosten and P. J. Tomson (eds.), *Voces Biblicae: Septuagint Greek and its Significance for the New Testament,* (Leuven 2007) 35–61.

This article examines the roots εὐλογ- and εὐχαριστ-, which are nearly synonyms, in the Greek Old and New Testaments and related texts. Philo's discussion of Abraham's blessing (Gen 12:1–3) in *Migr.* is briefly treated. The gift of εὐλογία includes both noble ideas and effective speech. As an example of Philo's use of εὐχαριστεῖν *QG* 1.64 is discussed, where εὐχαριστεῖν means giving thanks to God. (ACG)

H. Tronier, 'Grænser for apologi. Er Filons brug af allegorese apologetisk?' [Limits for Apologetics: Is Philo's use of allegory apologetic?],' in A. Klostergaard Petersen, J. Hyldahl and K. S. Fuglseth (eds.), *Perspektiver på Jødisk Apologetik*, Antikken og kristendommen 4 (Copenhagen 2007) 207–231.

In discussing Philo and his allegories (pp. 218–231), Tronier takes his point of departure in the distinction made by W. Bernard between allegory as 'substitutive' and allegory as 'diaeretic'. The former is the more traditionally Stoic one: something (A) is said, but something else (B) is meant. The latter is associated with Platonic tradition and works within the dualistic understanding of a phenomenal and an ideal world. Reading Philo from the viewpoint of the substitutive kind of allegory would make him an apologist. Reading him as a representative of a diaeretic allegory would not. According to Tronier Philo should primarily be seen as a representative of the latter kind of allegory. Hence he should not be categorized as an apologist. (TS)

R. M. Victor, *Colonial Education and Class Formation in Early Judaism: A Postcolonial Reading* (diss. Texas Christian University 2007).

Philo is one of the sources used to determine how the institution of the gymnasium was used to educate the elites and enable Greek citizens, Hellenes, and Hellenistic Jews to function politically, ethnically, and economically within the larger Greek empire and particularly in Judea, by creating a separate class of 'Hellenized Jews' among the Jewish population. (DTR; based on author's abstract)

D. Winston, 'Philo of Alexandria on the Rational and Irrational Emotions,' in J. T. Fitzgerald (ed.), *Passions and Moral Progress in Greco-Roman Thought*, (London–New York 2007) 201–220.

Philo's theory of the passions is essentially that of the Stoics with occasional modifications. Although Posidonius' Platonizing version of the Stoic theory was of considerable help to Philo, he nevertheless used this paradigm rather selectively. Philo's knowledge of Stoic philosophy is quite extensive, and he even makes use of some of the most esoteric of the technical terms of the school. Philo's portrait of Moses is that of a 'supersage' who transcends even the impossible ideal projected by the many Stoic paradoxes that attracted the ridicule of their numerous critics. Moreover, in the final analysis, the most effective therapy for removing the passions is to counter them with the most powerful emotion of all, the love of God. (DTR; based on author's summary)

S. M. B. Zorzi, *Desiderio della bellezza (ἔρως τοῦ καλοῦ). Da Platone a Gregorio di Nissa: tracce di una rifrazione teologico-semantica*, Studia Anselminana 145. Historia theologiae 1 (Rome 2007), esp. 181–199.

As part of a broad study which investigates the concept of Desire (or Love) of Beauty in its evolution from Plato to Gregory of Nyssa, the author discusses Philo and sees in him a 'lethal transition', because it is in Philo that *erôs* reaches the point of being completely spiritualized and separated from all physicality. Contributing to this process in the first place is Philo's identification of the 'image of God' in man with the *nous*—and the original as well as final state of the nous is *apatheia*, absence of passion or desire. Since desire is associated with physical pleasure and such pleasure is branded as sin, the pure soul should be possessed only by desire or love of God. Interestingly, *apatheia* in Philo does not signify a complete absence of emotions: there is a place for virtuous emotions such as joy, contrition, compassion, and piety. But Philo does separate the physical meaning of *erôs* completely from what for him is the only positive meaning, i.e. the spiritual. An analogous process happens in the case of beauty: de-personalized, cosmic beauty is separated from the human beauty of the body. The latter, with its physical pleasures, is seen only as a dangerous trap of sin. Beauty, although not much mentioned by Philo, is—maybe for the first time in Jewish writings—identified with God. So *erôs*, though reduced to the spiritual, 'vertical' dimension, nevertheless acquires a new aspect of reciprocity and personal focus which would be unthinkable in Plato, thanks to the fact that there can be friendship with God. (HMK)

Extra items from before 2007

S. AHBEL-RAPPE, 'Plato's Influence on Jewish, Christian, and Islamic Philosophy,' in H. H. BENSON (ed.), *A Companion to Plato*, (Oxford 2006) 434–451, esp. 435–437.

Philo begins the story of the influence of Plato on the formation of Jewish, Christian and Islamic philosophy. A number of pages are devoted to his thought under the heading Middle Platonisms, focusing on his interpretation of creation in *Opif.* and his mystical reading of the Pentateuch as an allegory of the flight of the soul from the lower material realm to divine knowledge. (DTR)

N. BELAYCHE, ''Hypsistos'. Une voie de l'exaltation des dieux dans le polythéisme gréco-romain,' *Archiv für religionsgeschichte* 7 (2005) 34–56.

The significance of the adjective ὕψιστος when it qualifies a divinity is debated. Does it imply that there was an evolution towards monotheism in the Greco-Roman world, maybe under the influence of Judaism, since the Septuagint translates *Elyon* by *Hypsistos*, a divine name used by Philo as well? Through the analysis of votive inscriptions, the author shows that the use of ὕψιστος by pagan worshippers is to be understood as a way to exalt the god, which is not exclusivistic and does not imply monotheism. Not only are several gods called ὕψιστος, but the god *Hypsistos* is sometimes mentioned together with other gods whom the devotee wishes to worship as well. True, in the majority of cases, the god *Hypsistos* is the only one to be invoked, but simply because in this specific religious context the devotion is directed towards this god in particular. Moreover, archaeological data show that gods which were called ὕψιστοι were worshipped in the same way and through the same rituals as the other gods. Finally, the adjective ὕψιστος, which emphasizes the god's greatness and might, represents a reflection on the essence of the divinity rather than on its unicity. (KB)

C. BENNEMA, *The Power of Saving Wisdom: an Investigation of Spirit and Wisdom in Relation to the Soteriology of the Fourth Gospel*, Wissenschaftliche Untersuchungen zum Neuen Testament 2.Reihe 148 (Tübingen 2002), esp. 71–83.

In this study on spirit and wisdom in the Gospel of John, a chapter is devoted to Philo and other Jewish writers. In Philo's thought πνεῦμα is seen as the essence of the rational soul breathed in by God. Because πνεῦμα is given by God, it functions as the principle of communication between God and man. It provides the basis for knowing and seeing God. Philo argues, however, that God cannot be known in himself, but only through lower levels of being. Wisdom is a guide on the way to the understanding of God. Salvation is given through a fuller measure of participation in the divine *pneuma*. (ACG)

M. L. COLISH, *Ambrose's Patriarchs: Ethics for the Common Man* (Notre Dame IN 2005).

The exegetical works of Philo are a constant point of reference in this first monographic study of the four treatises that Ambrose devoted to the Old Testament patriarchs, *De*

Abraham, De Isaac, De Jacob and *De Joseph.* See the list of references in the index on p. 189 (but there is no index of passages). The author argues that in these treatises Ambrose develops 'an ethics for the common man' (p. 153). (DTR)

F. FRAZIER, 'Une «biographie allégorique» chez Philon? Sur l'emploi de l'interprétation allégorique dan le *De Josepho,'* in B. PÉREZ-JEAN and P. EICHEL-LOJKINE (eds.), *L'allégorie de l'Antiquité à la Renaissance,* Colloques, congrès et conférences sur la Renaissance européenne 43 (Paris 2004) 255–286.

The paper was presented as part of a conference on the practice of allegory from antiquity to the Renaissance held at the Université Paul-Valéry in Montpellier, France in January 2001. A key characteristic of Philo's allegorical method is its flexibility, as evidenced by the variety of application in the two series, the Allegorical Commentary and the Exposition of the Law. In the latter it is combined with biography in the treatises *Abr.* and *Ios.* The allegorization works at two levels, in a general way for the treatises as a whole and in particular detail for their individual sections. Moreover in the former treatise the main character belongs to the spiritual realm, whereas in the latter Joseph must be active in the context of the city situated in the material realm. The first two sections of the article compare the structure and contents of the two treatises. In the third section the author outlines how the treatise *Ios.* explores the key features of the political life, its apparent grandeur and its precarious nature as it seeks to find stability in a world of fundamental uncertainty. There are limits, however, to this allegorization and these are explored in the fourth and final section of the paper. Just like Abraham, Joseph declares that he belongs to God and receives his reward from Him. This 'pious interpretation', it should be noted, falls outside the allegorical interpretation proper, but can be illustrated by a comparable passage in *Migr.* 17–22. Frazier concludes her article by emphasizing the richness and complexity of Philo's allegorical reflection. Allegory as practised in the service of spiritual meditation is a highly flexible instrument. In the case of Joseph it leads to the paradoxical result that one may rise to the level of the soul, but at the same time is constantly reminded of the inferiority of the material realm. (DTR)

C. HOFFMANN and A. KAMESAR, 'Wilamowitz and Heinemann II: Three Letters from the 1920's' *Illinois Classical Studies* 31–32 (2006–07) 130–144, esp. 140–142.

In the second of the three letters written in 1927 by the great German classicist Ulrich von Wilamowitz to Isaac Heinemann, he makes some brief observations on Philo's Greek style and wonders whether his former pupil Moshe Schwabe, now teaching at the Hebrew University of Jerusalem, would measure up to the difficult task of translating him. No doubt this relates to the German translation of Philo, which Heinemann was editing. (DTR)

M. A. JACKSON-MCCABE, *Logos and Law in the Letter of James: The Law of Nature, the Law of Moses, and the Law of Freedom,* New Testament Studies 100 (Leiden 2001), esp. 87–95.

Revised version of the University of Chicago dissertation completed in 1998 (see summary in *SPhA* vol. 13 p. 265). Although there are many decidedly Stoic terms and concepts in Philo's treatment of natural law, his presentation of such ideas is scarcely typical of the Stoics in every respect, because it is also informed by his dependence on other traditions of discourse, whether Middle Platonic, Neo-Pythagorean or Jewish. The result is a quite distinctive presentation of the Stoic correlation of *logos* and law. (DTR)

J. KIEFER, *Exil und Diaspora: Begrifflichkeiten und Deutungen im antiken Judentum und in der hebräischen Bibel*, Arbeiten zur Bibel und ihrer Geschichte 19 (Leipzig 2005), esp. 399–412.

In this broad-ranging investigation into the themes of exile and diaspora in ancient Judaism and the Hebrew Bible, a section is devoted to Philo. First Philo's use of the terms ἀποικία, παροικία and μετοικία is analysed. Only once does he affirm that the diaspora of the Jews is a consequence of divine judgment. Elsewhere he argues that it is motivated by the desire to 'colonize' or by the search for better living conditions. Various key texts such as *Flacc.* 45–46, *Legat.* 214–216, 276ff., *Mos.* 2.225–232, *Praem.* 165, and *Spec.* 2.162ff. are cited and analysed. It remains difficult to determine whether the tension between the hope of the return of the exiles and the positive view of the Diaspora represents a contradiction that is real, i.e. psychological or biographical–chronological, or whether it only appears to be such. But elsewhere the juxtaposition of acceptance of the diaspora situation and adherence to eschatological expectation is quite common. (DTR)

J. LUST, *Messianism and the Septuagint: Collected Essays*, Bibliotheca Ephemeridum Theologicarum Lovaniensium 178 (Leuven 2004), esp. 81–86.

In this volume of collected essays which have as a common theme the subject of messianism in the Septuagint, mention should be made of a discussion of Philo's citation of the messianic text Num 24:7 & 17 in *Mos.* 1.290 and *Praem.* 95 in an article entitled 'The Greek version of Balaam's third and fourth oracles: the ἄνθρωπος in Num 24,7 and 17: messianism and lexicography' first published in 1995. In both cases Philo cites the verses with the term ἄνθρωπος, i.e. 'there shall come forth a man ...' This is perhaps evidence that the original LXX text contained the term, yet early Christian quotes do not contain it, so it is also possible that later Christian authors inserted it on the basis of Philo, who may have included it in his own rewording of the text. (DTR)

M. F. MACH, 'Philo's 'Philosophical' turn to 'Religion',' in U. BIANCHI, F. M. MORA and F. BIANCHI (eds.), *The Notion of 'Religion' in Comparative Research. Selected Proceedings of the XVI IAHR Congress*, Storia delle Religioni 8 (Rome 1994) 403–413.

Philo is one of the most disputed figures in both the history of philosophy and the history of religion, and his use of Greek-philosophical doctrines is one of the greatest difficulties for the modern interpreter of his thought. The question must be posed: why should Philo use elements of general Greek culture and of Greek philosophy to interpret the Jewish Bible? Philo's writings give the impression of a theological attempt at exegesis 'which does not yet crystallize into a clear terminology and suffers from the effort to verify it by re-finding it in biblical phrases' (p. 405). Greek philosophy helped Philo formulate his view of religion, firstly because the problem of cognition had long been disputed and secondly because the transcendence of the truly Existent was well and truly established, at least in Platonism. Philo, however, wants to go a step further and establish a personal

relation with the divine which is more than an intellectual one. Here his 'religiosity over-
comes Plato's more mechanical theology and it may be the reason for the ambivalent role
of Greek philosophy in his thought' (p. 413). (DTR)

M. J. MARTIN, *The School of Virtue and the Tent of Zion. An Investigation
into the Relationship between the Institutions of the Greco-Roman Diaspora
Synagogue and the Jerusalem Temple in the Late Second Temple Judaism: Philo — a
Case Study* (diss. University of Melbourne 2000).

In this Melbourne dissertation it is argued that an inherent tension existed between the
institutions of the Graeco-Roman Diaspora synagogue and the Jerusalem Temple in the
pre-70 C.E. first century The relationship between these two institutions was characterised
by an inherent ambiguity, thus contrasting with attempts to demonstrate the existence of
either a complementary relationship or an overt opposition between the Temple and synagogue in this period. This ambiguous relationship derives from the fact that both institutions functioned as loci of divine worship, yet each embodied quite distinct constructions
of the locus of sanctity. A structuralist model of sacred spaces in Judaism is drawn upon in
an attempt to describe these conceptions of the locus of sanctity and characterize their
ambiguous relationship in first century Judaism. The relationship is placed in the context
of the transition from a temple-centred locative worldview to an anthropocentric utopian
worldview taking place in the religious thought of the Mediterranean world during this
era which a number of scholars have proposed. Proceeding from a position admitting the
existence of a plurality of Judaisms in the post-Maccabaean era, the writings of Philo of
Alexandria are taken as a discrete body of evidence to serve as a case study to test the
proposed hypothesis. It is shown that Philo betrays a notable tension in his thought concerning the relationship between the institutions of the Temple and the synagogue. Whilst
Philo vociferously defends the relevance of the Jerusalem Temple, examination of his exercises in idealizing speculation—his description of the life of the Therapeutic community of
De Vita Contemplativa and his vision of the eschatological endtime—reveals that ultimately
the Temple is irrelevant to the mode of spiritual worship, the life of the virtuous man,
which he consistently and wholeheartedly advocates and which is embodied in the life of
the synagogue, a 'school of virtue'. The Temple retains relevance for Philo only insofar as it
functions as a symbol of Jewish corporate identity in the Gentile Roman world. The notion
of the 'centrality' of the Jerusalem Temple, commonly ascribed to the Judaisms of the Late
Second Temple period, is revealed to be a dubious and ill-defined concept. Some implications of the ambiguous relationship thus revealed for the issue of synagogues associated
with Greek-speaking Diaspora communities in pre-70 C.E. first century Jerusalem (such as
that of Acts 6) are examined. (DTR; based on author's summary)

B. C. McGING, 'Philo's adaptation of the Bible in his "Life of Moses",' in
B. McGING and J. MOSSMAN (eds.), *The Limits of Ancient Biography*,
(Swansea 2006) 117–140.

This article examines some aspects of the composition of Philo's *Mos.*, especially the
way in which Philo deals with his main source, the Septuagint. The author discerns several
techniques, the most important of which is his adaption of the biblical text. Philo rewrites
the text in words that are an echo of the biblical verses. In most circumstances Philo
elaborates on what he finds in the Bible. On a few occasions, however, he makes an abridg-
ment of the biblical narrative. Although allegory does not fit very well into a retelling of
Moses' life, occasionally Philo offers an allegorical interpretation. A strange feature is that

Philo avoids the use of proper names with the exception of Moses himself. An appendix presents an overview of the structure of the treatise. (ACG)

G. W. E. NICKELSBURG, *Jewish Literature Between the Bible and the Mishnah: A Historical and Literary Introduction.* Second editon (Minneapolis 2005), esp. 212–221.

For this new edition of the classic introduction to the literature of Second Temple Judaism (first edition published in 1981) the author has broadened his approach and so has added sections on Philo and Josephus missing previously. The section on Philo is located in the chapter entitled 'Israel in Egypt' and is, as the author indicated in n. 108, an abridged version of his paper in the Philo and the New Testament volume published in 2004 (see *SPhA* vol. 19 p. 270). Philo is regarded as an important and significant figure among Hellenistic Jews around the turn of the era, but in Nickelsburg's view he was not unique. His works do, however, furnish a unique window into the world of Hellenistic Judaism. Without his corpus, our knowledge of this phenomenon would be greatly impoverished and our view of the Judaism of this period would be less balanced. (DTR)

D. T. RUNIA, Art. 'Philon [12] Philon von Alexandreia (Philo Iudaeus),' in H. CANCIK and H. SCHNEIDER (eds.), *Der Neue Pauly: Encyclopädie der Antike,* (Stuttgart 2000) 9.850–855 (columns).

Philo of Alexandria is the twelfth of nineteen Philos listed in this new Encyclopedia, which sits halfway between the great Pauly Wissowa *Realencyclopädie* (83 vols. published 1890–1978, for Philo see R–R 4109) and the *Kleine Pauly* (5 vols. published 1964–1975, article on Philo by B. Schaller, 4.772–776). The article is divided into four sections: Life and Context; Works; Teachings; *Nachwirkung*. It is completed with a listing of editions, translations and a limited bibliography. An English translation was published in 2007. See also above under M. Landfester. (DTR)

P. SERRA ZANETTI, 'Note su Tertulliano e Filone d'Alessandria,' in A. CACCIARI, F. CITTI, C. NERI and L. PERRONE (eds.), *P. Serra Zanetti, Imitatori di Gesù Cristo. Scritti classici e cristiani,* (Bologna 2005) 37–61, esp. 48–61.

Review of *Philon d'Alexandrie: La migration d'Abraham. Introduction, texte critique, traduction et notes* par R. Cadiou, SC 47 (Paris 1957) = R–R 1551. After a survey of Cadiou's introduction, with some critical observations, Serra Zanetti critically discusses Cadiou's text constitution and/or translation regarding the following sections of *Migr.*: 26, 41, 42, 47, 67, 68, 76, 77, 80, 82, 83, 98, 104, 120, 122, 126, 131, 138, 145, 146, 149, 150, 157, 158, 160, 174, 180, 192, 195, 211, 216, 218, 225. The article was originally published in *Memorie dell'Accademia delle Scienze dell'Istituto di Bologna, Classe di scienze morali* s. 5 VII (1957–59 [1960]. **Check cross-reference** (HMK)

O. S. VARDAZARYAN, 'Meknoghakan ənt'ercanut'yunnerə ew P'ilon Alek'sandracu erkeri hayeren meknut'younnerə' [in Armenian: Readings with commentaries and Armenian scholia of the works by Philo the Alexandrian], *Banber Erevani Hamalsarani. Hasarakakan gitut'yunner [Proceedings of the Yerevan University: Social Studies]* 102.3 (2000) 110–118.

Some works by Philo and Pseudo-Philo, which were translated into Armenian in about the fifth century, were actively commented on in twelfth–fourteenth centuries by Armenian ecclesiastical doctors (*vardapets*). While observing the hermeneutic 'coat' of the 'Armenian Philo', as well as the description of the 'class-reading' given in medieval Armenian manuscripts, it is possible to reconstruct the stages of preparing and digesting philosophical and theological texts which were included in the school curriculum. As such, the procedure did not differ from grammatical and rhetorical methods of analyzing, memorizing and paraphrasing texts, as they are described in *Ars Grammatica* by Dionysius Thrax and especially in the three chapters at the end of *Progymnasmata* by Theon of Alexandria which were lost in Greek but are preserved in Ancient Armenian translation. The correlation may be noted between these stages of commenting and the genres of commentaries: (a) the introductory lection about an author under the study (Gr. *hypothesis*, Lat. *causa*, Arm. *patčar*); (b) an exposition of the text(s), i.e. piece by piece paraphrase with sporadic explanations (the *scholia* in proper sense, Arm. *lucmunk'*); (c) a concise rhetorical composition on the basis of the studied text, an epitome (arm. *hawak'umn*). (DTR; based on the author's summary)

O. S. VARDAZARYAN, 'P'ilon Alek'sandrac'u yerkeri hayeren lucmun-k'nerə' [in Armenian: The Armenian scholia to the works by Philo of Alexandria], *Patma-Banasirakan Handes [The Historical-Philological Journal (Yerevan)]* 168.1 (2005) 185–206.

The paper contains a bibliography of the Armenian medieval scholia (12th–13th century) to the Armenian translations of several genuine and non-genuine works by Philo of Alexandria. The sigla used in the present description, although referring to the scholia which are found in the manuscripts preserved in Matenadaran ('Mashtots' Institute of Ancient Manuscripts, Yerevan, Armenia), may be applied to the more precise and compact introduction of the same material preserved in foreign collections of Armenian manuscripts. The failure of attributions of these scholia, offered by G. Grigoryan, is demonstrated: they cannot be taken as two different compositions by Hovhannes Sarkavag and Hovhannes Yerznkatsi Pluz respectively. The above-mentioned scholar was misled by the identical preambles, which could adhere to the *different* scholia on the same work by Philo. Full texts of these preambles are published in the appendix to the description of the scholia. It is proposed that two recensions of the scholion 'Preface to Philo' originated in the school of Vardapet Vanakan; in addition the series of scholia in the codex of Yerevan Matenadaran No 1672 may be ascribed to the school of Mxit'ar Gosh. (DTR; based on the author's summary)

O. S. VARDAZARIAN, 'Patčark' groc' P'iloni. Usumnasirut'yun ew bnagir' [in Armenian: The 'Introductions' to the writings by Philo. Texts and studies], *Proceedings of the 'V. Brusov' Yerevan State University of Linguistics. Social studies* 3 (2005) 185–233.

The *Patčark'*, introductory summaries (Gr. *hypotheseis*, Lat. *argumenta, causae*, Syr. *elta*) of the class-readings of authors included in school curriculum, represents the most interesting part of the medieval Armenian commentaries on the 'Armenian Philo'. They display the notions about Philo and his literary heritage which circulated in Armenian monastic schools in 12th–13th centuries. The commentators have used the scheme of the *eisagoge*, with a biographical chapter of encomiastic character at the beginning. Four compositions of this genre are preserved in Armenian manuscripts: Anonymous A, Anonymous B, the argument by David Kobayrec'i's and—related to the latter—'Introduction to Philo'. The critical edition of these texts is accompanied by a brief introduction, which contains the description of the manuscript tradition and the comparative dating within the group, and also by notes which mainly focus on the sources of the concepts used by the Armenian scholiasts or give literary parallels for their phraseology. (DTR; based on the author's summary)

O. S. Vardazarian, *Filon Aleksandrijskij v vosprijatii armjanskogo sredneve-kovja. K voprosu ob istokakh* tradicii [in Russian: Philo of Alexandria in the perception of the Armenian Middle Ages. On the source of tradition] (Yerevan 2006).

This study, written in Russian, opens up a new and hitherto virtually unknown area of Philonic studies. For this reason the abstract is more detailed than is usual in the Philo bibliography project.

Introduction (pp. 3–8). The monograph is devoted to probable cultural channels through which the unique collection of Philonic and pseudo-Philonic works has been transmitted to the Armenian milieu. Circumstantial characteristics of these channels can be found in the scholia (12th–14th centuries) to the Armenian corpus Philonicum, especially in scholiasts' view of Philo's biography and in the categories which Armenian interpreters applied to the exegetical method used by the Alexandrian. The analysis of these concepts, while extending beyond the Armenian context, presents an ideal opportunity for the reconstruction in general outline of an intellectual atmosphere, which enabled Philo's works to be adopted by early Christian tradition and later transferred to Armenian soil.

Chapter I: 'Armenian version of the legend about Philo: literary sources and historical implications' (pp. 9–28). The Armenian Church doctors' notions concerning Philo's biography were mostly formed on the basis of the well known sources, such as Eusebius' *Ecclesiastical History* and *Chronicle* and the apocryphal *Vita Ioannis*, and in this regard are nothing more than secondary literary fictions. However, the most original details of the narratives about Philo, namely the line connecting him with the Jacob the Just and messianic movements in Palestine about the time of the Jewish War may conceal the remnants of the most ancient variant of the legend, which presented Philo as a Christian author. Nevertheless, judging from medieval Armenian practice, the body of Philo's works has been included in school curricula not because of the legend, but rather the latter served as a justification of its inclusion.

Chapter II: 'Philo's exegetical method in interpretation by Armenian hermeneutists: formulating the problem' (pp. 29–54). The Armenian scholiasts perceived the Armenian Corpus Philonicum not as a set of casual translations, but as a well structured whole, connected together by the ideas of virtue and spiritual perfection. The complementary use of both these characteristics, as well as the general conviction of the Armenian monastic doctors about the spirituality of Philo's exegesis, seems to be at variance with utterances concerning Philo's method by Photius and especially by Ambrose. The latter made use of Philo's 'merely moral', as he claims, interpretation for constructing his own spiritual exegesis of Gen. 2:15. The evidence for the particularity of the exegetical position of Armenian medieval teachers can be seen also in their tendency to identify Philo's allegorical method with exegetical methods used by the apostle Paul and described in his term ἀλληγορούμενα (Gal 4:24).

Chapter III: 'Terms of contemplative exegesis in their application to Philo's method' (pp. 55–89). There is a set of kindred terms, by means of which Armenian commentators tried to define the exegetical method of the Alexandrian: 'intelligible', 'intellectual contemplation', 'new vision (or contemplation)', 'incorporeal', 'subtle contemplation'. In investigating the provenance of this terminology it emerges that it was used by Greek and Latin authors to characterize the 'spiritual' and 'anagogic' interpretations of the Bible.

Chapter IV: 'Philo as a 'spiritual' author in the Armenian commentators' view: on the source of tradition' (pp. 90–110). One can trace the essential concepts of spiritual exegesis in the Book of Wisdom, and especially in the encomium of *sophia* in 7:13–29. From the same tradition, probably, the notion on Philo as a spiritual author could arise, precisely because by conveying the philosophical sense of the Law, the Alexandrian gave the reader of the Holy Scripture the opportunity to contemplate the Divine Wisdom directly in its activity. While reinterpreting the spiritual exegetical method, the early Christian authors began to attribute to the Bible with a merely dogmatic meaning. The habit of ascribing explicit or concealed dogmatic views to Philo probably should be connected with this very meta-morphosis. It seems that the gradually fading tradition of spiritual exegesis resulted in a loss of interest toward Philo's heritage as well. However, in the same epoch some works by Philo were translated into Armenian, and the Armenian scholiography of subsequent centuries diligently preserved the early Christian and possibly pre-Christian notions concerning Philo's exegesis as well.

Afterword (pp. 111–115). In order to form at least a rough idea of the source from which the described notions might have been borrowed, one should note the considerable number of famous catechists who demonstrate knowledge of Philo's works, especially of those included in the Armenian corpus. If the adoption of the Philonic heritage by Armenian scholars has happened due to the institution of catechization, the nearest point of transmission might be the Jerusalem Church, with which the Armenian Church always had very active relations. As the comparison of one of Cyril of Jerusalem's catechetical homilies with the respective passus of 'Evangelical Preparation' by Eusebius suggests, the collection might have been formed as a manual for the purpose of training future catechists, the spiritual preceptors of the church, or have been transmitted through some other, especially monastic, modifications of the catechetic rite.

Notes (pp. 116–152). Literature (pp. 153–170). Index of names (pp. 171–175).

Appendix I: '*Skizb ew patčar̲ ant'erc'uacin, i Yakobay asac'eal* [The beginning and 'introductory summary' of the (scriptural) readings, delivered by Yakob]' (pp. 176–187). Publication of the text of the introductory summary by *vardapet* Yakob (probably the future katholikos Yakob Klayec' I, † 1286) dedicated to the Armenian Lectionary. The summary presents, mostly in a legendary way, the history of the Lectionary and discusses some controversial points concerning calculation of some dates of the ecclesiastical year. From the Philonist point of view the most noteworthy aspect is the narration about Christian community of Jerusalem, which was led by Jacob the Brother of the Lord, who, in scho-liast's view, compiled the skeleton of the Jerusalem Lectionary. Before the siege of Jerusalem the community had migrated to Egypt (especially to the Thebaid), where Philo became acquainted with them and gave the evidence about them in his treatise *Contempl.*

Appendix II: *Eraneloj tearn Grigori Niwsacwoj episkoposi eghbawr Barsghi T'ught' yaghags Ergoj Ergocs* [Beati episcopi Grigorii Nysseni Basilii fratris Epistula de Cantico Canticorum (Praefatio ad Olympiadem)] (pp. 188–210). Publication of the Armenian translation of Gregory of Nyssa's Preface to his Commentary on the *Song of Songs*, with Greek parallels to the passages, which may be interpreted as containing ideological shifts that aim to present Gregory's exegetical method not as Alexandrian, but as moderate Antiochean. The text is important as a probable source of the terminology used by Armenian scholiasts in their description of Philo's exegesis.

Summary in Armenian (pp. 211–225). Summary in English (pp. 226–243). (DTR; based on the author's summary)

O. S. Vardazarian, 'Hovhan Orotnec'u Hawak'umn Yaytnabanut'ean i Philone Imastnoy, or "Yaghags Naxaxnamut'ean"' [in Armenian: The Epitome of the Explanation of the (Treatise) On Providence by Philo the Wise, (made) by Yovhannēs Orotnec'i], *Banber Matenadarani [Journal of the Matenadaran, Yerevan]* 17 (2006) 213–259.

The critical edition of the text of the epitome of the *Prov.*, made in the school of the famous medieval Armenian *vardapet* Yovhannēs Orotnec'i (1315–1386), was prepared on the basis of three manuscripts, which are all preserved in Yerevan. In the Introduction to the edition the problem of authorship of the epitome is first discussed. Judging from the title, there are two possible inferences: (a) Yovhannēs Orotnec'i could have composed it by using some scholia of previous authors; (b) the explanations given by the above-mentioned *vardapet* were recorded during class-readings and transformed in a rhetorical composition by one of his disciples. In the latter case the most probable candidate is Grigor Tathevatc'i (†1409), who was known as a recorder of some other lectures delivered by Orotnec'i and who was familiar with several specific phrases of the epitome. Although it is a concise paraphrase of the *Prov.*, the epitome differs from its source text in its general tendency and the proportions of its exposition. Contrary to Philo, who claims to discuss the theses stated by Alexander only in the most friendly manner, the author of the epitome is intent to make a *refutation* against all those who do not believe in Divine Providence. Such a shift in perception is very ancient; it can be noted already in citations from *Prov.* in the *Praeparatio Evangelica* (see esp. τὰς τῶν ἀθέων ἀντιθέσεις in 8.13.7). There are some large gaps in the exposition, but they should not be interpreted as *lacunae*: the omissions can be explained as a desire to counterbalance the scope of the first and second books of *Prov.* and to avoid items unknown to the Armenian audience. In the 'Notes' the additional sources of several passages of the epitome are pointed out: these are Armenian translations of Ps.-Aristotle's *De Mundo* and Plato's *Timaeus*.). (DTR; based on the author's summary)

SUPPLEMENT

A Provisional Bibliography 2008–2010

The user of this supplemental Bibliography of the most recent articles on Philo is reminded that it will doubtless contain inaccuracies and red herrings because it is not in all cases based on autopsy. It is merely meant as a service to the reader. Scholars who are disappointed by omissions or are keen to have their own work on Philo listed are strongly encouraged to contact the Bibliography's compilers (addresses in the section Notes on Contributors).

2008

F. ALESSE (ed.), *Philo of Alexandria and Post-Aristotelian Philosophy*, Studies on Philo of Alexandria 5 (Leiden–Boston 2008).

F. ALESSE, 'La sabbia e la materia: una polemica filosofica di Filone,' *Adamantius* 14 (2008) 24–30.

M. ALESSO, 'Qué es la felicidad según Filón,' *Circe* 12 (2008) 11–27.

J. S. ALLEN, *The Despoliation of Egypt in Pre-Rabbinic, Rabbinic and Patristic Traditions*, Supplements to Vigiliae Christianae 92 (Leiden–Boston 2008), esp. 91–117 and passim.

M. A. BADER, *Tracing the Evidence: Dinah in Post-Hebrew Bible Literature*, Studies in Biblical Literature 162 (New York 2008).

S. BADILITA, 'Retraite au désert et solitude du prophète chez Philon,' *Adamantius* 14 (2008) 43–51.

S. BADILITA, 'Philon d'Alexandrie et l'exegese allegorique,' *Foi et vie* 107 (2008) 63–76.

S. BAE, *Jesus' Resurrection as the Climactic Semeion in the Fourth Gospel* (diss. The Southern Baptist Theological Seminary 2008).

C. T. BEGG, 'Jacob's Descent into Egypt (Gen 45,25–46,7) according to Josephus, Philo and Jubilees,' *Ephemerides Theologicae Lovanienses* 84 (2008) 499–518.

C. T. BEGG, 'The Marah Incident according to Philo and Josephus,' *Laurentianum* 49 (2008) 321–336.

P. J. BEKKEN, 'The Controversy on Self-Testimony According to John 5:31–40; 8:12–20 and Philo, Legum Allegoriae III.205–208,' in B. HOLMBERG and M. WINNINGE (eds.), *Identity Formation in the New Testament*, Wissenschaftliche Untersuchungen zum Neuen Testament 2.227 (Tübingen 2008) 19–42.

R. M. VAN DEN BERG, *Proclus' Commentary on the Cratylus in Context: Ancient Theories of Language and Naming*, Philosophia Antiqua 112 (Leiden–Boston 2008), esp. 52–56.

M. BOERI, 'Estrategias argumentativas filonianas en *De aeternitate* y *De providentia*,' *Nova Tellus* 26 (2008) 39–65.

G. BOHAK, *Ancient Jewish Magic: a History* (Cambridge 2008).

M. BONAZZI, 'Towards Transcendence: Philo and the Renewal of Platonism in the Early Imperial Age,' in F. ALESSE (ed.), *Philo of Alexandria and Post-Aristotelian Philosophy*, Studies on Philo of Alexandria 5 (Leiden–Boston 2008) 13–52.

L. BORMANN (ed.), *Schöpfung, Monotheismus und fremde Religionen: Studien zu Inklusion und Exklusion in den biblischen Schöpfungsvorstellungen*, Biblisch-theologische Studien 95 (Neukirchen-Vluyn 2008).

P. C. BOUTENEFF, *Beginnings: Ancient Christian Readings of the Biblical Creation Narratives* (Grand Rapids 2008), esp. 27–32.

E. Bovo and C. LÉVY, 'Le 'je' de l'être juif chez Philon d'Alexandrie et Lévinas,' *Antiquorum Philosophia* 2 (2008) 137–156.

G. J. BROOKE, 'Moving Mountains: from Sinai to Jerusalem,' in G. J. Brooke, H. NAJMAN and L. T. STUCKENBRUCK (eds.), *The Significance of Sinai. Traditions about Sinai and Divine Revelation in Judaism and Christianity*, Themes in Biblical Narrative 12 (Leiden–Boston 2008) 73–89.

J. BYRON, 'Cain's Rejected Offering: Interpretive Approaches to a Theological Problem,' *Journal for the Study of the Pseudepigrapha* 18 (2008) 3–22.

F. CALABI, '*Eremia*. Il deserto di Filone Alessandrino,' *Adamantius* 14 (2008) 9–23.

F. CALABI, *God's Acting, Man's Acting: Tradition and Philosophy in Philo of Alexandria*, Studies in Philo of Alexandria 4 (Leiden–Boston 2008).

F. CALABI, 'Filone di Alessandria: tra pensiero greco e tradizione ebraica,' *Materia Giudaica* 13 (2008) 23–34.

C. CARLIER, *La Cité de Moïse*, Monothéismes et Philosophie 11 (Turnhout 2008).

D. CIARLO, 'De mutatione nominum. L'interpretazione del cambiamento dei nomi biblici da Filone Alessandrino a Giovanni Crisostomo,' *Augustinianum* 48 (2008) 149–204.

N. G. COHEN, 'Philo Judeaus and the Torah True Library,' *Tradition* 41 (2008) 31–48.

C. DEUTSCH, 'Visions, Mysteries and the Intellectual Task: Text Work and Religious Experience in Philo and Clement,' in F. FLANNERY, C. SHANTZ and R. A. WERLINE (eds.), *Experientia, Volume 1: Inquiry into Religious Experience in Early Judaism and Early Christianity* (Atlanta 2008) 83–104.

J. Dillon, 'Philo and Hellenistic Platonism,' in F. Alesse (ed.), *Philo of Alexandria and Post-Aristotelian Philosophy*, Studies on Philo of Alexandria 5 (Leiden–Boston 2008) 223–232.

H. Dörrie, M. Baltes, C. Pietsch and M.-L. Lakmann, *Die philosophische Lehre des Platonismus: Theologia Platonica. Bausteine 182–205: Text, Übersetzung, Kommentar*, Der Platonismus in der Antike 7.1 (Stuttgart-Bad Cannstatt 2008), esp. 108–110, 414–415.

E. Eliasson, *The Notion of That Which Depends on Us in Plotinus and its Background*, Philosophia Antiqua 113 (Leiden–Boston 2008), esp. 126–130.

T. R. Elssner, *Josua und seine Kriege in jüdischer und christlicher Rezeptionsgeschichte*, Theologie und Frieden 37 (Stuttgart 2008).

L. H. Feldman, 'Philo's Interpretation of Korah,' in K. E. Pomykala (ed.), *Israel in the Wilderness. Interpretations of the Biblical Narratives in Jewish and Christian Traditions*, Themes in Biblical Narrative. Jewish and Christian Traditions 10 (Leiden–Boston 2008) 55–70.

E. Filler, 'Description of the Creation by Philo in the Light of the Neopythagorean Theory of Numbers [Hebrew],' *Daat* 62 (2008) 5–26.

E. Filler, 'The Nature of Number Seven in Propensity Towards Number One in Philo [Hebrew],' *Daat* 63 (2008) 5–26.

S. D. Fraade, 'Hearing and Seeing at Sinai: Interpretive Trajectories,' in G. J. Brooke, H. Najman and L. T. Stuckenbruck (eds.), *The Significance of Sinai. Traditions about Sinai and Divine Revelation in Judaism and Christianity*, Themes in Biblical Narrative 12 (Leiden–Boston 2008) 247–268.

S. Golberg, 'The Two Choruses Become One: The Absence–Presence of Women in Philo's On the Contemplative Life,' *Journal for the Study of Judaism in the Persian, Hellenistic and Roman period* 39 (2008) 459–470.

R. Gounelle and J. M. Prieur (eds.), *Le Décalogue au miroir des Pères*, Cahiers de Biblia Patristica 9 (Strasbourg 2008).

M. Graver, 'Philo of Alexandria and the Origins of the Stoic ΠΡΟΠΑΘΕΙΑΙ,' in F. Alesse (ed.), *Philo of Alexandria and Post-Aristotelian Philosophy*, Studies on Philo of Alexandria 5 (Leiden–Boston 2008) 197–221.

L. Gusella, 'Il deserto dei Terapeuti a confronto con quello di Esseni e Qumraniei,' *Adamantius* 14 (2008) 52–66.

M. Hadas-Lebel, 'Le désert lieu de la parole,' *Adamantius* 14 (2008) 39–42.

H. Hanafi, 'Philo of Alexandria: A Contribution to the Greek–Egyptian–Jewish Dialogue,' *Diotima* 36 (2008) 74–78.

A. Harker, *Loyalty and Dissidence in Roman Egypt: The Case of the Acta Alexandrinorum* (Cambridge 2008).

I. Heinemann, *The Reasons for the Commandments in Jewish Thought: From the Bible to the Renaissance*, translated by L. Levin (Boston 2008).

J. Herzer, 'Zwischen Loyalität und Machtstreben. Sozialgeschichliche Aspecckte des Pilatusbuldes bei Josephus und im Neuen Testament,' in C. Böttrich and J. Herzer (eds.), *Josephus und das Neue Testament. Wechselseitige Wahrnehmungen*, WUNT 209 (Tübingen 2008) 429–450.

R. A. Horsley, *Wisdom and Spiritual Transcendence at Corinth: Studies in First Corinthians* (Eugene 2008).

K. Klun, 'From the Decalogue to Natural Law: from the Philosophy of Philo of Alexandria [Slovenian],' *Phainomena: Journal of Phenomenology and Hermeneutics* 17 (2008) 27–61.

G. H. van Kooten, 'Image, Form and Transformation: a Semantic Taxonomy of Paul's "Morphic" Language,' in R. Buitenwerf, H. W. Hollander and J. Tromp (eds.), *Jesus, Paul, and Early Christianity*, Novum Testamentum Supplements 130 (Leiden–Boston 2008) 213–242.

G. H. van Kooten, 'Balaam as the Sophist par excellence in Philo of Alexandria: Philo's Projection of an Urgent Contemporary Debate onto Moses' Pentateuchal Narratives,' in *The Prestige of the Pagan Prophet Balaam in Judaism, Early Christianity and Islam*, Themes in Biblical narrative 11 (Leiden–Boston 2008) 131–161.

G. H. van Kooten, *Paul's Anthropology in Context. The Image of God, Assimilation to God, and Tripartite Man in Ancient Judaism, Ancient Philosophy and Early Christianity*, Wissenschaftliche Untersuchungen zum Neuen Testament 232 (Tübingen 2008).

E. Koskenniemi, 'Moses—A Well-Educated Man: A Look at the Educational Idea in Early Judaism,' *Journal for the Study of the Pseudepigrapha* 17 (2008) 281–296.

S. M. Lee, *The Cosmic Drama of Salvation, the Law, and Christ in Paul's Undisputed Writings: From Anthropological and Cosmological Perspectives* (diss. The Claremont Graduate University 2008).

C. Lévy, *Les Scepticismes*, Bibliographie thématique «Que sais-je» 2829 (Paris 2008), esp. 84–87.

C. Lévy, 'La conversion du scepticisme chez Philon d'Alexandrie,' in F. Alesse (ed.), *Philo of Alexandria and Post-Aristotelian Philosophy*, Studies on Philo of Alexandria 5 (Leiden–Boston 2008) 103–120.

C. Lévy, 'Études philoniennes,' *Bulletin de l'Association Guillaume Budé* 2 (2008) 156–166.

A. A. Long, 'Philo and Stoic Physics,' in F. Alesse (ed.), *Philo of Alexandria and Post-Aristotelian Philosophy*, Studies on Philo of Alexandria 5 (Leiden–Boston 2008) 121–140.

S. Lorenzen, *Das paulinische Eikon-Konzept. Semantische Analysen zur Sapientia Salomonis, zu Philo und den Paulusbriefen*, Wissenschaftliche Untersuchungen zum Neuen Testament 2.250 (Tübingen 2008).

L. LUGARESI, *Il teatro di Dio. Il problema degli spettacoli nel cristianesimo antico (II–IV secolo)*, Supplementi Adamantius (Brescia 2008), esp. 463–489.

H. MARGARITOU ANDRIANESI, 'On Philo's Platonism. The Natural Laws of Consequences in Philo,' *Diotima* 36 (2008) 52–73.

M. W. MARTIN, 'Progymnastic Topic Lists: A Compositional Template for Luke and Other Bioi,' *New Testament Studies* 54 (2008) 18–41.

E. F. MASON, *'You are a Priest Forever': Second Temple Jewish Messianism and the Priestly Christology of the Epistle to the Hebrews*, Studies on the Texts of the Desert of Judah 74 (Leiden–Boston 2008).

A. M. MAZZANTI, 'L'Egitto e il deserto: la dispersione e l'aggressione all'anima. Note a *Legum allegoriae* II.84–87,' *Adamantius* 14 (2008) 31–38.

P. MPUNGU MUZINGA, *La pratique des rituels de Nombres 19 pendant la période hellénistique et romain*, Études bibliques 58 (Pendé 2008).

E. MUEHLBERGER, 'The Representation of Theatricality in Philo's Embassy to Gaius,' *Journal for the Study of Judaism* 39 (2008) 46–67.

E. MÜHLENBERG, 'Das Problem der Offenbarung bei Philo von Alexandrien,' in E. MÜHLENBERG (ed.), *Gott in der Geschichte* (Berlin–New York 2008) 73–90.

H. NAJMAN, 'La recherche de la perfection dans le judaïsme ancien,' in J. RIAUD (ed.), *Les élites dans le monde biblique*, Bibliothèque d'Études Juives 32 (Paris 2008) 98–116.

J. H. NEWMAN, 'The Composition of Prayers and Songs in Philo's *De vita contemplativa*,' in A. HOUTMAN, A. D. JONG and M. MISSET-VAN DE WEG (eds.), *Empsychoi Logoi—Religious Innovations in Antiquity. Studies in Honour of Pieter Willem van der Horst*, Ancient Judaism and Early Christianity 73 (Leiden–Boston 2008) 457–468.

M. R. NIEHOFF, 'Questions and Answers in Philo and *Genesis Rabbah*,' *Journal for the Study of Judaism* 39 (2008) 337–366.

J. S. O'LEARY, 'Japanese Studies of Philo, Clement and Origen,' *Adamantius* 14 (2008) 395–402.

R. PEROTTA, *Haireseis: Gruppi, movimenti e fazioni del giudaismo antico e del cristianesimo (da Filone Alessandrino a Egesippo)* (Bologna 2008).

M.-Z. PETROPOLOU, *Animal Sacrifice in Ancient Greek Religion, Judaism, and Christianity, 100 BC to AD 200*, Oxford Classical Monographs (Oxford 2008).

T. E. PHILLIPS, ''Will the Wise Person Get Drunk?' The Background of the Human Wisdom in Luke 7:35 and Matthew 11:19,' *Journal of Biblical Literature* 127 (2008) 385–396.

R. RADICE, 'Philo and Stoic Ethics. Reflections on the Idea of Freedom,' in F. ALESSE (ed.), *Philo of Alexandria and Post-Aristotelian Philosophy*, Studies on Philo of Alexandria 5 (Leiden–Boston 2008) 141–167.

I. Ramelli 'Philosophical Allegoresis of Scripture in Philo and Its Legacy in Gregory of Nyssa,' *The Studia Philonica Annual* 20 (2008) 55–100.

G. Ranocchia, 'Moses against the Egyptian: the Anti-Epicurean Polemic in Philo,' in F. Alesse (ed.), *Philo of Alexandria and Post-Aristotelian Philosophy*, Studies on Philo of Alexandria 5 (Leiden–Boston 2008) 75–102.

G. Reydams-Schils, 'Philo of Alexandria on Stoic and Platonist Psycho-Physiology: the Socratic Higher Ground,' in F. Alesse (ed.), *Philo of Alexandria and Post-Aristotelian Philosophy*, Studies on Philo of Alexandria 5 (Leiden–Boston 2008) 169–195.

J. M. Rist, *What is Truth? From the Academy to the Vatican* (Cambridge 2008), esp. 35–38, 163–165.

A. Runesson, D. D. Binder and B. Olsson (eds.), *The Ancient Synagogue from its Origins to 200 C.E.: A Source Book* (Leiden–Boston 2008).

D. T. Runia, 'Worshipping the Visible Gods: Conflict and Accommodation in Hellenism, Hellenistic Judaism and Early Christianity,' in A. Houtman, A. D. Jong and M. Misset-van de Weg (eds.), *Empsychoi Logoi—Religious Innovations in Antiquity. Studies in Honour of Pieter Willem van der Horst*, Ancient Judaism and Early Christianity 73 (Leiden–Boston 2008) 47–61.

D. T. Runia, 'Philo and Hellenistic Doxography,' in F. Alesse (ed.), *Philo of Alexandria and Post-Aristotelian Philosophy*, Studies on Philo of Alexandria 5 (Leiden–Boston 2008) 13–52.

D. T. Runia, 'The Place of *De Abrahamo* in Philo's *Œuvre*,' *The Studia Philonica Annual* 20 (2008) 133–150.

D. T. Runia, E. Birnbaum, K. A. Fox, A. C. Geljon, H. M. Keizer, J. P. Martín, M. R. Niehoff, J. Riaud, G. Schimanowski and T. Seland, 'Philo of Alexandria: an Annotated Bibliography 2005,' *The Studia Philonica Annual* 20 (2008) 167–209.

D. T. Runia and G. E. Sterling (eds.), *The Studia Philonica Annual*, Vol. 20 (Atlanta 2008).

K.-G. Sandelin, *Sophia och Hennes Varld. Exegetiska uppsatser från fyra årtionden* (Åbo 2008).

K.-G. Sandelin, 'Måltidens symboliska betydelse i den alexandrinska judendomen. Ett bidrag till frågan om den kristna eukaristins bakgrund,' in K.-G. Sandelin (ed.), *Sophia och Hennes Varld. Exegetiska uppsatser från fyra årtionden* (Åbo 2008) 77–81.

K.-G. Sandelin, 'Vishetens måltid,' in Idem, *Sophia och Hennes Varld. Exegetiska uppsatser från fyra årtionden* (Åbo 2008) 82–100.

K.-G. Sandelin, 'Dragning till frammande kult bland judar under hellenistisk tid och tidlig kejsartid,' in Idem, *Sophia och Hennes Varld. Exegetiska uppsatser från fyra årtionden* (Åbo 2008) 101–159.

K.-G. SANDELIN, 'Filon från Alexandria och den grekisk-romerska kulturen,' in Idem, *Sophia och Hennes Varld. Exegetiska uppsatser från fyra årtionden* (Åbo 2008) 160–170.

M. L. SATLOW, 'Philo on Human Perfection,' *Journal of Theological Studies* 59 (2008) 500–519.

L. SAUDELLI, *Eraclito e la testimonianza di Filone di Alessandria* (diss. Università di Urbino–École Pratique des Hautes Études 2008).

R. W. SHARPLES, 'Philo and Post-Aristotelian Peripatetics,' in F. ALESSE (ed.), *Philo of Alexandria and Post-Aristotelian Philosophy,* Studies on Philo of Alexandria 5 (Leiden–Boston 2008) 55–73.

P. M. SHERMAN, *Translating the Tower: Genesis 11 and Ancient Jewish Interpretation* (diss. Emory University 2008).

P. M. SPRINKLE, *Law and Life: the Interpretation of Leviticus 18:5 in Early Judaism and in Paul,* Wissenschaftliche Untersuchungen zum Neuen Testament 2.241 (Tübingen 2008).

E. STAROBINSKI-SAFRAN, 'Le thème du désert dans le Midrach et chez Philon d'Alexandrie,' *Adamantius* 14 (2008) 67–78.

G. E. STERLING, '"Turning to God": Conversion in Greek-Speaking Judaism and Early Christianity,' in P. GRAY and G. O'DAY (eds.), *Scripture and Traditions: Essays on Early Judaism and Christianity in Honor of Carl R. Holladay* (Leiden 2008) 69–95.

C. TASSIN, 'Un grand pretre ideal? traditions juives anciennes sur Pinhas,' *Revue des Études Juives* 167 (2008) 1–22.

C. TERMINI, 'La speranza come cifra della relazione teandrica: Filone e Paolo a confronto,' in *Nuovo Testamento: Teologie in dialogo culturale. Scritti in onore di Romano Penna nel suo 70° compleanno,* Supplementi alla Rivista biblica 50 (Bologna 2008) 433–447.

M. TIWALD, ΕΙΝΑΙ ΒΕΒΑΙΩΣ ΙΟΥΔΑΙΟΣ (Ant XX,38). "Authentisches Jude-Sein" bei Josephus und Paulus,' *Protokolle zur Bibel* 17 (2008) 105–125.

J. C. DE VOS, 'Die Bedeutung des Landes Israel in den jüdischen Schriften der hellenistisch-römischen Zeit,' *Jahrbuch für biblische Theologie* 23 (2008) 75–99.

E. WASSERMAN, *The Death of the Soul in Romans 7: Sin, Death, and the Law in Light of Hellenistic Moral Psychology,* Wissenschaftliche Untersuchungen zum Neuen Testament 2.256 (Tübingen 2008).

E. WASSERMAN, 'Paul among the Philosophers: The Case of Sin in Romans 6–8,' *Journal for the Study of the New Testament* 30 (2008) 387–415.

L. WEHR, 'Hat der Mensch einen freien Willen? Parallelen zu einer aktuellen Debatte im Neuen Testament und dessen antiker Umwelt,' in T. SCHMELLER (ed.), *Neutestamentliche Exegese im 21. Jahrhundert. Grenzüberschreitungen. Für Joachim Gnilka* (Freiburg im Bresgau 2008) 394–409.

D. Westerkamp, 'The Philonic Distinction: German Enlightenment Historiography of Jewish Thought,' *History and Theory* 47 (2008) 533–559.

M. A. van Willigen, *Ambrosius' De Ioseph. Inleiding, filologisch commentaar en vertaling* (Zoetermeer 2008).

D. Winston, 'Philo and Maimonides on the Garden of Eden Narrative,' in C. Cohen, V. A. Hurovitz, A. Hurvitz, Y. Muffs, B. J. Schwartz and J. Tigay (eds.), *Birkat Shalom: Studies in the Bible, Ancient Near Eastern Literature, and Postbiblical Judaism Presented to Shalom M. Paul on the Occasion of His Seventieth Birthday* (Winona Lake 2008) 989–1002.

B. G. Wold, 'Ethics in 4QInstruction and the New Testament,' *Novum Testamentum* 50 (2008) 286–300.

J. Woyke, 'Nochmals zu den 'schwachen und unfähigen Elementen' (Gal. 4.9): Paulus, Philo und διε στοιχεῖα τοῦ κόσμου,' *New Testament Studies* 54 (2008) 221–234.

D. Zeller, 'Schöpfungsglaube und fremde Religion bei Philo von Alexandrien,' in L. Bormann (ed.), *Schöpfung, Monotheismus und fremde Religionen*, Biblisch-Theologische Studien 95 (Neukirchen-Vluyn 2008) 125–148.

X. Zhang, *Feiluo sixiang daolun II: youtai de lüfa he ziwo de zhiliao [An Introduction to the Thought of Philo (II): The Jewish Law and Self-Therapy]* (Beijing 2008).

2009

R. Alciati, 'Monachesimo come tempio: il cantiere di Cassiano nuovo Chira,' *Adamantius* 15 (2009) 246–269, esp. 255–258.

M. Alexandre Jr, 'Philo of Alexandria and Hellenic Paideia,' *Euphrosyne* N.S. 37 (2009) 121–130.

C. Anderson, *The Ambiguity of Nature: Philo of Alexandria's Views on the Sensible World* (diss. Southampton 2009).

J. M. G. Barclay, 'Grace Within and Beyond Reason: Philo and Paul in Dialogue,' in P. Middleton, A. Paddison and K. Wenell (eds.), *Paul, Grace and Freedom: Essays in Honour of John Kennith Riches* (London 2009) 9–21.

M. V. Blischke, '"Die Gerechten aber werden ewig leben (Sap 5,17)": begrenzte und entgrenzte Zeit in der Sapientia Salomonis,' in R. G. Kratz (ed.), *Zeit und Ewigkeit als Raum göttlichen Handelns*, Beihefte zur Zeitschrift für die alttestamentliche Wissenschaft 390 (Berlin–New York 2009) 187–212.

P. Borgeaud, T. Römer and Y. Volokhine (eds.), *Interprétations de Moïse: Égypte, Judée, Grèce et Rome*, Jerusalem Studies in Religion and Culture 10 (Leiden–Boston 2009).

A. P. Bos, 'Philo on God as 'arche geneseôs',' *Journal of Jewish Studies* 60 (2009) 1–16.

F. Calabi, 'Il re in Filone di Alessandria,' in S. Gastaldi and J.-F. Pradeau (eds.), *Le philosophe, le roi, le tyran*, Collegium Politicum 3 (Sankt Augustin 2009) 53–69.

F. Calabi, 'Dio e l'ordine del mondo in Filone di Alessandria,' *Études Platoniciennes* 5 (2009) 23–39.

N. De Lange, 'The Celebration of the Passover in Greco-Roman Alexandria,' in C. Batsch and M. Vârtejanu-Joubert (eds.), *Manières de penser dans l'Antiquité méditerranéenne et orientale: Mélanges offerts à Francis Schmidt par ses élèves, ses collègues et ses amis*, Supplements to the Journal for the Study of Judaism 134 (Leiden–Boston 2009) 157–166.

D. Flusser, *Judaism of the Second Temple Period. Volume 2: The Jewish Sages and their Literature* (Grand Rapids 2009).

S. Gambetti, *The Alexandrian Riots of 38 C.E. and the Persecution of the Jews. A Historical Reconstruction*, Supplements to the Journal for the Study of Judaism 135 (Leiden–Boston 2009).

G. S. Goering, *Wisdom's Root Revealed. Ben Sira and the Election of Israel*, Supplements to the Journal for the Study of Judaism 139 (Leiden–Boston 2009).

J. Gundry, '"Or Who Gave First to Him, so that He Shall Receive Recompense?" (Rom 11,35): Divine Benefaction and Human Boasting in Paul and Philo,' in U. Schnelle (ed.), *The Letter to the Romans*, Bibliotheca Ephemeridum Theologicarum Lovaniensium 226 (Leuven 2009) 25–53.

A. van der Hoek, 'God Beyond Knowing: Clement of Alexandria and Discourse,' in A. B. McGowan, B. E. Daley, S.J. and T. J. Gaden (eds.), *God in Early Christian Thought: Essays in Memory of Lloyd G. Patterson*, Supplements to Vigiliae Christianae 94 (Leiden–Boston 2009) 37–60.

A. Kamesar, 'Biblical Interpretation in Philo,' in A. Kamesar (ed.), *The Cambridge Companion to Philo* (Cambridge etc. 2009) 65–91.

A. Kamesar (ed.), *The Cambridge Companion to Philo* (Cambridge etc. 2009).

M. B. Kartzow, *Gossip and Gender: Othering of Speech in the Pastoral Epistles*, Beihefte zur Zeitschrift für die neutestamentliche Wissenschaft und die Kunde der älteren Kirche 164 (Berlin 2009).

A. Kerkeslager, 'Agrippa I and the Judeans of Alexandria in the Wake of the Violence in 38 CE,' *Revue des Études Juives* 168 (2009) 1–49.

C. Köckert, *Christliche Kosmologie und kaiserzeitliche Philosophie*, Studien und Texte zu Antike und Christentum 56 (Tübingen 2009).

M. Landfester and B. Egger (eds.), *Dictionary of Greek and Latin Authors and Texts*, Brill's New Pauly Supplements 2 (Leiden 2009).

J. R. Levison, *Filled with the Spirit* (Grand Rapids 2009), esp. 142–159 and passim.

C. Lévy, 'Philo's Ethics,' in A. Kamesar (ed.), *The Cambridge Companion to Philo* (Cambridge etc. 2009) 146–171.

Y. Liebes, 'The Work of the Chariot and the Work of Creation as Mystical Teachings in Philo of Alexandria,' in D. A. Green and L. S. Lieber (eds.), *Scriptural Exegesis* (Oxford 2009) 105–121.

S. D. Mackie, 'Seeing God in Philo of Alexandria: The Logos, the Powers, or the Existent One?' *The Studia Philonica Annual* 21 (2009) 25–48.

J. P. Martín (ed.), *Filón de Alejandría Obras Completas*, Vol. 1 (Madrid 2009).

J. P. Martín (ed.), *Filón de Alejandría Obras Completas*, Vol. 5 (Madrid 2009).

G. Maschio, 'Ambrogio di Milano: note sulla formazione e sul metodo di lavoro,' *Augustinianum* 49 (2009) 145–175.

M. D. Matlock, *Traditions of Prose Prayer in Early Jewish Literature* (diss. Hebrew Union College—Jewish Institute of Religion (Ohio) 2009).

G. W. E. Nickelsburg and M. E. Stone (eds.), *Early Judaism: Texts and Documents on Faith and Piety*, Revised Edition (Minneapolis 2009).

R. A. Norris, 'Who is the Demiurge? Irenaeus' Picture of God in *Adversus haereses* 2,' in A. B. McGowan, B. E. Daley S.J. and T. J. Gaden (eds.), *God in Early Christian Thought: Essays in Memory of Lloyd G. Patterson*, Supplements to Vigiliae Christianae 94 (Leiden–Boston 2009) 9–36.

T. Novick, 'Perspective, Paideia, and Accommodation in Philo,' *The Studia Philonica Annual* 21 (2009) 49–62.

B. A. Pearson, *Ancient Gnosticism: Traditions and Literature* (Minneapolis 2009).

R. Radice, 'Philo's Theology and Theory of Creation,' in A. Kamesar (ed.), *The Cambridge Companion to Philo* (Cambridge etc. 2009) 124–145.

T. Rajak, *Translation and Survival. The Greek Bible of the Ancient Jewish Diaspora* (Oxford–New York 2009).

J. R. Royse, 'The Works of Philo,' in A. Kamesar (ed.), *The Cambridge Companion to Philo* (Cambridge etc. 2009) 32–64.

D. T. Runia, 'Philo and the Early Christian Fathers,' in A. Kamesar (ed.), *The Cambridge Companion to Philo* (Cambridge etc. 2009) 210–230.

D. T. Runia, 'The Theme of Flight and Exile in the Allegorical Thought World of Philo of Alexandria,' *The Studia Philonica Annual* 21 (2009) 1–24.

D. T. Runia, 'Philo of Alexandria,' in G. Oppy and N. Trakakis (eds.), *The History of Western Philosophy of Religion. Volume 1: Ancient Philosophy of Religion* (Durham 2009) 133–144.

D. T. Runia, E. Birnbaum, A. C. Geljon, H. M. Keizer, J. P. Martín, M. R. Niehoff, J. Riaud, G. Schimanowski and T. Seland, 'Philo of

Alexandria: an Annotated Bibliography 2006,' *The Studia Philonica Annual* 21 (2009) 73–122.

D. T. RUNIA and G. E. STERLING (eds.), *The Studia Philonica Annual*, Vol. 21 (Atlanta 2009).

P. SCHAEFER, *The Origins of Jewish Mysticism* (Tübingen 2009), esp. 154–174.

D. R. SCHWARTZ, 'Philo, his Family, and his Times,' in A. KAMESAR (ed.), *The Cambridge Companion to Philo* (Cambridge etc. 2009) 9–31.

F. SIEGERT, 'Philo and the New Testament,' in A. KAMESAR (ed.), *The Cambridge Companion to Philo* (Cambridge etc. 2009) 175–209.

P. SOISSON, 'Un avatar du paganisme : un Christ nommé Jesus,' *Cahiers du Cercle Ernest Renan* 245 (2009) 5–30.

G. E. STERLING, 'How Do You Introduce Philo of Alexandria? The Cambridge Companion to Philo,' *The Studia Philonica Annual* 21 (2009) 63–72.

H. SVEBAKKEN, *Philo of Alexandria's Exposition of the Tenth Commandment* (diss. Loyola University of Chicago 2009).

C. TERMINI, 'Philo's Thought within the Context of Middle Judaism,' in A. KAMESAR (ed.), *The Cambridge Companion to Philo* (Cambridge etc. 2009) 95–123.

D. C. TIMMER, *Creation, Tabernacle, and Sabbath. The Sabbath Frame of Exodus 31:12–17; 35:1–3 in Exegetical and Theological Perspective*, Forschungen zur Religion und Literatur des Alten und Neuen Testaments 227 (Göttingen 2009).

F. TRABBATONI, 'Philo, *De opificio mundi* 7–12,' in M. BONAZZI and J. OPSOMER (eds.), *The Origins of the Platonic System: Platonisms of the Early Empire and their Philosophical Contexts*, Collection des Études Classiques (Leuven 2009) 113–122.

D. WINSTON, 'Philo and the Rabbinic Literature,' in A. KAMESAR (ed.), *The Cambridge Companion to Philo* (Cambridge etc. 2009) 231–253.

A. YOSHIKO REED, 'The Construction and Subversion of Patriarchal Perfection: Abraham and Exemplarity in Philo, Josephus, and the Testament of Abraham,' *Journal for the Study of Judaism* 40 (2009) 185–212.

2010

P. ASHWIN-SIEJKOWSKI, *Clement of Alexandria on Trial: The Evidence of 'Heresy' from Photius' Bibliotheca*, Supplements to Vigiliae Christianae 101 (Leiden 2010).

A. P. Bos, 'De uitleiding uit Egypte in de Openbaring van Johannes, bij Philo van Alexandrië en in de Hymne van de Parel,' in K. van der Ziel and H. Holwerda (eds.), *Het stralend teken. 60 jaar exegetische vergezichten van dr. D. Holwerda* (Franeker 2010) 18–27.

D. K. Burge, *First Century Guides to Life and Death in the Roman East: a Comparative Study of Epictetus, Philo and Peter* (diss. Macquarie University, Sydney 2010).

F. Calabi, *Storia del pensiero guidaico ellenistico* (Brescia 2010).

M. DelCogliano, *Basil of Caesarea's Anti-Eunomian Theory of Names: Christian Theology and Late-Antique Philosophy in the Fourth Century Trinitarian Controversy*, Supplements to Vigiliae Christianae 103 (Leiden 2010), esp. 79–87.

L. Duprée Sandgren, *Vines Intertwined: A History of Jews and Christians from the Babylonian Exile to the Advent of Islam* (Peabody, Mass. 2010), esp. 217–224, 565–568.

A. C. Geljon, 'Philo's Interpretation of Noah,' in M. E. Stone, A. Amihay and V. Hillel (eds.), *Noah and his Book(s)*, Early Judaism and its Literature 28 (Atlanta 2010) 183–191.

A. Klostergaard Petersen, 'Alexandrian Judaism. Rethinking a Problematic Cultural Category,' in G. Hinge and J. Krasilnikoff (eds.), *Alexandria. A Cultural and Religious Meltingpot* (Aarhus 2010).

M. Mira, 'Philo of Alexandria,' in L. F. Mateo-Seco and G. Maspero (eds.), *The Brill Dictionary of Gregorius of Nyssa*, Supplements to Vigiliae Christianae 99 (Leiden–Boston 2010) 601–603 and passim.

H. Najman, *Past Renewals: Interpretative Authority, Renewed Revelation and the Quest for Perfection in Jewish Antiquity*, JSJSup 53 (Leiden 2010).

M. R. Niehoff, 'The Symposium of Philo's Therapeutae: Displaying Jewish Identity in an Increasingly Roman World,' *Greek, Roman, and Byzantine Studies* 50 (2010) 95–117.

M. R. Niehoff, 'Philo's Scholarly Inquiries into the Story of Paradise,' in M. Bockmuehl and G. G. Stroumsa (eds.), *Paradise in Antiquity: Jewish and Christian Views* (Cambridge 2010).

BOOK REVIEW SECTION

TESSA RAJAK, *Translation and Survival: The Greek Bible of the Ancient Jewish Diaspora*. Oxford; Oxford University Press, 2009; xvi + 380 pages. ISBN 978-0-19-955867-4. Price $140, £74.

Tessa Rajak, professor of Ancient History at the University of Reading (UK), has published an eminently readable, elegantly written, well-researched, and fascinating book on the first Jewish Greek Bible translation as a cultural artefact and icon. This is not a traditional introduction to the study of the Septuagint. On the contrary, it presupposes quite some knowledge of research on the LXX and other early Greek translations of the Hebrew Bible ('The Three') on the part of its readers. Her thesis is (*inter alia*): "The existence of a Bible in Greek made possible the remarkable flowering of the diaspora in the Graeco-Roman Mediterranean (p. 7)." Based on six Grinfield lectures given at Oxford University in 1995-96, the book now contains ten chapters, followed by an impressive bibliography (pp. 314-365) and an index of names and subjects (alas, there is no *index locorum*).

After having set out in the introductory chapter what is the aim of her study and having given a brief summary of its results, in chapter one Rajak deals with the *Letter of Aristeas*. She argues that in this document memory and myth are intertwined, it is a mixture of fact and fiction, but tradition is not wholly to be dismissed. "Rather, the *Letter* is an embodiment of Alexandrian Jewish identity, a literary vehicle precisely for its collective memory (p. 51)." Interestingly, a degree of ambivalence towards the royal benefactor (Ptolemy II) lurks within it. Rajak stresses that, whatever the origins of the LXX, this large-scale translation enterprise was unique in the Hellenistic world. Chapter two is about culture and power in Ptolemaic Alexandria and in it Rajak argues at length that, although Ptolemy's involvement in the translation project is not demonstrable, the claim that he commissioned the translation of the Torah is quite credible when set against the background of that king's ambitious cultural imperialism and the intellectual concerns of his age. In the early days of Alexandria, the legacy of Alexander the Great kept alive curiosity about other cultures and their laws. "The Jewish Torah, defined as a subject people's legal system, would thus recommend itself to the King as a proper object of his attention (p. 84)." Chapter three deals with the variegated nature of the Jewish Diaspora. Rajak presents a short but vivid sketch of the landmarks in its eventful history, stressing the continuity of its social and religious institutions, especially the synagogue where the LXX played such a central role, and discussing the various levels of individual and group integration into city life. In this connection, she also deals with the phenomenon of pagan sympathizers ("Godfearers") and with manifestations of tension and anti-Jewish violence. This is a fine chapter with many useful insights. In chapter four, on language and identity in the Greek Bible, Rajak discusses the Jews' adaptation to the "colonial language"and contends that the translators shaped the Koine Greek in such a way as to make it possible both to "go Greek" and to "stay Jewish." The fact that LXX Greek is often more oriented towards the source than the target language made a connection for readers and hearers with the traditional language of the Jews, Hebrew. Rajak emphasizes the symbolic role of the Hebrew language as a cultural reference point, a source of unity and a preserver of tradition, even in the Greek-speaking Diaspora. The language of the LXX "with its deliberate mirroring of Hebrew balance, syntactic patters, and semantic structures (…), reflects a kind of recalcitrance, a reluctance to accede totally to a Hellenizing 'project,' which by the same token could not be ignored" (p. 153) and it was "a vehicle for quiet cultural resistance"(p. 156)—hence the word "survival" in the book's title. But Diaspora Jews did not speak Hebraizing Greek in daily life. In chapter five, on representing and subverting power, Rajak shows how translations of late biblical texts (Daniel and Wisdom, among others) could have worked as response or resistance to external political authority, often markedly subversive. Here belong, e.g., representations of tyrannical rage but also polemics against idol worship, where motifs from Greek political philosophy and those of oriental Wisdom literature were brought together. Chapter six deals with uses of Scripture in Hellenistic Judaism. Here Rajak asks how the centrality of the Bible functioned in Jewish lives and how far it made the Jews different from other groups (here she also explains why the term "centrality" is to be preferred to "canonicity"). She shows how the Greek Bible created a unity across place and time, even if differently read in different circles. Jewish Diaspora culture was built upon the Greek Bible. The many (fragmentary) products of Graeco-Jewish writers, never without elements of scripturalization, pass review here, with Rajak's acute comments. Chapter seven, "Parallels and Models," discusses the comparison that is often drawn between the role of the Bible for the Jews and the position of the Homeric poems among the Greeks, but she highlights the differences between the two rather than the similarities. She also assesses the role of the Bible in the Dead Sea Scrolls and in the New Testament, both of them products of "Bible-soaked" communities, and contrasts them with the Greek Diaspora Jews who, however Bible-centred they were, "perhaps lived *by* but not *through* Torah" (p. 13), or "lived *with* Torah, rather than fully *by* or *through* Torah" (p. 256), probably because they lacked an apocalyptic mindset. Rajak's formulation betrays her awareness of the speculative nature of this observation. But indeed, direct biblical quotes are almost lacking in Graeco-Jewish literature, except for Philo. "The main thrust in Hellenistic-Jewish literature is typically not inward, towards community building and resistance to the environment, but outward, towards making connections" (p. 250), with the non-Jewish world, that is. Chapter eight traces the influence of the Greek Bible among pagan Greeks and Romans and Rajak is here unabashedly a maximalist, refreshingly so. All well-known texts (the Alexandrian antisemitists, Pseudo-Longinus , Numenius, etc.) are well discussed, but in this chapter I found some glaring omissions. In her discussion of reflections of the story of Solomon's judgement in the dispute between two mothers she does mention the papyrus of Philiscus (p. 267) but not the famous fresco in Pompeii that is often deemed to represent that story (see, e.g., J. Berry, *The Complete Pompeii*, London 2007, p. 88). Moreover, she states that Numenius "manifests the most extensive acquaintance with the Greek Bible of all pagan thinkers" (p. 269). That can only be said when one leaves Porphyry out of account, and he is nowhere mentioned in the book, even though there was no pagan author who had a more profound knowledge of the LXX than Porphyry (see my "Porphyry and Judaism" [forthcoming]; also G. Rinaldi, *La Bibbia dei pagani* [2 vols., Bologna 1997-98)] could have served Rajak well here). Finally, there is a good discussion of the Jewish elements in the magical papyri (but Morton Smith's seminal article on this topic is not mentioned (see his *Studies in the Cult of Yahweh* [Leiden 1996] 2.242-256)). The last chapter (nine) is an excellent and original treatment of "The Septuagint between Jews and Christians." Here, among other things, Rajak deals very critically with the traditional "abandonment theory," i.e., the theory that after the appropriation of the LXX by the Christians, the Jews dropped it and turned to the more literal versions of Aquila and others. "The abandonment theory can be easily dismantled and the evidence points rather to a growth of Jewish interest during the second century c.e. in a multiplicity of Greek versions, including their own 'old Greek'." This dismantling is done in an exemplary way and Rajak clearly shows how a Christian agenda (beginning with Christian authors in the second century c.e.) kept alive this ill-founded theory till recently. Rajak is certainly right that the LXX remained in use among Jews till the early Middle Ages.

Apart from my critical remark on chapter eight, there are some other points to be criticized, albeit mostly non-essential ones. In bibliographical matters there are some irregularities. Apart from inconsistent use of italics, in the cumulative bibliography several items are lacking which are referred to in the footnotes: Daiches 1941, Nicolson 2003, Barclay 2002, Rajak 2001 are all referred to (see p. 90 n. 74, p. 258 n. 2, p. 259 n. 4) but not mentioned in the bibliography. At pp. 43 and 301 Pausanias and Augustine are referred to but without indication of the *locus*. At p. 123 Sardis is said to be a city in Phrygia (it should be Lydia). At pp. 148-152 Rajak argues that knowledge of Hebrew was not lost in Alexandria but the evidence she adduces is at best circumstantial; and I do not believe there was a situation of trilingualism among the Jews there (see p. 163). At p. 182 *apothegm* should be *apophthegm*; and *stratiôtês* is not "army" but "soldier" (p. 189). At p. 219 Rajak says of Philo the Elder's poem on Jerusalem "we know nothing more than the title," but in fact we do have six fragments of that poem (see Holladay, *Fragments* 2.205-299)—he is the same as Philo the epic poet mentioned by Rajak at p. 115 (see A.-M. Denis, *Introduction à la literature religieuse judéo-hellénistique* [Turnhout 2000] 2.1192, a book not mentioned by Rajak). And on my interpretation of *Exagôgê* 74-5, the dramatist Ezekiel does not say that Moses received God's throne only "temporarily" (p. 229). But these are mere quibbles that do not detract at all from the great value of this fine book that I recommend unreservedly to all scholars who are interested in the early Jewish Diaspora. Needless to say, I recommend it also to all students of Philo, who figures prominently in this book.

Pieter W. van der Horst
pwvdh@xs4all.nl

MANFRED LANDFESTER, with Brigitte Egger, eds., *Geschichte der antiken Texte: Autoren- und Werklexikon. Der neue Pauly*, Supplemente Band 2. Stuttgart and Weimar: J. B. Metzler, 2007.
MANFRED LANDFESTER, with Brigitte Egger, eds., trans. and ed. Tina Jerke and Volker Dallman, *Dictionary of Greek and Latin Authors and Texts. Brill's New Pauly*, Supplements Volume 2. Leiden and Boston: Brill, 2009.

The volumes of *Der neue Pauly*, presented as an updated, more compact replacement for the older but still useful *Real-Encyclopädie* of Pauly-Wissowa, began to be published in 1996. This new Pauly has been further provided with three supplemental volumes, of which vol. 1 presents an overview of ancient chronological systems (via reigns, kings, emperors, and so on) while vol. 3 is a beautifully printed historical atlas. Vol. 2, which concerns us here, "illustrates how the principal works of Greek and Latin literature have inscribed themselves upon the cultural memory of Europe and its intellectual relatives" (ET, vi). We thus find entries for 250 authors from the Greek and Latin world (ranging in alphabetical order from Achilles Tatius to Zosimus the historian), a survey of their principal writings, along with their manuscript tradition, early and modern editions, and translations and commentaries. That the entries provide a concise overview of the manuscript attestation of the authors is a noteworthy and valuable feature of the volume. All of this material was first published in German and then translated into English.

As would be expected, Philo of Alexandria receives due attention. But there are, of course, many other entries that will interest any student of antiquity. Much valuable information will be found here on the major (and not so major) writers, from Homer through the Athenian age, and on into the Hellenistic and Roman periods. There are substantial entries on Josephus and on the Bible, both the MT/LXX and the NT. These last two entries have some shortcomings, but succinctly present important aspects of the transmission history of the Bible.

My focus here will be on the article on Philo, which was written by Landfester, so let us turn to that in the German version.[1] After an overview of the material, we find a listing of twelve of Philo's works, by title in Greek, Latin, and German, along with a synopsis of each work. One idiosyncrasy here is that the works are designated, for further reference in the article, by abbreviations taken from the Greek titles. Thus, e.g., *De animalibus* is cited as *"Alog. z."* (from the end of the Greek title: ἄλογα ζῷα), *De providentia* as *"Pron."* (from Περὶ προνοίας), and *De aeternitate mundi* as *"Aphthars."* (from ἀφθαρσίας). Surely it would have been more useful to readers to follow some more or less standard abbreviations, since those are what will be found in the literature.[2] Citing only a small portion of Philo's works, even if they are perhaps the principal ones, is probably an inevitable result of trying to cover all of ancient Greek and Latin literature in one volume. (I note, e.g., that of Plato's thirty-six works only sixteen are listed. On the other hand, all of Josephus's much smaller number of works are cited.) Nevertheless, since there is much blank space on many pages, I wonder whether some alternative page layout might have allowed a fuller

---

[1] Manfred Landfester, "Philon aus Alexandreia (Philo Iudaeus)," *Geschichte*, 456–59; "Philo of Alexandria (Philo Judaeus)," *Dictionary*, 479–83. By the way, it is unusual to find "Philon aus Alexandreia" rather than "Philon von Alexandreia."

[2] Similarly, the reader of the Aristotle article is not well served by having Περὶ ψυχῆς cited as *"Psych."* rather than *"De anima,"* or Περὶ οὐρανοῦ cited as *"Uran."* (English *"Ouran."*) rather than *"De caelo."*

listing.[3] But it would be uncharitable to complain of the choices that had to be made.

Regrettably, though, the information provided for these twelve works is not always accurate. For example, regarding *Aet.* (to use the usual term) we are told "frg. erh." (ET: "extant in frgs.") since this work seems to break off before its conclusion, although we are not given that qualification for *Contempl.*, a considerably shorter work. The description of *Opif.* as "im Wesentlichen wörtliche Erklärung des Pentateuch-Inhalts" (ET: "essentially a literal explanation of the content of the Pentateuch") seems to miss something crucial. It is certainly misleading to say of *Prob.* "erster Teil verloren" (ET: "first part lost") simply because its companion piece, as cited in *Prob.* 1, is lost. And the Latin title of *Prob.* begins "Quod probus omnis" in the German but "Quod omnis probus" (correctly) in the English.

Next, the article turns to the manuscripts. Naturally, one could hardly expect that such an article could provide more than a cursory glance at the material that occupies hundreds of pages in the Cohn–Wendland–Reiter prolegomena, not to speak of the many further books and articles. In fact, what we find is a listing of seven manuscripts: V, M, A, U, G, H, and Laurentianus 85,10.[4] While any discussion of the textual evidence for Philo is certainly to be commended, I must confess to having some doubts as to the usefulness of such a listing. V (Vindobonensis theol. gr. 29) is a well-known manuscript, both for its text of *Opif.* and for its *pinax* containing an important list of works of Philo.[5] But the others are, I believe, rarely if ever cited in the modern translations into German, English, and French. What would, I believe, be more important would be some notice of the Coptos papyrus, which contains the complete text of *Sacr.* and *Her.* and was used by Cohn and Wendland, and perhaps even of the Oxyrhynchus papyrus, which preserves fragments of several books, including at least one book not otherwise extant. These are both of the third century, thus antedating by some 800 years any of the manuscripts cited. In fact, in other articles the significance of the papyri for the transmission of texts is often emphasized.[6]

---

[3] And note that indeed almost half of p. 459 is blank.

[4] This is "F" in PCW, but that siglum is not utilized here, in contrast to the other manuscripts.

[5] See the photograph in David T. Runia, *Philo in Early Christian Literature: A Survey* (CRINT 3.3; Assen: Van Gorcum; Minneapolis: Fortress, 1993), 21.

[6] For the New Testament, of course, papyri provide extensive evidence within a century or two of the works themselves. Nevertheless, Landfester, in his entry "Bibel (Novum Testamentum)," says: "Im Einzelnen ist der Wert der Papyri für die Textkonstitution wegen ihres geringen Umfangs eher gering" (ET: "Because of their small size (and limited content), the value of individual papyri for the textual constitution is minimal"). This assertion hardly reflects the important role that the papyri (especially the early and exten-

We then find citations of important editions (including the *editio princeps* by Turnebus, Mangey's 1742 edition, and PCW), early translations (into Latin and Armenian), modern translations (PCH, PLCL, and PAPM), and commentaries. All of these should be familiar to anyone doing research in Philo, and Landfester generally gives a clear overview of their dates and contents. However, here also there are some errors to be found. For example, Conybeare was not the editor of the 1892 Venice edition of the works of Philo found in Armenian beyond those already edited by Aucher. Under the "early translations" (ÜF = Frühe Übersetzungen) the ancient Latin translation is correctly assigned to the fourth century; however, it is said to contain the *Quaestiones* in two volumes, although the arrangement in "two volumes" is hardly the fourth century format, but derives from Petit's 1973 edition, presented in two volumes, which is cited here. On the other hand, we are not given a date here for the Armenian translation, but only for Aucher's two volumes of 1822 and 1826. Fortunately, the reader was told under the listing of *QG* and *QE* (works #11) that the Armenian in fact dates from the sixth century. Finally, it seems that Mangey's Latin translation of his Greek text is misinterpreted as a commentary.

The translation by Marcus of *QG* and *QE* in PLCL Supp 1–2 is cited. But we are told explicitly that the older English translation by Yonge (reprinted in 1993) and the German and French translations (PCH and PAPM) do not include the works preserved in Armenian. A reader would thus miss the following resources: Yonge's translation of *QG* 1–3, the translation by Früchtel of *Prov.* (via Aucher's Latin) in PCH 7, as well as the translation by Hadas-Lebel of *Prov.* (via Aucher's Latin for the parts not preserved in Greek) in PAPM 35, the translation by Terian of *Anim.* in PAPM 36, the translation by Mercier of *QG* in PAPM 34A and 34B, and the translation by Terian of *QE* in PAPM 34C. While PLCL is cited, there is no indication that it includes in PLCL 9 a translation by Colson of the Greek fragments of *Prov.* preserved by Eusebius. Since no notice is taken of *De Deo*, the translation, with much valuable additional commentary and references, by Siegert is also not listed. From what is cited by Landfester, the reader wishing to consult the cited works found in Armenian other than *QG* and *QE*, i.e., *Anim.* and *Prov.*, both of which contain much material of interest to classical scholars, might proceed to Aucher's 1822 edition, surely not the

---

sive $\mathfrak{P}^{45}$, $\mathfrak{P}^{46}$, $\mathfrak{P}^{47}$, $\mathfrak{P}^{66}$, $\mathfrak{P}^{72}$, and $\mathfrak{P}^{75}$, as well as the more than one hundred others) have played in New Testament textual criticism since at least the 1930s. For example, Eldon Jay Epp, "Textual Criticism, New Testament," *ABD* 6.420, comments on the papyri and majuscules from before the fourth century: "These mss, because of their extraordinarily early dates, occupy a position of supreme importance in all aspects of NT textual criticism, especially its history and theory."

most accessible source for the usual scholar of antiquity, rather than to the volumes in PAPM. However, Terian's earlier 1981 edition of *Anim.* with commentary is listed.

The listings conclude with the citation of three recent commentaries: Radice on *Leg.*, Runia on *Opif.*, and van der Horst on *Flacc.* It is pleasing to find as the last two entries here the volumes of the Philo of Alexandria Commentary Series.

I have so far been speaking of the German original. The English translation follows the German very closely, in format and in details. But there are a few slips here and there. Under the listing for *Aet.* (works #4) "De mundo" in German has become "De mando" in English. In the description of *Opif.* (#8) "Exegetic Works" should be "Exegetic work," and "bases" should be "basis." The English title of *Legat.* (works #10) is cited as "On the Embassy to zu Gaius." And PCW is said to be "without the work extant in Armen.," where we should have "works" (for "Werke").

Of the shortcomings noted here, some are simply the inevitable results of the format of the work. It is, of course, difficult to know what to choose to say about the reception history of Philo or other important figures in only a few pages, and any selection is bound to create problems and to leave out aspects that will seem important to some scholars. Also perhaps inevitably any volume that covers all of Greek and Roman antiquity will fall short on occasion. Nevertheless, the scholar seeking orientation with respect to the transmission of the works of Philo and of other important authors of antiquity will find much helpful material here.

James R. Royse
Claremont, CA

José Pablo Martín (ed.), *Filón de Alejandría. Obras Completas Volumen I.* Madrid: Editorial Trotta, 2009, 358 pp. ISBN 978-84-9879-022-1. Price €20.

Two millennia after the monumental contribution of Philo of Alexandria to Jewish Hellenistic philosophy and the interpretation of Scripture, this master philosopher remains alive as a significant Greek author. He left us a corpus within preserved Greek literature only exceeded in size by authors like Plato, Aristotle, Diodorus Siculus, Josephus and Plutarch, and the interest in his work has been surprisingly on the increase, especially in the last three decades.

In Spanish, we already had Triviño's incomplete translation in five volumes and the more recent versions of S. T. Tovar, *Sobre los sueños* and

Sobre José, and S. Vidal, *Los terapeutas: De vita contemplativa*, among others. But the need for a new and complete critical translation of Philo was so strongly felt by J. P. Martín, that he inspired the creation of a translation project entitled *Philo Hispanicus*. The first fruits of *Filón de Alejandria. Obras completas*, to be published in eight volumes, are now available. Volume I is the first of the collection, and two others are already finished: Volume V (2009), and Volume II (2010).

Martín justifies the relevance and opportunity of this project of a critical translation, which emerges from a judicious work of academic research. In his own words, the aim of the translation presented here is "to integrally contain the authentic treatises of Philo received in the original Greek or in the Armenian version; to have a critical introduction by experts in each language of origin; to express the original content as faithfully as possible . . . ; to contain introductions and annotations on the language, the ideology and the history of the texts; to be followed by bibliographies and indices in order to facilitate access for the general reader and also for the scholar interested in internal information or willing to expand his research in the complex aspects of the work" (p. 87).

This first volume of the complete works of Philo opens with a "General Introduction" to the edition and includes the translation of four of his most significant treatises: *De opificio mundi*, and *Legum allegoriae 1-3*. In his introduction to the whole corpus, J. P. Martín magisterially accomplishes three convergent objectives: illuminating issues in need of new research on the life and work of Philo, harmonizing information transmitted by scholars in different periods and situations, and suggesting new perspectives of analysis that will give a better understanding of the structures that inform his philosophical and theological thinking. This invaluable introduction, which has the length of a mini-dissertation, is developed in six parts, in which the following themes are treated and discussed:

1. "Philo of Alexandria": his life, his family and education; his audience; political and philosophical activity; the political and social situation of the Jewish community in Alexandria.

2. "Philo's works": (1) literary genre and classification of the corpus according to his own methods of biblical interpretation. Classification of the treatises in four sections: biblical hermeneutics, historical-theological treatises, apologetic treatises, and treatises on philosophical issues; (2) presentation of the special and programmatic books (*De vita Mosis 1,2; De opificio mundi*); (3) the zetematic method, involving question and answer: *Quaestiones et solutiones in Genesim, Quaestiones et solutiones in Exodum*; (4) the method of allegorical interpretation; (5) the (subordinate) series *On dreams*;

(6) *Exposition of the Law of Moses*; (7) historical–theological books; (8) apologetic books; (9) philosophical issues; and (10) Philo's Greek language.

3. "The Ideas in Context": the philosophy of Moses; keys for the interpretation of Mosaic philosophy; text interpretation and allegory; the double creation in the perspective of Platonism; the difference between being and non-being: God as the Existent one; the Logos of God and his powers; Israel, the people of philosophy and freedom; individual, particular, universal: paradoxes of anthropology; the Roman Empire and the Temple of Jerusalem.

4. "Reception and interpretations": Philo's presence in the first two centuries; from the third onwards, in Jerome and Augustine and in Byzantine culture; on the identity of Philo as a diaspora Jew in Jewish scholarship.

5. "The Text, transmission and editions": importance of Caesarea in the transmission of the *corpus philonicum*, justification for the critical edition adopted in this translation, and reference to other translations and commentaries that have been taken into account.

6. "This Castilian Translation": attention to its main characteristic traits, and the ordering of the fifty-one books in the set of the eight volumes that will comprise the whole collection. This section ends with a list of the signs and abbreviations used.

The first text in the collection is *La creación del mundo según Moisés* [*De opificio mundi*], a fundamental treatise translated by Francisco Lisi with exemplary rigor and correctness. It is articulated in six parts, each with its own title, while all of these are sub-divided in sixty-one brief chapters with their respective subtitles. This method of presentation is much appreciated for the ease of searching that it provides. The footnotes through the varied richness of their content are also a precious source of information and clarification, though containing few references to bibliographic discussions. In the introduction (pp. 97–106), themes such as the characteristics of the work and its place in the corpus, explanation and justification of its structure, and the cosmologialc thought of Philo, also provide valuable information to help the reader penetrate to the deeper message of the treatise. The comments related to manuscript transmission and questions of translation not only justify the choices made by the translator, but also reflect his concern to reach the best results in his attempt to be as faithful as possible to the author's original intended meaning.

The three treatises on the *Alegorías de las leyes* [*Legum allegoriae* 1-3] mark the beginning of Philo's Allegorical commentary, where the Alexandrian philosopher gives an exegesis of Gen 2.1-17 and 3.8-18 in order to give a hermeneutic description of the spiritual itinerary of the soul. Marta Alesso provides the reader with a meticulous and faithful translation, which respects the exact arrangement of the text.

These treatises occupy almost half of this first volume. In the first short introduction to all three together, the translator examines them in the larger context of the nineteen that compose the Allegorical commentary on Gen 2-17, in order to elucidate how the themes of allegory consistently exceed the limits of the biblical text and form networks of meaning that provide an articulate vision of hermeneutics, theology, cosmology, anthropology and ethics. She also reflects on the nature and complexity of the allegorical method, justifying the adopted text as well as the criteria which she follows in her translation.

In the introduction to the first book Alesso tries to define its relation with *De opificio mundi* as well as with the whole corpus, reflecting on how the allegorical method structures and illumines the text, and how it redefines, reconfigures and reconstructs meaning at a higher and lower level, apparently incorporating elements of Alexandrian culture and the work of Jewish allegorists, combined with ideas from classical Greek authors such as Heraclitus, Plato, Aristotle, the Pythagoreans and the Stoics. Alesso uses a similar strategy in the other two introductions. In addition, besides mentioning the specific philosophical and theological topics in each treatise and its particular formal structure, the translator also reflects on the philosophical language in the second and on themes such as the soul's gradual progress, logos mediation and revelation in the third.

With regard to the translation, each treatise is well structured, retaining the exact divisions of the Cohn-Wendland edition, with paragraphs and chapter numbering. The only difference lies in the addition of titles and subtitles, which facilitate and guide the reader's work. The footnotes are very enlightening in their explanation of historical, philological and mythical issues and in the discussion of the problems of translation to which many passages give rise.

The bibliography and the indices that complement this edition are in themselves two precious tools in the hands of the reader who wishes to examine the Philonic treatises and look for older or recent bibliographical materials on the author and the themes that are connected with him. The bibliography is exhaustive and up-to-date. It is divided in three sections: (1) editions, commentaries and translations; (2) classical sources; and (3) critical bibliography. The indices are also very complete and varied: (1) Biblical citations; (2) Philonic index; (3) Ancient authors index; (4) Modern authors index; (5) Greek terms index; (6) Subjects index; (7) General index.

We must be really grateful to the editor and the translators for the significant contribution that they have made to Philonic studies, and especially for their philological and lexicographic investment on behalf of a critical translation that is most helpful for a better understanding of the text in its proper environment and also in ours. The general introduction and the introductory sections connected to each individual treatise are also very useful and enlightening for a better understanding of the Philonic corpus.

Manuel Alexandre Jr.
University of Lisbon, Portugal

José Pablo Martín (ed.), *Filon de Alejandria. Obras Completas V.* Madrid: Editorial Trotta, 2009, 358 pp. ISBN 978-84-9879-023-8. Price €20.

This Volume V is the second of the collection which aims to produce an edition of the *Complete works* of Philo of Alexandria in Spanish. The project is directed by José Pablo Martín, a learned scholar in the field of ancient philosophy with a particular focus on the Alexandrian thinker.

In this volume, the editor includes the treatises that are described as historical because they contain "documentation, description and interpretation of events of the past as well as the present of the people of Israel, the city of Alexandria and the Roman Empire" (p. 9). But he prefers to classify them in the historical–theological genre, as being historical in terms of genre, but with a specifically theological content. The *Vida de Moisés* I, II [*Life of Moses* I, II] is basically a narration of the life of the leader of the Jews "combined with an explanation of his four areas of ministry." *La vida contemplativa o de los suplicantes* [*The contemplative life, or The suppliants*] contains a description and encomium of the Therapeutae. The two remaining treatises, *Contra Flaco* [*Against Flaccus*] and *Embajada a Gayo* [*Embassy to Gaius*], respectively narrate the iniquitous conduct of the prefect of Alexandria and his unfortunate destiny and the vicissitudes of the delegation of the Jews of Alexandria sent to the Roman emperor Caligula.

The translation of each treatise is preceded by an explanatory introduction that has the mark of its own translator, generally following a similar model of structure. The two books of the *De vita Mosis* and the *De vita contemplativa* are individually introduced and translated by Martín and edited by Marta Alesso. The remaining two, formally presented as historical–theological treatises, are introduced and translated by Sofía Torallas Tovar, with a single introduction before the first. The revision has been done by Lena Balzaretti.

In his introduction to *Vida de Moisés*, Martín focuses his special attention on the following topics: the position of the work among the treatises of

Philo, its transmission and literary genre, the contents of the work and its sources, and the formal structure of both books. The uniqueness of Philo's work is clearly justified in the first topic, since the figure of Moses is magnificently presented, not only for having received the inseparable articulation of the four faculties—political leadership, legislative competence, priesthood and prophecy (p. 17), but also for having engraved in his soul the marks of virtue that coincide with the paradigms which inspired the configuration of the world, the Torah and the liturgical structures of the sanctuary in the desert (p. 18). The unique nature of this work is seen, he adds, in its independent conception, development, genre and destiny, but through its language and content it remains related in many ways to the rest of the corpus (p. 19).

In his reflections on the work's literary genre, the translator analyses explicit references in the text and considers various solutions that have been proposed. He concludes convincingly that *De vita Mosis* "is a historical–theological treatise which, based on the method of the Hellenistic *bios*, combines a rewriting of the hero's *life* with a theological explanation of the *faculties* which allow him to have a mediating role in cosmology and in relation to humankind" (p. 24). As regards the contents of this work, Martín examines the main aspects implicit in the literary genre and provides a synthesis of its main themes. Regarding the formal presentation of its structure, both books are divided in three parts, with exordium and conclusion. Those of the first book are: preparation for Moses' mission (5–84), liberation of the Jews from Egypt (85–213), the land's occupation and distribution (214–333). The second book's parts are: Moses as legislator (8–65), Moses as priest (66–186) and Moses as prophet (187–291). Each of these sections is then divided into chapters and paragraphs, more or less regularly ordered for better consultation and reading. The translation, as may be expected from a scholar with Martín's extensive experience, is accurate. Criteria related to particular lexical decisions are presented in footnotes.

Noting that *De vita contemplativa* has been the object of more discussion than any other of Philo's treatises, Martín attentively discusses issues like the historical enigma of the text, the relationship of Philo and his writings with this treatise, the text's reception up to modern times, the question of the position of Therapeutae within contemporary Judaism, and the work's literary genre. After establishing the authenticity of the text and its relationship to the rest of the corpus, the translator nevertheless questions the identity of the group since there are no other literary, epigraphic or archaeological sources that convincingly testify to its existence. He concludes that the literary genre is a combination of various types; it is at the same time a protreptic work that exhorts to appreciate or imitate a philosophical school, an apologetic treatise defending Mosaic philosophy and Judaism, "a book of theology that shows 'the royal way' which leads to God through the written word of Moses, and also a diatribe against dominant practices in the imperial Roman-Hellenistic society" (p. 155). In short, to use his formulation, it is a historical-theological apology. The formal structure of the text also follows the paragraph and chapter divisions, with titles not always coinciding with chapters. In addition, the translation follows the adopted model of taking into account antecedent versions.

The last two translated texts, also classified as historical–theological treatises, are *In Flaccum* and *Legatio ad Gaium*. After treating issues raised by the texts and the historical circumstances connected with their content, themes such as: the Jewish population of Egypt, the confrontation involving Jews and other groups, and the conflict of Palestine, Tovar discusses the nature of the treatises to clarify her understanding of their literary genre and to determine a coherent view on the formal structure of both of them.

In accordance with the structural model previously used, both treatises are divided in two parts: *In Flaccum* into "The persecution of the Jews" (1–96) and "Punishment and death of Flaccus"; the *Legatio ad Gaium* into "The reign of Caligula" and "The Embassy." No comments are given on the translation, but the method generally adopted by the collection is followed and the final product is equally faithful to the original. Like volume of the series, this volume is also supplemented with a very complete bibliography and the same seven useful indices.

It is hardly necessary to say that the present volume, as well as the other seven in the process of publication, will constitute a most valuable resource for all those who study Philo and his work in Spanish-speaking communities around the world.

Manuel Alexandre Jr.
University of Lisbon, Portugal

SARAH J. K. PEARCE, *The Land of the Body: Studies in Philo's Representation of Egypt*. Wissenschaftliche Untersuchungen zum Neuen Testament 208; Tübingen: Mohr Siebeck, 2007. xxviii + 365 pages. ISBN 978-3-16-149250-1. Price €109, $215.

The story of Israel in the Pentateuch involves several regions and countries outside the promised land. Perhaps the most important of these is Egypt. The treatment of Egypt in the biblical tradition posed challenges for first century Egyptian Jews who honored the biblical text and lived in a country that had oppressed their ancestors. Unlike many communities of the

Diaspora that could create their own aetiological legends to legitimate their origins, e.g., Cleodemus Malchus, Egyptian Jews had to come to grips with existing traditions. Sarah Pearce has provided a thorough and careful analysis of ancient Egypt's most famous and prolific Jewish author's presentation of Egypt.

She opens with an introduction that surveys recent research and sets out two basic principles. She follows the *opinio communis* that Philo is an exegete and must be understood on the basis of his interpretations of Scripture—her first principle. She distinguishes herself by following through on this principle. She recognizes the three different commentaries that Philo wrote and refuses to collapse them into a single perspective with a common audience (pp. 23-25, 179-80). She routinely opens sections in her work with a summary of the biblical text and scrupulously attempts to anchor her analysis of Philo's views by indicating his indebtedness to specific biblical texts. These practices allow her to provide a systematic treatment of a theme without ignoring either differences within the Philonic corpus or the influences of specific biblical texts on his thought. She also recognizes that Philo cannot be read in a vacuum and deals appropriately with his *Umwelt* —her second principle. Again, her principle is more than profession; it is practice. She supplies an impressive survey of contexts throughout the monograph, making the work a rich resource not only for the texts in Philo that she treats but for other texts that she introduces as part of her larger discussion.

True to her second principle, she sketches the larger context in the first two chapters. Chapter one sets out the historical and intellectual contexts of Philo. The overview is an excellent summary of the contemporary understanding of Philo and could be used as a basic introduction. As would be the case of virtually any summary, other Philonists will have a few quibbles. So, for example, she dismisses the existence of the organization of the Alexandrian Jewish community as a *politeuma* in a single sentence (p. 9 n. 55), although a recently discovered inscription that documents the existence of a *politeuma* in Herakleopolis in the second century B.C.E. has made many rethink the reference to the *politeuma* of Alexandria in *Ep. Arist.* 310 (J. M. S. Cowey and K. Maresch, *Urkunden des Politeuma der Juden von Herakleopolis (144/3–133/2 v. Chr) (P. Polit. Jud.): Papyri aus den Sammlungen von Heidelberg, Köln, München, und Wien* (Abhandlungen der Nordrhein-Westfälischen Akademie der Wissenschaften. Sonderreihe Papyrologica Coloniensia 29; Wiesbaden: Westdeutscher Verlag, 2001), no. 5). She suggests that Philo's three commentary series are a "scholarly convention" (p. 20). While the titles that we give to the series are modern conventions, the division of the treatises into three separate commentary series is the work of Philo himself. This is evident not only from the very different character of the three series and their overlapping treatments of the same biblical texts, but from the references that Philo makes. He provides secondary prefaces for six of the treatises in the Allegorical Commentary, suggesting that he considers them units within a larger work (*Plant.* 1; *Ebr.* 1; *Sobr.* 1; *Her.* 1; *Fug.* 2; *Somn.* 1.1). He does even more for the Exposition: he gives us the plan of the whole (*Abr.* 2-5; *Mos.* 2.45-47; *Praem.* 1-3). Scholars have only given labels to what Philo has done.

Pearce continues her survey of the historical context by exploring how Egyptians were understood at the time of Philo (chapter two). She explores different perspectives including the Roman view that thought of residents of Egypt in three groups: Romans, Greeks, and Egyptians. She points out that while there were different assessments of Egyptians, Octavian championed the hostile view as part of his propaganda against Anthony and Cleopatra. She then examines Philo's presentation in *In Flaccum* and the *Legatio*. She concludes that Philo did not draw a firm distinction between Greeks and Egyptians and created a negative image of the mixed group in Egypt.

The next three chapters explore Philo's portrait of Egypt and the Egyptians in the biblical tradition. Chapter three sets out the Alexandrian Jew's presentation of the land of Egypt. Pearce sets out the mental map of the Near East in the Pentateuch in which Egypt is either the oppressor that frames the Pentateuch (Gen 15:18; Deut 26:6-7) or a threat (Genesis) from which Israel must migrate (Exodus) and remain away (Leviticus–Deuteronomy). Philo picks up the migration theme and presents Egypt as the body from which the soul must migrate. She works her way through Philo's treatment of all the major texts in which Egypt plays a role. Her analysis of the texts is impressive. While she has set her task as an exposition of the biblical texts, one wants to ask how Philo could have had such a negative image of Egypt and, at the same time, been proud of his native Alexandria, a local patriotism that Pearce notes (pp. 14-15). Perhaps he might have said that the second largest city in the Roman Empire was distinct from Egypt— at least it was in ancient sources where it is *Alexandria ad Aegyptum* ("Alexandria near Egypt" a translation of the earlier Greek Ἀλεξανδρεία ἡ πρὸς Αἰγύπτῳ [e.g., *OGIS* 193]).

Pearce works through Philo's presentation of specific Egyptians in chapter four. She notes that there are four Pharaohs in the Pentateuch: the Pharaoh with whom Abram interacted, the Pharaoh with whom Joseph interacted, the Pharaoh who oppressed Israel, and the Pharaoh of the exodus. Philo only dealt with these in the Allegorical Commentary. Pearce groups his treatments into thematic portraits of Pharaoh as the scatterer (based on an etymology), a Typhonic figure (Typhon=Seth), the enemy of God, a self-lover, the overly proud mind, the atheist (a particularly good treatment [pp. 153-57]), and the opponent of Moses. She then tackles the Egyptian overseer whom Moses killed, the Egyptian sophists who opposed Moses, and Hagar, symbol of the encyclia in the Allegorical Commentary and an Egyptian by race but Hebrew by life in the Exposition. The survey is balanced and insightful. Again, one wonders how Philo could have been as positive about a non-biblical figure such as Ptolemy II Philadelphus (*Mos.* 2.29-30). The praise in this singular text is undoubtedly due to his role in the legendary origins of the LXX. Still it demonstrates how Philo could be positive.

The fifth chapter examines the role of the Egyptians as wicked hosts in contrast to the Jews as perfect guests. Philo went beyond the LXX and his Jewish predecessors in presenting the Egyptians in this light. In doing so, he transferred the charge of inhospitality often leveled against Jews by Greek and Roman authors to the Egyptians, playing off of an earlier Greek theme of the Egyptians as xenophobic, e.g., Aeschylus, *Supplices* 893ff. He rehabilitated the image of the Jews by presenting them as good guests who were forced to become suppliants before God.

The final three chapters explore Philo's exposé of Egyptian religion. She opens with his treatment of the Nile (chapter six). Philo was the first to criticize the Egyptians for their veneration of the Nile, drawing on a Greek tradition that collapsed Hapy and the inundation of the Nile with the river itself. She turns to animal worship in chapters seven and eight. She begins with an overview of how others critiqued Egyptian animal worship (chapter seven). She points out that the Egyptians did not offer a normative explanation of their practice; presumably the live animals demonstrated the vitality of the deity in the temple. The views of outsiders range from Herodotus who considered animal veneration a *paradoxon* to Juvenal who was sharply critical. Jewish authors also had different perspectives that extend from condemnation to Artapanus who argued that Moses invented the Egyptian cults! Philo wrote more extensively on the Egyptian cults than any other Jewish author in antiquity (chapter eight). He identified the worship of animals with Egyptian religion. He thought that it was against the law of nature for a rational being (a human) to worship an irrational being (an animal). In this way the Therapeutae and Egyptians form opposite ends of a spectrum in *Contempl.* He denied the counter utilitarian argument that the veneration is an expression of gratitude for the animals' usefulness, since the Egyptians worship savage animals such as crocodiles. It is against this background that we should read Philo's multiple treatments of the golden calf: they were polemics against Egyptian animal cults.

Pearce's analysis is comprehensive, clear, and insightful. The work is an excellent example of how a scholar can explore a theme that runs throughout Philo's works while remaining true to the realities of his exegetical orientation and indebtedness to other thinkers. It is a solid contribution to scholarship and a good model for those who want to tackle a theme that spans the corpus.

Gregory E. Sterling
University of Notre Dame

MARTIN GOODMAN, *Judaism in the Roman World: Collected Essays.* Ancient Judaism and Early Christianity 66. Brill: Leiden, 2007. xi + 275 pages. ISBN 978-90-04-15309-7. Price €108, $154.

MARTIN GOODMAN, *Rome and Jerusalem: The Clash of Ancient Civilizations.* Vintage Books: New York 2007. xi + 598 pages. ISBN 978-03-75-41185-4. Price $35.

Since the 1980s, scholars in the field of ancient Judaism have been profiting from the stunning knowledge and the many insights provided by Martin Goodman in his large and impressive scholarly oeuvre. Goodman's major publications include the monographs *The Ruling Class of Judea* (1987) and *Mission and Conversion* (1994), as well as several edited books such as *Jews in a Graeco-Roman World* (1998) and *The Oxford Handbook of Jewish Studies* (2002). Goodman is known for always pursuing clear and strong theses, in books as well as in articles. Often his contributions have been questioning *communes opiniones*, as is the case in his book on Jewish mission, where Goodman argues that Jewish proselytism was not an important aspect of ancient Judaism (about the same time, the French scholars E. Will and C. Orrieux in their *"Prosélytisme Juif"? Histoire d'une erreur* [1992] arrived at similar conclusions). Goodman's scholarship is among the most cited in the field.

Thesis-driven scholarship is also what makes the two new books under review so valuable, one (*Judaism in the Roman World*) more so than the other (*Rome and Jerusalem*). *Judaism in the Roman World* makes nineteen previously published articles more easily accessible. To the specialist, not all of these articles will be equally important, but many certainly (still) are. The first paper is a brief "tour d'horizon" of what should be included by the term "Early Judaism": for Goodman this is roughly the time from 200 B.C.E. to 500 C.E., from the late second temple to the closure of the Talmud. One may doubt, however, that the term "Early Judaism" is an appropriate one for the period from 200 B.C.E. onwards. First, the term is an apologetic one in the sense that it replaces the heavily biased term "Late Judaism" ("Spätjuden-tum") by its opposite. And second, such a definition excludes the Persian period, so important for the development of Judaism. Maybe "Ancient Judaism" as a term including Persian, Hellenistic and Rabbinic Judaism would be a more adequate one for the early periods of Judaism (very much in the sense of the Brill series in which this book was published: *Ancient Judaism and Early Christianity*).

Goodman argues repeatedly, and rightly so, for a grand variety within Judaism. The Diaspora as such was part of this variety: Diaspora commu-nities were independent of priestly influence from Jerusalem. Priests could not impose their will on the Diaspora (p. 22). More importantly, the variety among Jews in Palestine was much larger than often assumed: According to Goodman the Pharisees and the *hakhamim* are to be understood as two separate groups (p. 40). And the marginalization of the Sadducees by the rabbis should not be read as a sign of their non-existence (p. 134f.). If the rabbis have very little to say about the *halacha* of the *minim*, it is because they avoided these "heretics" (p. 172), not because they were not there. It is not least the scrolls from Qumran which can be taken as another indication of the great variety of first-century Judaism. Goodman does not exclude that the Qumran sectarians were Essenes, but tends to understand them as an additional subgroup of first-century Judaism (p. 143). And in "Saddu-cees and Essenes after 70 C.E." Goodman rightly questions the "standard assumption" (p. 154, is it still one?) that the Jewish "sects" disappeared soon after 70. They may very well have continued to exist for centuries (p. 161).

Judaism in the Roman World brings together a series of relatively short papers, all with important conclusions: Goodman shows how for Jews, in an unparalleled way in Greco-Roman antiquity, the scrolls containing the sacred scriptures "were themselves sacred objects" (p. 74). Therefore any-thing attached to the scrolls can defile the hands as much as the text itself (*tYad.* 2:12 and p. 75). The next paper follows up on this. In "Texts, Scribes and Power in Roman Judaea" Goodman shows how for Jews the writing of sacred texts brought power (while reading did not, p. 79). The paper on "Jewish Proselytizing in the First Century" (pp. 91–116) originally led to Goodman's book on conversion, already mentioned in this review. Good-man rightly stresses that there was no proselytizing movement in first-century Judaism. However, I doubt that there was a shift soon afterwards, as Goodman is arguing: "At some time in the second or third century some Jews seem to have begun looking for converts in just the way they were apparently not doing in the first century." More likely is that, while Jewish mission surely never became a mass movement, in antiquity there were always individual Jews actively looking out for converts. In one of the following papers ("The Persecution of Paul by Diaspora Jews") Goodman argues that it was Paul's missionary activities among the gentiles to which the Jewish authorities reacted when they persecuted him. Jews were afraid that a Jewish missionary activist might needlessly provoke their pagan neighbours.

It has to be said that this collection of papers is not free of repetition, but this should also be interpreted as a sign of the author's consistency. Goodman's argumentation is always sound, sometimes also provocative: might the sun god on the synagogue mosaics from Hammat Tiberias have represented the god of the Jews (p. 206f.)? Rarely are there points made by Goodman which are less convincing. That Titus had not intended to destroy the Jewish temple in Jerusalem (p. 54), an argument also defended in *Rome and Jerusalem* (p. 421), is highly unlikely. Exactly because Josephus relied on imperial patronage, Josephus was willing to write apologetically on Titus' behaviour before the fall of Jewish temple.

Rome and Jerusalem: The Clash of Ancient Civilizations is an amazing book. Goodman must have enjoyed writing these 557 pages, with very few notes, on these two cultures he knows so well. The subtitle is certainly awkward, given how loaded the phrase "clash of civilizations" is and, especially, given that for most of the book Goodman is arguing that between Romans and Jews for a very long time there was the exact opposite of a clash: coexistence and *laissez vivre*. At the same time, the destruction of the Jewish temple in Jerusalem by the Romans in 70 c.e., already the topic of the prologue, lies like a constant shadow over the whole book: To some extent the book reads like Josephus' *Jewish War* with its climax in Jerusalem's *halosis*.

But the Jewish-Roman war did not lead to a "clash of ancient civiliza-tions." Goodman generally places, it seems to me, too much weight on the consequences of the war. The Flavians certainly needed the victory over the Jews and used it widely for their political propaganda for many years to come. But how important was it to the Romans to prevent the Jews from rebuilding the Temple? While the Romans took over the holy space of the Temple, they probably would not have prevented the Jews from building the Temple elsewhere and they did not prevent the Jews from having synagogues. And how much interest in rebuilding the Temple did the Jews themselves really show? As Goodman writes in one of the papers in *Judaism in the Roman World*: "For most Jews, Judaism did not need to be recon-structed, because it was not shattered" (p. 158).

And did the Roman comments on the Jews really become much more hostile after 70 C.E., as Goodman writes (366ff.)? Seneca, before the war, famously once calls the Jews a *sceleratissima gens*. Goodman surmises that Seneca mixed the Jews up with the Christians who at the time were accused of having caused the great fire in Rome in 64 C.E. (p. 373). But this sneer is more likely to be understood as just another anti-Jewish remark by a Greek or Roman author. The Jewish-Roman war had probably less of an influence on how Jews were viewed by pagans than Goodman suspects.

Rome and Jerusalem is both impressionistic and expressionistic at the same time. The reader will find many (maybe too many) details on many different aspects of Jewish and Roman lives. On the other hand, Goodman draws portraits of each of the two cultures which are sometimes simplistic. Here and there he speaks of *the* Romans and of *the* Jews. As for the latter, while in his collected essays Goodman cautiously and convincingly shows how diverse Judaism was in the first few centuries C.E., in his monograph Goodman allows himself to simplify. In the context of ornamental gardens, for example, Goodman writes (p. 263): "For Jews, delight in nature was generally limited to appreciation of the useful: the ploughed field, the dressed vine or the carefully tended fig tree." Is there really enough evidence for such a statement?

Martin Goodman has provided us with a fascinating and impressively learned "diptychon" of Jewish and Roman culture, on a great variety of themes such as lifestyles, war, and justice (to name just a few). Of course, Jews were to some extent simply part of Roman culture and one may wonder whether Goodman's "parallel lives" is the best approach to understand Rome and Jerusalem.[1] But there is no doubt that *Rome and Jerusalem*, written for a larger audience, also deserves the full attention of scholars of ancient Judaism. Even if one does not share all of Goodman's conclusions, this is a delightfully written book, full of insights and knowledge.

René Bloch,
University of Bern

---

[1] Cf. S. Schwartz, Sunt Lachrymae Rerum. *JQR* 99 (2009) 60-64.

JEAN RIAUD, ed. *Les élites dans le monde biblique.* Bibliothèque d'Etudes Juives 32. Paris: Honoré Champion, 2008. 266 pages. ISBN 978-2-7453-1718-6. Price €50.

This volume is the outcome of a conference that took place at the Faculty of Catholic Theology of the University of Angers in February 2006, following two years of regular meetings of the faculty members. The book is divided into three parts: biblical texts (from the Hebrew Bible), local elites in Palestine and in the diaspora at the turn of the era, and Christian communities. The first article, by Hedwige Rouillard-Bonraisin, deals with elites in a sense that is not expected from the outset, that is, with the election of the youngest son over the first-born, a prominent motif in several biblical stories. Then Jean Riaud addresses the issue of biblical elites from a more sociological-political perspective, by analyzing the category of the "elders" ($z^e qenim$) in biblical texts. Their role in villages and towns, or at the royal court, is described in several passages, but one wonders how much these descriptions correspond to an actual historical reality. The last article of the first part, by Paul Mottard, focuses on the first judge of Israel, Othniel, who benefits from his marriage with the daughter of Caleb, but is also chosen by God. The notions of social elite and divine election are thus mixed in this case.

The second part of the book opens with an erudite article by Jérôme Gaslain that oscillates between an analysis of the Parthian invasion of Judaea and a study of the military elites of the Arsacide kingdom as such, two related but nevertheless different topics. Hindy Najman's article tackles the issue of perfection in Philo and the *Fourth Book of Ezra*, and reflects upon two distinct ways to perfection already found in Plato, that which is based on the desire to become like the sage (Abraham, Moses, …) and that which implies death and the liberation of the soul from the body. The search for perfection is only remotely linked to the issue of elites, except if one moves from the sociological, political or economic level and from a functional analysis to a more philosophical or religious approach. The next article adopts this perspective as well. Laura Gusella's contribution focuses on the Therapeutae and compares them with the Essenes and with the Qumran community. Then David Hamidovic describes the functioning of the local Jewish socio-economic elites (especially women) around the Dead Sea in the second century C.E., through a careful and meticulous analysis of the personal archives of Babatha found at Nahal Hever. In particular, he shows how this illiterate woman who possessed lands and palm trees had recourse to Jewish and Nabatean scribes and used Roman, Jewish and Nabatean law according to her purposes. In the last article of part II, Jens Herzer tackles the topic of the relationship of Pontius Pilate with the Judean elites and shows that the former was rather successful in establishing a kind of collaboration with the latter in the interest of Rome.

Part III, on Christian communities, opens with an article by Philippe Léonard on rhetoric in Paul's writings, in which he argues that rhetoric, one of the values of the elites, was not renounced by Paul, but adapted to the needs of preaching, focusing on the Cross and not on the beauty of discourse. Marie-Laure Chaieb then asks whether ministers in the Church in the second century C.E. were considered elites by Christians. After having examined criteria such as birth, power, wealth, strength, intelligence, age and function, she concludes that they constitute a spiritual elite characterized by holiness and charity. Paul-André Turcotte addresses the issue of the relationships between Christians and the Roman imperial or local elites, arguing that the former occasionally were among the latter. But he does not provide concrete examples. Finally, Madeleine Scopello analyzes the notion of elites in Manicheism, showing that it is conceived of in terms of election. The Manichean "church" itself is divided into two groups, the "elects" and the "auditors."

In the book the articles are classified more or less according to a chronological order, as well as to "cultural-religious" areas (Bible, Judaism, Christianity, Manicheism). In his stimulating essay at the end of the book, Michel Meslin attempts instead to elaborate a *typology* of elites. He asks a crucial question, that of the definition of the word "elites." He first reminds the reader of the criteria used in the definition of the Roman senators and the knights, whose status was based on money on the one hand, on birth or imperial choice on the other hand. Then he distinguishes between socio-economic elites like the "elders" of the Bible or Babatha, the more political elites like the Parthian aristocracy or Pontius Pilate, and the more religious elites for whom divine election or charisma play a large role, such as in the case of Othniel or that of the youngest son in the biblical narratives, or—shifting from literary characters to religious communities in the first centuries—of Christian leaders and Manichean elects.

This is a worthwhile collection of essays, some of which are especially stimulating for further research. But in my opinion the book as a whole needed an introduction to help the reader grasp the set of issues addressed therein. Above all, the absence of a definition of "elites" at the beginning of the work is problematic. Michel Meslin's contribution responds to this *desideratum* to some extent, but the problem is that it comes at the very end of the book. A thorough reflection about the relationship between the notion of elites and that of election and vocation is particularly needed. In that same line, one also wonders about the connection between elites, election and asceticism, the latter being mentioned in several contributions (in those dealing with perfection, with the Therapeutae and with the Manicheans, at least). Finally, the issue of the amount of people that can be numbered among the elite deserves to be raised. Can the elite represent 20% of a population, for instance, or 30% of a religious group (or 50%, as in the case of the youngest son being chosen instead of the first-born)? Or does the category imply that a smaller number of people be involved? This is just an example of the questions that arise from reading the book. In spite of these reservations, it is a fine collection of interesting studies, covering a wide range of issues and from which a lot can be learnt.

Katell Berthelot
CNRS, Centre de Recherche Français à Jérusalem

PER JARLE BEKKEN, *The Word Is Near You: A Study of Deuteronomy 30:12–14 in Paul's Letter to the Romans in a Jewish Context.* Beihefte zur Zeitschrift für die neutestamentliche Wissenschaft und die Kunde der älteren Kirche 144. Berlin, New York: de Gruyter, 2007. xiii + 294 pages. ISBN 978-3-11-019341-1. Price $143.

Bekken's work, apparently completed in 2006, develops his dissertation produced under Peder Borgen, and provides more detail than his earlier helpful publications on the subject. He notes (vii) that he undertook most of the research in 1988–1992; nevertheless, he does interact with more recent work, some as late as 2006. Naturally he interacts most extensively with his Doktorvater, Peder Borgen (through 2000), who has displayed special acumen in bringing to bear hellenistic Jewish context on early Christian literature. He also interacts, however, with a range of scholars known both for their work in early Judaism more generally (e.g., E. P. Sanders) and Pauline studies (especially Paul's letter to the Romans; e.g., James Dunn and J. Ross Wagner).

He cites Philo over three hundred times, Josephus about twenty times, and other clearly hellenistic Jewish works over forty times. Unlike some works that focus exclusively on some ancient circles to the exclusion of others, he also cites other early Jewish sources (e.g., the Qumran scrolls over thirty times; *1 Enoch* over thirty times; and sixteen references from *2 Baruch*) and some non-Jewish philosophers (with Stoics predominating, but also sources from the Platonically-inclined moralist Plutarch).

Bekken notes Philo's frequent use (in six extant contexts) of Deut 30:12-14 and chooses two of the most relevant examples (*Virt.* 183-184; *Praem.* 79-84) for detailed comparison with Paul's application of the text in Romans 10:6-8. He seeks to demonstrate (successfully, in my opinion) that Paul's eschatological and christological use of the passage is not idiosyncratic, but reflects an interpretive approach familiar to his contemporaries. He also rightly recognizes that Paul's literary context involves a special approach to the law rather than a repudiation of it.

Bekken shows that Paul's selective citation of Deut 30:12-14, including his omissions and substitution of vocabulary, fits contemporary expectations; scholars familiar with Christopher Stanley's work on citations in antiquity might have expected as much. More significantly, the third chapter of Bekken's work demonstrates that Paul's exegetical paraphrase is not arbitrary, but reflects a standard expository method, one indeed employed for this very text in Baruch. Paul's paraphrase includes exposition following citation three times in 10:6-8, as well as expository development in 10:8-17 (a unit framed by literary inclusio). Even Paul's "this is" (three times in 10:6-8) is specifically paralleled in contemporary interpretive texts (both Jewish and non-Jewish).

Not only does Bekken establish that Paul's interpretive style fits the exegetical conventions of his day, but he also suggests a more specific interpretive tradition for Deut 30:12-14 against which Paul may be read. He notes that Philo (in *Praem.* 79-84) reads Deut 30:11-14 as addressing how Jews as distinct from Gentiles can obey God's law. Viewing Philo's approach as covenant nomism, Bekken argues that Paul presupposes knowledge of such a usage of Deut 30, against which he formulates his own approach. He also situates Philo's use of Deut 30 in *Virt.* 183-184 in the larger context of conversion (both Jewish repentance and proselytes) in *Virt.* 175-186.

In Bekken's exegesis, the flow of thought in Paul's literary context reveals Christ as the "goal" of the law (Rom 10:4), and this eschatological goal of the law is the hermeneutical key to 10:5-8. In contrast to contemporary, ethnically exclusivist interpretations that emphasized Jewish lawkeeping as against Gentiles' inability to do so, Paul contends that the law's message can be fulfilled by faith rather than by works (see 9:31-32). Thus Bekken rightly recognizes Paul's emphasis on continuity with what he regards as the message of the law.

At the same time, Bekken also argues (in chapter 5) that Paul's approach is consonant with another aspect of his contemporaries' approach to the law. When Paul insists that the law should be read in light of its eschatological fulfilment in Christ (10:4), his reading may parallel the approach of contemporaries. Philo links Deut 30:11-14 with the promised blessings of the covenant in *Praem.* 79-84, and such promised blessings could be understood eschatologically (he cites *Praem.* 87-97, noting parallels with Is 11 LXX and some other eschatological texts). Some of us would find

Bekken's connections here more difficult; Philo's primary exegetical canon is the Pentateuch, and his future ideals differ significantly from aspects of Paul's eschatology (especially in, say, the Thessalonian correspondence). Nevertheless, Bekken makes an extensive case for Philo's eschatology, and parallels with *Opif.* 79-82 suggest a correspondence between his future hopes and his protology. In any case, at least the connection between obedience and future corporate blessing is clear.

Those interested in comparing Philo with another important first-century Diaspora Jewish voice (Paul) will find much of interest in this work, and not only in the observations most directly relevant to the passage at hand. Thus, for example, Bekken's comparison of *Praem.* 152 with Rom 11:17-24 may be illuminating for both sources. Although his primary objective is to illumine a Pauline text, his thorough engagement with the Philonic corpus (including periodic discussions of Philo's meaning, as in, for example, his exploration of Philonic eschatology above; of ideas of repentance and conversion on pp. 85-93; and of loving and being loved by God on pp. 102-106) will render this book of interest to students of hellenistic Judaism more generally as well as to students specialized in early Hellenistic Jewish Christianity.

Scholars might debate some of his Philonic arguments (e.g., the extent to which *Virt.* 175-186 addresses Jews or Gentiles), but Bekken is well-informed and takes into account Philo's broader lexical usage in constructing his arguments. Readers will thus find this work a stimulating and thoughtful conversation partner. The work's focus, of course, remains the light that Philo sheds on Paul. In my view, Bekken achieves his primary objective of setting Paul's argument in his broader Diaspora Jewish context.

Craig Keener
Palmer Theological Seminary

GEORGE H. VAN KOOTEN, *Paul's Anthropology in Context: The Image of God, Assimilation to God, and Tripartite Man in Ancient Judaism, Ancient Philosophy and Early Christianity.* Wissenschaftliche Untersuchungen zum Neuen Testament I 232; Tübingen: Mohr Siebeck, 2008. xxiv + 444 pages. ISBN 978-3-16-149778-0. Price €119.

This ambitious monograph argues that Paul's understanding of the image of God is closest to Philo of Alexandria's understanding. Both authors drew from Jewish and Hellenistic philosophical traditions in response to the Second Sophistic movement that championed form over substance.

Although the author does not lay out the argument in major parts, the work naturally falls into three major sections. The first (chapters one and two) explores Pauline anthropology against the background of Hellenized Judaism and Hellenistic philosophy. Van Kooten opens with a *religionsgeschichtlich* study of the image of God. He points out the infrequent nature of the concept in the Hebrew Bible/LXX and then surveys the multiple understandings of the concept in Second Temple Jewish literature. He concurs with John Levison that there was not a uniform understanding of Adam or the image of God (J. R. Levison, *Portraits of Adam in Early Judaism: From Sirach to 2 Baruch* [JSPSup 1; Sheffield: JSOT Press, 1988], 159–60), although Van Kooten argues that the concept is not wholly subservient to the *Tendenzen* of individual authors, especially with respect to the anti-idolatrous, intellectual, and physical understandings (pp. 44–47). The survey sets up the unique understandings of Philo and Paul. He summarized Philo's view in five points: the Alexandrian's interpretation of the plural, "let us"; the preposition "in" in the phrase "in the image"; the cosmos as a copy of the image; his emphasis on the "likeness" between God and humanity; and the two creation accounts. His treatment of the Philonic material is good, although it suffers from the cursory nature of a survey. For example, he does not address Philo's motive in emphasizing the plural (*Opif.* 75; *Conf.* 168–82, esp. 179–82; *Fug.* 68–72, esp. 70; *Mut.* 31–32) nor does he know all of the major literature, e.g., he does not interact with Thomas H. Tobin, *The Creation of Man: Philo and the History of Interpretation* (CBQMS 14; Washington, D.C.: The Catholic Biblical Association, 1983). The treatment of Paul is similarly good but better in detail. He summarizes Paul's use of image in the Corinthian correspondence and provides a particularly helpful analysis of μορφή and εἰκών in his treatment of Phil 2:6.

The second chapter explores Philo's and Paul's understanding of God's image as a model in which humans are reshaped. Van Kooten opens with a summary of understandings of the "image of God" in the larger Greco-Roman world and then moves to an overview of ὁμοίωσις θεῷ κατὰ τὸ δυνατόν (Plato, *Theat.* 176a–b) in the Platonic tradition with some attention to diverging paths. He points out that "likeness to God" could be understood intellectually or ethically in the tradition. It became the *telos* of Middle Platonism with Eudorus. With this background, he works through Philo's and Paul's understandings and demonstrates how they share a perspective that had been influenced by the philosophical tradition. His overview of Philo is quite good. He points out Philo's open debt to and acceptance of the Platonic tradition in this regard (*Fug.* 62–64, 82) and accurately summarizes his thought, although once again, he does not appear to know some major works. For example, he says that "it may well be that Clement is dependant on Philo in this, since he mentions Philo's writings regularly among his sources" (p. 184), but never refers to Annewies van den Hoek's, *Clement of Alexandria and His Use of Philo in the Stromateis: An Early Christian Reshaping of a Jewish Model* (VCSup 3; Leiden: Brill, 1988). The treatment of Paul is again good, but there are some similar gaps. For example, in his exposition of baptism in Rom 6:1–11, Paul unpacks the meaning of baptism by means of the old confession that Christ died, was buried, and was raised (1 Cor 15:3–5), a connection that is missing in Van Kooten (pp. 206–08). Van Kooten's work with the primary texts is careful enough that he offers sound treatments, but they could be nuanced and strengthened if he had engaged more of the secondary literature.

The second part of the monograph argues for a Sophistic background to both Philo and Paul (chapters three through six). Van Kooten uses the work of Bruce Winter as a launching pad (*Philo and Paul among the Sophists: Alexandrian and Corinthian Responses to a Julio-Claudian Movement* (2nd ed.; Grand Rapids: Eerdmans, 2002)). Winter had shown the development of the Second Sophistic prior to Nero by using the works of Philo and Paul among other sources. Van Kooten begins with Philo's references to the sophists (chapter three). He posits Balaam as a paradigm since he spoke out of both sides of his mouth. He rehearses the narrative of Israel and situates the references to sophists within it. He claims that "there is an uninterrupted anti-sophistic reading of these narratives." This leads him to conclude that "the scale and scope of this undertaking suggests that Philo deliberately chose the Mosaic Pentateuch as the vehicle to convey his warning to the Greek-educated Jewish youth concerning the dangers of the anti-philo-sophical, social and political lures of the sophist movement" (p. 244). This extends well beyond the evidence in my judgment. Philo's three commentary series are very different in nature. Van Kooten has lumped them together and assumed that they had a common audience and function. These are problematic assumptions. It might be possible to argue that Philo had the sophists in mind when he wrote the Allegorical Commentary since thirty-four of the forty-three references to σοφιστής and twelve of the fourteen references to σοφιστικός are in the Allegorical Commentary (*Leg.* 2.232 (*bis*); *Cher.* 8, 10; *Det.* 38, 39, 71, 72; *Post.* 35, 86; 131, 150; *Agr.* 136, 143, 144, 159; *Ebr.* 71; *Sobr.* 9 (*bis*); *Conf.* 39; *Migr.* 72, 76, 171; *Her.* 246; *Congr.* 67, 129; *Fug.* 209, 211; *Mut.* 10, 208, 257; *Somn.* 1.102, 220; 2.281 and *Leg.* 1.174; 3.41, 233; *Det.* 41, 42; *Post.* 53, 101; *Agr.* 162; *Migr.* 82, 85; *Her.* 304; *Mut.* 263). It is more difficult to argue that they are a target in the Exposition of the Law that only has five references to σοφιστής and one to σοφιστικός (*Ios.* 103, 106; *Mos.* 1.92; 2.212; *Praem.* 58 and *Opif.* 157) or the *Quaestiones* that only contain one reference to each (*QG* isf 3 and *QE* isf 26). Yet even this is not without challenges: the sophists are not the only group Philo critiques. Why select these over against the radical allegorizers (*Migr.* 89–93)? While Philo often contrasts the sophists with the message that he is presenting, it is almost always as a device to urge the reader to consider true wisdom and virtue rather than accepting a cleverly crafted argument (e.g., *Post.* 86; *Sobr.* 9; *Migr.* 72, 171; *Her.* 246; *Congr.* 67; *Fug.* 209; *Mut.* 10, 208; *Somn.* 2.281). The statement that Philo warns his readers against the sophists is true, but this does not appear to be the function of the Allegorical Commentary which invites the reader to experience likeness to God through conformity to the Logos.

Van Kooten provides a helpful overview of Paul's stance versus what is known generally about the sophists (chapter four). In this case, the Apostle does not call anyone a sophist; the evidence is a series of analogies between Paul's opposition to practices at Corinth and what is known about the sophists in the Second Sophistic movement. Van Kooten argues that Paul's battle with the sophists at Corinth led him to develop inner values. One issue that he does not address in detail but should have is whether the sophists knew Jewish exegetical traditions that would have influenced the Corinthians.

He explores the two types of humans in Philo and Paul in chapter five. He notes the double creation tradition. In his explanation he makes the curious argument that the reference to Adam as "the second man" in *Leg.* 2.4–5 "cannot be used as evidence that as a matter of fact, 'the first man' is the heavenly man in Philo" (p. 278). His conclusion is problematic. While it is true that this is unusual language for Philo, it reflects an exegetical tradition that he has inherited. This is an instance where van Kooten's failure to interact with Tobin is evident (see Tobin, *The Creation of Man*, 102–34). Van Kooten has an intriguing analysis of 1 Corinthians. He argues that Paul faced three forms of opposition: those who denied the resurrection, the sophists or *psychikoi* in 1 Cor 1–4, and the excessive *pneumatikoi* in 1 Cor 10–14. While one might question whether it is possible to break down the opposition into such discrete groups, it is a provocative analysis. He expands his treatment of Paul's relationship to the Corinthians by exploring the Apostle's treatment of Exod 34 in 2 Cor 3–4 (chapter six). He argues that the sophists introduced Moses positively as an example of power and glory; Paul countered by drawing on the inner person as a contrast.

The third part consists of chapter seven that tackles Romans. Van Kooten argues that the situation is now different: the sophists have fallen out of the picture and have been replaced by the tensions between Jewish and Gentile Christians. Paul extended his earlier views, worked out in his battle against the sophists, to develop a universal ethic. He opened the letter with a form of natural theology in keeping with the view of Varro and others that championed Rome's imageless cult for its first 170 years (Frg 18; Plutarch, *Numa* 8.7–8). He argues for assimilation to Christ through the "inner person." He maintains that Paul had a trichotomic anthropology that focused on the renewal of the mind (Rom 12:1–2). While Philo and Paul shared an emphasis on the renewal of the mind, there is a significant difference in their anthropology. Philo did not envision a resurrected body and soul; he anticipated the liberation of the soul from the body and was content to conceive of a naked soul (*Abr.* 236 vs. 2 Cor 5:1–10).

This work is a careful treatment of a complex development within the history of religions. Van Kooten is best in chapters one and two where he sketches the *religionsgeschichtlich* background of Philo's and Paul's understanding of the image of God and assimilation to God. Van Kooten's careful treatment of a wide range of texts is exceptionally good, although there are some weaknesses in the secondary literature. The work is more problematic when it argues that the sophists are the catalysts for the development of Philo's and Paul's unique perspective. While he is correct to call attention to the value of Winter's work, he makes too much of it in my opinion. Further, van Kooten does not adequately explain how Philo and Paul came to share such similar perspectives. A summary chapter might have been useful to come to terms with this issue.

It is easy to be critical of a work that attempts to do so much over controversial ground. This is a serious piece of scholarship that deserves careful reading. While I have found a number of aspects problematic, the work is responsibly stimulating and provocative. This is enough to win praise.

Gregory E. Sterling
University of Notre Dame

EMMA WASSERMAN, *The Death of the Soul in Romans 7: Sin, Death and the Law in Light of Hellenistic Moral Psychology.* Wissenschaftliche Untersuchungen zum Neuen Testament II 256. Tübingen: Mohr Siebeck, 2008. x +171 pages. ISBN 978-3-16-149612-7. Price €44, $83.

This exquisitely documented book, a development of a dissertation published in 2005, focuses on the impassioned monologue in Romans 7. Wasserman structures her analysis by first describing the principles of moral psychology found in Plato and developed and modified by the Stoics and later Middle Platonists. She then looks to Philo of Alexandria and his participation in a "Platonic Discourse" and the resultant analysis of the "Death of the Soul." She contends that Paul engaged in the same discourse and that this is the underlying determinant in his plaintive cry for deliverance in Rom 7:24. She next discusses the life and death of the soul in Romans 1–8, focusing especially on Rom 1:18–32 as it applies to chapters six and 8:1–13. Wasserman's analysis can be seen as a solution to the debate between Bultmann and Käsemann as to the referent to Paul's personal pronoun "I" in the chapter seven monologue.

In her introduction, Wasserman suggests that the scholarship on Rom 7 has thus far not achieved an accepted and coherent consensus about who is speaking and what the person is speaking about. For her part, she draws from the research of Stanley Stowers and Troels Engberg-Pedersen, who have looked to the influence of Hellenistic moral traditions upon Rom 7 for answers. Her contention is that the Hellenistic moral philosophers view the character of people's actions as ranging along a spectrum, from habitual goodness to habitual evil. Here she introduces a most appropriate segment from Philo's *Legum Allegoriae* (1.105–107) where he defines the "death of the soul" to be the soul's "becoming entombed in passions and wickedness." Wasserman writes that "Life and death function as analogies that convey the dominance of one faculty of the soul over another. This use of death metaphors is also consistent with more common Platonic metaphors and analogies for domination such as imprisonment, military conflict, slavery and rule" (p. 8). On the basis of the foregoing, Wasserman interprets Rom 7:7–25 as depicting the "plight of reason or mind imprisoned by the passions and appetites" (ibid.).

In chapter one, she relies upon scholarly advances in the past few decades in understanding Hellenistic and Roman preoccupation with human emotions and passions in constructing ethical theories. She proposes that it is not necessary to rely upon specific quotations of a particular philosophical work to develop a writer's reliance upon a tradition, but instead she focuses on "Platonic traditions" and "show(s) that intellectuals sustain a distinctive Platonic discourse about the soul that is appropriated by different types of intellectuals. . ." (p. 16). "Discourse" refers to the set of writings that arise out of "shared concepts, language, motifs, metaphors and assumptions about their relationships that enable and constrain intellectual production" (p. 18). Paul, she contends, appropriated and participated in the on-going discourse that was occurring in the Hellenistic world. Later in chapter one, Wasserman traces the patterns of appropriation of Plato's and Aristotle's moral psychologies through a broad range of Hellenistic writers, including Cicero, Seneca, Plutarch, Epictetus, Philodemus, Galen and Philo.

In the discussion of Aristotle's therapeutic spectrum, Wasserman points out that Aristotle includes θηριότης as one end of the moral spectrum; but in a footnote, she excludes this end of the spectrum. Aristotle, however, in both the *Nichomachean Ethics* (1150a) and *Magna Moralia* (1200a) describes Θηριότης as exceeding the limits of vice and not having a name, in the same manner that virtue cannot be ascribed to gods, since they transcend men. In other words, a "bestial" person, for Aristotle, has lost his/her nature as an ἄνθρωπος. I suggest that this might be important later in her analysis.

In chapter 2, Wasserman deals specifically with the death of the soul in Rom 7, applying the elements of the Hellenistic discourse that she established in chapter 1. Central to her thesis is Philo's adoption of a tripartite structure of the soul (though he is not averse to the Stoic structure, as in *Her.* 232–233) which consists of the νοῦς, θυμός and ἐπιθυμία. She shows that Philo visualizes that the insubordination of the latter two elements to the first produces the death of the soul.

The only problem this reviewer sees in her discussion is that she constantly characterizes the "death of the soul" as a metaphor. She cites Dieter Zeller's excellent article in *Studia Philonica Annual* VII (1995, 21) where Zeller described Philo's treatment specifically as metaphorical, with the use of "death" as having a "shocking effect." If the "death of the soul" is merely a metaphor, then it is merely a substitute for another phrase, such as calling one a "sinner," "evil" or "immoral." By characterizing the "death of the soul" as a metaphor, Wasserman seems to suggest that there is no "ontological" impact to the phrase.

In *Agr.* 139, Philo discusses a hierarchical structure of beings, ranging from the lifeless to the immortal. Further, Abraham Terian provided scholars with *Philonis Alexandrini de Animalibus* (Chico: Scholars Press, 1981) in which he described the "metaphysical pyramid of his understanding of the universe," based on this text. The critical bifurcation in the pyramid is that between the λογικά and the ἄλογα, or the Rationals and the Irrationals (Terian, 35). Terian quotes *Spec.* 3.99, "For everyone who is left forsaken by reason, the better part of the soul, has been transformed into the nature of a beast, even though the outward characteristics of his body still retain their human form" (Terian, 39). This perception is significantly different from that which suggests that the "death of the soul" is a mere metaphor. It suggests that there is a level of ontological change that occurs when the passions overcome the intellect. I suspect that Aristotle had this in mind when he spoke of "beastliness"; for this state, worse than vice, actually transforms a person into the character of a beast. This does not necessarily mean that the ontological degradation is permanent; in fact, Wasserman quotes Zeller's fragment of Menander (in Zeller, ibid., 51) where the subject had been "dead" but upon arrival in Athens, "I have become alive again for all the rest of my life, as if I had lain down in the temple of Asclepius and had been saved." Hence, while the soul may die due to the conquest of the intellect by the passions, and thereby lose that specific character that causes a person to be a human person, i.e., ruled by one's intellect, such a state of affairs is not necessarily permanent and one's humanity can be restored.

Chapter three places Rom 7:7–25 within the context of the overall argument of Rom 1–8. Wasserman begins with the expressions of "extreme immorality" identified by Paul in 1:18–32, at the end of which passage Paul maintains that those engaging in such depraved activities deserve death (ἄξιοι θανάτου εἰσίν). Wasserman does not, however, elucidate the meaning of "death" that Paul intends here; it clearly cannot be physical death, as that would be too extreme for some of the faults, such as being a "gossip" (ψιθυριστής). I suggest that here as well, Paul means "death of the soul," but uses the word ἄξιος in a manner that expresses "a corresponding" or "equivalent" perspective, as opposed to being "worthy." (See BDAG, ἄξιος). In this case, the types of actions listed by Paul are indeed those which bring about the "death of the soul."

In this final chapter, Wasserman points out that in Rom 6:15–23 Paul shows that "the mastery of sin (in one's life) leads to death at the final judgment." Regrettably, there is no evidence in 6:1–23 for the attribution of death at that time, but in 6:23, ". . .the wages of sin is death" certainly cannot mean physical death, as living sinners are evidence to the contrary; hence, "death of the soul" would be a superior interpretation of this use of θάνατος. Further, there is no evidence for his phrase pointing to death at final judgment. Paul's usage would be consistent, however, with a non-metaphorical use of "the death of the soul," insofar as it would have a vastly superior parenetic value over its characterization as a metaphor. Life indeed is truly at stake; and its opposite, a real, ontological death, is the consequence of "sin" however it is characterized.

In her conclusion, Wasserman recognizes one of the larger problems in dealing with the "death of the soul." As she describes the difficulty of understanding Paul's apocalyptic world-view, she points out the need for more study. "An important first step in this project will be to develop criteria for distinguishing between the metaphorical and literal uses of language" (p. 147). I wholly agree. Indeed, Paul is inconsistent in his own uses of the word "death;" sometimes it is clearly metaphorical (i.e., dying to sin); but in other places (6:23) I believe he takes a non-metaphorical stand, holding that sinful actions are destructive of one's soul.

John T. Conroy, Jr.
Blessed Edmund Rice School for Pastoral Ministry

KENNETH L. SCHENCK, *Cosmology and Eschatology in Hebrews: The Settings of the Sacrifice*. Society for New Testament Studies Monograph Series 143. Cambridge: Cambridge University Press, 2007. xi + 220 pages. ISBN 978-05-21-88323-8. Price $93, £52.

Kenneth Schenck's study of Hebrews continues his earlier engagement with this endlessly fascinating text. In his earlier work, he argued that one can best understand what is going on in Hebrews if one uncovers the story that underlies the homily. Using the techniques of Greimasian narrative analysis he recounts that story, which stretches from creation to heavenly glory, with the action of the Great High Priest as the pivotal point. A similar analysis undergirds this monograph, which focuses, as the title suggests, on the relationship between cosmology and eschatology in the text.

In the process of unpacking these two dimensions of Hebrews, Schenck begins with a survey of the contemporary scholarly scene and argues that attempts to read Hebrews against a single simple "background" fail to do justice to the homily's narrative and rhetorical complexity. Schenk then offers a detailed exegesis of some of the most controversial passages. His discussion is marked by a masterful command of the secondary literature. He carefully notes the range of scholarly opinion on all the issues that he addresses and offers a carefully reasoned and closely argued account of his own positions. Anyone interested in Hebrews will learn much from his careful treatment of all the issues and, whether or not one agrees with him, will have to take his arguments with utmost seriousness.

The results of the analysis involve an interesting assessment of what Hebrews takes to be the relationship between creation and ultimate glory. Schenck argues, for instance, that Hebrews has a rather low view of the created order, expecting it to be eliminated or displaced in the eschaton, leaving only the "heavenly realm" which Christ's priestly action has made accessible to his followers. In sketching this relationship between cosmology and eschatology, Schenck echoes many earlier students of Hebrews, particularly those who have found Platonic or Philonic influences at work in the text. This is where his monograph becomes of particular interest to readers of this journal.

As already noted, Schenck begins with the premise that one ought not try to squeeze Hebrews into one or another of the "backgrounds" that have been proposed in the history of scholarship. Our homilist instead should be seen as someone who combines models in new and interesting ways. Schenck's instincts are certainly sound and move the interpretation of Hebrews in a useful direction. Far too much ink has been spilled on whether or not Hebrews fits some pre-ordained category. What Schenck suggests instead is that at those points where "background" issues are often disputed, metaphor is at work, a mode of discourse that refuses to be pinned down to a single, specific meaning. Thus the heavenly high priesthood of Christ, the heavenly sanctuary, with the various possibilities of its construal, the veil that is the flesh of Christ (10:20), all are part of a complex of metaphors that serve the rhetorical purpose of encouraging fidelity in the face of circumstances hard, as always, to define with precision.

The general approach is refreshing and the results generally persuasive. The summary of those results in the last chapter, which lays out the "story" presumed by the homily and the circumstances to which it might have been addressed (a mainly Gentile community in late first-century Rome dismayed by the destruction of the Temple) are a plausible reconstruction of the text's rhetorical situation, even if not all students of Hebrews would agree.

The study is thorough, engaging, and in many ways persuasive, but despite all its strengths and its very reasonable recognition of the rhetorical flexibility of Hebrews, Schenck does not fully capture the rhetorical dynamics of this most sophisticated bit of early Christian homiletics. The problem comes at precisely those many points where Hebrews suggests some connection to a Platonic/Philonic realm of speculation. On point after point, Schenck marshals the arguments pro and con, the meaning of *hypodeigma* (8:5; 9:23), the use of *skia* (8:5; 10:1) or *eikôn* (10:1), the treatment of the heavenly realities that need cleansing (10:23), the designation of heaven "itself" (10:24). In each case he suggests why commentators might have been tempted to see a Platonic or Philonic scheme at work and why that scheme cannot work. He even recognizes that some passages, such as the conclusion of chapter 9, have a very Platonic/Philonic "feel," but cannot with any degree of ease be subsumed into a Platonic metaphysics.

Schenck, of course, is right, both in what he recognizes as a Platonic "feel" and why that feeling seems to be wrong. What he doesn't account for is the fact of the "feeling" itself. The reason, I believe, is that he assumes that the text finally has a single coherent, if complex, model of cosmology and eschatology. Hence the apparently vertical dichotomy between heaven and earth of chapter 8 must ultimately mean the same thing or have the same referent as the horizontal/eschatological dichotomy of chapter 10. He seems to insist on this, despite the fact that he recognizes the complexity of the models at work in the language of Hebrews. He is particularly clear on this complexity in discussing the work's Christology, which, despite the sapiential reference to Christ as instrument of creation in the proem, seems thereafter to focus almost exclusively on Christ as the eschatological agent of redemption.

The assumption at work here may be a function of the underlying narratological model of Schenck's analysis. Like most forms of structuralist analysis, a quest for the underlying framework or skeleton of a text seeks for stability. Despite Schenck's recognition of the importance of "rhetoric" for understanding Hebrews, he subordinates the rhetorical dynamics of the text to its narrative structure, leaving room only for "metaphor" that enables multiple senses or referents. What is missing is a sense of the ways in which the homilist uses metaphor (and other tropes), with their complex possible referents, for rhetorical effect. He does so to toy with the expectations of his audience, to lead them along a path that seems to point in one direction until he subverts those expectations and takes them in a new and unexpected direction.

Students of narrative, especially ancient narrative (see Aristotle's *Poetics*), recognize that something similar could happen in stories as well, in the *peripateia* that comes with a moment of recognition or *anagnoresis* within a plot. Interestingly enough, modern students of homiletics such as Eugene Lowry (*Homiletical Plot, the Sermon as Narrative Art Form* [Atlanta: John Knox, 1980; Louisville: Westminster John Knox, 2001]) have made the same point about the ways in which really good sermons work, by revolving around a pivot point that leads an audience to new insight. But a *structuralist* approach to an underlying *narrative*, which fits pieces of the narrative plot into a preconceived actantial pattern, leaves little room for such rhetorical dynamics.

Hebrews is a text that does precisely what Eugene Lowry says good homilies should do. The language and structures that it puts into play with a Platonic or Philonic "feel," odd though they may be from a strict philosophical point of view, do what they were designed to do. They constitute a gesture in a certain direction, which sets up expectations about where ultimate reality is to be found and how it is to be accessed. Many modern commentators have been led down that path to try to find a simple and consistent Platonic/Philonic world view expressed in the text. But having made its gesture in a Platonic direction, Hebrews dramatically changes its course. The pivotal point in Hebrews comes very clearly at the beginning of chapter 10, where the previously dominant vertical dichotomies, pushed to a point of absurdity, suddenly and unmistakably shift to a horizontal plane, and with that shift comes a revaluation of where ultimate reality is to be encountered, in the shadow casting "body" (10:10) of the One who offers himself in faithful conformity with the will of God. That shift implies the kind of transvaluation of values that the homilist calls his audience to undergo, giving up the security of past relationships to follow the shamefully executed Christ "outside the camp." Schenck's efforts to pin down the cosmology and eschatology of Hebrews miss that rhetorical play, which, however, is quite compatible with the ultimate rhetorical aim that he assigns to Hebrews.

Schenck, then, has given us a learned and carefully argued study of important themes in Hebrews, one that will certainly stimulate further fruitful discussion of this masterful Christian homily.

Harold W. Attridge
Yale Divinity School

PETER C. BOUTENEFF, *Beginnings. Ancient Christian Readings of the Biblical Creation Narratives.* Grand Rapids, Mich.: Baker Academic, 2008. 256 pages. ISBN 978-0-8010-3233-2. Price $24.99.

Written at least in part to address the position of the Eastern Orthodox Church on how to read the first three chapters of Genesis from a faith perspective, the author has produced a wide ranging and readable account of the exegesis of early Greek Christian writers from the New Testament to the Cappadocians (Tertullian also appears, though not the Syriac writers Aphrahat and Ephrem). The relevant work of each major figure is contextualized in terms of his general approach to Scripture and the major theological challenges faced by his generation.

Bouteneff also explicitly leaves out the late fourth century Latin writers Jerome and Augustine. Though he does not overemphasize this, he points out that Western Christian notions of "the fall" and of "original sin" are due to Augustine in particular. Bouteneff notes that St Paul does have a concept of a "fall," but that by portraying Adam as both the first human being and first sinner, Paul broadened the scope of salvation to incorporate non-Jews. Death is a consequence of sin rather than its punishment, a theme developed in later writers. The Adam–Christ/death–life polarity put forward in 1 Cor 15 is the result of Paul's contemplation of the meaning of salvation in Christ, which led Paul back to consider the beginnings of humanity and why it needed redemption.

Irenaeus emerges as one of the most interesting writers, the key to whose thought is the concept of *anakephalaiosis*, "recapitulation." He argued that since God as Saviour existed eternally, the creation of the one to be saved was necessary. Irenaeus also saw mankind's apostasy as allowed by Providence, in that God knew that human maturity is impossible without the knowledge of good and evil. Though fallen humanity remains in the image of God (Gen 1:26), it has lost the divine likeness, which can only be recovered through assimilation to Christ. (This contrasts strongly with a strand in early Syriac thought, in which the goal of spiritual endeavour is a return to a state of Edenic innocence and angelic purity, largely by means of sexual abstinence and ascetical practices.)

In fact Adam is rarely depicted primarily as an historical figure by early Greek Christian authors. They view him rather as the "emblem and originator of transgressive patterns of human behaviour" (p. 174), with Origen considering Cain's fratricide as far worse than Adam's eating of the fruit. And throughout the period under consideration there is an insistence that humans have free will and that Adam's disobedience does not mean that all his descendants will automatically become sinners.

A number of times Bouteneff notes that despite the Church Fathers' knowledge of the cosmology and science of their day, they very rarely try to square it with the biblical account. For them the focus of the Hexaemeron, or account of the six days of creation, was its testimony to divine Providence and the nature of the Creator. There is a variety of interpretations of the "days," from twenty-four hour periods to entire eras, and a tendency to interpret what was described as having been created (water, trees, animals etc.) as real things, but this was largely a reaction to the tendency of Origen and also gnostic heretics to allegorize the account completely. There was a growing stress on the doctrine of creation *ex nihilo* in the face of pagan and gnostic claims. The new insistence on the role of the Son as present in the beginning and as agent of creation represented a markedly different understanding of Genesis 1 from that of rabbinic Judaism.

In terms of the methodology of reading Scripture, Bouteneff reviews the range of practice within both allegorical and typological exegesis. Allegory could represent a denial of the plain meaning of the text, but it could also involve an additional, higher sense. There was also a debate over whether the type had to have a concrete historical existence (as required by the Antiochenes in the subsequent period) or whether it received meaning only through its fulfilment in the event or person it prefigured. Bouteneff also briefly discusses the Fathers' avoidance of the term "myth," which had negative, pagan connotations, even if theologians favour its use today as "true fiction."

From the point of view of readers of this journal, and for scholars of Jewish studies more widely, it is a pity that the short section on Philo ("Coda," pp. 27–32) is not better integrated into the book. Bouteneff acknowledges Philo's influence on Greek Christian writers in terms both of subject matter and of allegorical methodology, which is why he includes him. However, Philo is hardly mentioned at all after the Introduction, and his contribution is passed over in the book's conclusions. One might also quibble at the author's statement that Philo "makes no pretense at being either scriptural or historical" (p. 27). Bouteneff may well have hesitated to say more, given that his readership is presumably a Christian one coming from a faith perspective and in view of the growing body of literature on Philo and Scripture. Also, as Bouteneff makes clear, by the fourth century a tradition had become established of interpreting Genesis chapters 1–3 in a strongly christological and eschatological framework. Thus while some forms of Christian exegesis (principally Alexandrian) still bore the hallmark of Philonic allegorical interpretation, they had also developed their own exegetical traditions in which the influence of philosophy and of Hellenistic Judaism was much diminished.

Alison G. Salvesen
Oriental Institute, University of Oxford

SABRINA INOWLOCKI, *Eusebius and the Jewish Authors: His Citation Technique in an Apologetic Context*. Ancient Judaism and Early Christianity 64. Leiden: Brill, 2006. xviii + 337 pages. ISBN 978-90-04-14990-8. Price $160, €112.

The study under review is a revised English translation of a doctoral dissertation originally titled *La citation comme méthode apologétique: les auteurs juifs dans l'Apodeixis d'Eusébe de Césarée*, which was prepared and defended at the University of Brussels under the supervision of Professor Michèle Broze. The first stage of the author's research was supervised by Martin Goodman (Oxford) and she also worked closely with Dr. Annewies van den Hoek during an academic stay at the Harvard Divinity School.

The study has a well-thought-out methodology and clear structure. It consists of six chapters. In the first, sources and method are introduced. The research focuses on Eusebius's two great apologetic works known as the *Praeparatio evangelica* (fifteen books) and the *Demonstratio evangelica* (twenty books, of which only ten are extant). The former is primarily directed at Greek readers versed in the traditions of Hellenism, the latter responds to Jewish accusations that Christians have adopted the Jewish Scriptures but have abandoned the Jewish way of life. In recent years scholars have concluded that the two works really form parts of a single undertaking that is meant to be read as a whole, which Eusebius himself calls the *Apodeixis* (Demonstration). It emerges in the study, however, that the way sources are cited in the two parts differs quite markedly. Although the study examines both parts, the main emphasis is on the *Praeparatio*. The four non-biblical Jewish authors that are studied are Philo, Josephus, Philo's Alexandrian predecessor Aristobulus, and Pseudo-Aristeas the author of *The Letter to Philocrates*. In addition it also discusses a group of minor Jewish authors quoted by Eusebius indirectly via Alexander Polyhistor. Since the main object of study is an apologetic work that makes frequent reference to philosophical and exegetical themes, of all the Jewish authors studied, Philo is the one who receives the most attention. Josephus plays a less central role. In the *PE* it is mainly the *Contra Apionem* that is cited; in the *DE* greater use is made of his historical works. The other authors receive only limited attention, but the use of Aristobulus is interesting, because surprisingly Eusebius sees him as the main representative of Jewish allegory.

The next three chapters continue to discuss background themes that prepare the reader for the main investigation. The second chapter gives a valuable overview of how authors were cited by other authors in the Greco-Roman world and how Eusebius develops such techniques in creating his own unique method. Far from just patching citations together, he formulates a complex argument through the agency of such citations, selecting and adapting them in the process. This study innovates by not placing the emphasis on the cited excerpts themselves, valuable though they are (often we only know these texts through Eusebius), but on what the author does with them. The next chapter gives an overview, for purposes of comparison, of the non-Jewish—i.e. pagan, Christian and biblical—authors that Eusebius cites. Chapter four introduces a crucial problem of nomenclature. Eusebius sometimes calls biblical and Jewish persons "Hebrews" (Ἑβραῖοι) and sometimes "Jews" (Ἰουδαῖοι). The distinction is not clear-cut and sometimes downright confusing. But it does yield important insights into his complex relation to the Jewish people and the Jewish religion.

The final two long chapters contain the bulk of the research. Chapter five presents the "labour of citation" (Inowlocki actually retains the French phrase "travail de la citation" in the chapter title for reasons that seem unnecessary to me), i.e. examination of the actual mechanics of the selection, cutting and arrangement of his citations and also detailed analysis of the degree to which Eusebius remains faithful to the text and intent of the excerpts he cites. In the final chapter it is his usage of the citations that comes under the microscope. It emerges that there are three main functions. Jewish authors are used (1) as an intermediary between Jewish-Christian and Greek thought, (2) as a source for apologetic and polemical themes against pagan authors, and (3) as a source for early Christian history (mainly in the *DE*). The use made of the various authors and their texts depends largely on the status which he accords them and this is quite varied. The same applies to the degree of approbation that he gives them. This depends strongly on the context of the usage. When Eusebius cites

"Hebrew" testimonies on theological and philosophical themes, he completely appropriates the content. But in the case of other themes he retains a certain distance from them. However, the testimony of the Jewish authors is never wholly rejected.

Having given the above account of the main contents of the study, I may be allowed to make a remark related to my own research. When I did the research for my book on *Philo in Early Christian Literature* (Assen 1993), I soon realized that it was not going to be possible to cover this subject, which had hitherto only been very superficially researched, in anything like the detail it deserved. So I decided to cover the field by means of a survey that gave an overview of the main areas and indicated where further research would be profitable, without doing all the detailed work myself. This would have been a lifetime's work and was not what the board of the series that commissioned the work wished me to do. So I expressed the hope that the study would inspire further research. The monograph by Sabrina Inowlocki now under review is exactly the kind of research that I envisaged. Because she has plunged into the fine-grained detail of Eusebius's appropriation of Philo (and other Jewish authors writing in Greek), she has been able to achieve new and significant insights into the use of these texts by one of the most influential Christian authors in the early Church. Let me now mention four of these new insights.

(1) Inowlocki shows how Eusebius, though living and working in Caesarea, stands very clearly in the Alexandrian tradition, which was mediated to him via Origen and Pantaenus. What is new is the way she can prove that many of his apologetic methods and thematics are inspired by the example of Clement of Alexandria, whose writings he had clearly studied very closely. But there is of course a crucial difference between the way the two men make use of earlier Greek and Jewish material. Clement rarely cites his authors but paraphrases them in complex ways. Eusebius prefers to cite the actual words of his authors, joining up the citations by means of his own interspersed comments. (2) Eusebius's relationship to Judaism is complex and has given rise to much scholarly discussion and dispute. Inowlocki's research into the way Eusebius uses the two terms "Hebrews" and "Jews," while perhaps not the last word on the subject, certainly yields fresh insight. She shows how Judaism plays many different roles in his writings depending on the context. Philo is regarded positively, not only because he provides important information on the beginnings of the Church, but also because through his writings he casts light on the ancient Hebrew tradition of the Patriarchs and Moses, the biblical heritage to which in his view the Christians, and not contemporary Jews, are the heir. Hence the title "the Hebrew" which Eusebius usually gives him.

(3) Inowlocki's analysis of the use of Philonic texts in Books 7 and 11 of the *PE* also yields important results. Just like in Clement, Philo is used as an intermediary between Greek philosophy and biblically-based Christian thought, with particular emphasis on the role of key terminology such as λόγος, εἰκών, παράδειγμα, γένεσις and so on. Eusebius is arguing for biblical Platonism, though—just like Philo—he is convinced that Plato is indebted to Moses. In a sense Moses and Plato are treated in a parallel way. Just as Philo is invoked to explain the philosophy of Moses, so later Platonists such as Arius Didymus, Plutarch and Numenius are used as witnesses to the Platonic tradition. This explains why of all the leading philosophers of the earlier period of Greek philosophy, only Plato is cited directly. There is not a single direct quotation from the works of Aristotle, Epicurus or Chrysippus in the entire *PE*. The key to Eusebius's treatment of Greek philosophy is the antithesis between agreement (συμφωνία) and disagreement (διαφωνία). If Greek philosophical doctrines agree with Moses and with each other, they can be useful. If they disagree with Moses and among each other, they are to be rejected. Inowlocki mentions this theme (p. 59, 93), but she might have developed it further. (4) The final two long chapters of the book are one long study in how Eusebius selects and adapts his citations from Philo and the other Jewish authors. Numerous insights are given to a whole range of texts. The excitement is in the detail and there is a huge amount to learn.

Of all the various aspects covered by the term "adaptation," perhaps the most intriguing is the extent to which Eusebius as citer of other writers' material remains faithful to the text he is citing. In many cases this cannot be checked when the original is lost. But in the case of authors such as Philo, Josephus and Plato we can almost always check exactly what he is doing (but not in the case of Philo's *Hypothetica*, where no other trace of the original survives). Inowlocki rightly argues that it is wrong and counterproductive to impose on the Church father our modern notions of intellectual property and responsibility towards the intentions of the original author. Nevertheless Eusebius does appear on the surface to be quite faithful to the texts he cites *verbatim*. Modern editors have understandably, but sometimes rather naively, used his texts as evidence of the state of their manuscript tradition in the third and fourth centuries c.e. The section entitled "Faithfulness to the text of the Jewish authors' citations" (pp. 190–220) is therefore one of the most fascinating and important in the whole book. I read it with great interest, agreeing with many interpretations, but also finding myself questioning or disagreeing with some. The following critical comments focus on this section.

p. 192. Cohn and Wendland do not claim that Eusebius's manuscripts of Philo's *Prob.* reflect the text of better codices that are no longer extant, but rather that his text is closest to the better Philonic manuscripts and are of considerable value in confirming their readings.

p. 195. I agree that it is tempting to regard the expression δεύτερος θεός as the result of an Eusebian intervention. But the fact that the Armenian translation has the same phrase must be a serious objection, because we would have to assume either that the sixth century Armenian translators had taken the Eusebian citation into account or the fact that both texts introduced the same phrase independently of each other. Both possibilities are quite unlikely. The reference to *QG* 2.86 is puzzling, since this text does not exist. There seems to be a mix up with *Leg.* 2.86 where Philo writes δεύτερος ὁ θεοῦ λόγος, which is not quite the same as δεύτερος θεός.

p. 197. In the translation of *Agr.* 51 the crucial words "as law" are missing ("and he shall set over them as law his true *Logos*...").

p. 200. The suggestion that the deletion of the words αἴτιον, τὸ δὲ παθητόν· καὶ ὅτι τὸ μὲν δραστήριον in *Opif.* 8 may have been due to Eusebius is certainly worth considering. But it is surely unexpected that he would delete the word αἴτιον. Grammatically too there are problems with the way the μέν . . . δέ construction works if the words are deleted. I think a case of *parablepsis* either by Eusebius or the manuscript tradition has to be the more likely option. Note also that the translation of ὁ τῶν ὅλων νοῦς by "the soul of the universe" is inexact ("intellect" is to be preferred). Philo is not attracted to the Platonic concept of a world-soul.

p. 205. The omission of θεῶν in the phrase θεὸς θεῶν νοητῶν τε καὶ αἰσθητῶν in *Spec.* 1.20 might well be deliberate, as Inowlocki argues. It should be noted, however, that the omission spoils Philo's clear allusion to Deut. 10:17.

Finally a few words should be said about the book's presentation. As noted at the outset of the review, it is a translation from the original French prepared by the author. She does not tell us why she went to all this trouble, but presumably it was done in order to increase the readership of the book. Because of the book's origin, it contains references to francophone literary theorists such as L. Rosier, G. Genette, M. Bakhtine and A. Compagnon who will be unknown to most English-speaking readers. I have no problems with this at all. It is profitable to be exposed to different traditions of scholarship. It is also not a real problem that the reader is introduced to some unusual English words such as "remindful," "ablation," "notoriousness," "Olymp," and so on. English readers should be grateful for all the effort that has gone into the translation and not carp about the occasional wrong term or infelicitous phrase. Nevertheless the book would have been aided by a more thorough process of revision and copy-editing. There are quite a few mistakes in the Greek (including a strange tendency to omit the iota in words starting with φιλ, see pp. 61, 64, 76, 143, 189 (twice)) and also in references to authors and texts. It is a pity that these errors were not removed.

But it would be quite inappropriate to end on a negative note. This monograph makes a significant, indeed exciting, contribution to our under-standing of the appropriation of Hellenistic-Jewish writings by one of the most influential figures in the early Christian tradition. I recommend it highly.

David T. Runia
Queen's College
The University of Melbourne

The Studia Philonica Annual 20 (2010) 313–315

NEWS AND NOTES[1]

New editor of The Studia Philonica Monograph Series

The Editorial and the Advisory Boards of *The Studia Philonica Annual*, in conjunction with the publisher SBL Publications (Atlanta), are most pleased to announce that Professor Thomas H. Tobin, S.J. has accepted the appointment as Editor of The Studia Philonica Monograph Series. In this role he succeeds Professor David Hay, who most sadly passed away suddenly in August 2006. Professor Tobin has been on the Advisory Board of *The Studia Philonica Annual* since its inception in 1989 and has been its Chair since 2007. So far five volumes have been published in the monograph series, the last in 2002. A new volume is planned to appear in the very near future. All lovers of scholarship should be most grateful to the publisher for continuing to provide this great opportunity for scholars to publish monographs in the area of Philonic and Hellenistic-Jewish studies. For further details on submission of manuscripts see above p. v.

> The Editorial and Advisory Boards
> *The Studia Philonica Annual*

Philo of Alexandria Group of the Society of Biblical Literature

At the 2009 Annual Meeting of the Society for Biblical Literature in New Orleans, Louisiana, the Philo of Alexandria Group met for two sessions, on November 22 and 23. The first session, presided over by Kenneth L. Schenck (Indiana Wesleyan University), was devoted to Philo's treatise *De Agricultura*, being prepared by Albert Geljon (Christelijk Gymnasium Utrecht) and David Runia (Queen's College, University of Melbourne) for

[1] Items of general interest to Philo scholars to be included in this section can be sent to the editor, David Runia (contact details in Notes on Contributors below).

the Philo of Alexandria Commentary Series (PACS). Albert Geljon opened the session by discussing aspects related to the treatise and to preparation of the translation and commentary (a sample of which for *Agr.* 1–25 had been distributed prior to the meeting). David Runia then presented a paper entitled "The Structure of Philo's Allegorical Treatise *De Agricultura*" (published in this volume). Responding to these presentations were James R. Royse (Claremont, California), who addressed Philo's use of biblical texts in *Agr.* (published in this volume); David Konstan (Brown University), who spoke about the organization of and rationale underlying the treatise (published in this volume); and Maren Niehoff (Hebrew University of Jerusalem), who discussed Philo's references in the treatise to other interpreters. (Maren Niehoff had kindly stepped in for Sarah Pearce, who was unfortunately unable to attend because of illness.) After questions and comments from the audience, a business meeting followed. This included a relay of greetings from absent and far-flung well-wishers, discussion of plans for future meetings, remarks by David Runia about *The Studia Philonica Annual* (which had a year earlier marked its 20th anniversary!), and a brief report by Gregory Sterling about PACS. Since this meeting, David Runia has rejoined the Philo Group Steering Committee (see "News and Notes," *SPhA* 18 [2009]: 146).

The theme of the second session, presided over by Robert Kraft (University of Pennsylvania) was "Philo and the Bible of Alexandria." Speakers and topics included Tessa Rajak (University of Reading), "Philo's Hebrew: The Etymologies Once Again;" Benjamin G. Wright III (Lehigh University), "The Septuagint in Philo: Translation and Inspiration;" Gregory E. Sterling (University of Notre Dame), "Which Version of the Greek Bible Did Philo Read?;" Maren Niehoff, "Did Alexandrian Jews Apply Text-critical Methods to Their Bible?;" and Hans Svebakken (Loyola University Chicago), "Philo's Reworking of a Traditional Interpretation of 'Clean' and 'Unclean' Winged Creatures." A group of Philonic friends representing no fewer than seven countries also gathered for dinner one evening at Bacco Restaurant in the French Quarter.

For the 2010 meeting of the SBL Philo of Alexandria Group in Atlanta, Georgia, two sessions are planned on the theme of "Philo and the Roman World."

Ellen Birnbaum
Cambridge Mass.

Philo conference to be held in Italy

An international conference on Philo will be held in Milan, Italy, on June 14–17, 2011. The conference is being organized by the following Universities: Università Cattolica di Milano, Università Statale di Milano, Università di Pavia, Université de Paris-Sorbonne, Université de Bordeaux and Institut Universitaire de France. The theme is "Potere e potenze. Pouvoir et puissance" (Power and potencies). It will be approached both in relation to ontology and the human possibilities of knowing God and from a political point of view.

The conference will bring together many distinguished Philonic scholars from Europe and abroad, including the editors of this Annual, David Runia and Gregory Sterling.

Francesca Calabi
Milan

New research on the Armenian Philonic tradition

In 2005 Olga Vardazarjan published in Yerevan, Armenia her dissertation on the medieval Armenian tradition of Philonic studies. For the first time an extensive study is devoted to the tradition of scholiasts and commentators on the Philonic corpus who were active in the twelfth–fourteenth century, notably the future Armenian *katholikos* Yakob Klayec' I (†1286) and Yovhannēs Orotnec'i (1315–1386). Dr Vardazayan has also written four further articles on this subject, which to my knowledge has not hitherto received scholarly attention in modern times. Summaries of her research are found in the Bibliography section on pp. 252–56.

David T. Runia
Queen's College
The University of Melbourne

The Studia Philonica Annual 22 (2010) 316–319

NOTES ON CONTRIBUTORS

TATJANA ALEKNIENE is Associated Professor of Ancient History in the Department of General History at the Vilnius Pedagogical University. Her postal address is T. Ševčenkos g. 31, 207 k., LT-03111, Vilnius, LITHUANIA; her electronic address is t.d.aleknos@takas.lt.

MANUEL ALEXANDRE JR is Professor of Classics Emeritus at the University of Lisbon, Faculty of Letters, Portugal, and Senior Research fellow of the Center of Classical Studies at the same University. His postal address is Rua Joly Braga Santos, Lote E - 3 Dto., Lisbon 1600-123, PORTUGAL; his electronic address is malex@fl.ul.pt.

HAROLD W. ATTRIDGE is the Rev. Henry L. Slack Dean and Lillian Claus Professor of New Testament at Yale Divinity School. His postal address is 409 Prospect St., New Haven, CT 06511, USA. His email address is: Harold.Attridge@Yale.edu.

KATELL BERTHELOT is Researcher at the National Center for Scientific Research (France), currently appointed at the French Research Center in Jerusalem. Her postal address is: CRFJ, PB 547, 3 Shimshon St., 91004 Jerusalem, ISRAEL; her electronic address is katell.berthelot@crfj.org.il.

ELLEN BIRNBAUM has taught at several Boston-area institutions, including Boston University, Brandeis, and Harvard. Her postal address is 78 Porter Road, Cambridge, MA 02140, USA; her electronic address is ebirnbaum@comcast.net.

RENÉ BLOCH is Professor of Jewish Studies at the University of Bern. His postal address is: Institut für Judaistik, Universität Bern, Länggassstrasse 51, 3012 Bern, SWITZERLAND; his electronic address is: rene.bloch@theol.-unibe.ch.

DULCINEA BOESENBERG is a graduate student in the Department of Theology at the University of Notre Dame. Her postal address is Department of Theology, 130 Malloy Hall, University of Notre Dame, Notre Dame, IN 46556, USA; her electronic address is dboesenb@nd.edu.

JOHN T. (JACK) CONROY is Assistant Professor at Barry University and the Blessed Edmund Rice School for Pastoral Ministry. His postal address is John T. Conroy, Jr., 636 Fifteenth Avenue South, Naples, FL 34102, USA; his electronic address is jconroy@alumni.nd.edu.

MICHAEL COVER is a doctoral student in theology at the University of Notre Dame. His postal address is Department of Theology, 130 Malloy Hall, University of Notre Dame, Notre Dame, IN 46556, USA. His email address is mcover@nd.edu.

RONALD R. COX is Associate Professor and Seaver Fellow in the Religion Division, Pepperdine University. His postal address is Religion Division, Pepperdine University, Malibu, CA 90263-4352, USA; his electronic address is ronald.cox@pepperdine.edu.

PIETER W. VAN DER HORST is Professor emeritus of Early Christian and Jewish studies at Utrecht University. His postal address is: Comeniuslaan 51, 3706XB Zeist, THE NETHERLANDS; his email address is: pwvdh@xs4all.nl. His website is: http://www.pietervanderhorst.com

ALBERT C. GELJON teaches classical languages at the Christelijke Gymnasium in Utrecht. His postal address is Gazellestraat 138, 3523 SZ Utrecht, THE NETHERLANDS; his electronic address is geljon@ixs.nl.

CRAIG KEENER is Professor of New Testament at Palmer Theological Seminary of Eastern University. His postal address is Palmer Seminary, 6 E. Lancaster Ave., Wynnewood, PA 19096, USA; his electronic address is ckeener@eastern.edu.

HELEEN M. KEIZER is Dean of Academic Affairs at the Istituto Superiore di Osteopatia in Milan, Italy. Her postal address is Via Guerrazzi 3, 20052 Monza (Mi), ITALY; her electronic address is h.m.keizer@virgilio.it.

DAVID KONSTAN is Professor of Classics at New York University and John Rowe Workman Distinguished Emeritus Professor of Classics and the Humanistic Tradition at Brown University. His postal address is 48 College Street, Brown University, Providence RI 22912, USA; his electronic address is dkonstan@brown.edu.

JUTTA LEONHARDT-BALZER is Lecturer in New Testament at the University of Aberdeen. Her postal address is School of Divinity and Religious Studies, King's College, University of Aberdeen, Aberdeen AB24 3UB, UNITED KINGDOM; her electronic address is j.leonhardt-balzer@abdn.ac.uk.

JOSÉ PABLO MARTÍN is Professor Consultus at the Universidad Nacional de General Sarmiento, San Miguel, Argentina, and Senior Research fellow of the Argentinian Research Organization (CONICET). His postal address is Azcuenaga 1090, 1663 San Miguel, ARGENTINA; his electronic address is philonis@fastmail.fm.

EKATERINA MATUSOVA is Associate Professor of Classics at the Institute for Oriental and Classical Studies at the Russian State University for the Humanities, Moscow. Her postal address is 125993 GSP-3, Miusskaya pl. 6, Moscow, RUSSIA; her electronic address is ek.matusova@yahoo.co.uk.

MAREN S. NIEHOFF is Senior Lecturer in the Department of Jewish Thought at the Hebrew University, Jerusalem. Her postal address is Department of Jewish Thought, Hebrew University, Mt. Scopus, Jerusalem 91905, ISRAEL; her electronic address is msmaren@mscc.huji.ac.il.

JEAN RIAUD is Professor in the Institut de Lettres et Histoire, Université Catholique de l'Ouest, Angers. His postal address is 24, rue du 8 mai 1945, Saint Barthélemy d'Anjou, FRANCE; his electronic address is jean.riaud@wanadoo.fr.

JAMES R. ROYSE is a Visiting Scholar at the Claremont School of Theology. His postal address is P.O. Box 567, Claremont, CA 91711-0567, USA; his electronic address is jamesrroyse@hotmail.com.

DAVID T. RUNIA is Master of Queen's College and Professorial Fellow in the School of Historical Studies at the University of Melbourne. His postal address is Queen's College, 1–17 College Crescent, Parkville 3052, AUSTRALIA; his electronic address is runia@queens.unimelb.edu.au.

TORREY SELAND is Professor and Research Coordinator at The School of Mission and Theology, Stavanger, Norway. His postal address is School of Mission and Theology, Misjonsmarka 12, 4024 Stavanger, NORWAY; his electronic address is torreys@gmail.com.

GREGORY E. STERLING is Dean of the Graduate School and Professor of New Testament and Christian Origins in the Department of Theology, University of Notre Dame. His postal address is 502 Main Building, University of Notre Dame, Notre Dame IN 46556, USA; his electronic address is sterling.1@nd.edu.

THOMAS H. TOBIN, S.J. is Professor of New Testament and Early Christianity at Loyola University Chicago. His postal address is Department of Theology, Loyola University Chicago, 1032 West Sheridan Road, Chicago, IL 60660-1537, USA; his electronic address is ttobin@luc.edu.

HORACIO VELA III is a graduate student in the Department of Theology at the University of Notre Dame. His postal address is Department of Theology, 130 Malloy Hall, University of Notre Dame, Notre Dame, IN 46556, USA; his electronic address is horaciovela1@gmail.com.

DAVID WINSTON is Emeritus Professor of Hellenistic and Jewish Studies, Graduate Theological Union, Berkeley. His postal address is 1220 Grizzly Peak, Berkeley, CA 94708, USA; his electronic address is davidswinston@comcast.net.

The Studia Philonica Annual 22 (2010) 320–326

INSTRUCTIONS TO CONTRIBUTORS

Articles and Book reviews can only be considered for publication in *The Studia Philonica Annual* if they rigorously conform to the guidelines established by the editorial board. For further information see also the website of the Annual:

http://www.nd.edu/~philojud

1. *The Studia Philonica Annual* accepts articles for publication in the area of Hellenistic Judaism, with special emphasis on Philo and his *Umwelt*. Articles on Josephus will be given consideration if they focus on his relation to Judaism and classical culture (and not on primarily historical subjects). The languages in which the articles may be published are English, French and German. Translations from Italian or Dutch into English can be arranged at a modest cost to the author.

2. Articles and reviews are to be sent to the editors in electronic form as email attachments. The preferred word processor is Microsoft Word. Users of other word processors are requested to submit a copy exported in a format compatible with Word, e.g. in RTF format. Manuscripts should be double-spaced, including the notes. Words should be italicized when required, not underlined. Quotes five lines or longer should be indented and may be single-spaced. For texts in Greek only Unicode fonts can be accepted. For Hebrew the font provided on the SBL website is recommended. In all cases it is **imperative** that authors give **full details** about the word processor (if it is not Word) and foreign language fonts used. Moreover, if the manuscript contains Greek or Hebrew material, a PDF version of the document must be sent together with the word processing file. If this proves difficult, a hard copy can be sent by mail or by fax. No handwritten Greek or Hebrew can be accepted. Authors are requested not to vocalize their Hebrew (except when necessary) and to keep their use of this language to a reasonable minimum. It should always be borne in mind that not all readers of the Annual can be expected to read Greek or Hebrew. Transliteration is encouraged for incidental terms.

3. Authors are encouraged to use inclusive language wherever possible, avoiding terms such as "man" and "mankind" when referring to humanity in general.

4. For the preparation of articles and book reviews the Annual follows the guidelines of *The SBL Handbook of Style for Ancient Near Eastern, Biblical, and Early Christian Studies*, Hendrickson: Peabody Mass., 1999. For members of the Society of Biblical Literature, a downloadable PDF version of this guide is available on the SBL website, www.sbl-site.org (if non-members need a copy, they are asked to contact the editors). Here are examples of how a monograph, a monograph in a series, an edited volume, an article in an edited volume and a journal article are to be cited in notes (different conventions apply for bibliographies):

> Joan E. Taylor, *Jewish Women Philosophers of First-Century Alexandria—Philo's 'Therapeutae' Reconsidered* (Oxford: Oxford University Press, 2003), 123.
> Ellen Birnbaum, *The Place of Judaism in Philo's Thought: Israel, Jews, and Proselytes* (BJS 290; SPhM 2; Atlanta: Scholars Press, 1996), 134.
> Gerard P. Luttikhuizen, ed., *Eve's Children: The Biblical Stories Retold and Interpreted in Jewish and Christian Traditions* (Themes in Biblical Narrative 5; Leiden: Brill, 2003), 145.
> Gregory E. Sterling, "The Bond of Humanity: Friendship in Philo of Alexandria," in *Greco-Roman Perspectives on Friendship*, (ed. John T. Fitzgerald; SBLRBS 34; Atlanta: Scholars Press, 1997), 203–23.
> James R. Royse, "Jeremiah Markland's Contribution to the Textual Criticism of Philo." *SPhA* 16 (2004): 50–60.

Note that abbreviations are used in the notes, but not in a bibliography. When joining up numbers in all textual and bibliographical references, the n-dash should be used and not the hyphen, i.e. 50–60, not 50-60. For publishing houses only the first location is given. Submissions which do not conform to these guidelines will be returned to the authors for re-submission.

5. The following abbreviations are to be used in both articles and book reviews.

(a) Philonic treatises are to be abbreviated according to the following list. Numbering follows the edition of Cohn and Wendland, using Arabic numbers only and full stops rather than colons (e.g. *Spec.* 4.123). Note that *De Providentia* should be cited according to Aucher's edition, and not the LCL translation of the fragments by F. H. Colson.

Abr.	*De Abrahamo*
Aet.	*De aeternitate mundi*
Agr.	*De agricultura*
Anim.	*De animalibus*
Cher.	*De Cherubim*
Contempl.	*De vita contemplativa*
Conf.	*De confusione linguarum*
Congr.	*De congressu eruditionis gratia*
Decal.	*De Decalogo*
Deo	*De Deo*

Det.	*Quod deterius potiori insidiari soleat*
Deus	*Quod Deus sit immutabilis*
Ebr.	*De ebrietate*
Flacc.	*In Flaccum*
Fug.	*De fuga et inventione*
Gig.	*De gigantibus*
Her.	*Quis rerum divinarum heres sit*
Hypoth.	*Hypothetica*
Ios.	*De Iosepho*
Leg. 1–3	*Legum allegoriae* I, II, III
Legat.	*Legatio ad Gaium*
Migr.	*De migratione Abrahami*
Mos. 1–2	*De vita Moysis* I, II
Mut.	*De mutatione nominum*
Opif.	*De opificio mundi*
Plant.	*De plantatione*
Post.	*De posteritate Caini*
Praem.	*De praemiis et poenis, De exsecrationibus*
Prob.	*Quod omnis probus liber sit*
Prov. 1–2	*De Providentia* I, II
QE 1–2	*Quaestiones et solutiones in Exodum* I, II
QG 1–4	*Quaestiones et solutiones in Genesim* I, II, III, IV
Sacr.	*De sacrificiis Abelis et Caini*
Sobr.	*De sobrietate*
Somn. 1–2	*De somniis* I, II
Spec. 1–4	*De specialibus legibus* I, II, III, IV
Virt.	*De virtutibus*

(b) Standard works of Philonic scholarship are abbreviated as follows:

G-G   Howard L. Goodhart and Erwin R. Goodenough, "A General Bibliography of Philo Judaeus." In *The Politics of Philo Judaeus: Practice and Theory* (ed. Erwin R. Goodenough; New Haven: Yale University Press, 1938; repr. Georg Olms: Hildesheim, 1967), 125–321.

PCH   *Philo von Alexandria: die Werke in deutscher Übersetzung*, ed. Leopold Cohn, Isaac Heinemann *et al.*, 7 vols. (Breslau: M & H Marcus Verlag, Berlin: Walter de Gruyter, 1909–64).

PCW   *Philonis Alexandrini opera quae supersunt*, ed. Leopoldus Cohn, Paulus Wendland et Sigismundus Reiter, 6 vols. (Berlin: Georg Reimer, 1896–1915).

PLCL   *Philo in Ten Volumes (and Two Supplementary Volumes)*, English translation by F. H. Colson, G. H. Whitaker (and R. Marcus), 12 vols. (Loeb Classical Library; London: William Heinemann, Cambridge, Mass.: Harvard University Press, 1929–62).

PAPM   *Les œuvres de Philon d'Alexandrie*, French translation under the general editorship of Roger Arnaldez, Jean Pouilloux, and Claude Mondésert (Paris: Cerf, 1961–92).

R-R	Roberto Radice and David T. Runia, *Philo of Alexandria: an Annotated Bibliography 1937–1986* (VCSup 8; Leiden etc.: Brill 1988).
RRS	David T. Runia, *Philo of Alexandria: an Annotated Bibliography 1987–1996* (VCSup 57; Leiden etc.: Brill 2000).
SPh	*Studia Philonica*
SPhA	*The Studia Philonica Annual*
SPhM	Studia Philonica Monographs
PACS	Philo of Alexandria Commentary Series

(c) References to biblical authors and texts and to ancient authors and writings are to be abbreviated as recommended in the *SBL Handbook of Style* §8.2–3. Note that biblical books are not italicized and that between chapter and verse a colon is placed (but for non-biblical references colons should not be used). Abbreviations should be used for biblical books when they are followed by chapter or chapter and verse unless the book is the first word in a sentence. Authors writing in German or French should follow their own conventions for biblical citations.

(d) For giving dates the abbreviations B.C.E. and C.E. are preferred and should be printed in small caps.

(e) Journals, monograph series, source collections, and standard reference works are to be be abbreviated in accordance with the recommendations listed in *The SBL Handbook of Style* §8.4. The following list contains a selection of the more important abbreviations, along with a few abbreviations of classical and philosophical journals and standard reference books not furnished in the list.

ABD	*The Anchor Bible Dictionary*, 6 vols. New York etc., 1992
AC	*L'Antiquité Classique*
ACW	Ancient Christian Writers
AGJU	Arbeiten zur Geschichte des antiken Judentums und des Urchristentums
AJPh	*American Journal of Philology*
AJSL	*American Journal of Semitic Languages*
ALGHJ	Arbeiten zur Literatur und Geschichte des hellenistischen Judentums
ANRW	*Aufstieg und Niedergang der römischen Welt*
APh	*L'Année Philologique*
BDAG	Bauer, W., F. W. Danker, W. F. Arndt, and F. W. Gingrich. *A Greek-English Lexicon of the New Testament and Other Early Christian literature.* 3^d ed. Chicago: University of Chicago Press, 1999
BibOr	Bibliotheca Orientalis
BJRL	*Bulletin of the John Rylands Library*
BJS	Brown Judaic Studies
BMCR	*Bryn Mawr Classical Review* (electronic)
BZAW	Beihefte zur Zeitschrift für die alttestamentliche Wissenschaft

BZNW	Beihefte zur Zeitschrift für die neutestamentliche Wissenschaft
BZRGG	Beihefte zur Zeitschrift für Religions- und Geistesgeschichte
CBQ	*The Catholic Biblical Quarterly*
CBQMS	The Catholic Biblical Quarterly. Monograph Series
CC	Corpus Christianorum, Turnhout
CIG	*Corpus Inscriptionum Graecarum*. Edited by A. Boeckh, 4 vols. in 8. Berlin, 1828–77
CIJ	*Corpus Inscriptionum Judaicarum*. Edited by J. B. Frey, 2 vols. Rome, 1936–52
CIL	*Corpus Inscriptionum Latinarum*. Berlin, 1862–
CIS	*Corpus Inscriptionum Semiticarum*. Paris, 1881–1962
CPh	*Classical Philology*
CPJ	*Corpus Papyrorum Judaicarum*. Edited by V. Tcherikover and A. Fuks, 3 vols. Cambrige Mass., 1957–64
CQ	*The Classical Quarterly*
CR	*The Classical Review*
CRINT	Compendia Rerum Iudaicarum ad Novum Testamentum
CPG	*Clavis Patrum Graecorum*. Edited by M. Geerard, 5 vols. and suppl. vol. Turnhout, 1974–98
CPL	*Clavis Patrum Latinorum*. Edited by E. Dekkers. 3rd ed. Turnhout, 1995
CSCO	Corpus Scriptorum Christianorum Orientalium
CWS	Classics of Western Spirituality
DA	Dissertation Abstracts
DBSup	*Dictionnaire de la Bible*, Supplément. Paris, 1928–
DPhA	R. Goulet (ed.), *Dictionnaire des philosophes antiques*, Paris, 1989–
DSpir	*Dictionnaire de Spiritualité*, 17 vols. Paris, 1932–95
EncJud	*Encyclopaedia Judaica*, 16 vols. Jerusalem, 1972
EPRO	Études préliminaires aux religions orientales dans l'Empire romain
FrGH	*Fragmente der Griechische Historiker*. Edited by F. Jacoby et al. Leiden, 1954–
GCS	Die griechischen christlichen Schriftsteller, Leipzig
GLAJJ	M. Stern, *Greek and Latin Authors on Jews and Judaism*, 3 vols. Jerusalem, 1974–84
GRBS	*Greek, Roman and Byzantine Studies*
HKNT	Handkommentar zum Neuen Testament, Tübingen
HNT	Handbuch zum Neuen Testament, Tübingen
HR	*History of Religions*
HThR	*Harvard Theological Review*
HUCA	*Hebrew Union College Annual*
JAAR	*Journal of the American Academy of Religion*
JAOS	*Journal of the American Oriental Society*
JAC	*Jahrbuch für Antike und Christentum*
JBL	*Journal of Biblical Literature*
JHI	*Journal of the History of Ideas*
JHS	*The Journal of Hellenic Studies*
JJS	*The Journal of Jewish Studies*
JQR	*The Jewish Quarterly Review*
JR	*The Journal of Religion*
JRS	*The Journal of Roman Studies*
JSHRZ	Jüdische Schriften aus hellenistisch-römischer Zeit

JSJ	*Journal for the Study of Judaism in the Persian, Hellenistic and Roman Periods*
JSJSup	Supplements to the Journal for the Study of Judaism
JSNT	*Journal for the Study of the New Testament*
JSNTSup	Journal for the Study of the New Testament. Supplement Series
JSOT	*Journal for the Study of the Old Testament*
JSOTSup	Journal for the Study of the Old Testament. Supplement Series
JSP	*Journal for the Study of the Pseudepigrapha and Related Literature*
JSSt	*Journal of Semitic Studies*
JThS	*The Journal of Theological Studies*
KBL	L. Koehler and W. Baumgartner, *Lexicon in Veteris Testamenti libros*, 3 vols. 3rd ed. Leiden, 1967–83
KJ	*Kirjath Sepher*
LCL	Loeb Classical Library
LSJ	*A Greek-English Lexicon.* Edited by H. G. Liddell, R. Scott, H. S. Jones. 9th ed. with revised suppl. Oxford, 1996
MGWJ	*Monatsschrift für Geschichte und Wissenschaft des Judentums*
Mnem	*Mnemosyne*
NCE	*New Catholic Encyclopedia*, 15 vols. New York, 1967
NHS	Nag Hammadi Studies
NT	*Novum Testamentum*
NTSup	Supplements to Novum Testamentum
NTA	*New Testament Abstracts*
NTOA	Novum Testamentum et Orbis Antiquus
NTS	*New Testament Studies*
ODJ	*The Oxford Dictionary of Judaism.* Edited by R.J.Z. Werblowsky and G. Wigoder, New York 1997
OGIS	*Orientis Graeci inscriptiones selectae*
OLD	*The Oxford Latin Dictionary.* Edited by P. G. W. Glare. Oxford, 1982
OTP	*The Old Testament Pseudepigrapha.* Edited by J. H. Charlesworth. 2 vols. New York–London, 1983–85
PAAJR	*Proceedings of the American Academy for Jewish Research*
PAL	*Philon d'Alexandrie: Lyon 11–15 Septembre 1966.* Éditions du CNRS, Paris, 1967
PG	Patrologiae cursus completus: series Graeca. Edited by J. P. Migne. 162 vols. Paris, 1857–1912
PGL	*A Patristic Greek Lexicon.* Edited by G. W. H. Lampe. Oxford, 1961
PhilAnt	Philosophia Antiqua
PL	Patrologiae cursus completus: series Latina. Edited by J. P. Migne. 221 vols. Paris, 1844–64
PW	Pauly-Wissowa-Kroll, *Real-Encyclopaedie der classischen Altertumswissenschaft.* 49 vols. Munich, 1980
PWSup	Supplement to PW
RAC	*Reallexikon für Antike und Christentum*
RB	*Revue Biblique*
REA	*Revue des Études Anciennes*
REArm	*Revue des Études Arméniennes*
REAug	*Revue des Études Augustiniennes*
REG	*Revue des Études Grecques*
REJ	*Revue des Études Juives*
REL	*Revue des Études Latines*

RGG	*Die Religion in Geschichte und Gegenwart*, 7 vols. 3rd edition Tübingen, 1957–65
RhM	*Rheinisches Museum für Philologie*
RQ	*Revue de Qumran*
RSR	*Revue des Sciences Religieuses*
Str-B	H. L. Strack and P. Billerbeck, *Kommentar zum Neuen Testament aus Talmud und Midrasch*, 6 vols. Munich, 1922–61
SBLDS	Society of Biblical Literature Dissertation Series
SBLMS	Society of Biblical Literature Monograph Series
SBLSPS	Society of Biblical Literature Seminar Papers Series
SC	Sources Chrétiennes
Sem	*Semitica*
SHJP	E. Schürer, *The History of the Jewish People in the Age of Jesus Christ*. Revised edition, 3 vols. in 4. Edinburgh, 1973–87
SJLA	Studies in Judaism in Late Antiquity
SNTSMS	Society for New Testament Studies. Monograph Series
SR	*Studies in Religion*
SUNT	Studien zur Umwelt des Neuen Testaments
SVF	*Stoicorum veterum fragmenta*. Edited by J. von Arnim. 4 vols. Leipzig, 1903–24
TDNT	*Theological Dictionary of the New Testament*. 10 vols. Grand Rapids, 1964–76
THKNT	Theologischer Handkommentar zum Neuen Testament, Berlin
TRE	*Theologische Realenzyklopädie*, Berlin
TSAJ	Texte und Studien zum Antike Judentum
TU	Texte und Untersuchungen zur Geschichte der altchristlichen Literatur, Berlin
TWNT	*Theologisches Wörterbuch zum Neuen Testament*, 10 vols. Stuttgart 1933–79.
VC	*Vigiliae Christianae*
VCSup	Supplements to Vigiliae Christianae
VT	*Vetus Testamentum*
WMANT	Wissenschaftliche Monographien zum Alten und Neuen Testament
WUNT	Wissenschaftliche Untersuchungen zum Neuen Testament
YJS	*Yale Jewish Studies*
ZAW	*Zeitschrift für die alttestamentliche Wissenschaft*
ZKG	*Zeitschrift für Kirchengeschichte*
ZKTh	*Zeitschrift für Katholische Theologie*
ZNW	*Zeitschrift für die neutestamentliche Wissenschaft*
ZRGG	*Zeitschrift für Religions- und Geistesgeschichte*